PROBLEMS IN LATIN AMERICAN HISTORY

Problems in Latin American History

The Modern Period

JOSEPH S. TULCHIN
University of North Carolina
Volume Editor

HARPER & ROW, PUBLISHERS
New York, Evanston, San Francisco, London

Problems in Latin American History: The Modern Period

Copyright © 1973 by Harper & Row, Publishers, Inc.

Standard Book Number: 06-046711-8

Library of Congress Catalog Card Number: 72-8255

CONTENTS

EDITOR'S INTRODUCTION

The survey course in Latin American history presents a number of unique problems to the student and the teacher. In its usual format, "From Columbus to Castro" in two semesters, it covers nearly 500 years of history. Only the Western Civilization course equals that time spread and its instructors have the singular advantage of building on earlier training and exposure. The typical student in the Latin American survey, on the other hand, knows little or nothing about the area. To compound this difficulty, the material embraces the histories of twenty different nations. All too often, both student and teacher are frustrated by the mass of detail and the bewildering variety. Texts in the field only contribute to the confusion. They offer narrative political histories of each country, *seriatum,* producing the impression that Latin American history is nothing more than a series of revolutions made by men on horseback and, in sum, somehow of less consequence and more sordid than the histories of other areas. To correct this distorted impression, the instructor must rely on lectures and supplementary readings. We believe appropriate reading material will attract students to the study of Latin America and we offer this book with the hope of stimulating that response.

The problem of selection is central to the organization of an effective reader in Latin American history. While we sought to identify the most significant issues in Latin America history since independence, we also tried to establish a geographical and chronological spread that would be useful to the broadest possible clientele. We did not try to be comprehensive; our objective was a flexible book that could be used in many different ways.

The book is divided into ten units, each of which is the work of a specialist. Aside from the fact that each has an introduction, a section of readings, and a bibliography, they do not follow a rigid model. Some of the introductions are descriptive narratives, others are historiographical, and still others are methodological and conceptual. The nature of the readings also varies—some include only primary sources, some use only secondary materials, and some mix the two. There is variety, also, in the ideological positions assumed by the editors. We hope the breadth of interpretation enhances the pedagogical utility of the volume; student and teacher will not be tied to the views of a single editor.

All of the units aim at conceptualization; that is, to explain broad ranges of events, not merely to describe specific moments in the past. Taken together, they illuminate basic themes in the history of Latin America since independence. To begin, Hugh M. Hamill, Jr., of the University of Connecticut, raises the question of continuity and change within a revolutionary context. By treating the struggle for independence from Spain as a dynamic movement Hamill throws light on two further questions which are central to the study of Latin America in the nineteenth century and, in one form or another, figure prominently in the discussion of contemporary problems. They are: Should political and social institutions be based on foreign models or strictly on local experiences? and, Is personalist government an aberration, a sign of political immaturity, or a peculiar but effective form of political organization based on cultural norms of Latin American society? Anthony P. Maingot, of Florida International University, considers the second of these questions in his unit on the caudillo. Relying on the instruments of functional analysis, he focuses on the style of political leadership and concludes that caudillos were not an aberration or an obstacle in the evolution of Latin American society. Charles A. Hale, of the University of Iowa, considers the first question in the unit on liberalism in Mexico, probing into the nature of political conflict from the perspective of intellectual history.

Moving forward chronologically, Roberto Cortés Conde, of the Torcuato Di Tella Institute in Buenos Aires, discusses the process through which the Latin American nations entered the world economy. As he points out, the "export oriented models of growth . . . have a renewed, contemporary interest." His analysis of historical phenomena suggests, in a manner similar to Maingot's essay, that theoretical models used to explain economic development often fail to consider factors because of ethnocentric biases. Cortés Conde's essay is a marriage of two disciplines, history and economics, to the advantage of both. Herbert S. Klein, of Columbia University, also touches on the themes of ethnocentric bias and the selection of models for national integration in his unit on slavery and race relations. This is a subject of obvious interest to students of North American society and it is no accident that the intense debate over different facets of the problem reflect such a strong comparative tendency.

The units by Thomas E. Skidmore, of the University of Wisconsin, on Getulio Vargas, and by Eldon Kenworthy, of Cornell University, on Juan Perón, are case studies of two efforts to solve the problems of modernization within the framework of popular democracy. Comparing and contrasting the experiences of Brazil and Argentina during the regimes of these leaders is a challenging exercise in which the differences are as enlightening as the apparent similarities.

Both Vargas and Perón fit Maingot's definition of the caudillo. Moreover, both came to power with the aid of the military; both fell at the hands of the military. The involvement of the military in politics is not a passing phase of Latin American development. At this writing, in Argentina, Brazil, Peru, Paraguay, Bolivia, Colombia, Ecuador, Honduras, Guatemala, Panama, and the Dominican Republic, the military either rules directly or is not far behind the throne. The eighth unit, by Anthony P. Maingot, puts the problem of civil–military relations in historical perspective, emphasizing that the problem is not new and that the military is not now, and probably never was, a homogeneous group.

But, if the military is heterogeneous, its participation in politics today more often than not stems from the shared conviction of its leaders that their nations shall not continue to wallow in the pit of underdevelopment and dependence. They seem to agree on the need for more rapid development. The question is, How? Some of them believe that a revolution is necessary before the development they seek can be achieved. In this, they are not alone. Hobart A. Spalding, Jr., of Brooklyn College of the City University of New York, brings together documents which represent the revolutionary ideologies in Latin America, the strident demand for revolutionary change in the structures of Latin American societies. The student of Latin American history will follow with interest the unfolding drama in Argentina, Brazil, Chile, Peru, Cuba, and Mexico—all ruled by avowedly revolutionary regimes—to see how they shall satisfy the universal demand for development.

The United States government will be another avid spectator of events in Latin America, for the demand for revolutionary change carries with it a potential threat to U.S. interests in the hemisphere. By the same token, the forces for change in Latin America must take the United States into account; its economic and political power are inescapable, its every action—or inaction—affects the destinies of the nations in the hemisphere. Of course, as I point out in my historical survey of inter-American relations, the final chapter in this volume, the overwhelming power of the United States is a recent phenomenon. Historical perspective requires that we attempt to understand the evolution of international relations in the hemisphere before the United States became a superpower and to understand how the Latin Americans view their northern neighbor.

The different uses to which this book can be put are, to a great extent, a function of the editors' interdisciplinary approach, thus a word on our approach is in order. We want students to appreciate and understand Latin America through its history. All of us share a dual commitment to Latin America. We are engaged professionally in the study of the past and we are concerned with the region's contemporary problems and its future prospects. We retain the historian's devotion to the particular while leaning on the social sciences in reaching for unifying concepts and generalizations both to convey the complexity of Latin American history and to help the student organize the basic historical material. To that end, we prefer not to rely on political narrative alone. We believe that the study of Latin American history should be integrated with the study of indigenous civilizations, literature and culture, the problems of development, social structure, and the region's quest for revolutionary change. It is in this spirit that we offer these chapters to students of Latin America.

One final point on the approach to Latin American history. Latin America is often considered part of the Third World because of certain shared traits summarized in the terms underdevelopment and external dependence. While a geat deal can be learned from a comparative study of contemporary problems, the study of history makes plain that the nations of Latin America bear the imprint of their European heritage to a degree that is true of no other Third World area. Perhaps for this reason social scientists join with historians to insist that a knowledge of the history of Latin America is indispensable to the study of the region from the point of view of any discipline. We hope this volume contributes to that knowledge.

Joseph S. Tulchin

I.
The Consequences of Spanish American Independence

⚑ HUGH M. HAMILL, JR.

The particular historical prism through which we commonly view the Spanish American wars for independence is found in those accounts generously provided by the winners, their heirs and admirers. Bookstalls and libraries are glutted with hundreds of volumes with such titles as *Men of Heroic Times, The Venezuelan Woman During Independence, Hidalgo: Torch of Liberty, The First Soldier of the Nation,* and *Birth of a World.* Even measured accounts pass under titles like *The Rise of the Spanish American Republics as Told in the Lives of their Liberators.* The assumption easily made by the most casual reader is that "liberty," "independence," and "the nation" are universals which, as positive goods, were wrested from a mother country at once monstrous and pathetic. The need to vest emancipation with patriotic champions in order to create nationalist ideologies has helped nurture a widespread belief that the years from 1810 to 1825 were characterized by prodigious exploits at arms, by eloquent and imaginative statesmen, and by resourceful generals who fought all day and danced all night.

This understandable impression of the Spanish American wars for independence creates interpretative problems for the student of early national history. For once past the conflict with Spain, the key word for most republican conditions is "instability." If independence had been such an age of heroic vision, sacrifice for the fatherland, and commitment by a people to nation building, then why were the postrevolutionary years marked by enervating civil wars, cynical personalist leaders, worthless constitutions, economic privation, and neocolonialism?

It is the purpose of this unit to treat the consequences of Spanish American independence from perspectives which allow the reader to explore the processes of change during, as well as immediately after, the resolution of the multiple struggles with Spain.

Socioeconomic changes within a body politic, which are in any sense profound, occur without regard for later periodization imposed upon them by social scientists who rejoice in chopping up what the English historian Frederick Maitland once called the "seamless web of history." If the wars of independence touched many sectors of the complex societies and regions of Spanish America, then those effects were often immediate, not hoarded for release upon some red letter day like December 9, 1824, at the Battle of Ayacucho. It is especially difficult for the inveterate periodizer to fit "independence" for all of Spanish America within the limits of terminal dates. The Creoles of La Plata, for example, began to move perceptibly toward independence at least as early as 1806. By 1810 they had gained effective control of Buenos Aires and the Litoral and had completed the formalities of their break with Spain by 1816. Upper Peru (Bolivia), on the other hand, was not free from Spanish control until 1825. And as for Cuba, it was almost the end of the century before it won an independence of sorts. In document 1, Richard Morse develops a perceptive interpretation of independence which employs a novel periodization. He places the era within a larger conceptual framework and obviates the need to dwell excessively on terminal dates.

When the question is asked "What were the qualities of change throughout the wars?" a host of related queries arise. How profound were the effects of the struggle on the socioeconomic components of New Spain, New Granada, Venezuela, Peru, La Plata, Chile, and other centers of conflict? May one or more of the movements in these areas be classified as "Revolution"? If so, by what criteria? Document 2 explores this matter of social and economic revolution. Its author, Charles Griffin, looks beyond the political effects of the Spanish ouster to inquire into the alterations in production and trade and into the shifts in social relationships. The article from which this selection has been excerpted was published in 1949 and has since stimulated much research by other scholars anxious to turn their attention away from military and political history. Each of the next two documents (3 and 4) owes some debt to Griffin's pioneer work. Magnus Mörner, writing in 1967, draws detailed attention to the degrees of social mobility and frustration experienced by the lower sectors during the chaotic years of civil conflict. The cogent essay by Stanley and Barbara Stein (document 4) bears upon economic disunity during the wars and the reasons for the emergence of postwar neocolonialism dominated by Great Britain.

Whether or not the reader opts for a revolutionary explanation, he should consider the possibility that accelerated change was not produced solely by the insurgents and that, perhaps, some significant alterations were the result of royalist efforts to preserve their control. The civil–military regulations for Mexico decreed in 1811–1813 by the Spanish general and Viceroy Felix María Calleja, for example, helped to create a militarized society which would later accept the army and its officers, like Antonio López de Santa Anna, as arbiters of political power (document 5).

That control over less dramatic alterations and the humdrum details of daily government were also often in royalist anti-insurgent hands over much of the area is demonstrated by the decrees of the governors of Antioquia in 1816 and Popayán in 1817 (document 6). These New Granadan decrees suggest another way to interpret the independence years. Just as inordinate attention may be paid to the patriotic derring-do of the rebels, so, too, excessive concentration on the question of "Revolution" may obscure the fundamental consideration of the years of independence as transmitters of established life-styles, value systems, and social organization. In selection 1, Richard Morse emphasizes the continuity of the Spanish American model of the traditional patrimonial state, and, as has been mentioned, sets up a radical periodization to reduce the significance of the independence "period" from its usual pivotal position. While independence brought some changes, the Creole corporate elites strengthened their positions vis-à-vis lower sectors of society and imposed their inherited value systems on the postwar republics. If the instability of the middle decades of the nineteenth century stands in sharp contrast to the relative prosperity and serenity of late colonial times, this, the counterrevolutionary argument goes, is only a function of the elimination of the moral authority of the crown. Independence served principally to expose the factionalism and local contests for power which had long characterized a colonial system in which the king was the ultimate arbiter of endless disputes. The dominant position of the *caudillo* in this shattered world is explored by Anthony P. Maingot in Unit II.

At the very least, attention to continuities inherent in the period raises the matter of motivations. What prompted some individuals, sectors, corporations, families and regions to associate actively with independence movements and prompted others to oppose them? Without getting into the problem of causation, it is plain enough that none of the varied struggles was simply a conflict of Americans against Spaniards. In every instance "civil war" is most descriptive. Triggered as the movements were in 1808 by Napoleon's elimination of the traditional moral authority of the Bourbon monarchy and the severance of the personal ties between king and kingdom, the question became not only a matter of home rule but, as Carl Becker has suggested with reference to the American Revolution, who shall rule at home. To explain quarrels lasting deep into the century, attention must be paid to such internal rifts as that between the mercantile Buenos Aires *porteños* and the western Argentine producers of textiles, wine, and other local commodities, which were old divisions intensified in the course of the war years.

It would also be well to ask, for example, why it was that some regions like Venezuela, Chile, and La Plata on the administrative or geographic periphery of the old viceroyalty of Peru were quick to experiment with independence (not always with initial success), while the viceregal center itself came but tardily to accept independence from Spain? Or to ask why a region like the Bajío in Mexico produced a powerful—if short-lived—social revolution under Hidalgo in 1810–1811 while the core around Mexico City remained solidly in royalist control, until the conservative Iturbide rescued the capital from a Spanish liberal regime in 1821? The answers to these questions may help unravel the complexities of much recent history as well as of the wars for independence themselves.

The contours of liberal and conservative political theory and their implications for such controversial matters as church-state relations which emerged in the wake of independence are explored in Unit III of this volume, edited by Charles A. Hale. Certain other ideological factors require attention, however, even though there has been a tendency to overemphasize the role of ideas in the struggles of the first quarter of the nineteenth century. For every Bolívar and Hidalgo, familiar with the literature of the Enlightenment, there were dozens of insurgent leaders who could not tell Pufendorf from Paine and who fought entirely for motives which had nothing to do with the rationalist ideology of which they were totally ignorant.[1]

In document 7, Simon Collier makes a case for the role which nationalism played in the particular case of Chile. He regards "the sense of national identity" "as the single most important aspect of the new ideology." The reader should weigh the evidence in this selection against Morse's conten-

[1]See Charles W. Arnade, "The Political Causes of the War of Independence in Spanish America," *Journal of Inter-American Studies,* II (April 1960), 125–132.

tion that nationalism was not "an ingredient of the Latin-American independence movement."

The concluding document (8) pits the utopian ideological dreams of a group of Mexican reform pamphleteers, or *proyectistas,* against the harsh realities of the newly independent country. Javier Ocampo skillfully X-rays Mexican ideology and opinion, to use his term, during the two months which followed Agustín de Iturbide's triumphal liberation of Mexico City on September 27, 1821. Enthusiastic optimism for a new society foundered quickly on the shoals of the powerful corporate indisposition to reform of the new ruling elite. The piece suggests the difficulties ahead for a new country cut loose from the restraints and order of the Spanish empire.

By exploring the independence years and their aftermath as part of a whole process, the reader should be able to develop his own opinions about the nature of social, political, economic, and ideological transformations which did or did not take place in the regions which had once been part of Spain's New World empire. The selections which follow only begin that exploration. The bibliographic suggestions at the end of this unit are the next step.

1.
INDEPENDENCE IN A PATRIMONIAL SOCIETY

RICHARD M. MORSE

This reading is presented first because Professor Richard Morse, an historian at Yale University, integrates independence into a broad conceptual scheme which establishes a critical basis for the rest of the readings. The context is a larger essay in which Professor Morse provides his version of the emergence of Latin American civilization as his contribution to a distinguished collection of studies of societies fragmented from the European matrix. In it he draws particular attention to the qualities of the medieval Catholic urban inheritance from Spain. His model of a patrimonial society, based on an essentially static Thomistic world view in which hierarchies prevail and the status of individuals is determined by lineage and corporate function rather than ability, is basic to an understanding of his treatment of independence.

The best historical analogue to the Spanish American wars for independence is the Protestant Reformation. Both movements occurred within a far-flung, venerable Catholic institutional order which was exhibiting decadence at its upper levels. Both movements developed as unco-ordinated patterns of dispersed and disparate revolt. Neither

From "The Heritage of Latin America," by Richard M. Morse, in *The Founding of New Societies: Studies in the History of the United States, Latin America, South Africa, Canada, and Australia*, pp. 159–169, notes omitted. Edited and copyright © 1964 by Louis Hartz. Reprinted by permission of Harcourt Brace Jovanovich, Inc.

was heralded by a coherent body of revolutionary doctrine, and each improvised its multiple "ideologies" under pressure of events. Indeed, each movement at its inception betrayed a strong conservative or fundamentalist character. Each was the final cluster of a centuries-old series of random and localized heresies, uprisings, or seditions; and, in the case of each, world events were finally propitious to transform the impromptu outbreak into a world-historical revolution.

On the South American continent it was not until a number of years after Napoleon's deposition of the Spanish king that the goal of independence became clearly defined and was pursued in the military campaigns conducted separately by Simón Bolívar and José de San Martín. Even then the mass of the people played no role in the movement. The independence of the Spanish South American countries was achieved under the auspices of the creole elites in the more outlying regions. The impetus for the two main campaigns was imparted from Venezuela in the north and Buenos Aires in the south. Both of these regions were offering fresh promise for agricultural and commercial development. After independence, both Venezuela and Argentina fell under strong-man rule. This served to entrench the somewhat reconstituted creole oligarchies, which were now unhampered by the presence of Spanish bureaucracy.

If we except the special case of Saint Domingue, where a massive slave revolt produced Haiti's independence from France, Mexico is the only Latin-American country where there occurred substantial popular uprisings. Under Hidalgo an inchoate crowd of humble Indians and mestizos in central Mexico was led to fight for land, for Mexican autonomy, and for an end to the caste system (1810–11). Under Morelos they were led to fight for independence (1813–15). Both leaders were liberal parish priests. Both were captured and executed. Well-to-do creoles resisted identification with the rebellion or with a French revolutionary spirit. Some creoles even suspected the Spaniards themselves of being tainted with freemasonry and Illuminism. The army, church, and landowners remained loyal to the crown during the Napoleonic interregnum and after the establishment of reaction and despotism under the restored Ferdinand VII (1814). The Mexican insurgent movement was flickered out when suddenly, in 1820, liberal, constitutional reforms were forced upon the Spanish monarchy. At this point, fearing for their privileges, the Spaniards in

Mexico and the upper creoles joined to embrace the separatist cause, setting up the short-lived emperorship of Agustín de Iturbide. Mexican independence was an act of counterrevolution.

It cannot be said, therefore, that "nationalism" was an ingredient of the Latin-American independence movement. Simón Bolívar, the *líder máximo* of independence, was torn between the generous vision of a transnational amphictyony of the Hispanic American peoples and a keen perception of the feuding local oligarchies and earthbound peasantries from which only phantom nations could be formed. One surmises that Bolívar's use of the term "amphictyony," dictated by the Enlightenment fashion of neoclassicism, was a surrogate for his instinctive sense of a Hispanic unity rooted in a political and religious heritage having medieval coloration. A modern Colombian writes, "Had Bolívar not feared to be Napoleon and had he abandoned the paradigm of George Washington, perhaps our national destiny would have been saved." The independence of the United States caused a bonding through compact of autonomous colonies. The independence of Spanish America caused the decapitation of a realm that had ever been, if not unified, at least unitary. In one case *e pluribus unum,* in the other *ex uno plures.* The Panama Congress of 1826, while it served as a first utterance of the Pan American ideal, symbolized the abandonment of attempts to regulate the internal affairs of the Spanish American peoples on a continental scale.

The extent of the politico-administrative crisis faced by the independent Spanish American nations of 1830 can be appreciated when we recall our model of the Thomist-patrimonial state. The lower echelons of administration had operated by the grace of an interventionist, paternal monarch, thoroughly sanctioned by tradition and faith. His collapse straightway withdrew legitimacy from the remnants of the royal bureaucracy. It was impossible to identify a substitute authority that would command general assent. Decapitated, the government could not function, for the patrimonial regime had developed neither: (1) the underpinning of contractual vassalic relationships that capacitate the component parts of a *feudal* regime for autonomous life; nor, (2) a rationalized *legal* order not dependent for its operation and claims to assent upon personalistic intervention by the highest authority.

Although legitimacy was withdrawn from the hierarchies of gov-

ernment and society by independence, no revolutionary change occurred. "Thus the social and spiritual structure of the past is preserved under new forms; its class hierarchy, the privileges of special
bodies . . . the values of the Catholic religion and Hispanic tradition
are maintained. At the same time its political and legislative forms
and its international status change." To state the case more fully, political or social revolution was neither cause nor concomitant of the
independence wars. . . .

The collapse of the supreme authority activated the latent forces of
local oligarchies, municipalities, and extended-family systems in a
struggle for power and prestige in the new, arbitrarily defined republics. These telluric creole social structures were direct heirs of social
arangements proliferated in the conquest period but held in check
by the patrimonial state. Now again they seized the stage. The *caudillo*
of the independence period, controlling a clanlike or an improvised
retinue through charismatic appeal, was the latter-day version of the
conquistador. In the absence of developed and interacting economic
interest groups having a stake in constitutional process, the new countries were plunged into alternating regimes of anarchy and personalist
tyranny. The contest to seize a patrimonial state apparatus, fragmented from the original imperial one, became the driving force of
public life in each new country.

There is abundant testimony that Spanish America universally suffered a collapse of the moral order during the early decades of independence. The face of anarchy was somewhat masked, however, by
that ancient habit of legalizing and legitimizing every public act which
had been so important a cement to the former empire. Each new
country duly produced its constitutional convention and one or more
Anglo-French-type constitutions. The political mechanism which
emerged was generally a biparty system. Party programs faithfully
reflected the rhetoric of Western parliamentary politics, though not
without occasional shrewd adaptation to local situations. Although
only an elite was politically active (as was the case in the England of
1830, for that matter), party adherence frequently reflected an alignment of "conservative" landed and monied interests, high clergy, and
former monarchists against the "liberal" professionals, intellectuals,
merchants, and those with a creole, anticlerical, and anticaste outlook.
Given a static rather than a dynamic social system, however, the game
of politics became a naked contest for power.

Chile was an example perhaps unparalleled of a Spanish American country which managed, after a twelve-year transitional period, to avoid the extremes of tyranny and anarchy with a political system unencumbered by the mechanisms and party rhetoric of an exotic liberalism. Despite its outlandish contour the country had a certain ecological cohesion around its central agricultural zone. Because the landholding class had been infiltrated by mercantile groups partly composed of recent immigrants from northern Spain, the elite represented a spectrum of moderately diverse economic interests. A Valparaiso businessman, Diego Portales, was shrewd enough to identify and co-ordinate those interests within a constitutional system having an aura of native legitimacy. The centralizing 1833 Constitution which bore his influence created a strong executive without stripping the congress and courts of countervailing powers. The first president had the aristocratic bearing which Portales himself lacked; a staunch Catholic and brave general who stood above party factionalism, he helped to legitimize the office itself. The first several presidents each served double five-year terms. The official candidate was generally victorious and hand-picked by his predecessor. Thus the structure of the Spanish patrimonial state was re-created, with only those minimum concessions to Anglo-French constitutionalism that were necessary for a nineteenth-century republic which had just rejected monarchical rule.

From our broad premises and from the specific case of Chile we may infer that for a newly erected Spanish American political system to achieve stability and continuity it had to reproduce the structure, the logic, and the vague, pragmatic safeguards against tyranny of the Spanish *patrimonial state*. The collapse of monarchical authority meant that this step required the intervention of strong *personalist* leadership. The energies of such leadership had to flow toward investing the state with suprapersonal *legitimacy*. The ingredients of legitimacy, in turn, were native psychocultural *traditions*, leavened or perhaps merely adorned by the *nationalism* and *constitutionalism* which had become watchwords of the age.

The usual political trajectory of a Spanish American nation can be plotted as one or another form of breakdown or short circuit in this model. The most notorious form is personalist leadership that constitutes its own untransferable legitimacy. In a telluric setting of moral and institutional collapse, the instances of personalism ranged from the superb, intellectually informed, yet tragically frustrated political genius of a Bolívar all the way to careers dominated by sheer enactment of impulse, such as those of the Argentine *caudillo* Facundo described by Sarmiento; or the Bolivian president who commanded his aides to play dead like poodles, and who had his ministers and generals troop solemnly around the table on which his mistress stood naked.

It is beyond our purposes to present even a perfunctory account of the careers of the twenty Latin-American nations during the past century and a half. At this point we will merely suggest a way of periodizing Spanish American history that allows us to explore the political dilemmas of the modern countries in the light of their Thomist, patrimonial heritage. The historical divisions conventionally used are the following:

Indigenous Period	To 1492
Colonial Period	1492 to 1824
National Period	Since 1824

Here is our radically revised schema (offered chiefly for heuristic purposes):

Indigenous Period	To 1520
Spanish Period	1520 to 1760
"Colonial" Period	1760 to 1920
National Period	Since 1920

We extend the Indigenous Period to 1520 because for a generation after Columbus' discovery Spanish colonization was restricted to the islands and shores of the Caribbean Sea and conducted on a trial-and-error basis, with commercial exploitation rather than effective colonization usually in the ascendant. Hernando Cortés, who conquered the Aztec empire in 1519–21, was the first of the explorers and conquistadors to make clear to the crown the full scope of the colonizing and civilizing venture upon which Spain had embarked.

The . . . Spanish Period . . . was the time of "incorporation" of the Indies into Hispano-Christian civilization.

The term "Colonial" . . . serves in the new schema to characterize the period when the creole, Catholic culture and institutions of Spanish America lay open to influences and pressures of the Western world which were on the whole ineffectually mediated to the ethos of the formative Spanish Period.

The National Period is still today in its inception. It is a time when political arrangements are being devised, erratically and painfully, which directly accommodate the traditions, structures, and psychology of the patrimonial state to the imperatives of a modern industrial world. It is a time when Spanish Americans are beginning to contemplate their countries' first sustained involvement with each other and with the world as autonomous nation states.

The start of the "Colonial" Period we set at 1760, the eve of the most important Bourbon reforms. As Octavio Paz sums up the case for it:

The reforms undertaken by the Bourbon dynasty, particularly Charles III, improved the economy and made business operations more efficient, but they accentuated the centralization of administrative functions and changed New Spain into a true colony, that is, into a territory subject to systematic exploitation and strictly controlled by the center of power.

As Paz goes on to make clear, the critical matter is not quantitative exploitation. It would be hard to make the case that the financial enrichment of Spain at the expense of the Indies or the cruelty to Indians and Negro slaves, was greater in 1780 than it had been in 1680 or 1590. The primary sense of "colonial" as here used designates not a unilaterally exploitative relationship, but a discontinuity of structure and purpose between two systems. The fact was that the "enlightened," rationalistic, technocratic Bourbon policies were an overlay upon and not a radical reform of Spanish American institutions.

Bourbon economic reforms aroused antagonism from creole merchants in Mexico City, Caracas, and Buenos Aires who were thriving under the old monopolistic system. It can even be concluded that "while Spain evolved toward [economic] liberalism, there were interests in America which obstructed those new currents." Administrative reform, and specifically the creation of the intendant system, "revealed a fatal lack of integration in Spanish policy." New officials were underpaid without being allowed the traditional extralegal fees and exactions. The division of authority between the intendants and the viceroys was unwisely or vaguely stipulated. The activities of the intendants aroused the town governments to greater activity without their receiving a commensurate increase of authority. "[The] reforms of Charles III, both in their administrative and in their commercial aspects, helped to precipitate the collapse of the imperial regime they were intended to prolong."

The assumptions and programs of Western liberalism continued to be a bone in the throat of Spanish America, whether their guise was enlightened despotism, Manchester economics, or Anglo-French constitutional democracy. The tendency of doctrinally liberal reforms was to withdraw legitimacy from the patrimonial state, to dismantle its apparatus, and to cancel the shadowy, paternalistic safeguards of status for the inarticulate masses. Since, however, the stimuli to economic change came from without—from the Western world—and not from within, there did not occur even among the new oligarchies that competitive differentiation of economic function which gives liberalism its *raison d'être*. Mexico's liberal Constitution of 1857 was informed by the vision of a prosperous independent peasantry. But its enactment merely hastened the delivery of traditional Indian communities to systems of debt peonage that were beyond the tutelage of church and state. A similar process occurred in the other Indian countries south to Bolivia. It gave to the landowning oligarchies a measure of absolute local power that would have exceeded even the dreams of the conquistadors.

The anti-Spanish rallying cries of Democracy! Liberalism! and Civilization! provoked by the Spanish American independence wars contained hopes which were persistently undermined by the drift of the nineteenth century. This trend is implied by the "two stages" into which Leopoldo Zea divides the period's intellectual history. The first was a romantic, eclectic phase when such diverse and often contradictory currents as Cartesianism, sensationalist psychology, physiocratic economies, Saint-Simonianism, utilitarianism, Scotch realism, and French traditionalism were all commingled in a multiple attack on the Hispanic, scholastic legacy. The second phase saw many of these streams of thought, and some new ones, merge to form a unified intellectual position, that of positivism.

Positivism occurred in many versions throughout Latin America, sometimes with an Anglo-Spencerian rather than a Franco-Comtean emphasis. Whatever its guise, it appeared to offer a unitary, constructive, systematic, scientific approach to the problems of stratified societies, stagnant economies, and archaic school systems. In practice, however, the watchwords of positivism could be used to justify systems of vested interest and entrenched privilege. Frock-coated bourgeois *caudillos* had replaced the soldier *caudillos* of the postindependence era. Their regimes were secured less by charismatic leadership and military prowess than by creation of orderly conditions for attracting foreign trade and investment in this heyday of European capitalism. Liberalism tinctured by social evolution could justify limiting economic freedom to those who already possessed it. Tinctured by nineteenth-century anthropology it acquiesced in the continued exploitation of Indians, Negroes, and those of "mixed race."

It might be imagined that Latin America's intellectual drift from romanticism to scientism, from eclecticism to determinism, merely reflected the general European movement. Zea offers us two caveats to correct this impression. One is that the acceptance of positivism in Latin America represented a search for the inclusive doctrine and instrument of order which might replace scholasticism. Seen thus, positivism appears to serve familiar casuistical purposes more importantly than those of speculative scientific inquiry.

Secondly, at the same time that . . . the Spanish American mind groped unconsciously to recover a habitual mold of thought, it was explicitly attacking the civilization within which that mold had been shaped. Spanish Americans were condemned to the impossible task of denying and amputating their past. Yet Spain was always with them. Unable to deal with their past by a *dialectic logic* which would allow them to assimilate it, they rejected it by a *formal logic* which kept it present and impeded their evolution. The Conquest, Colonialism, and Independence were problems never resolved, never placed *behind*. They are still alive in our own century. . . .

Not only did ideas from nineteenth-century Europe assume new coloration and use in the Latin-American setting, but some were screened out before reaching it. Marxism, for example, made virtually no impact whatsoever. A philosophy which identifies an engine of political demolition in society will scarcely win general acceptance among a people groping to recover and legitimize an overarching patrimonial state. The clarion call to a single solidary and militant class echoes weakly in a society where all groups look separately to a patrimonial structure for accommodation, tutelage, and salvation. The model toward which the Thomistic society tends must be formulated in statistics, not dynamics. Its ultimate law is natural and moral, not scientific and sociological. These strictures were for the most part overlooked in nineteenth-century Latin America. But they continued in clandestine operation.

2.
WERE THERE REVOLUTIONS?

CHARLES C. GRIFFIN

Prominent among the provocative essays in Latin American historiography, published since World War II, is this call for new research and interpretation of the wars for independence. Unlike Richard Morse's effort to locate independence in a panorama of Spanish American civilization, Dr. Charles C. Griffin, Professor Emeritus of History at Vassar College, focuses directly on the socioeconomic impact of the conflicts. By reference to the Jameson thesis which concerns the social impact of Anglo-American independence (and, implicitly, to the debate about that thesis), Professor Griffin pointedly raises the question of profound Revolution within the context of Spanish America during the independence struggles and offers some tentative conclusions. The rich footnotes in the original version should be consulted by the inquisitive.

The revolutions which brought about the establishment of independent governments in America differed in marked degree from the

From Charles C. Griffin, "Economic and Social Aspects of the Era of Spanish-American Independence," *The Hispanic American Historical Review, XXIX* (1949), pp. 170–187, selection from pp. 170, 174–187, footnotes omitted. Reprinted by permission of the publisher. Copyright 1949, Duke University Press, Durham, North Carolina.

For Professor Griffin's own revision and expansion of this article, see *Los temas sociales y económicos en la época de la Independencia* (Caracas: Fundación John Boulton, 1962).

classic revolutions of modern Europe—the French and the Russian—in that their primary effect was to throw off the authority of a transatlantic empire rather than to bring about a drastic reconstruction of society. In the case of the United States, however, it has long been recognized that the revolutionary struggle did not confine itself to the political sphere, i.e., to independence and the establishment of a new federal government. Almost a generation ago the late J. Franklin Jameson published his essays on *The American Revolution Considered as a Social Movement* in which he suggested relations between the revolution and the manifold changes of the era, some already recognized, and others destined to be more fully charted by a subsequent generation of scholars. Because many of these changes were not the result of conscious revolutionary planning, but came about under the stimulus of new conditions created during and after the revolution, they had not earlier been sufficiently closely related to the revolution and to each other.

It is possible that the time may be ripe for a similar shift in emphasis in the interpretation of the revolutions for independence in Spanish America. . . .

The presentation of a general view, however exploratory, is complicated by regional diversity in the character and course of the independence movement in its various centers. Differences in geography, in population, in tradition, as well as in the duration and intensity of military operations must be considered, together with variations in the extent of contact with Europe and the United States. These differentiating factors modified certain general tendencies: the destructive force of war, and the stimulation produced by free intercourse with foreign countries.

The immediate economic consequence of revolution, except in a few favored areas, was disaster. The prosperity of the later colonial economy of Spanish America was shattered by warfare which was everywhere waged with little regard for the rights of private property and the lives of non-combatants. It is only possible to suggest here the terrible destruction suffered by many regions. This reached its maximum in Venezuela, where both the human and the livestock population declined, the latter by more than one-half between 1810 and 1830. Almost as severe were the losses in the Banda Oriental and in certain parts of the Viceroyalty of New Spain. New Granada and

Chile represent areas which were less continuously theatres of military action, and with a consequently lighter incidence of destruction. The extreme horrors of the *guerra a muerte* in Venezuela and the slaughter in Mexico during the early stages of revolution were not often matched in scale elsewhere, but, even where loss of life was less severe, interruption of normal economic life was serious. People were uprooted from their homes in various ways. Men were recruited, often by force, for the rival armies. Even when they escaped death they frequently never returned, taking up life again elsewhere. There were also many examples of emigration on a substantial scale. These dislocations of population had unfavorable results for agriculture and mining, removing the necessary labor force, and on business in general owing to the flight of capital along with its owners.

The interruption of normal lines of trade and communication also had serious adverse effects. Northwest Argentina suffered from the halting of trade with Peru. Montevideo, while in hands hostile to Buenos Aires, lost part of its commercial function. Guerrilla warfare in New Spain at times disrupted internal communications except by armed convoys. Wartime financial extractions, ranging from confiscation to forced loans, appropriation of goods for the use of the rival armies, forced acceptance of depreciated currency, and high and arbitrary taxation brought ruin to many. Cattle-raising countries like the Banda Oriental and the Venezuelan hinterland suffered from wholesale robbery and expropriation of the livestock on which the economy of these regions was based. Mining regions were paralyzed by flooding of the workings and destruction of equipment.

It is impossible to measure exactly the total effect of these varied consequences of war, but it is probably safe to say that from 1810 to 1820 Buenos Aires and Peru, the strongholds of the rival forces in South America, were least affected. Regions like Paraguay and, to a lesser extent, Central America suffered from isolation but were little damaged. Chile, New Granada, and Mexico underwent severe destruction at times, but were not equally affected throughout the decade. On the other hand, Venezuela and Uruguay saw no real peace during the period and their normal economic activities were totally upset.

In the second decade of revolution theatres of military operations shifted. Warfare on a large scale was over in Mexico in 1821, and in Colombia after 1822. Fighting in Chile ceased, except for guerrilla warfare in the far south. On the other hand, Peru, which had previously escaped, became the center of the fighting. Though devastation here was not so widespread nor long continued as in some other areas, the burden of supporting large armies (patriot and royalist) in the field for several years was a heavy one. The duration of military activity in what is now Ecuador was briefer, but this region gave a good deal of support to the later Peruvian campaigns. For the war as a whole, therefore, only the province of Buenos Aires and its immediate neighbors to the north and west were able to escape the direct scourge of war. Even here there were intermittent skirmishes between patriot factions especially after the year 1820.

The upheaval caused by war was not limited to destruction of life and property and the disorganization of business; it also brought changes in society which were not envisaged by the creole aristocrats and intellectuals who headed the revolts of the *cabildos* in 1809 and 1810. Except in Mexico, the revolutions had begun with efforts to dislodge the peninsular bureaucracy without otherwise changing relations among classes, but war unleashed forces that these early revolutionists were unable to harness. Race and class antagonisms flared up which could only be brought under control by the exaltation of nationalism and a parallel minimizing of class distinctions. Without any general upset in these relations, there was a blurring of lines. None of the new independent governments recognized legal disabilities for *pardos* or *mestizos*. In Mexico, the clergy no longer kept the elaborate records of caste as a part of their parochial registers.

The "career open to talents" seems to have been the rule. A *mestizo* general might rise to the presidency of his country; a *mulato* colonel might become a large landowner. This does not mean that an equalitarian society grew out of the wars, but it does indicate that the wars brought new blood into the ruling class and simplified the social distinctions in lower strata of the population.

The annals of revolution in Mexico and Colombia are well sprinkled with the names of prominent military officers with Indian or Negro blood in their veins, or both. Piar and Padilla in Colombia were conspicuous examples. In Mexico, Guerrero and Morelos reached even higher renown. In the lower ranks officers with similar racial antecedents were numerous. In Peru and Bolivia *mestizos* also held high military rank. Santa Cruz, who became president of the latter republic, was the son of an Indian woman and a Spaniard. In the naval service of Colombia a number of *mulatos* held commissions. The large percentage of color in the ranks of Bolívar's officers was frequently commented on by the race-conscious European officers who served in Colombia.

The tendency toward greater racial tolerance was not unchecked. White creole fear accounts in part for the severe treatment meted out to such officers as Piar and Padilla. Their insubordination might well have been condoned if it had not been for their race. If there had not been great gains for the mixed bloods, such severity as that which led to the execution of both, in spite of the brilliant military services they had rendered to the cause of independence, might not have been considered necessary.

In Río de la Plata and in Chile there do not seem to have been instances of high military commanders of recognized mixed blood. We can cite, however, the cases of politicians and journalists like Vicente Kanki Pazos (an Indian from Upper Peru) and the meteoric career of Bernardo Monteagudo (a *mulato* from Tucumán). The strength of the creole element in the population in the Viceroyalty of Buenos Aires, except in the north, and the fact that it was not heavily depleted by the wars may be one explanation for the less conspicuous place of the *mestizo* in military leadership. The relatively stable agrarian economy of Chile with its strong personal ties between landowner and *inquilino* provided fewer opportunities for social change than the more elaborately stratified population of Peru, Colombia, and Mexico. In these southern regions, however, the revolution brought increasing fluidity among economic groups. "Self-made men," among them many foreigners, began to make themselves increasingly evident, beginning the process which was to ease their way into the upper social ranks of *estancieros* and merchants. This tendency was stimulated by the procedure followed by many governments in paying off officers and men with land confiscated from royalists or from the public domain. Land had been for so long a badge of social position that it proved impossible to discriminate for more than a generation against the owner of a large estate.

Another series of important social and economic changes grew out of the increasing contact with foreign lands during the course of the wars of independence. In this respect local differences are also notable. Buenos Aires, without question, developed a new economy based on foreign trade earlier than any other Spanish-American country. The accumulated demand for free trade during the later years of the viceroyalty had paved the way and the absence of Spanish power to interfere, after 1810, gave the development free rein. This ushered in the cattle boom which was to fix the character of the Argentine economy for generations. It led to expansion on the Indian frontier and to the rapid growth of the city of Buenos Aires, as population flowed in to serve the needs of an expanded commerce. Small shops and factories on a handicraft basis multiplied and the accumulation of wealth created new luxury trades. On the other hand, . . . free trade brought depression to Cuyo and to the northern provinces from Tucumán to Jujuy, which lost much of their market for home manufactures to foreign competition.

In Chile, with interruptions due to the wars, similar changes can be seen. Free trade meant a larger market for the grain and other food surpluses which before the revolution had been shipped almost exclusively to Peru. Valparaíso became a port of call for ships bound to the Orient and for the northwest coast of America. The export of Chilean silver and copper increased under the pressure of need to balance imported manufactures. By 1825 a number of English mining experts were planning developments in the Coquimbo region. Chilean naval activity stimulated the work of shipyards and attracted both business men and laborers to the port city, which soon lost its sleepy colonial aspect. Free trade, however, had a less violently stimulating effect on the economy of Chile than in Río de la Plata. The immediately available resources of Chile were less vast, and depended, for expanded exploitation, on growth of population and on a long-range development of mining equipment and transportation which could not be carried through at once.

The ports of Peru and Colombia were opened to world trade at a later time and these republics were less favorably situated than those of the far south from a commercial point of view. Trade did not develop here on a healthy basis. In Peru it began with a hectic wartime flush, with government purchases of munitions of war and naval stores and even of food (including flour from the United States), and with considerable speculative purchases of luxury goods. This drained the country of its currency and saddled it with large commercial and governmental debts. The economic situation was still further complicated by a heavy flight of capital which took the form of specie exports in British and American warships. Silver mining did not recover quickly from wartime interruption and nitrates and guano had not yet appeared on the scene to provide a temporary solution to the balance of payments problem. At the same time, the domestic production of coarse textiles in Peru was largely displaced by foreign goods and did not recover after the war.

Free trade in Venezuela began, except for the brief interlude of the first republic in 1810–1811, with operations which bear little resemblance to regular business. Private ownership of the livestock of the Orinoco valley was largely disregarded, and after Bolívar established himself at Angostura, the livestock resources of the region were swept up by his agents and shipped to the West Indies to pay for the war supplies sold on credit at high prices by British, Dutch, and American merchants. There was no expansion of the agriculture of the coastal area of Venezuela during the period under review. It continued to seek an outlet in the *colonias extrangeras* in the Caribbean, as it had under Spanish rule, though it was now a legal trade. Privileged products like Barinas tobacco and the cacao of Caracas lost the protected markets of later colonial times and production declined. New Granada's economic recovery was also slow. There was a flurry of imports, chiefly for government account, from 1822 to 1825, financed by the loans floated in London. Apart from these years, foreign trade grew much more slowly than in Buenos Aires or Chile. Only in Guayaquil, in the southern part of Colombia, did a business boom develop. This was based on the export of lumber, rice, and cacao and the exploitation of the favored situation of this port.

In Mexico free trade did not actually begin until 1823. Until that time, all but a trickle of irregular trade had continued to follow traditional colonial channels to Spain and Cuba. When commerce with Spain was suspended, great difficulty arose owing to the disappearance of Spanish commercial capital at Veracruz. It was to take time to build up a new system of credit depending on agents of European manufacturers, established at Mexico City. In spite of English interest in Mexican mining, production of the precious metals, which accounted for most of Mexico's export surplus, did not wholly recover in the period before 1830.

The foregoing would appear to indicate some correlation between commercial progress and a lesser degree of severity in military operations in the different regions mentioned. This factor, however, cannot have been decisive. The extent to which free trade brought economic revolution also depended on the existence of resources in demand in the world markets and on adequate transportation facilities for bringing these to the seaports. Obviously, Buenos Aires, with its easily traversed *pampa,* and Chile, with production located never very far from the sea, had a great advantage over Peru, Colombia, and Mexico.

That the statesmen and politicians of Spanish America recognized the vital importance of transportation at this time is evident in the many efforts to develop steam navigation on South American rivers during the revolution. Plans were put forward involving the Orinoco, the Magdalena, the Atrato, and the Paraná. Several concessions were granted to foreigners, but none brought significant results until a later time. Interest in road construction in Ecuador, Mexico, and Colombia also failed to bring results in view of government financial embarrassments.

The rate and extent of trade expansion varied considerably from region to region, but the direction of change was the same. All the new republics headed toward a broader production of resources demanded by the world market and became increasingly intimately linked with the expanding economy of the nineteenth century, centered on and directed by Great Britain. This trade expansion brought other economic developments in its wake. Taxation shifted from the complex system of colonial days, with its multiple excises, monopoly franchises, and sales taxes, toward reliance on the customs duties on imports as the all-important source of revenue. Consumption of imported goods tended to outrun the ability of exports to balance them, leading to the negotiation of foreign loans on highly disadvantageous terms. Buenos Aires, Chile, Peru, Mexico, and Colombia all experienced the beginnings of their troubles with foreign creditors during this epoch. The too rapid expansion of imports may have been one cause of the financial crises which contributed to widespread political instability after the establishment of independence.

Along with the economic liberalism, of which the removal of trade barriers was concrete evidence, there developed a broader liberalism which also influenced society. The story of the abolition of slavery has often been told and need not be repeated here. It should be remembered, however, that outright abolition in some countries and gradual emancipation in others had reduced slavery to insignificant proportions in republican Spanish America before 1830. This was, of course, preceded by the manumission of slaves on a considerable scale in the course of the revolutionary wars. Freedmen formed part of San Martín's liberating forces that fought at Chacabuco and of the army of Sucre that completed the liberation of Peru at Ayacucho.

The Indian fared less well in this era. In spite of frequent references to their ancient woes in propaganda directed against the Spanish regime, the achievement of independence meant little to the native race. Though frequently involved in revolutionary fighting, Indians never wholeheartedly sided with either party in the struggle. In southern Chile they were active as royalist guerrillas. In Mexico they fought and bled with Hidalgo. In Peru and Colombia they fought on both sides, either because they were forced to do so, or because they followed some leader who had a personal reason for taking sides. The lapse of colonial protective legislation exposed them to exploitation under the increasingly individualistic republican legal codes and the war of independence ruined many of the missions which had preserved their existence, even if they did not succeed in fitting them for the competitive society they now had to face.

Perhaps the most marked social change of the era was the growth of the rift between the society of the seaports and capitals, on the one hand, and rural and provincial society, on the other. At the seats of government and in the ports upper and middle classes began to be affected by the streams of foreigners (diplomats, visiting scholars, pedagogues, merchants, soldiers and sailors) which began to appear on the scene. Fashions began to ape the styles of London and Paris; new sports and pastimes replaced colonial recreations; even habits of food and drink changed. Provincial cities were but little affected by these newfangled notions and the countryside was largely unconscious of them. Thus, the wider, European outlook of the elite in almost every country began to show itself in minor ways long before it was enshrined in law, educational institutions, and in the arts.

The hypothesis suggested by the foregoing remarks may be summarized as follows: the revolutionary wars which led to independence were a profound shock to the society and to the economic life of the

Spanish colonies. Wartime destruction left many countries less able to maintain traditional ways and opened the way for new developments. Ensuing changes were brought about, first of all, by the expansion of foreign trade, which in turn, had repercussions on the whole economic and social structure. Nevertheless, only the beginnings of a basic transformation took place and there were many ways in which colonial attitudes and institutions carried over into the life of republican Spanish America. Liberal ideas, however, used at first to buttress the rising power of landowners and business men, weakened paternalistic aspects of colonialism.

The Río de la Plata region was most deeply changed by the revolution. Throughout the continent, too, the greater cities and the ports were more affected by the new than were the provinces and the countryside. There emerged, therefore, no single clearly identifiable pattern of change, and developments noted were not so much revolutionary as they were examples of an accelerated tempo of evolutionary transformation.

3.

THE SOCIETY OF CASTES: Mobility and Frustration

MAGNUS MÖRNER

Social alterations, both progressive and regressive, resulted from the breakdown of traditional administrative machinery, the recruitment of armies, and the internal migrations of refugee peoples. They are among the most significant aspects of the independence movement. The Swedish scholar Magnus Mörner, formerly Professor of History at Queens College, explores these effects with particular attention to the lower sectors of the Society of Castes. As Professor Mörner points out elsewhere in his book *Race Mixture . . .* , "the Society of Castes, with its legal sanction and deep roots in social attitudes and values" formed "the basis of social stratification until the very end of the colonial era" (p. 70). The reader who is absorbed in the problem of "Revolution" will be especially interested in the discussion of Creole ambivalence on the matter of freedom.

Within the colonial society, the resentment and aggression of the oppressed masses manifested themselves from time to time in rebellions and riots. Indian uprisings were in fact usual, and most were quite easy to put down. . . .

The uprisings of mestizos were usually more moderate, directed as they were against some new tax or other unpopular administrative measure. Even so, they often reflected deep hatred between mestizos and whites. . . .

We must emphasize, however, that the emancipation movement in Spanish America, anticipated by a great many crushed conspiracies, was above all the work of the criollo elite, set in motion when the Napoleonic invasion of Spain had brought about a series of disruptive events. The only exceptions of any importance were the popular rebellions in New Spain, led by the two parish priests, Hidalgo and Morelos, and defeated with the help of frightened criollos. In Brazil, socioracial tensions on the eve of emancipation had created a dangerous situation. The abortive movement of 1798, known as the "Inconfidencia" of Bahía, apparently was directed by mulattoes of modest origin. In Bahía, there were also frequent uprisings of slaves (no fewer than eight between 1807 and 1835). But, as we know, Brazil obtained independence in an extraordinarily tranquil way, thanks to fortunate circumstances that preserved the monarchy. Hence, no events were explosive enough to release a large-scale socioracial struggle.

Humiliations suffered by individuals under the Society of Castes helped to create revolutionaries. The great example is Francisco Javier Eugenio de Espejo, the zambo intellectual of Quito, whose tragic life was a daring challenge to a society based on privilege and social inequality. But we must also realize that by far the majority of single conspirators and revolutionaries were criollos. Espejo's example shows how difficult it was for one of the disdained castas to obtain the education required to create an "enlightened" revolutionary.

The wars of emancipation were civil wars. Both sides drafted Indians, Negroes, and castas to do a great part of the fighting. Most men in the loyalist army in Peru and Alto Peru, the present Bolivia, were Indians. Between 30 and 40 per cent of the patriot army that General San Martín brought across the Andes to liberate Chile seem to have been Negroes. For all their bravery, these fighting men of color were pawns, driven on by the interests more or less alien to their own.

But during the wars there were occasions when all the tensions and hatreds, bottled up under the Society of Castes, threatened to explode, bringing on a socioracial struggle. Let us first look at Venezuela. In 1813, as is well known, two Spanish officers, Tomás Boves and Francisco Morales strove to incite the llaneros against the criollo rebels, inaugurating the most savage phase of the struggle. "We are going to fall into the hands of the Negroes. May God grant that I am mistaken!" one of the criollo leaders wrote in anguish to his wife, darkly foreshadowing racial warfare. And Archbishop Coll y Prat reported to Madrid about the 1,500 "Zamboes and Mulattoes," who entered Caracas proclaiming "general slaughter of the whites." In spite of everything, it seems that the fears as well as the many descriptions of the cruelty of Boves and his men were somewhat exaggerated. We should not forget that history was written by the victors. In 1817, Bolívar succeeded in persuading the new llanero chieftain, José Antonio Páez, to join the patriots instead. From that moment, the llaneros' savage heroism was in the service of the criollo revolutionaries. In the same year, Bolívar caused a sensation when he had one of his best generals, Manuel Piar, executed for insubordination. It is impossible to escape the impression that Piar was so harshly punished because he was a mulatto. Bolívar wrote to a friend that Piar had started "to provoke the war of colors." In fact, the loyalist generals harbored the same fear. Captain General Francisco Montalvo wrote to the Spanish government in 1814 that Boves had been able to rally between ten and twelve thousand "Zamboes and Mulattoes who now fight to destroy the white Criollos, their masters, because of the community of interests [with us] that they find in this. It will not take long before they start to destroy the white Europeans, who are also their masters, and whose death will give them the same benefit as that of the former." A prophesy that proved to be true! The new general-in-chief of the loyalists, Pablo Morillo, in 1817 sent a very courageous colored officer to Spain explicitly because he had proved to be "a stalwart foe of all whites. He has also commanded people of his own color and exercises too much influence over them. . . ." We may conclude that the risk of a clear socioracial struggle in Venezuela, already a battle ground for years, was removed because neither patriot nor loyalist commanders wanted this kind of struggle.

In Mexico, it is well known that, incited by the fiery speeches of Miguel Hidalgo, the Indian hordes now and then took bloody revenge on the whites, as in the horrible massacre of the public granary of Granaditas in Guanajuato. When the criollos realized that the war cry of "Death to the Gachupines," the invective for peninsulars, included themselves as well, they did not hesitate to help suppress the uprising. But it is most interesting that José María Morelos, at first the principal aide of, and thereafter successor to, Hidalgo and a mestizo or "moreno" himself, did intervene as soon as he considered a race war to be clearly imminent. By a decree issued in Tecpán on October 13, 1811, Morelos declared that:

. . . our system is only intended to invest the political and military government that now resides in the Europeans, in the Criollos instead . . . and that consequently there be no distinction of [racial] qualities but that we should all call ourselves Americans . . . from which it follows that everybody ought to know that there is no reason for whites to fight Negroes, or Negroes to fight natives. . . . As the whites are the first representatives of the Kingdom and the first to take up arms in defense of the people and the other "castes" . . . the whites, by virtue of these merits, should deserve our gratitude and not the hatred that one has tried to instill against them. . . .

To underline his words, Father Morelos had the two patriot leaders, whose behavior had directly provoked the decree, executed.

The attitude of the criollo elite was strikingly ambivalent when criollos had to face the socioracial consequences of the very movement they had brought into being. On the one side were their fears, as we have already illustrated, and their desire to maintain their privileged position; on the other, was the influence exercised over them by the equalitarian ideas of the French revolution. In Venezuela, the first Spanish American nation to declare its independence, the fathers of the constitution of 1811, after much debating, prohibited the importation of slaves, made the Indian equal with other citizens, and abolished "the ancient laws that imposed civil degradation on part of the free population of Venezuela hitherto known under the name of Pardos. They are to enjoy the natural and civil reputation and to cover the inalienable rights that correspond to them as to all other citizens." Other early constitutions of the new Spanish American republics granted citizenship to all those born in the country in question, without explicitly referring to previous discrimination. In Mexico, Morelos, then acting in the name of Hidalgo, prohibited the use of labels such as Indian, mulatto, and casta in November, 1810.

Hence, political emancipation tangibly affected every parish in the immense region, when one day the traditional classification into ethnic groups suddenly was discontinued. Let us take as an example an entry found in the register of marriages in one of the churches of Mexico City in 1822:

By order of the Superior government a proclamation was made public on the 14th of this month of January ordering that the qualities of Spaniards, Indians, Mulattoes, etc, no longer be specified in parish registers, but that everybody receive the qualification of American, and this order will be carried out from today onwards. . . .

Applying the new equalitarian concept did not always prove easy. High authorities themselves sometimes found it difficult to abandon the word "Indian," even in their decrees. For some time, the courts were reluctant to cease treating the Indians as legal minors. Nevertheless, legal and administrative equalization was an innovation of great importance. No longer did prejudice and different forms of socioracial discrimination find endorsement in legislation. On the other hand, the indigenous population did not find in the new legislation the special protection that it often required.

While we are considering constitutionalism and civil rights for the dark-skinned, we should examine briefly the Liberal Assembly at Cadiz, Spain, which was to produce the Constitution of 1812, even though that constitution was doomed to a short life. Here the anti-discriminatory attitude of the Spanish American deputies was intimately related to the problem of the popular basis of constitutional monarchy. By virtue of an equalitarian representative system, the overseas possessions with their 15 or 16 million inhabitants would necessarily dominate a common parliament, since Spain held only 10 or 11 million people. The "liberal" Spanish deputies then found a means of reducing the American basis by appealing to the division dictated by the Society of Castes. However prejudiced they were personally on race and class questions, the Spanish American deputies offered determined resistance. At first, the peninsulars tried to exclude the Indians, but in this respect the Laws of the Indies were too openly in favor of the natives, so they had to give way. Then they concentrated on trying to exclude those of African blood. Despite rather loud opposition by the Americans, they succeeded. A clever compromise suggested by a Peruvian, would have had the castas enjoy suffrage but not be eligible; it, too, was rejected. By a formula as astute as it was entangled, the constitution came to state that the "basis of national representation . . . is the population composed by

the natives who on both sides derive from the Spanish dominions."
But the individual possibility of "passing" allowed already by the
Cédulas de Gracias al Sacar was not annulled, because another para-
graph stated:

For those Spaniards who on either side are reputed [!] to originate
from Africa, the door of virtue and merits remains open to become
citizens. Consequently, the Cortes [the Spanish parliament] will grant
letters of citizenship to those who render qualified services to the
Fatherland, to those distinguished by their talent, application and
conduct, granted that they are born in legitimate marriage of free
parents, that they are married to a free woman . . . and that they exercise some profession, office or useful industrial occupation with
capital of their own.

A decree of 1812 also opened the doors of universities, seminaries,
and the priesthood to the pardos, but with reservations that reduced
considerably the value of the decree. Under these circumstances, the
triumph won at Cadiz by the peninsular "liberals" only served to
provide patriot propaganda with ammunition. And, after Ferdinand
VII returned from French capitivity, the restricted liberalism initiated
by the Constitution of 1812 also disappeared. Intelligent loyalist commanders realized the adverse psychological effect produced by the
Spanish government's indifference toward socioracial issues. The
captain general of Venezuela, now José Ceballos, wrote to the king
in 1815, asking him to concede some favors that might attract pardos,
suggesting at least the possibility offered by the suspended constitution
of 1812. The point of departure of his discussion was that "Venezuela
has returned to the domination of the King thanks to the efforts of
the inhabitants themselves and the armies under the Royal banner
were composed almost entirely of Pardos and people belonging to the
other castes." How could they be compensated? For slaves, manumission was the obvious compensation, but how about the pardos?
Ceballos referred to his own experience of the past campaigns, in
which "the darkest Pardo became accustomed to giving orders to
whites and to treating them on at least equal terms." He concluded
that ". . . in the case of these people no other means remains than to
take them legally from their inferior class." But Ferdinand VII, sub-
limely stubborn and stupid as always, did not heed sound advice.

Colored people finally had no choice but to join the patriot cause.

The situation could not be better illustrated than by the dialogue that Pedro Molina of Guatemala wrote for the periodical *El genio de la Libertad* in 1821. When discussing the passionate subject of emancipation with loyalist Don Gómez, Pedro Mulato says that he has seen "Negro slaves who were very much esteemed and generously treated by their masters flee to the forest to live naked only in order to be free." Don Gómez interrupts: "These are savages, but we who descend from Spaniards and Christians. . . ." Pedro Mulato: "We should be free for that very reason. Is it my fault that I am a Mulatto so that Spaniards, the compatriots of my father but not of my mother, do not want me to become anything at all?" Don Gómez: "This is because the mixture of white and black breeds bad blood." Pedro Mulato has the last word: "In that case I would find myself ill, my friend."

The promise of manumission also helped to swell the ranks of of patriot armies and the fighting qualities of the former slaves won general recognition. General San Martín confessed that "the best soldier we have is the Negro and Mulatto," whereas the whites "are only fit for the cavalry." Bolívar promised freedom to any slave who took up arms against the loyalists and tried to fulfill his promise to President Pétion of Haiti to abolish slavery as such. It was not his fault that abolition only got started during his time. His abolitionist attitude undoubtedly was sincere, based as it was on humanitarian considerations but also on political and military convenience. But Simón Bolívar, at the same time, is a fascinating example of the criollo elite's ambivalent attitude toward the race issue.

A draft of Bolívar's from 1815 stresses the relative harmony of racial relations in Spanish America, denying that the "difference of castes" forms any obstacle to independence. In this draft he even tried to explain away the secret of Boves' success by stating that slaves and mulattoes had been forced to attack the patriots. The division that mattered for the Liberator was, of course, that between American-born and peninsulars. In his famed Letter of Jamaica from the same year, written under the shadow of the Black Legend, with explicit reference to Father Las Casas, Bolívar displayed a romantically pro-Indian attitude. Interestingly, he took the historical fact of the mestizaje as the point of departure for the political and constitutional theorizing that fills most of the document: ". . . we are . . . neither

Indian nor European but a species midway between the legitimate proprietors of this country and the Spanish usurpers. . . ." In his famous message to the Congress of Angostura, Bolívar pursues the same theme:

We must bear in mind that our people are neither European nor North American; they are a mixture of Africa and America rather than an emanation of Europe. Even Spain herself has ceased to be European because of her African blood, her institutions, and her character. It is impossible to determine with any degree of accuracy to which human family we belong. The greater portion of the native Indians has been annihilated. Europeans have mixed with Americans and Africans, and we have all been born of the same mother, our fathers, different in origin and in blood, are foreigners, and all differ visibly as to the color of their skin, a dissimilarity which places upon us an obligation of the greatest importance.

He concluded that politically the Democratic Republic offered the only solution because "legal equality is indispensable when there is physical inequality to correct, to some extent the injustice of Nature."

The documents of Bolívar to which I have hitherto referred are all of a public character, and the Jamaica letters are obviously propagandistic. There is, nevertheless, no reason to doubt the sincerity of the Liberator's belief that the historical fact of miscegenation formed the very basis for the Spanish American peoples' national existence. But the race question for him was even more serious and profound. He had been raised in the aristocratic environment of the slave plantation. Since he was a delicate child and early became an orphan, it would be natural if he retained special affection for the obligatory Negro nanny. From Peru he writes to his sister María Antonia in 1825:

I enclose a letter from my "mother" Hipólita so that you give her all she wants and do for her as if she really were my mother, because her milk has nurtured my life and I have also had no other father than she.

But Bolívar had also inherited the fears and the guilt complex of the slavocrat proprietor class. There was also, it seems, some uncertainty as to his own lineage. Whether or not a great-grandmother of of his was a mulatto is, of course, a trivial detail. But the very uncertainty in this matter may have profoundly concerned Bolívar himself. Toward the end of his life, when admittedly his whole attitude became increasingly somber and pessimistic, he included in some of his letters passages that disclose both fears and guilt with regard to colored people. A letter to General Santander in 1826 is especially revealing. Informed about the insubordination of General Páez, the Liberator found himself in anguish:

We are very far from the wonderful times of Athens and Rome, and we must not compare ourselves in any way to anything European. The origins of our existence are most impure. All that has preceded us is enveloped in the black cloak of crime. We are the abominable offspring of those raging beasts that came to America to waste her blood and to breed with their victims before sacrificing them. Later the fruits of these unions commingled with slaves uprooted from Africa. With such physical mixtures and such elements of morale, can we possibly place laws above heroes and principles above men?

In these naked words, Simón Bolívar expresses the "tragic sense of life" of which Unamuno speaks, intimately related to the idea of criminal rape as the origin of existence and awareness of the eternal stigma of slavery. At the same time, he remains the aristocrat who regards the masses with contempt mixed with fear. His concept of men of more or less dark skin, like Piar, Padilla, and even Páez shows mixed disdain and envy, because he feels that they embody the real spirit of America. By virtue of their origin, they will be the victors of tomorrow. Referring to Padilla, Bolívar writes to Santander: ". . . legal equality is not enough to satisfy the spirit of the people who want absolute equality, both in the public and the domestic sphere. Later, they will request 'Pardocracy' which is their natural and only inclination before exterminating the privileged class. . . ." In shocking contrast to his optimistic declaration of 1815, Bolívar now speaks of the "natural enmity of the colors," prophesying gloomily about the day "when the people of color will rise and put an end to everything." In a way reminiscent of Spengler, Bolívar admits the impotency of his own class and "race." Referring to Padilla and Páez, he exclaims: "These two men have the elements of power in their blood, because my [blood] is of no value in the eyes of the people." There can be no doubt that the "Götterdämmerung," the last battle that loomed before the eyes of the declining and dying Bolívar, had a strong flavor of racial conflict.

But the great battle between the races never took place. In the long wars for independence, many individuals of more or less dark skin were able to climb the social ladder because of their military merits, such as Andrés de Santa Cruz, José Antonio Páez, Vicente Guerrero, and Agustín Gamarra. But, instead of replacing the traditional criollo elite, they were assimilated into it abandoning any intention they might have had to represent the interests of the socioethnic group from which they sprang. Furthermore, for all the contrast between the lighter skin of the upper strata and the darker skin of most of those below, the new Society of Classes did not offer the rigid and well-defined borders that directly provoked attack. There were always some of darker skin who, thanks to military or professional merit, or by sheer astuteness, participated in the upward mobility, whereas, now and then, "whites" were sinking to the bottom of the social structure. It is true that, by the middle of the nineteenth century, intellectuals and professionals of the middle strata, conspicuous among them the mestizos, began to form a most influential part of the liberal parties, especially in Mexico under the *Reforma* (the period of turmoil and profound political change, 1854–1876). But their attack against the elite (still mostly criollo) was not ethnically dictated. The oligarchy was attacked for being an oligarchy, not for being composed of criollos.

The rebellions of the indígenas, which had been frequent under the Spanish regime, continued during most of the national era. Among the leaders, not a few mestizos can be found by the mid-nineteenth century, such as José María Barrera in the so-called Caste War among the Maya Indians of Yucatán. But such mestizos had identified themselves with the Indians.

Apart, perhaps, from the Dominican Republic with its border problem with Negro Haiti, in Spanish America only Venezuela seems to have experienced any major "racial" influence on its political life. If we can trust the testimony left by some contemporary observers, the Monagas brothers' regime demogogically fomented the hatred of the masses for the more white-looking elite. These tensions culminated in the sanguinary so-called Federal War of 1859–1863. This horrid civil war, excellently described by novelist Rómulo Gallegos in his *Poor Negro,* succeeded in bringing about extensive socioracial leveling, a great achievement that contrasts strikingly with the utter sterility of its political consequences. From that time onward, Venezuela, for all its political instability and lack of equilibrium, was able to achieve more harmonious (or less disharmonious) relations between the ethnic elements than almost any other Spanish American country. . . .

If we were to try to summarize the facts presented in this chapter, we should make it clear that the built-in tensions of the Society of Castes really threatened to produce a civil struggle along socioethnic lines. But the criollo elite understood how to preserve its control, with the peninsulars attracting much of the accumulated hatred. The legal framework defining the Society of Castes was abolished. Nevertheless, the stratification into classes preserved most of the traditional distance between the basic ethnic groups, even though, on an individual level, social mobility, upward as well as downward, now and then affected persons of different colors. Naturally enough, socioracial prejudice did not disappear, but its expression became more subtle. Therefore it was less easily exposed than that of colonial society.

4.
ECONOMIC DEPENDENCY AND THE WARS OF INDEPENDENCE

STANLEY J. STEIN and BARBARA H. STEIN

When the economic history of Spanish America is examined, it may be significant to recall that Mexicans date their economic independence not from 1821 but from the expropriation of foreign petroleum holdings in 1938. Whether or not they are correct in so pinpointing that event or whether other Spanish Americans should also emphasize economic self-reliance only in this century, if at all, are debatable questions. Among recent efforts to explore this theme is that by an historian at Princeton, Stanley Stein, and his wife, Barbara Stein. In a collection of essays, the Steins define an elaborate pattern of dependence between the Peninsular metropolis and the crown's American possessions which developed over three centuries. In this selection, they treat the effects of political severence from Spain upon economic sectors in America. Did economic self-sufficiency emerge to replace the dependency status or did some brand of neocolonialism fill the void?

. . . [T]he colonial heritage and external conditions before, during, and after independence in Latin America both created new and exacerbated old conflicts of interest which remained unresolved for

From Stanley J. Stein and Barbara H. Stein, *The Colonial Heritage of Latin America: Essays on Economic Dependence in Perspective*, pp. 131–137. Copyright © 1970 by Oxford University Press, Inc. Reprinted by permission.

decades after 1824 and led to the option of internal war rather than constitutional compromise. When French armies invaded the Iberian peninsula, the English chose to make the peninsula a bleeding ground of French continental military supremacy; long smoldering colonial conflicts erupted in a series of disconnected, continent-wide civil wars between 1810 and 1824. Early, two major currents in all anti-colonial wars fused: resistance to further transatlantic economic control and struggle over who would then rule at home. The Spanish colonial policy of ruling by dividing, of balancing one interest group against the other, collapsed in 1810. It left a colonial legacy of sectional and regional conflict.

It is widely held that the Latin American independence movements were aimed at ending metropolitan monopoly of economic decision-making and that therefore they represent a struggle for economic liberty. No one can deny that this is what they achieved, but it would be a gross oversimplification to state that this was the principal goal of the early insurgents. In fact, acceptance of this generalization has clouded the interpretation of the post-independence decades. Perhaps it would be more accurate to argue that many of the colonial elite hoped to maintain allegiance to embattled Spain while enjoying the right to trade directly with all Europe and the United States. They did not desire to overturn society but rather to enlarge somewhat access to, and enjoyment of, positions of profitable monopoly. Open conflict ensued when Spanish intractability on the key issue of direct trade was backed by Spanish readiness to employ military force against the reformers.

Segments of the elite in colonial Latin America were attempting to make the colonial economic system rational for their interests. While the United States by 1793 could profit from European conflict, the Spanish colonies were both stimulated and frustrated. Their output of sugar, cacao, coffee, hides, and salt beef rose, but Spanish shipping was interrupted by the omnipresent British navy, and Spanish colonial policy had blocked the creation of a shipping industry in the colonies. Foodstuffs and manufactures were denied the colonies, and could be obtained only by massive participation in smuggling with English and United States ships off their coasts. Hence the mounting pressure for direct trade, for legalizing reality. But when independence solved the problem of direct trade, there was no political nor economic unity to permit rapid utilization of economic decision-making. Serious internal disunity, in fact, prolonged the civil wars of independence.

Hence post-independence decades were wasted in trying to settle highly divisive problems imbedded in the colonial heritage. The most conspicuous of the Spanish and Portuguese colonial elite, military officers, high bureaucrats, merchants—the core of opposition to independence—emigrated. A large majority remained, a significant contrast with the high percentage of émigrés from the new United States and from revolutionary France. In the immediate post-independence decades the influence of well-connected enclaves of such traditionalists upon Latin America was decisive. The new national capitals, generally the hub of the colonial economic network, wished to maintain their monopolistic position in national and international trade. To them, this was the reward of independence. But the sub-regions, many of which had developed in the eighteenth century, often stimulated by contraband activities, insisted on regional economic autonomy; this is why they often became federalists, not centralists. In Mexico, Guadalajara attacked the Mexico City–Veracruz commercial axis; in Argentina, the western interior provinces resisted expansionist Buenos Aires, and they were joined by the Litoral provinces and by Uruguay and Paraguay, former divisions of the colonial viceroyalty. The western provinces of Argentina wished to protect the local production of cotton, woolen, and linen textiles, leather goods, sugar, wines, and brandies. Having lost access to former markets in what was now Bolivia, they sought to expand in the new Argentina. But Buenos Aires merchants were interested solely in selling cheaper European imports. The conflict of regional economic interests versus those of the older mercantile centers was repeated everywhere in Latin America.

In Mexico, those involved in the artisan textile industry wanted to preserve the national market for their output, but the Mexico City merchants preferred to import English manufactured products. In sum, the new nations were torn by conflicts: between those who wished to monopolize all domestic and foreign trade from one national point and those who sought a local distribution monopoly; between those who wished to protect local artisan production and those who distributed cheaper imports; between those who favored agriculture and those who favored mining or industry. Each sub-area under the assumed protection of federal constitutions and provincial or state autonomy sought to create regional economic enclaves by internal tariffs or tolls. Thus no national unity was readily forged; there was no immediate possibility of a unified, national economic policy as was created early in the United States.

In any event, other factors would have made it difficult to escape the combined legacy of colonialism and civil war. After independence attempts to create new industries were hampered by the absence of banking institutions and capital markets and by the low level of capital accumulation. Civil war had destroyed livestock and estates, dispersed manpower, disrupted the mines. The major sources of funds, the church and the merchants, were reluctant to diversify investment. Industries in underdeveloped areas do not make demand, they respond to it. And the nature of the colonial economy of Latin America, like that of the southern United States, had concentrated income, held the per capita income of the masses at a minimal level and inhibited capital formation in liquid assets; in a word, it reduced the possibility of sustained local demand for high cost products of infant industry. Massive imports of British manufactures simply crushed local industry based upon primitive technology. Inevitably, like the southern United States, Latin America was drawn to the search for export staples, traditional or new, to pay for imports. They were drawn to the land and to external sources of dynamism.

In this way, the colonial economic heritage was reinforced by local conditions and, in particular, by the economic pressure of Great Britain, which now harvested more than a century of sustained interest in the Iberian colonial world. British manufacturers, merchants, bankers, insurance companies, shippers—all consolidated their success in the struggle against French competitors. Everywhere in Latin America, British merchants entrenched themselves—in Buenos Aires, Rio de Janeiro, Valparaiso, Caracas, in Veracruz, Cartagena, Lima. Great Britain, technologically and industrially advanced, became as important to the Latin American economy as to the cotton-exporting southern United States. At this point, Latin America fell back upon traditional export activities, utilizing the cheapest available factor of production, the land, and the dependent labor force. The land in Mexico, Brazil, and Argentina emerged as what it had always been, a source of security, income, prestige, and power.

The achievement of economic self-determination in ex-colonial areas does not necessarily lead to its efficient long-term use. The failure of Latin American movements for independence to create the bases of sustained economic growth through balanced agricultural, ranching, and industrial diversification only indicates the continued strength of a colonial heritage of externally oriented economies linked closely to essential sources of demand and supply outside the new national economies. This colonial heritage has a parallel in the southern United States after independence that is heartening even in a negative fashion. It suggests that an export-oriented economy based upon the large-scale production of staples by a coerced labor force has resilience, even when it exists in the same nation-state with its antithesis, a modern, egalitarian, industrializing economy and society. The South was an internal colony of the mercantile, industrial, and financial North. Yet even in the South paternalism, elitism, and plantation agriculture have ensured until recent times the survival of institutions and attitudes, ways of living and thinking, which come remarkably close to those of other plantation areas of the New World. The colonial heritage has effectively delayed the formation of what we term today modernized societies.

Ex-colonies, then and now, cannot readily shed the economic legacy of centuries of colonialism, they cannot rapidly close the gap between backwardness and modernity, between primitive and advanced technology, between low and high levels of income, saving, and investment, between literacy and illiteracy, between obscurantism and enlightenment, between closed and open societies, between—as the sociologists phrase it—societies based upon adscription and those based upon achievement. It is not surprising, then, that Latin America did not begin to modernize its economy through industrialization until a century after independence.

Under these circumstances the major consequence of the anti-colonial movements in Latin America between 1810 and 1824, the crushing of the ties of transatlantic empire, led—one is almost tempted to say, inevitably—to neo-colonialism. Leaving aside for the moment socio-political and psychological elements of the colonial heritage, we can see how the economic growth of Latin America through diversification and industrialization could not occur while colonial patterns of production, capital accumulation and investment, income distribution and expenditure survived. We are now readier to accept the fact that institutional factors or barriers play a determining—perhaps *the* determining—role in affecting the rate of economic and social change. Thus, in all the major areas of Latin America after 1824 there emerged a search for a viable basis of export economies, for the production and export of primary products or, as they were then termed, "colonial staples." Not until about a half-century after independence was the new basis firmly established, and its establishment coincided with the onset of political stability. Yet stability in whatever form it takes —republic or monarchy—may be a necessary, but not a sufficient basis for economic sovereignty. The absence of an autonomous, self-sustaining economy strengthened the heritage or heritages of colonialism in Latin America after 1824. This is the rationale that Latin Americans and others have evoked in calling post-colonial Latin American economy and society neo-colonial.

5.
COUNTERINSURGENCY AND THE MILITARIZATION OF SOCIETY

FELIX MARÍA CALLEJA

The boost given to the military by the wars of independence has long been identified as one of their most conspicuous and pernicious consequences. It has frequently been observed that the armed exploits of Bolívar, Sucre, Belgrano, and a host of lesser patriots drew attention to the soldier as the pivotal figure in public affairs. What has not been so obvious, however, is the contribution that royalist defenders made to the development of a militarized society. Indeed, the prewar emergence of a Creole militia officer caste, sponsored by the Bourbons themselves to shore up the empire's defenses, had already begun the creation of a corporate power bloc. This was as vital in Buenos Aires as it was in Mexico. When the Spanish General Felix María Calleja presented the following counterinsurgency plan to the viceroy of New Spain in 1811, he wrote shrewdly and prophetically that

The extinction of the revolution can be brought about; but there will be drawbacks, and the most important of these is [that] in arming the kingdom, [we are] arranging [matters] so that if [its citizens] should be turned against us someday, we can be caused much anxiety. For the present [however], if our divisions are strategically positioned, the towns may not only be held in obedience and confidence but they will also

From Felix María Calleja, "Civil Defense Regulations of June 8, 1811," in Carlos María de Bustamante, *Campañas del General D. Felix María Calleja* (Mexico, 1828), pp. 119–122. My translation.—HH.

pledge themselves to pursue the insurgents, they will become their natural enemies . . . and it will be difficult once they have successfully warred against the enemy and suffered the consequence of his evil actions for them to resolve to join him. . . .

When Calleja became viceroy himself (1813–1816), he reiterated his civil defense program. Years later the patriot journalist Carlos María de Bustamante wrote: "This simple plan . . . made soldiers of all America."

Article 1.   Divisions of the armies will be stationed at points from which they can come to the rescue without the need for long marches and [so] destroy the bandit gangs, which have frightened the towns because of their number, . . . [and to achieve this] all authorities, [and] owners or administrators of haciendas will be obliged to report to the commander; and he who does not comply exactly with this order will be treated as an insurgent.

Article 2.   In each city, villa or *cabecera* [provincial capital] of the territorial district a *comandante de armas* will be named by the respective generals, simplifying if possible royal jurisdiction with the end of appointing no more than one chief and avoiding competition and delays, [which commandant] will immediately form an urban corps of cavalry or infantry according to the size of his jurisdiction, in which will serve without exception all *vecinos honrados* [citizens], according to their class; and if someone resists (which I do not anticipate), for this sole act he will be exiled as a bad patriot to a distance of fifty leagues from his home.

Article 3.   These corps will be armed for the time being with weapons [already] scattered through the towns, which the commandant shall arrange to gather up, and with lances and machetes for those [communities] which do not have them.

Article 4.   Daily service in each one of these corps shall involve a hundred or a hundred and fifty men who shall be paid according to local resources, and a fund shall be formed out of provisional municipal taxes, and if they should not have them, they shall be based upon a forced contribution which with equity and according to the fortunes of each person will be arranged by the *cabildo* [town council], naming for this purpose a commission of three individuals who merit confidence and a treasurer into whose control the funds will come.

Article 5. The military commanders and the royal justices will have to observe the most exact and severe discipline with this permanent force, arranging regulations and circumstances; and drawing the most severe charges if they are not fulfilled.

Article 6. The remainder of the urban corps will drill on holidays in the manual of arms and will always be ready to muster.

Article 7. Everyone in a neighborhood will be enlisted by *barrio* [precinct] in charge of a magistrate, including in the enlistment every man able to bear arms, and it will be the latter's obligation to muster with such [weapons] as he can; and if lacking his whole [kit], to present himself to his superior [equipped] at least with slings and stones when the military commander gives the order.

Article 8. For each one of these barrios or its musters there shall be named an ecclesiastic who inspires confidence by his virtue and patriotism . . . [who shall] serve as confessor and exhort and animate [the troops] on all occasions.

Article 9. The owners of each hacienda within the respective districts shall establish a company of fifty men along the same lines as in the towns, which will be commanded by a captain with respective subordinates. In [haciendas] of lesser importance, a [troop] of thirty under the orders of a second lieutenant, and on ranches a squad of six or eight under the orders of a sergeant.

Article 10. The commandant of the cabecera will have muster rolls from all [the haciendas], and everyone shall patrol the roads of his district, arresting suspects, and providing information about relevant incidents worthy of note; and if it should happen that a gang of bandits should gather, the commandant in charge of the cabecera shall muster all or part of the haciendas, according to necessity, and shall sally forth to disperse them and to punish the delinquents.

Article 11. The [contingents of the] barrios of the cabeceras shall also go forth with their respective leaders, if it be necessary: even when not [necessary], they shall be kept mustered, although occupied in their business affairs; and the individual who is absent in these cases without a thoroughly sound excuse, will be treated without pardon as an insurgent.

Article 12. The prohibition of arms of all sorts among all classes of persons who are not military is absolute and in order to distinguish [the military] each individual of these companies shall carry with him a certificate signed by the respective captain and countersigned by the military commandant of each cabecera.

Article 13. Those who are found with [weapons] without permission shall lose them and for the first offence be fined six pesos, which [sum] shall be applied appropriately enough to the funds of the urban corps of the cabecera, twelve for the second, and exile to fifty leagues for the third.

Article 14. Muleteers and others who require hardware shall use only an ax and a short knife without a point in order to cut ropes.

6.
LIFE GOES ON: Royalist Local Government

JOSÉ MARÍA OTS CAPDEQUÍ

Dramatic events always attract attention away from the un-
newsworthy fabric of daily existence. Destructive warfare,
however, did not affect all areas of Spanish America throughout the emancipation process. Some areas, like Buenos Aires,
came quickly under patriot rule and suffered little damage.
There were also areas where royalist authorities maintained
control over routine government for extended periods when
the insurgents were not battering down the gates. The two
New Granada decrees which follow have been distilled by
the eminent Spanish refugee historian José María Ots Capdequí as part of his institutional study of Colombia during
independence. The flavor of the original documents is en-
hanced by leaving portions in Spanish. The reader should
note the law and order, business-as-usual approach mixed with
a measure of Spanish patriot righteousness for propaganda
effect. These decrees, and thousands like them throughout
the hemisphere, emphasize the continuity of life-styles, manners, and petty distractions no matter the colors or symbolism
of the flag flying in the *plaza mayor*.

From José María Ots Capdequí, "The Impact of the Wars of Independence
on the Institutional Life of the New Kingdom of Granada," *The Americas,*
XVII (October 1960), pp. 111–198; selection from pp. 167–170, footnotes
omitted. Reprinted by permission of the publisher.

There is also considerable historical interest in the edicts or proclamations of some of the governors during these final moments of the Spanish domination in America.

The governor of Antioquia, under date of August 21, 1816, ordered: (1) that all citizens, without exception, work in carrying materials for the rebuilding of the streets, "that they begin immediately, each one taking care of the roads where their house and lot are." (2) "En la misma proporción facilitarán el curso de las aguas, cuidando de remover los obstáculos que la hagan formar cienos y dificultar el paso de una a otra." (3) "On the first days of every month landlords shall clean the exterior of their buildings, and every four months they shall repair and whitewash them." (4) "Over the principal entrance of the houses shall be painted a shield which says 'Viva Fernando VII.' It shall be made within a circle formed of two branches, one of olive and one of palm, with the royal crown above it." . . .

The political and military governor of Popayán, Lieutenant Colonel D. José Solis, also published a printed edict on February 27, 1817. In this proclamation, written in a high-sounding and moralistic tone, the governor ordered the following: (1) Prohibition of blasphemies—"quite common since the turbulent recent events"—against which he would react "with all the just anger of the laws." (2) Prohibition of all seditious propositions. (3) A demand made to every person who possesses "seductive or declamatory works against monarchical government," that they surrender them to the government "and that they denounce all those who possess them." (4) A notice that harborers of criminals will be severely punished—only when the criminals are guilty of sedition—as will those be punished "que lo fueran de rufianes, mugeres deshonestas que ganan por sus personas, esclavos, hijos de familia vagamundos, hombres casados o personas sospechosas, leones o alcahuetes." (5) An order that all citizens of other cities of the country or foreigners "who are found in this city or within its jurisdiction without a known legitimate reason" must be returned to their rightful place within three days. (6) Citizens of other cities of the province or foreigners who for any reason arrive in the capital city or in any place within the district must present themselves to the authorities. (7) "Ningun mercader, tendero o pulpero tendrá tratos con hijos de familia, esclavos o cualquiera otra persona sospechosa de que sólo puede tenerlos como consecuencia de hurto y malversación."

(8) An announcement that idleness and laziness would be persecuted, without exception of persons, "for not even women or nobles are immune or exempt from the universal law that condemns every man to work at an honest occupation, lucrative and useful to the fatherland," therefore "it should be prudently and respectfully found out what are the inclinations, life, and customs of the citizens and inhabitants [in this regard]. (9) It was ordered, therefore, that the "leyes de vagos" be applied, sending those so condemned to the armed services, to the presidios, to public works, to the learning of some art, to the plantations, etc. according to the individual case. "Girls and adult women will be placed in the homes of honorable matrons,—since the houses of Mercy and the hospices are lacking,—or to service in hospitals. (10) A prohibition against begging. (11) An announcement that prohibited games would be prosecuted without stop. (12) No artisan or mechanic—whether he be "maestro, oficial, aprendiz o jornalero"—shall be permitted to play lawful card games on work days from six in the morning to midday and from two in the afternoon until five." (13) On Sundays and feastdays no lawful games—"gallos, truco, villar, boliche, etc."—can be played before midday. In these games there shall not be permitted the entrance of "hijos de familia," slaves, or vagabonds, nor the using of strong liquors. The games called "villares" and "truco" can stay open only until nine at night. (14) A warning that prostitution, concubinage and "amistades torpes" would be prosecuted implacably. (15) "Voluntary drunkenness will be castigated. After two in the afternoon no liquors can be sold to the Indians." (16) "Dances at night are prohibited without previous written permission of the authorities." (17) "No one can walk masked, nor in clothing 'que no le convenga.'" (18) "Those who use prohibited arms shall be prosecuted." (19) "Those who adulterate coins shall be prosecuted." (20) "Solo tendrá curso la moneda legítima, debiendo admitirse toda la de cruz que no fuese falsa." (21) "Cleanliness of the streets shall be carefully carried out, and no one is allowed to throw into them 'inmundicias, vasos inmundos o suciedades.'" (22) "Owners of city lots and open areas shall enclose them and seed them within 30 days and if they do not, it shall be done at their cost." (23) "Buildings in ruins must be repaired." (24) "Pigs who populate the plaza and the streets must be kept confined during the day." (25) "It shall not be permitted to butcher pigs in the streets, nor to keep

chicha jars there—these can be broken by any person passing by—nor to tie saddle-horses to the doors or windows." (26) Those who sell spoiled food shall be prosecuted. To avoid "the hated monopolies," it shall not be allowed that the grocers intercept and buy at the entrances to the city the foods that should circulate and be sold with all liberty." (27) "No one shall go out without a light after nine o'clock at night. The use of firecrackers is prohibited unless they are part of some church solemnity or previous permission has been obtained." (28) "It is likewise prohibited to allow young or full-grown bulls to run through the streets, unless with the governor's permission." (29) "The *Alcaldes Hermandarios, Provinciales y Pedáneos* shall carry out with all rigor their obligation of patrolling the plains and mountains to assure the security of the roads." (30) "The same alcaldes shall take care to see that the bridges are in good repair and that the rural and public roads are in good condition."

7.
NATIONAL CONSCIOUSNESS AND ALTERNATIVE MYTH

SIMON COLLIER

In his treatment of Chile's revolutionary ideology, Simon Collier, an historian at the University of Essex, remarks that "the theme of national genesis was a strong one in the revolution." In this selection from Dr. Collier's study of ideas and politics during Chilean emancipation, there is a thorough examination of the need to justify rebellion. It was an awkward but necessary task for Chilean propagandists to destroy the myths of the Spanish conquest and to replace them with an autochthonous mythology which would bolster Chilean patriotism. The amazing dexterity with which this was accomplished, using the feared Araucanian Indians who had terrorized generations of Chileans, is explained in detail by Dr. Collier. Readers should consider to what degree nationalism was a significant result of the wars of independence.

The revolutionary rejection of Spain and the Empire was, it is fair to say, closely linked to what may be regarded as the single most important aspect of the new ideology: the sense of national identity which was growing up. The revolution undoubtedly extended and enlarged that feeling of regional and provincial pride which can be observed at the end of the colonial period. The events of 1808 and

From Simon Collier, *Ideas and Politics of Chilean Independence, 1808–1833,* pp. 207–217, footnotes omitted. Copyright © 1967 by Cambridge University Press. Reprinted by permission of the publisher.

1810 compelled the creole leaders to act in a distinctively "national" manner. As [the revolutionary journalist] Henríquez put it in 1811, "In the present circumstances [Chile] should be considered as a nation. Everything has combined to isolate her. Everything impels her to seek her security and happiness on her own." The need to *form* a new nation, and to give it specific national characteristics, was implicit in Juan Egaña's treatise on education, presented to Congress in 1811. Egaña's aim in the treatise was to persuade Congress "not so much to reform abuses and to correct a People inveterate in its habits, as to create, give existence, politics and opinions to a Nation which has never had them before." Chile, thought Egaña, was in a good position to undergo this treatment; she was "free from the influence and violences of corrupt Europe" and "placed at the extremity of the earth." Egaña, then, appreciated the inner significance of the events of 1810–11. Later on, after independence, many others shared this appreciation that a new nation was being built. *La Clave* was able to exhort its readers in 1827: "Let us not lose sight of the epoch in which we live, and the fact that we are the founders of a nation."

It can be argued, I think, that many attitudes . . . point to a new and more concrete sense of nationality. . . . The rejection of Spanishness and the total condemnation of the colonial period reflect the torments of emergence from the chrysalis, . . . but more direct evidence of national feeling should be noted. The word 'patriot' itself is significant. The word *patria* (homeland, fatherland), frequently used at the start of the revolution to denote the whole Spanish Empire, soon began to acquire a much more exclusively local character. An unknown patriot writer of early 1811 considered it essential, for instance to uphold the "integrity and good name of the homeland" by opposing the pretension of the Peruvian Viceroy. During the wars of the *"Patria Vieja,"* the cry of "¡Viva la Patria!" became common, and it was the permanency of the Chilean homeland rather than the imperial community that was being encouraged.

O'Higgins, in a draft proclamation to Chilean soldiers fighting on the royalist side, included an openly nationalistic note in his propaganda: "How could you forget that you are Chileans, our brethren, from the same homeland and with the same religion, and that you must be free despite the tyrants who are deceiving you?" The fact that Chileans of the lower class could fight on the royalist side (as they did in large numbers) as well as on the patriot side shows that patriotic sentiment had not penetrated very far below a certain level of society. But amongst the creole intelligentsia and the aristocracy it was already a major theme. The concept of *patria* as it developed through the revolution was not a narrow racial one, though it was certainly geographical. European Spaniards and foreigners were welcomed into the community of the homeland provided they supported the cause. Thus Carlos Spano, a *peninsular,* died in battle against the royalists and was suitably honored by the government, which publicly recalled that his last words had been, "I die for my Homeland, for the land which adopted me as one of its children!"

When Chile was liberated in 1817 by the Army of the Andes, the same themes of patriotism recurred. Those creoles who returned from a harsh and bitter exile on Juan Fernández could take renewed delight in the land they had lost, as did Juan Egaña: "Oh, adorable fatherland! How delightful is your beautiful aspect to one who has suffered! He who had lost you blesses your soil on seeing you once more!" "Our dear homeland, beautiful Chile," triumphantly proclaimed Bernardo O'Higgins as his army descended the Cordillera, "once again occupies the rank of nation!" Up and down the country, Chileans celebrated their return to freedom with tributes of a lyrical kind to their native earth. At Ligua a patriot styling himself "El Americano del Sud" produced a typical effusion, part of which may be quoted here.

There is no single being whose soul is not cheered merely by pronouncing . . . *beloved, adorable homeland.* . . . Did the enemies of American freedom perhaps imagine that the sweet word *'homeland'* would once again be proclaimed in Chile, as has been done today? . . . Those monsters succeeded in silencing it for more than two years, not even permitting the word to be framed on the lips of men. (Oh, enchanting homeland!) But now, freed from her oppressors, she calls on her sons publicly to name her as Mother. . . . Thus the despotic name of *King* will never more be revived in our territory, and the enchanting name of MOTHER COUNTRY alone will resound even in the forests.

Chileans had a very clear notion of what constituted their homeland. Definite geographical limits were always borne in mind. Differences of opinion between the provinces of the country did not mean that these provinces had ceased to form part of the homeland. "There," wrote Carrera in 1812, referring to Concepción, "are our brothers, the sons of the same mother." Chile was no exception to the general Latin American pattern in this. Most of the former viceroyalties or captaincies-general had accepted what Giménez Fernández has called the "provincialist thesis" as far as their boundaries were concerned, though it might just as well be referred to as the "commonsense" thesis. Bernardo de Vera y Pintado observed as early as 1813 that Spanish America would, on the whole, choose to divide itself along the lines of "those limits which the provinces have comprehended up to now." Within these limits, however, Chileans were agreed that a basic political uniformity should prevail. This was shown very clearly in the case of the island of Chiloé. In the 1823 Congress, it was maintained that "Chiloé, as an integral part of the state, must yield to the majority, and since the majority has freely expressed its will to become constituted, Chiloé must submit." Some deputies then chose to argue that Chiloé had signed no "pact" with Chile, but the main arguments expressed amounted to a claim that Chiloé had always "belonged" to Chile (which, administratively speaking, was untrue) and that if Chiloé were left free to opt out of "the great family of Chileans," then small townships within the state like Melipilla or Parral could claim the same privilege if they so desired. Such, quite apart from less theoretical considerations, was the argument in favour of liberating Chiloé from Spanish rule.

There can be small doubt that many men experienced a genuine and profound affection for their fatherland during the revolutionary period. Juan Egaña, born a Peruvian but emotionally a Chilean, could write of his "love for this country, which I regard as my only fatherland." Nicolás Matorras . . . could proclaim that "there is no fate, no glory equal to that of being a Citizen of our great Chile." Supreme Director Freire was able to denounce "innovations contrary to the *national spirit.*" The Cabildo of Santiago could urge greater efforts in the military struggle against the Spaniards, for "we shall, in the end, possess a land of our own."

This national sentiment invested the revolution with its fundamental significance. It was not merely a question of political rights rediscovered; it was the birth of a nation. "Chile is raised to the rank of nation," ran a line from a poem recited in the theatre on 12 February 1820. The Proclamation of Independence of February 1818 made this fact known, finally and unequivocally, to "the great confederation of the human race," of which Chile now became a member. . . . The colonial epoch, then, was not simply an earlier epoch, but different in kind. It was, in Egaña's words, a time "before there was a fatherland."

In short, the theme of national genesis was a strong one in the revolution, and it may fairly be regarded as the one emotion which carried all the others in its wake. . . .

National feeling, having fiercely rejected the legacy of Spain, was compelled to turn elsewhere for an alternative myth. The *conquistadores* had to be condemned as monsters: they could no longer be regarded as the legitimate heroes of the nation. But the Chileans did not have to travel far to find a suitable and acceptable object for their historical reverence. The new national myth was waiting for them on the doorstep, in the form of the Araucanian Indians, "the proud republicans of Araucania," as Simón Bolívar called them in his Jamaica Letter. Here, the Chileans quickly discovered, was a pantheon of timeless heroes who could hold their own in any company.

What are the Demi-Gods of antiquity alongside our Araucanians? Is not the Greeks' Hercules, in every point of comparison, notably inferior to the Caupolicán or the Tucapel of the Chileans?

. . . Alonso de Ercilla's epic poem *La Araucana,* with its stirring description of the Araucanian resistance to the Spanish conquest, had played its part in the stimulation of Chilean self-consciousness at the close of the colonial period. The example of Araucanian valour now began to inspire the patriots in their first military campaigns against the royalists. At a celebration in honour of one patriot success, Henríquez toasted "Araucanian valour, superior to European tactics," and not long afterwards the names of the ancient heroes were invoked to spur on the armies to greater victories.

Oh, patriots . . . recover your rights, imitating in unity and constancy your Araucanian ancestors, whose ashes repose in the urn of the sacred cause of liberty. . . . May Colo Colo, Caupolicán, and the immortal Lautaro (the American Scipio) be reborn amongst us, so that their patriotism and valour can serve . . . to frighten the tyrants.

The creoles regarded themselves as the true heirs of the Araucanians. Freire could speak of "our fathers, the Araucanians," Francisco Calderón could toast the Chileans as "the sons of Caupolicán, Colocolo and Lautaro," and Henríquez could proclaim, somewhat condescendingly, that "ancient and meritorious Araucania . . . looks with pleasure on the youthful and glorious exploits of Colombia, Peru and Buenos Aires." The adjective "Araucanian" became a poetic way of saying "Chilean." Thus Carrera referred to Chile's struggle as "the war of

Araucanian independence." Many of the newspaper titles of the period also indicated the identification very clearly.

The realities of Araucanian life, past and present, did not influence the Chilean vision of the ancient Indian as the true precursor of the modern patriot. Juan Egaña saw Araucania as "the happy region ignorant of the usages of Europe and the vices of the outside world." The distinctly aggressive and bloodthirsty nature of the Indians at the time of the Conquest was either ignored or presented as "valour," "constancy," and so on. . . .

The Chileans found many parallels, however idealized and artificial, between the Araucanian situation in the sixteenth century and their own in the early nineteenth. The Indians had after all, put up a commendably tough resistance to oppression.

The territories of Concepción and Valdivia will always be classic lands of liberty. Oh! The whole of America had bent the knee, and was kissing the hand of the oppressor, and only the standard of Araucania opposed the banners of the House of Austria!

Araucanian government, too, was superior to the government which had attacked it: "The Araucanians governed themselves according to democratic standards which were infinitely more perfect than those of the Republics in Europe at that time.". . .

Given these historical precedents, it became important to establish a sense of solidarity with the remaining Araucanians of the South. Purely political considerations doubtless helped in this process. O'Higgins, for instance, tried to attract Indian support against the royalists by proclaiming to them: "We know no enemy but the Spaniard; . . . we are all descended from the same fathers, we inhabit the same clime." But a rejection of the Spanish Empire and a cultivation of the Indians did not mean that the creoles, descendants of the conquerors, had to vacate the lands formerly occupied by the Indians. If the Spaniards, in their efforts to maintain control of America, claimed the "right of conquest," then the creoles could retort, with Henríquez, "If conquest gives rights, then we alone are the owners of these lands. For we can all indisputably claim descent from the *conquistadores*." The conquest might be condemned. But it was, after all, an accomplished fact, and after three hundred years the creoles surely had rights of tenure. As Henríquez asked, "Who can find a region which has always been inhabited [only] by natives?"

This practical consideration did not, and could not, absolve the creole Chileans from trying to form a common community with the Araucanian brethren they now idealized. A most interesting reflection of this optimistic aspiration is to be found in a short dramatic sketch written by Bernardo de Vera y Pintado during the O'Higgins government. The scene is set at the mouth of the River Bío-Bío. The last descendant of the old Araucanian heroes stands meditating alone. A Chilean frigate approaches from the sea. Significantly enough it bears the name *Lautaro*—the "name of a chief whose eternal fame inspires pride and draws forth tears of tender gratitude to the native." The frigate draws closer, the crew shouting suitably patriotic slogans. The captain then prophesies utopia in a stirring invocation to the trees of Araucania:

Oh, sturdy *maitenes,* whose trunks were once watered by unmixed blood—the indomitable Araucanian's blood with which he sealed his eternal independence. Today behold beneath thy shade the patriots who are renewing liberty in all the land. A day will come when, associated with the natives of this beautiful forest, we shall form a single family together. Her brilliant ferocity softened, Araucania will then taste the fruits of trade, the arts and the sciences. Agrarian laws will regulate her fields. Industry, and those connections which bring pleasure and wealth, will replace rusticity and indigence.

Having delivered this oration, the captain of the frigate informs the Indian of the liberation of Chile and of O'Higgins' martial prowess. The Indian fetches his wife to join in the celebrations. She is somewhat diffident at first, but the captain reassures her: "We are not enemies; we are your compatriots." The two Araucanians finally go aboard the frigate, where everybody sings an appropriate paean of praise to O'Higgins. Much of the mystique of the revolution is present in these lines of Vera's: the utopian optimism, the identification of the modern patriot cause with the ancient Araucania, and the belief that all Chileans, whether white or Indian, could live together in a reformed and ideal state.

When it came to practical approaches to the Araucanians, ironically enough, relatively little was achieved by successive Santiago governments. In fact the revolutionaries experienced one set of troubles after another in their dealings with the Indians, who remained stubbornly unappreciative of the advantages of the new liberal order. The patriots' failure to propagandize effectively along the Southern "Frontier" was exacerbated by the vigorous activity of the royalists. The Peruvian task-forces of 1813–14 were able to mobilize the Indians on their side, and the Church was active in promoting the royalist cause. After the liberation in 1817, Indians were more often than not involved in pro-royalist guerrilla activities under Benavides and later the Pincheiras. Their recalcitrant attitude proved a recurrent problem for the army in the South. . . .

In view of the rosy attitude of the revolutionaries towards the glorious Araucanian past, it was unfortunate that the Indians did not take a more positive stance in relation to the revolution. Nevertheless, this did not prevent a few moves in the direction of greater justice for the Indian, even though the question remained largely academic as long as the vast majority of Indians lived beyond the influence of the central government. The first Congress provided for the admission of Indians on equal terms into the Colegio Carolino and other schools, hoping that this would end "the shocking discrimination that maintains them in their depressed condition." In 1813 the Junta decreed certain economic aid measures which, it believed, would destroy "the caste difference" in what by rights should be "a nation of brothers." In O'Higgins' time the principle of equal rights was used to establish that the Indians were eligible for military service, perhaps a somewhat unhappy way of indicating their equality. Amongst the instructions which O'Higgins' Senate tried to force on San Martín before he set off to liberate Peru (where the Indian issue had a far greater practical importance than in Chile) was an article insisting that the Indians there should be granted the same civil rights as everybody else. Later governments were more interested in crushing the last remnants of royalist resistance in the South and the endemic lawlessness which followed, an aim finally achieved by Prieto. Despite this, there were some signs that earlier attitudes were being maintained. In the 1828 Congress, some deputies urged that the Araucanians should be regarded as an integral part of the nation, even if in the past they had been treated separately. In 1829 Nicolás Pradel recommended the appointment of a Consul for Araucania, a measure designed to bring creoles and Indians closer together. A scheme of wider and more utopian proportions, embracing the whole Amerindian race, was sponsored by O'Higgins in exile. It illustrated with some force the philanthropic motives so prominent in the revolutionary attitude towards the "noble savage."

8.
THE MOODS OF ITURBIDE'S MEXICO

JAVIER OCAMPO

Through an intensive study. of the massive pamphlet literature which was published during the first two months after
Agustín de Iturbide brought off the triumphant liberation of
Mexico from Spain in September 1821, Javier Ocampo reveals how the initial mood of exuberance to achieve a model
independent nation was undercut. In his summary, Sr.
Ocampo pits the utopian ideals of thoughtful reformists
against the harsh realities of a war-ravaged economy and a
rigidly stratified social order, and reveals the studied lack
of enthusiasm for basic changes among the ruling elite.
Ocampo's final statement might be enlarged to encompass
other areas of Spanish America and is a fitting conclusion
to this unit on the consequences of independence.

Analysis of specific ideas has brought us to dwell upon the personality of the revolutionary [of 1821] and especially upon his vehement
desire to have basic reforms quickly achieved. Revolutionary Mexicans
looked forward to the urgent realization of the model of an ideal
society; . . . [and to] the immediate destruction of ancient colonial
institutions. . . . The memorable oath [of independence] fed his hopes

From Javier Ocampo, *Las ideas de un día: El pueblo mexicano ante la
consumación de su Independencia,* pp. 316–317, 307–309, 317–319. Copyright © 1969 by El Colegio de México. My translation—HH. Used by
permission of the publisher.

of a total rupture with the traditional Spanish order, infused him with confidence in the general situation of the country, impressed upon him an optimism for the future . . . and stimulated his impatience to solve [his country's] problems.

His impatience was faced, nevertheless, with a vexatious political, economic, social, religious and cultural reality and with the inertia and sluggishness of those governors charged with achieving the changes so urgently desired. This explains why in the short period of two months which followed the entrance of General Iturbide and the Army of the Three Guarantees into the Capital the revolutionary experienced both frustration . . . and pessimism. . . . So it was that he confronted the government by exploiting freedom of the press, stimulating non-conformity and attacking those institutions which he considered inadequate to bring about his dream society.

In contrast to his impatience we encounter slowness in the development of official policy. The leadership, impeded as it was by chiefly bureaucratic matters and conscious of the necessity to maintain order and tradition in order to achieve gradual changes without great trauma for the State, bottled itself up in inaction which did not permit it to realize the dynamism which the historic moment required. . . .

The inaction of the Provisional Governing Junta and the assumption of all [political] power, including that of the Regency was [a particular cause] of the atmosphere of pessimism breathed late in 1821. . . . This [inertia] . . . was denounced . . . by the writer Rafael Dávila when he wrote:

Nobody doubts that some occult hand intends to retard our happiness, using every means to thwart the wise and beneficent acts of men who are truly jealous of our well-being and happiness: We are all painfully aware that [our leaders] are distracted from the [business] of convening a congress by matters less important to the nation. . . .

In Puebla there was published on November 21, 1821, a "Diario curioso de las sesiones y fiestas" of the Provisional Junta. Among the curious sessions [reported] are the following:

October 28:   A pontifical Mass was celebrated; at 11 o'clock there was a session but nothing in particular occurred.
October 29:   There was no session . . . it was ceremonial court day [día de besamanos].
November 1:   Today there was no session. The nobility and the most

stylish and attractive of both sexes gathered in the Plaza de Armas. . . . There was a bull fight. The bells rang announcing that the flag waved in Veracruz.

November 2: Reading of the minutes and various official documents. The discussion about convoking a Congress was continued. Various proposals were made to include foreigners, declaring them citizens, if they were settled; to alter the final plan of the convocation; to publish manifestos instructing the people in their [civic] duties; but all without resolving anything because [the Junta] was waiting for judgments from the Regency about these matters.

November 3: Nothing of particular interest was treated in the session unless it was the reading of an opinion of the commerce commission about the arrangements for importation and prohibition of goods. . . .

November 4: [The Junta] approved judgment of the commission on freedom of the press to the effect that [penalties for] abuses do not apply to the clergy. [I.e. The *fuero,* or clerical immunity from civil prosecution, was upheld.]

November 5: There were elections for the third secretary of the Sovereign Junta; salaries were assigned to the secretaries and the discussion about convoking the Congress was continued but nothing was accomplished. . . .

November 6: In this session the only noteworthy event was the reading of the judgment of the Regency to the effect that the future Congress should be composed of two chambers, after the fashion of the English and Angloamerican government: [this] paper was tabled so that those who wished could read it and discuss it tomorrow. . . . Today a balloon was released in the plaza . . . with the following inscription: "Eternal glory to the unconquerable Iturbide" and beneath the balloon was suspended an effigy representing Fame, with a banner which read "Liberty". . . .

[Meanwhile] the consummation of independence of the Mexican nation presented reformers with the ideal opportunity to bring about the shift toward a new society. . . .

In their dream to mold the ideal nation many Mexican writers revealed the same tendency [which had beset the old] Spanish policy of good intentions. . . . In the same manner Mexican writers . . . , avoiding stark reality, projected themselves into an indeterminate future in which utopia would be approached [and] into a perfect society free from the grave ills which had besieged it during the terrible colonial nightmare. . . .

It was not long before the utopian ideas of the writers confronted the actual state of things. Enthusiasm over the oath of independence could not completely veil latent reality: A country with great economic problems, as much through the decay of production, the stagnation of mining, agriculture, commerce and industry, as through the severe fiscal problems of the State. A nation endowed with rigid social stratification, with little or no social mobility; with a large poverty-stricken and ignorant mass, lacking a sense of progress and good government, lacerated by the multiple problems of malnutrition, unemployment, illiteracy and misery, and with a minority possessed with wealth and culture, conscious of the necessity to create an independent nation in which representative democracy and the law would be imposed for their own benefit. A reality which exhibited the coexistence of people in different cultural stages, and in which the pressure groups, represented principally by the clergy, the landed aristocracy, the upper bureaucracy and the military wove a net of interests in order to impede the realization of those fundamental reforms which were projected for the great transformation. The Mexican panorama presented, then, major difficulties for the fulfillment of those revolutionary projects to construct an ideal society. . . .

Two months after the official consummation of independence, the decay of [the initial] enthusiasm and optimism was already a fact. This brings us to conclude that the political ideas which were suggested to reform Mexican society clashed, in the first place, with political, economic, social, cultural and religious reality . . . ; in the second place, with the revolutionary impatience of individuals desirous of rapid, radical and visible transformations; and, in the third place, with the astounding sluggishness of the leading figures toward the realization of [those] transformations. This explains the moods of pessimism, decline and frustration and the multitude of problems which appeared in a short period of two months after the patriotic enthusiasm of September 21, 1821. This, it seems, is the obligatory reference point for the narration and interpretation of all subsequent Mexican history.

BIBLIOGRAPHIC SUGGESTIONS

The best point of departure for reading and research on the wars of independence and their aftermath is Charles C. Griffin (ed.), *Latin*

America: A Guide to the Historical Literature (Austin: University of Texas Press, 1971). A provocative series of papers on the continuity of values and life-styles which remained in spite of independence are those prepared by Woodrow Borah, Charles Gibson, and Robert Potash, "Colonial Institutions and Contemporary Latin America," *The Hispanic American Historical Review,* XLIII (1963), 371–394. An older work, first published in 1918, which explores the period through biographical sketches, is William S. Robertson, *The Rise of the Spanish-American Republics as Told in the Lives of Their Liberators* (New York: Free Press, 1965). As much attention tends to focus upon Bolívar in the years up to 1830, see David Bushnell (ed), *The Liberator, Simón Bolívar: Man and Image* (New York: Knopf, 1970) for a balanced introduction to the life and mind of this complex figure. For a full-dress biography, see Gerhard Masur, *Simón Bolívar* (Albuquerque: University of New Mexico Press, 1969, rev. ed.). Sample studies of other leaders involved with the later transition years include W. S. Robertson, *Iturbide of Mexico* (Reprinted; New York: Greenwood Press, 1968); Wilfred H. Callcott, *Santa Anna* (Reprinted, Hamden, Conn.: Archon, 1964); Louis E. Bumgartner, *José del Valle of Central America* (Durham, N.C.: Duke University Press, 1963); David Bushnell, *The Santander Regime in Gran Colombia* (Newark: University of Delaware Press, 1954); Ricardo Rojas, *San Martín, Knight of the Andes* (New York, 1945); and Stephen Clissold, *Bernardo O'Higgins and the Independence of Chile* (New York: Praeger, 1969).

Other works that open a wide range of inquiry include Charles W. Arnade, *The Emergence of the Republic of Bolivia* (Gainesville: University of Florida Press, 1957); Roger M. Haigh, *Martín Güemes: Tyrant or Tool?* (Fort Worth: Texas Christian University Press, 1968), a study of the power of extended families; Robert L. Gilmore, *Caudillism and Militarism in Venezuela, 1810–1910* (Athens: Ohio University Press, 1965); Miron Burgin, *The Economic Aspects of Argentine Federalism, 1820–1852* (Cambridge, Mass.: Harvard University Press, 1946); Ralph L. Woodward, Jr., *Class Privilege and Economic Development: The Consulado de Comercio of Guatemala, 1793–1871* (Chapel Hill: University of North Carolina Press, 1966); Arthur P. Whitaker, *The United States and the Independence of Latin America, 1800–1830* (Reprinted; New York: Norton, 1964); and for insight into British economic activity, see R. A. Humphreys, *Liberation in South America, 1806–1827: The Career of James Paroissien* (London, 1952). The numerous accounts of foreign observers are represented by H. G. Ward, *Mexico,* 2 vols. (London, 1828; 2nd ed., 1829), and R. A. Humphreys (ed.), *British Consular Reports on the Trade and Politics of Latin America, 1824–1826* (London, 1940). For a study of a country that postponed independence until 1898, see the relevant sections of Hugh Thomas, *Cuba: The Pursuit of Freedom, 1762–1969* (New York: Harper & Row, 1971).

II.
The Caudillo:
Representative Leader or Deviant Personality?

⚔ ANTHONY P. MAINGOT

So much of Latin American political history has been dominated by strong, charismatic[1] personalities that political historians have often been tempted to reduce the analysis of that politics to political biography. Not only are periods known in terms of particular leaders, but given political movements are called by the leader's name. Today Perón's movement is called "Peronismo" in the same way that Bolívar's movement was called "Partido Bolivariano."

The importance of the subject to Latin American intellectuals is apparent in the frequency with which their surveys of Latin American national politics end up focusing on the nature of leadership. Moreover, their explanations of that leadership have quite often reflected the kinds of deep-seated despair noticeable in the following conclusion of an Argentine scholar:

Do not try to find complications of pure social interests in the technique and genius of our primitive politics, because once stripped of its externals, the sentiment which generates

---

[1]Max Weber defined charisma as "The absolutely personal devotion and personal confidence in revelation, heroism or other qualities of individual leadership." But if we know what charisma is, do we know what brings it about, what causes this devotion and confidence in an individual leader?

all party action is adherence to the *caudillo*. . . . And as in reality there is no organic government, no political system, *tyranny, disorder, liberty, regeneration* is a man, or when several, a limited group of men.[2]

But, of course, many Latin Americans have tried to "find complications" to explain the technique and genius of Latin American political leadership or caudillismo, revealing in their efforts to do so schools of thought perhaps best described as "pessimist" or "optimist." Starting from a basic theoretical similarity, that is, the basis of legitimacy of the leadership was charismatic, and that that leadership tended to be dictatorial and authoritarian, the two schools diverge in their descriptions of the social realities, in their normative judgments of those realities, and, flowing from these differences, in their policy recommendations.

The "pessimist" school had its great flowering in Argentina. Not just the often cited Domingo F. Sarmiento and Juan Bautista Alberdi, but also such authors as Carlos Octavio Bunge, José Ingenieros, and Alfredo Colmo portray the Latin American personality or national character in psychopathological terms. Apathy, indolence, verbosity, arrogance, an exaggerated sense of theatrics, heroics, and acute personal susceptibilities—all characterized a New World "race." An inherent submissiveness to strong authoritarian types—or, as Bunge called it, *cacicability*—was the result of that collective character and the fundamental cause of caudillismo. Redemption, insisted the pessimists, had to come from the outside; the diseased Latin American body politic could not produce its own antibody to infection. Their policy recommendations invariably included the infusion of new blood into the system through North European immigration.

To the pessimists the caudillo as a leader embodied the intrinsic malaise of the society. He represented that malaise through his violent authoritarian actions. According to this school, leaders who did not remember the sordid social realities of their environment were destined to fall. Thus the

[2]Lucas Ayarragaray, *La anarquía argentina y el caudillismo* (Buenos Aires, 1925), pp. 139–40.

darkly pessimistic Bolivian, Alcides Arguedas, in his aptly titled book *Pueblo enfermo: contribución a la psicología de los pueblos Hispano-Americanos* (2nd ed. Barcelona, 1910), explains that the caudillo Linares lost his authority and power because he was a man of character: "He forgot that in certain areas, among peoples of doubtful morality, to have character [*tener carácter*] is to fall into disgrace."

The optimists, while agreeing with the pessimists that deep and serious problems characterized their societies, differed in their evaluation of the caudillo. Rather than being symptomatic of a disease-ridden body the caudillos were "rude agents of progress and peace"—the best the disturbed system had to offer. "The history of these Republics," noted the most widely read of this group, the Peruvian Francisco García Calderón, "is reduced to the biography of its representative men. The national spirit is concentrated in the caudillos, absolute chiefs, constructive tyrants."[3] Only the charismatic leader could engender the loyalty and affection of his people; only he functioned as a potent cohesive social force.

To the question what are the traits of leadership and the sources of power of the successful caudillo, the optimists nearly invariably answered that these caudillos dominate through valor, personal prestige, and aggressive audacity. Hence this school was optimistic in the sense that it did not turn to foreign sources for redemption, but rather expected that redemption to come from the caudillo—the democratic Caeser as Vallenilla Lanz called him—who represented the best traits of his own disturbed people.[4]

Despite different interpretations, it is clear that both schools saw caudillismo as a product of society and the caudillos as "representative" men. Unfortunately, this did not emerge explicitly in a working hypothesis of caudillismo. The literature was more concerned with condemning or praising the cau-

[3]Francisco García Calderón, *Latin America: Its Rise and Progress,* trans. Bernard Biall (London, 1913).
[4]Laureano Vallenilla Lanz, *Cesarismo democrático. Estudios sobre las bases sociológicas de la constitución efectiva de Venezuela,* 4a ed. (Caracas, 1961).

dillo as a political type. When this literature, especially of the pessimistic school, began to influence American scholarship on the subject, the underlying implicit premise of the representational character of caudillismo somehow got lost in the process.

What emerged were two central ideas which have become embedded in much of the literature on caudillismo: first, that the caudillo was characteristic of a certain period of Latin American history. The literature spoke of an "Age of the Caudillos," visualized as a distinct period of history in which a certain type of leadership was dominant. The second idea was that the characteristic or "typical" leaders of that period reflected a style of behavior which was deviant if not outright psychopathological.

Both premises are central to the work of one scholar who was the most active student of caudillismo some decades ago, Charles E. Chapman (document 1). Chapman saw caudillismo as the dominant factor in Latin American history. He, and his many students, drank deeply from the font of the pessimist school described above. Armed with the severe normative scale of white Anglo-Saxon society, Chapman measured caudillos in terms of their personal social and moral behavior and their contributions to the state. One begins to understand something of Chapman's orientation when one analyzes the nature of the "evidence" utilized in their studies —largely contemporary eyewitness accounts of foreign diplomats. J. Fred Rippy's piece (document 2) clearly indicates the difficulties of interpreting leadership in a foreign sociocultural context. What to the outsider seems psychopathological, may, in fact, be completely rational given the sociocultural context of the actor. Yet it is largely from outsider eyewitness accounts that the historian has drawn much of his data to reconstruct the "typical" caudillo.

Aside from the distortions caused by ethnocentric moralism, there are, on the surface, two additional weaknesses in the approach of both these schools and their American counterparts. The first weakness stems from the danger of studying only those leaders who achieved political power—called caudillos in *post facto* fashion. This approach disregards the effects which the mantle of power itself might have on leadership characteristics. Power lends prestige by the very fact of its occupancy. What Tucker calls "situational charisma" expresses the point very nicely: holding power *per se* can create the impression that the individual is a charismatic leader when in reality he may not be so. This weakness leads to the second. While it is clear that the personality characteristics form an important aspect of leadership studies, overemphasis on those traits, especially what are regarded as psychopathological ones, can produce a distorted view of leadership in a given social and cultural context. The attempts of historians at explaining motives, the psychological derivations of the leader's behavior, at "putting the caudillo on the couch," to borrow a suitable phrase, are usually not productive.

It is advisable, therefore, to bring the level of analysis down a peg or two; at the sociological level attention can center on the way in which political ideas, beliefs, and actions are formulated and expressed, fundamentally, on the style with which the leader presents himself to his political audience. Political style includes speech patterns, dress, manual expressions; in general, the total image of himself which he purposefully displays and projects.

The focus on political style is certainly not a new one. To cite but a few important studies: two decades ago V. O. Key, Jr., described the political style of the important state of Virginia as an extension of the plantation society's ingrained sense of honor and gentility *among peers*. The late Richard Hofstadter noted a certain "paranoic" style in much of American politics. Similarly the political style of Huey Long has been interpreted to represent that of Louisiana politics in general as a "demagogic" political style.

By stressing political style rather than political type, thus avoiding involvement in the leader's motives, the way is pointed to the study of the *representational character* of leadership, in the sense that leadership is dependent on group and public acceptance; it is part of the broader political culture. As Lucien Pye has noted, the style and operating codes of a society's leaders like the society's traditions as a whole are not just random products of historical experience, but, rather, they fit together as part of a meaningful and intelligible network of social relationships.

The view that leadership is representational in character is well established in sociological theory.[5] According to this theory leadership depends on acceptance within given contexts, i.e., it does not reside exclusively in the individual but rather in his functional relationship to other members of their group.[6] Two of the more obvious of these characteristics are interests and social background. Although the basic thrust of these early theoreticians still holds (for as Muzafer Sherif has asserted, the leadership status itself is within a group and not outside it),[7] more recent studies of leadership have corrected somewhat the tendency of these early studies to lean too heavily on "situational determinancy" and point to the leader's personality as an important factor. Emphasis on the leader's personality tends to be more important in situations where the definition of roles is undergoing change or at least being challenged, where traditional structures and value systems are in flux. Revolutionary situations bring about such changes. The years of the Latin American Wars of Independence are examples of this; so are the many cases of revolutionary or near-revolutionary situations in which new groups have challenged the right of Latin American traditional elites to rule.

Crucial for the understanding of political leadership in the

[5]Cf. Irving Knickerbocker, "Leadership: A Conception and Some Implications," *Journal of Social Issues, 4* (Summer 1948), pp. 23–40. For further discussion of the literature on this point see Ralph M. Stogdill, "Personal Factors Associated with Leadership: A Survey of the Literature," *Journal of Psychology, 25* (January 1948), pp. 66 *passim.*

[6]William O. Jenkin, "Review of Leadership Studies with Particular Reference to Military Problems," *Psychological Bulletin* (January 1947), pp. 54–79.

[7]See the following studies on leadership in the *International Encyclopedia of the Social Sciences, 9* (New York, 1968): Cecil A. Gibb, "Leadership: Psychological Aspects" (91–101); Arnold S. Tannenbaum, "Leadership: Sociological Aspects" (101–105); Lester G. Seligman, "Leadership: Political Aspects" (107–113).

multiethnic societies of Latin America is the concept of marginality developed by Robert Park and his student Everett V. Stonequist[8] to describe cases of conflicting role-commitments, of individuals caught between two cultures or two ideological worlds. One manner of resolving marginality is by seeking an outlet in leadership, often political leadership. The individual combats one part of himself by aggressively pursuing the leadership of the group which represents the other part of him. Commenting on marginal nationalist leaders, Stonequist remarked that "By losing himself in a cause larger than himself [he] overrides, if he does not solve, his own personal conflicts." In document 3 Madariaga describes Bolívar as a man straddling two distinct worlds, torn between them; in a sense marginal to both. This affected Bolívar's style and made him a complex and difficult person to understand but a man driven that much harder to assert leadership. The mixed Spanish, Indian, African aspects of his social milieu are artfully woven together by the author to show the leader's social context—the constituency to which his style of leadership appealed.

With these theoretical insights in mind the task becomes clearer. Studies of leadership styles would do well to begin with social history before entering into biography. The group, perhaps as much if not more than the individual, should be the point of primary focus. And the questions should reflect that focus. What is the nature of the social structure, the shape and orientation of the dominant groups? How long has that group or groups held its present position? What are the styles of behavior perceived by that group as the qualities desired in a leader? Which are the personal characteristics that provide an advantage in the competition to become a leader, that facilitate ascent to leadership status? In document 4 we see how the newly dominant elite in Colombia in

[8]Everett V. Stonequist, *The Marginal Man* (New York: Charles Scribner's Sons, 1937. Introduction by Robert E. Park). See also, Jesse R. Pitts, "Personality and the Social System," in Talcott Parsons *et al.* (eds.), *Theories of Society*, Vol. II (New York: Free Press, 1962), p. 711.

the early 1830s publicized the criteria of comportment, the style required of present and potential members of the "in" group.

An individual's style of life, characteristic attitudes, behavior and life chances are intimately, though of course never automatically or irrevocably, associated with his position in the social structure. The more stable the social structure the less chances there are of "marginal" situations arising, and the more clearly defined the expectations of the dominant groups are as to what constitutes "proper" behavior.

Candidates for leadership are not exempt from these expectations since it appears self-evident that the political style cannot deviate too drastically from the styles stressed by the particular stratum to which he belongs. Of course, if the prospective leader's intentions were revolutionary in the sense of overturning the social structure, he might very well purposely reject the style of his stratum and adopt that of the new group he is appealing to for power. But where the individual accepts the ideology of his stratum and shares its value system, his style will reflect the standards acceptable to that stratum.

That caudillos, without obliterating their unique personality configurations, depended very much on the group and social context is illustrated by the four subsequent documents. Ulises Heureaux responded to what Hoetink calls the "aristocratic culture" of the Dominican Republic (document 5); Emiliano Zapata embodied the traditional values of his village as defined by the village elders (document 6); Francisco Julião adopted a new style to appeal to a potentially powerful new sector of Brazilian society (document 7). Leadership in each of these studies is placed within a definite sociocultural context.

The final selection (document 8) points to the institutional or legal framework within which the role of leader is played out at the national level. It is clear that if at one time strong leaders were the cause of highly centralized forms of government with provisions for a powerful Executive, once established, these forms themselves became instrumental to continued executive dominance. The Latin American political systems are essentially executive-dominated ones. Both societal and institutional factors conspire to accentuate the importance of personal leadership.

The documents in this unit point to several characteristics of caudillismo which deserve special emphasis. First, caudillismo is not limited to one region nor to a distinct period of Latin American history. Fidel Castro is as much a caudillo as was Simón Bolívar, Ulises Heureaux, or Emiliano Zapata. Second, caudillismo is not to be confused with militarism or military rule. Not all military leaders are caudillos and not all caudillos military men. The terms are not synonymous, neither are they mutually exclusive.[9]

In Latin America social groups continue to project their political aspirations and social values onto "representative" men. These men come to embody the complex network of social relationships which forms their context. Some are "marginal" men, others are not. But they all, in one way or the other, take on the "style" most appropriate to their social milieu. Once a caudillo rises to national political prominence, the political and legal structures enhance the charismatic aspects of his role because they are executive-oriented structures.

It is crucial to understand that the caudillo's appeal will depend on the support of those groups who have the economic and social power to define what that style should be.

Finally, it is not altogether redundant to repeat one of the central themes of this introduction: caudillismo is not something of Latin America's past, it persists to this day. Vivid evidence of this fact has been the return to prominence in the late 1960s and early 1970s of a number of "fallen" caudillos. It was not too long ago that a keen observer of Latin American politics, Tad Szulc, wrote, "The long age of dictators in Latin America is finally in its twilight." His book was, it seemed, appropriately called *Twilight of the Tyrants*

[9]See Unit VIII, "Civil–Military Relations in the 20th Century," in the present volume.

(New York: Holt, Rinehart and Winston, 1959). Of the four caudillos still alive, three have made phenomenal comebacks in their nation's politics, this time electoral politics. The appeals of Juan Domingo Perón of Argentina, Marcos Pérez Jiménez of Venezuela, and Gustavo Rojas Pinilla of Colombia are remarkably similar; they are strongest in urban centers among the working classes, a sector only relatively recently articulate. The appeal of populist leadership is common to all three. They have made the transition from military leaders holding power through the military to populist leaders strongly opposed by the military. But at all times they have been individual leaders who embodied in their style and image the aspirations of major sectors of their societies. There has been no twilight of the Latin American caudillo.

1.

THE AGE OF THE CAUDILLOS: A Chapter in Hispanic American History

CHARLES E. CHAPMAN

As Professor of History at the University of California, Berkeley, Charles E. Chapman directed numerous Ph.D. dissertations on well-known Latin American caudillos. Chapman's approach to the study of caudillismo had a strong influence on much of the subsequent literature on the subject.

One of the dominant facts—one might almost dare to say *the* dominant fact—in the political history of Hispanic America in this era has been the existence of the institution of "caudillism," based on the rule of individuals commonly called "caudillos." Somewhat weaker terms occasionally employed to imply the same thing are the words "caciquism" and "caciques.". . .

Generally, the more violent of the caudillos appeared in the early years of the republican era, while those of later years were somewhat less crude and barbarous. On a smaller scale, much the same sort of evolution manifested itself in the careers of individual caudillos, whose measures were much harsher during the years when they were insecure in their power than they were after they had established control. In other words, the caudillos changed, just as did the people whom they

From Charles E. Chapman, "The Age of the Caudillos: A Chapter in Hispanic American History," *Hispanic American Historical Review,* Vol. 12 (August 1932), pp. 281–300. Reprinted by permission of the publisher. Copyright 1932, Duke University Press, Durham, North Carolina.

ruled, and tended to adapt themselves to public opinion in so far as it did not conflict with their own interests. . . .

. . . In any event, by whatever device, their rule was military and despotic, though often to the accompaniment of pomp and pageantry, display and etiquette, in order to produce glamor as of royalty to impress the crowd.

Once in office, the caudillos ruled permanently, or until defeat overcame them. . . .

It is hardly necessary to say that caudillism grew naturally out of conditions as they existed in Hispanic America; institutions do not have the habit of springing full-blown and without warning into life. One of the essential antecedents of caudillism is to be found in the character of the Hispanic races which effected the conquest of the Americas. Spaniards and Portuguese, then as now, were individualists, at the same time that they were accustomed to absolutism as a leading principle of political life. . . . In America, the conquerors were a dominant minority among inferior races, and their individualism was accentuated by the chances now afforded to do as they pleased amidst subjugated peoples. It must be remembered, too, that they did not bring their families, and in consequence not only was there an admixture of blood on a tremendous scale with the native Indians and even the negroes, but also tendencies developed toward loose and turbulent habits beyond anything which was customary in the home land. In other words, Hispanic society deteriorated in the Americas. To make matters worse, there were no compensating advantages in the way of political freedom, for the monarchy was successful in establishing its absolutist system in the colonies, a system which in practice was a corrupt, militaristic control, with scant interest in, or attention to, the needs of the people over whom it ruled. The Anglo-American colonies were settlements of *families* in search of new homes. They did not decline in quality, as there was no such association with the Indians as there was in Spanish America and Brazil. In Hispanic America, society was constituted on the basis of a union of white soldiery with Indian or negro elements. It tended to become *mestizo* or mulatto, with a resulting loss of white culture and the native simplicity of life. Soon the half-castes far surpassed the whites in numbers, and, especially in the cases of the *mestizos,* added to the prevailing turbulence in their quest for the rights of white men. . . .

Ignorance, turbulence, and what proved to be their great ally, universal suffrage, combined to assure the rise and overlordship of the caudillos. The overwhelming majority of the people of Hispanic America were illiterate. Certainly, it would be a generous estimate to assert that as many as ten per cent of the inhabitants could read and write. With this impossible background, democratic institutions were attempted. . . . The turbulence of the new alleged democracy could accept nothing less than universal suffrage, which of course was duly proclaimed. That meant the demogogue in the city. Much more important, it meant the caudillo in the rural districts, for the "sacred right of voting" became the principal legal basis of the power of the caudillos. Out of this there developed that curious phenomenon, the Hispanic American election. Elections were habitually fraudulent. The only question about them was whether the fraud should be tame or violent. If there were no resistance, various devices were employed to obtain the vote desired. . . . All that remained for the caudillos to do was to conquer the demagogues. Then at last the work was complete. The castout and wandering spirit of Hispanic absolutism had found a new home in the personality of the caudillos. The "Cowboyocracy" of the Río de la Plata and its parallels elsewhere in Hispanic America had established themselves in the seat of power.

The typical caudillo of the early independence era has been described in these terms:

Tenacious and astute, capable of converting himself into a dictator by means of his cynicism of temperament and his systematic cruelty, he was part cowboy, part actor, avaricious of omnipotence, manufacturer of terror, without any uneasiness of conscience, and with an obstinate contempt for human nature.

Under the caudillos there was no hierarchy, no division of powers. They themselves were absolute. Their will was the law. Caudillism became the real constitution, despite imported "fundamental documents." The caudillos ruled on behalf of themselves and their following, and protected such others among the wealthy as made fitting arrangements with them. . . . The most successful caudillos were those who combined audacity and animal-like courage with the methods of the braggart and bully. . . .

Eventually, the age of the violent or "muscular" caudillos, as they are sometimes called, came to an end. In most parts of Hispanic America there continued to be caudillos, but they were now of the "tame" and "semi-cultivated" variety. A few countries, notably Argentina, Chile, and Uruguay, banished caudillos altogether, but their ghosts remained in the offing, ready to materialize in a political emergency. . . .

So outwardly the caudillo changed. All legal forms were now carefully observed. If the constitution stood in the way, great pains were taken *to make a new constitution,* instead of open departure from the old. The "tame" caudillo preferred intrigue to violence, or if violence were necessary sought to place the burden of guilt upon others. Indeed, one of the oustanding traits of the tame caudillos was a certain feline duplicity. They were now afraid or ashamed of being thought to be caudillos. Nevertheless, caudillos they still were. . . .

It might be fitting, in closing this paper, to refer very briefly to Mariano Melgarejo, the most notorious of all the violent caudillos of Bolivia. An illegitimate child, and reared in poverty and neglect, he developed into a rude, ignorant, violent, and quarrelsome ruffian, and he was notoriously sensual and a confirmed drunkard. . . .

. . . As president he gave himself up to continual debauchery, and his personal vanity was so great that he was susceptible to the grossest of flattery.

By revolution he gained his power. By revolution he lost it—fleeing rather ignominiously from La Paz when it seemed that he had a chance of gaining the day, and barely escaping to Peru. This flight, so at variance with his whole life, seems to have been caused partly because of his fears for his mistress to whom he was devotedly attached. . . . His mistress had declared that she would no longer live with him, and while trying to force an entrance into the house, he was shot to death by José (the brother). It was the typical end of a typical caudillo. In Bolivia he was succeeded in the presidency by General Morales, himself a notorious caudillo.

2.
BOLÍVAR AS VIEWED BY CONTEMPORARY DIPLOMATS OF THE UNITED STATES

J. FRED RIPPY

That perception is selective is a common assertion and a fact. A product of his particular social and cultural environment, man judges behavior according to those normative scales approved and stressed by his society. Once out of that environment man continues to utilize his culturally centered frame of reference, but this often leads to distorted interpretations especially if normative judgments are attached to his observations. J. Fred Rippy, Professor Emeritus of History at the University of Chicago, demonstrates here how North American diplomats tended to judge Simón Bolívar by their own value system and thereby partly misrepresented his leadership qualities and public appeal.

In the earlier days of his brilliant career he was given only slight attention by the few Yankee agents in the theater of his activities, but whenever they mentioned him it was usually to praise him. . . .

Apparently there was little but praise for Bolívar the "Passionate Warrior." It was not until the Spaniards had been driven from South America and the agents of the United States began to observe and listen to reports of the political movements of the victorious general

From J. Fred Rippy, "Bolívar as Viewed by Contemporary Diplomats," *Hispanic American Historical Review*, Vol. XV (August 1935), pp. 287–297, footnotes omitted. Reprinted by permission of the publisher. Copyright 1935, Duke University Press, Durham, North Carolina.

that they first uttered adverse criticisms. Soon afterward, however, sentiments of disapproval came in to Washington in ever-increasing number until by 1829 the condemnation was almost unanimous.

In 1827, Consul William Wheelwright wrote from Guayaquil:

I have data for stating that General Bolívar who has been the pride and boast of every patriot has been and is the cause of all our evils: ambition and intrigue have marked his career since he last landed on the shores of Colombia.

From Chile, in 1829, Samuel Larned expressed the view that the machinations of the Liberator were behind recent successful revolutions in Peru and Bolivia. "Thus," remarked Larned,

. . . will this fortunate and ambitious man, through force, intrigue, corruption, and the prestige of his name, soon see his sway over these countries, either directly or indirectly, restored . . .

Harrison even went so far as to write Bolívar a long letter (September 27, 1829) warning the Liberator against his supposed despotic course and urging him to mend his ways. . . .

John Quincy Adams, after he was no longer Secretary of State or President, wrote that the

conduct of Bolívar has for many years been equivocal. As a military leader, his course has been despotic and sanguinary. His principles of government have been always monarchical, but for himself he has repeatedly played off the farce of renouncing his power and going into retirement. He still holds out this pretense, while at the same time he cannot disguise his hankering after a crown.

Even Henry Clay, hitherto an ardent admirer, penned a mild remonstrance in 1828. . . .

And Martin Van Buren, as secretary of state, and doubtless speaking for himself as well as for President Jackson, remarked:

The President is unwilling to believe that he who has made such liberal sacrifices and exerted such great powers, physical and moral, to redress the wrongs and secure the liberties of his country, can ever consent to exchange the imperishable renown which posterity will doubtless award to the constant and untiring patron of public liberty for the fleeting and sordid gratification of personal aggrandizement.

But the most severe criticism of Bolívar came from the pen of William Tudor, consul of the United States at Lima. Tudor had been an admirer of the Liberator until the late spring of 1826 and had more than once expressed the view that the presence of the General was necessary for the tranquillity of Peru and Bolivia. In May of this year, however, a closer view of the hero finally removed the halo. The first disillusionment was occasioned by Bolívar's alleged high-handed dismissal of the Peruvian Congress and by the discovery of what Tudor believed to be a trustworthy account of an ambitious project of the Liberator's to subdue all of South America:

The deep hypocracy [sic] of General Bolívar has hitherto deceived the world, tho' many of his former friends have for more than a year past discovered his views and abandoned him. With the violent dissolution of the Congress, the mask must fall entirely, and the world will see with indignation, or with malicious delight, that he who was occupying the attention of politicians in all countries, and for whom fate by a fortunate combination of circumstances, had prepared the means for leaving one of the noblest reputations that history could record, may be handed down as one of the most grovelling of military usurpers, loaded with the execration of his contemporaries for the calamities his conduct must bring upon them. . . .

This unfortunate state of things has partly been brought on by the base and excessive adulation that he has admitted, until it has become necessary to him. There is no individual among those about him, who dares tell an unpleasant truth, and at the slightest opposition he gives way to an unrestrained violence. At the present moment when they [the Peruvians] are in such distress for money, the only public work that is going on, is an equestrian statue of himself, the execution of which now is a project . . . to pay him court. . . . A great number of gold medals have been distributed with the arms of Peru on one side, and his bust on the other; and these medals are given to both men and women, with the diploma of being *benemerito de la patria:* and no one of either sex approaches him, who possesses one, without having it dangling from the neck; and those who neglect this are at once proscribed from all further audience. On his arrival at any of the towns, expensive fetes are to be got up for him, which bear excessively hard on an impoverished country; but his generals who are in command, will take care to vex those who are reluctant. . . . With these demonstrations he deceives himself, or is deceived by the crawling, despicable flattery of those about him, [and assumes] that they are the spontaneous effects of attachment.

. . . On August 1, [Tudor] mentioned the following extravagant incident which occurred at the celebration of Bolívar's forty-third birthday. In response to a toast that was given at his table, he declared himself a greater man than any which history has recorded, that not only the heroes of antiquity were inferior to him in "liberal ideas," but Washington and Napoleon he had left much in the rear.

A few weeks later Tudor related two more anecdotes regarding the Liberator's alleged vanities:

Some months since at a supper in Arequipa, at which were present upwards to twenty persons, after the champagne had circulated rather freely, talking of the character of Napoleon, he [Bolívar] said, if he had been in his [Napoleon's] situation, he would have conquered all Europe without difficulty. Some one remarked that he would have found an obstacle in England,—perhaps it might be so, he said, and then jumping on the table and kicking about the bottles and glasses, he exclaimed in this manner I would have marched over France and Spain.

Late in August, 1826, a group of ladies met in the palace at Lima to "intreat" [sic] the Liberator not to abandon Peru.

Three young girls delivered him short addresses on this occasion. . . . To these he answered that he regretted he could not remain, that he was sensibly affected by their kindness, but that his duty called him to Colombia. On this answer, two or three ladies whose husbands are in place, exclaimed: "he has said nothing, he has not promised, he must not go," and a general cry was raised, "he must not go:" those nearest to him then caught him in their arms, insisted that he should promise to stay, and with the exception of a very few, about seventy ladies being present, the whole went forward to embrace him. He said it was impossible to resist so much beauty and attraction, and that he would stay. . . .

In more abstract terms Tudor described Bolívar in 1827 in the following severe language:

His character is ardent, vehement, arrogant; his passions uncontrollable and restrained by no principle . . . : and with frequent sallies of frankness or rather indiscretion, he is capable of a most profound, solemn hypocrisy. He considers words as conveying no obligation, but wholly subordinate in whatever shape or profession, to promoting his designs.

In the chorus of condemnation raised by diplomats of the United States in service south of the Río Grande during the last five years of Bolívar's life, one finds only two notes of discord; and one of these was sounded under the impulse of emotion caused by the death of the Liberator.

Such was the hero of the war of liberation in northern South America as viewed by the diplomatic agents of the United States who served their country near the large stage whereon he acted. It is well to note the exact limitations of their dispraise. Most of them condemned the monarchical tendencies, the ambitions, the petty vanities, and the alleged political intrigues of his later years; some of them accused him of hypocrisy, of Machiavellianism; but none denied his power to sway the multitudes, or his military ability, or the remarkable achievements of his earlier years.

What of the reliability of the witnesses? They were men of strong political prejudices. They believed that the democratic federal republic was the best form of government ever framed and supposed it to be adapted to all peoples and all times. Bolívar, on the other hand, favored a more centralized and aristocratic system and expressed a preference for the English form of government. Thus to doubt the universal applicability of democracy, thus to express a predilection for the English political system, was, according to the conception of these agents, to flout the North American creed and arouse deep suspicion. Bolívar's views, once [they] became known to the representatives from the capital on the Potomac, tended to colour all their observations and place them in sympathy with the Liberator's enemies, men whose passionately biased statements they received with childish credulity. Obviously it would be unfair to accept the criticisms of the North American diplomats at their face value.

3.
BOLÍVAR

SALVADOR DE MADARIAGA

The noted Spanish historian, Salvador de Madariaga, stresses
here the mixed heritage of Bolívar, a mixture which made him
at first "marginal" and then "representative" as the context
changed. The English term *blood* is not as broad as the
Spanish word *sangre* which is often used, and is here used by
de Madariaga, to signify also cultural factors and loyalties. De
Madariaga's assertion that Bolívar wanted to be "King of
History" takes on broader relevance when seen in the light
of H. Hoetink's study (document 5).

The lineage of Bolívar and others like those of Villegas, Infante,
Martínez de Madrid, Ladron de Guevara, brought to the Liberator
the sap of old Spanish oak and laurel. But Simón Bolívar would have
been less representative as an historical figure, less complex as a
human soul, and less rooted in the soil of the New World, had he
been a pure white. Though the ambient forces and spirits might have
influenced him, he would have been unable to gain access—as he did—
to the deeper layers of the soul of the Indies if his family had not
at one time or another—probably more than once—taken in both
Negro and Indian blood. . . .

From Salvador de Madariaga, *Bolívar*. Reprinted by permission of the
University of Miami Press, the original publisher. Also by permission of
the author and the Bodley Head Ltd, London. (The excerpt presented here
is from the Schocken Paperback edition, 1969, pp. 16, 71–80 *passim*.)

. . . His temperament was jovial and earthly, his whole being plebeian; . . . [An] aristocratic sense remained very much alive in Bolívar in spite of the influence of his intellectual and republican self. . . .

These glimpses into Bolívar's mind illustrate the cause of his sadness in repose and of his vivacity in motion. He was aware of a gap between his faiths and his ideas; and his being was ever taut in an endeavour to conciliate the two irreconcilable parts which composed it. That is why Bolívar's eye never gained either the steadiness or the serene brilliancy of Napoleon's glance. He never looked at his interlocutor. And as for the fire of his eyes, which all observers praise, it was for all a sign of energy, for none a sign of peace. . . .

Bolívar shared the three bloods of the New World. Though a white for practical purposes, small proportions of Indian and Negro blood flowed in his veins; enough, even had they been ten times smaller, to gain him access to the collective memories and reactions of the two varieties of man on which in the New World fell the burden of labour and obedience. Without them, Bolívar would be neither representative of a continental awareness at a given moment in history nor even coherent; since many of his utterances which, under the assumption of his three-blood American nature, are explicable and natural, would, were he a pure white, become the ravings of an irresponsible demagogue.

As a white, Bolívar was heir to a tradition of power and government which took itself for granted to the point of ceasing to be aware of itself. That the white owned the land, the cattle, the slaves and whatever Indians were "reduced" or assimilated, was no more the subject of doubt and discussion than that day is day and night is night. . . . Such a tradition, deeper than any thought or theory, gave the whites of America, "conquerors' sons" to a man, their superb assurance about their right to rule and not to work. . . .

. . . Glory, for these men, is personal, not transferable; upwards not forwards; an end in itself, no means for anyone or anything; a spire, not a bridge. Bolívar was not thinking of becoming wealthier than he was; he was not even really thinking of becoming a crowned king or emperor of Venezuela or of the Great Colombia. He was not thinking at all. He was feeling, rising, tending, aspiring to his highest self. Both from his native idealism and from the influence of his philosophic friend, he had gained a Castillian contempt for the trappings of power. He was enchanted with the austerity of Napoleon's appearance —as he would have been with the austerity of Philip II—and felt how far more majestic it was than the jewel-shop-window chests of the imperial marshals and attendants. The crown Bolívar sought was not that of any kingdom on the map: he wanted to be King of History, which covers all the space of the earth and all the time of mankind.

So far, the white. But, even if in small proportions, Bolívar was also a *pardo* and a *mestizo*. . . . The negro in him was indifferent to Spain, with which he was connected with nothing but ties of resentment for a liberty and a country lost. But this resentment of the negro towards Spain was much weaker and far less dangerous than the feelings harboured by the Indians and made vocal by the *mestizos;* and for two reasons. There was no community, no mass behind the blacks; only loose individuals coming from different parts of Africa at different times. And the black knew that in Spanish lands his brethren were treated better than under any other flag in the New World and could gain their liberty more easily. Withal, the fact that Bolívar had black blood in his veins must have made it much easier for him to rise against that Spanish world which also lived in him and was the most forceful tradition in his soul.

Less apparent (though not altogether absent) in his features, the Indian was also an element in Bolívar's complex composition, and lent him traits both of the pure native and of the *mestizo* psychologies. That sadness we noted in him as the normal attitude of his quiescent moments, Spanish and particularly Galician though it is, has also a definite connection with the passive sufferings of the patient Indian overcome by a stronger people. There are in Bolívar's life stretches of passivity in which he seems incapable of action. . . .

. . . Whatever the view that may be taken on this evolution, one fact is clear. Bolívar's thought was as composite and complex as the rest of his character. In fundamentals, he was not at one with himself

We may now be able to attach a new meaning to his constant need of movement. It was most difficult for him to reach spiritual equilibrium. Between the many rival centres of force which ruled his inner horizon, wide spaces of indetermination stretched in fearful and solitary emptiness. Bolívar kept in constant motion in flight from that void. His diarists have left on record how unhappy he was till he had reached a decision. "H. E. is at times silent and taciturn: then it means that he has some worry or some scheme in the making, and until he has taken his decision, which usually is not long in coming, he remains ill-humored and uneasy." It was this vast empty space, crossed and recrossed by tensions, which he feared most. And it was because of the horror of it in which he lived that he could not suffer quietness and physical repose. As with aircraft, he could only hold the air by dint of speed.

4.

THE STYLE OF THE COLOMBIAN ELITE

EL CACHACO DE BOGOTÁ

El Cachaco de Bogotá was the main journalistic vehicle for the government of President Francisco de Paula Santander (1832–1837), who himself contributed occasional pieces. The following selections are from the year 1833, a crucial year for the consolidation of Colombian *santanderista* politics through the final defeat and expulsion of the "military party," self-appointed followers of Simón Bolívar's ideas.

Items 1 through 5 reflect the "style" of the Colombian elite *(cachacos):* politically intolerant, with a great emphasis on courtly and urbane behavior, and a clear recognition of the stratification of society into "good society" and the rest. Item 6, letter from the *llanero,* illustrates how that elite served as a "reference group" to "outsiders" aspiring to it or invoking its mercy.

Item 1

On Moderation

Much has been said concerning moderation in politics and in morality. If this type of moderation is a virtue, we declare, as of right now, that we unfortunately, or perhaps, fortunately, do not

"The Style of the Colombian Elite" as described in *El Cachaco de Bogotá,* 1833. Translated by Consuelo S. Maingot.

possess it. *Moderate* men, of moderate ways, are rightly exposed to the pity and disdain of truly patriotic, wise and magnanimous men; because they do everything only halfway . . . they are . . . people who are incapable, because of their apathetic and cowardly hearts, of taking any active and decisive part in the common cause, . . . (May 19, 1833)

Item 2

On Popularity
One gains popularity by behaving in a manner which is acceptable to the community, and you lose it when one stops behaving in this fashion, . . . (June 7, 1833)

Item 3

On July 23, 1833 conspiracy of the Bolivarian José Sarda
We have already seen it: there should be no comparison with our enemies: it is necessary that they die or that we die; and given that alternative, it is clear which path should be followed. The law condemns them all; they should disappear from the number of the living, so that, with this exemplary cleansing, one exterminates forever even the seeds of revolutions. (July 28, 1833)

Item 4

Sociability
[Note: This editorial takes note of those who criticize "the friendly reunions which are formed by people of the good society *(las gentes de la buena sociedad)*." The Editor disagrees with these critics.]
The frequent reunions of well-educated people improve social cus-

toms, manners and knowledge. It is there that the young are observed and studied, and there there is developed between the two sexes those sweet relationships which one day will unite them in conjugal ties; cultured and courtly manners are acquired because each and everyone makes an effort to appear more worthy of the esteem of the participants through an affable and moderate treatment. . . . Another of the benefits which they produce is the reconciliation of the parties: men, when they associate frequently, have a propensity to forget those things which divide them. . . .

For the youth which is being shaped, and which one day will play a distinguished role in the country, and maybe in the world, the association with people who are already formed is absolutely necessary. The principles of urbanity, even though they are known theoretically, if they are not put into practice, rarely serve on the opportune occasions. Cultured manners have a powerful influence on those things which are the object of particular and public transactions and nothing is as important as knowing how to use them. The courtly manners of a negotiator have achieved many times what the channels to politics and the most sublime talents could not. (August 1, 1833)

Item 5

Urbanity

[Note: The Editorial complains that among the youths there are those who have no manners. At dances they show lack of respect for "respectable persons" and "distinguished personages."]

Some young men who lack the most simple principles of urbanity want to pass as people of good standing, and give themselves importance in select society.

They show a detestable lack of courtesy, proper only to uncouth youth, who have had careless education, unworthy of cultured people.

There are, however, a considerable number who, because of their cultured manners, their moderation and other good qualities, bring to themselves attentions which perhaps otherwise they could not aspire to because of their age. (August 1, 1833)

Item 6

Letter to the Editor by a llanero ex-Bolivarian officer

I was born in the plains *(llanos)* of Apure; I have been a patriot since 1810, and not merely with my mouth, but also with my woolen blanket *(mocho)* and my lance, going anywhere I was taken: my hair has turned gray from going up and down the savanna looking for the Spaniards *(godos)*. When there was a Colombia I was a Captain with effective rank of Major: now I do not know what I am in reality. . . . So that therefore, *cachaco* gentlemen, do not believe that I am one of those officers, who because they do not have a salary go and offer themselves for revolutions, and here there are more than four of us who do not understand that kind of wrongdoing *(picardias)*: we who have fought for our country are not bad men *(malucos)*. Here is my general Juan Gómez, who is a brave fighter *(lanza brava)*, my companion Lira and other blanketed ones *(tapados)*. . . .

There remain over in the Congress some papers of mine which say whether I am an officer, or what it is that I am, and they have lost them. Mister Yerbas, the Secretary, will please do me the favor of looking for them, because now that the gentleman with the eye-glasses, who complained all the time, has left the Senate maybe I shall fare better. I belong to the party of the *cachacos,* friends of the constitutional government, and because of my dress *(por mi traje)* I am really a cachaco, but always with the government standing firm until death.

(Signed) The Major graduate of the old army of Colombia Augustin Hernandez, who lives on the street of San Miguel (September 8, 1833).

5.

NINETEENTH-CENTURY DOMINICAN REPUBLIC: A Case Study of a Latin American Political System

H. HOETINK

In this work Dutch sociologist H. Hoetink deals with the image of their leaders which is held by members of societies with aristocratic cultures. The leaders in turn adopt that image of themselves. Religious beliefs and imagery play an important part in the structure of such a society's expectations of its leaders. Hoetink notes that aspects of this self-image among Dominican caudillos is not limited to those of the past century, but is found in twentieth-century leaders. Caudillismo is not limited to any given period of Latin American history.

[Dominican] society is roughly divided into two sectors, of which the highest calls itself the thinking class (*la clase pensante, la gente bien, la gente culta*), while the lowest sector is referred to as the vulgus (*el vulgo, la clase baja*), or the unhappy ones (*los infelices*). . . .

In an aristocratic culture the theme of vertical distance is not limited to the image of social structure. The cultural goods are also subject to hierarchization: there is a distinction between higher and lower objects of knowledge, "higher" and "lower" branches of science, the highest being of course those that deal with spiritual questions.

The highest social group does not deem it correct to dwell at

From H. Hoetink, "19th Century Dominican Republic: A Case Study of a Latin American Political System," *Caribbean Review* (Winter 1970). Reprinted by permission of the publisher.

length on low matters, such as everyday needs, food and money. The idea that truth is reserved to a small number of select and blessed individuals fits well in this aristocratic model of thought, in which quality and essence are dominant over quantity and non-essence. . . .

It is clear that in an aristocratic culture, limited freedom of expression is not necessarily felt as an infringement of essential rights of all the people.

As President Heureaux, who governed the Dominican Republic in the two last decades of the former century, put it:

"The political thoughts which the Government cherishes and which must lead to a maintenance of international harmony, (...) cannot be handed over to the vulgus, which does not know how to measure the distance between throwing words in the air in cafes or (...) in the public square, and working and decision-making with the responsibilities which duty and conscience demand of a respectable government." The strict patterns of behaviour which the emphasis on distance produces have their psychological correlate in the value attached to predictable behaviour: in an aristocratic culture, impulsiveness and spontaneity are not appreciated, except in specific, well-defined spheres of activity and institutions, where emotional outlets are provided.

The general stress on *formalistic* and *disciplined* behaviour makes it so that also the distance between equals or near-equals, that is, the *horizontal distance* tends to be enlarged in an aristocratic culture. The political leader, the caudillo, also *before* he has reached the top of his career, is therefore like the Dominican Santana "austere (...) with a passion for order to the point of being inexorable": he will possess, like Heureaux, a formidable self-control, and, like Trujillo, not lose his sense of distance with his closest collaborators, not only because these qualities are functional in the selection of leaders per se, but also because they are valued as a close approximation of a cultural norm.

In the caudillo's meticulous care for his clothing and general appearance we recognize again this formalistic trait but here accompanied by a *narcissism* that is also culturally determined. *Narcissism* and *formalism* are of course interconnected, mutually reinforce each other, and help create the image of a distinct, autonomous, personality. Mannheim speaks in this context of "self-distantiation." Next to vertical and horizontal distance, I have to mention the stress on *temporal distance,* which shows itself in the rigid separation between profane and sacred time (holi-day), and which certainly still is a striking trait in Iberian culture.

In another context I will refer to the strengthening influence which Iberian Catholicism has on certain structural forms and mobility-types in the area under discussion. Here I may repeat Mannheim's remark that the Father-God-concept of Christian religion fits far better in a culture that emphasizes distance, than, for example, a pantheistic interpretation would do.

Maybe this explains partly the penetrating force of religious symbolism in the Dominican secular culture, and the ease with which national leaders are compared, or compare themselves to Christ. Thus Heureaux could write: "Things are going well and I go on playing the role of Christ," and: "I will have to walk with the cross to Calvary." One of the contemporary politicians, who by some of his followers is called "the Christ of Democracy," wrote a book on the Dominican Founding Father Juan Pablo Duarte; "the Christ of Liberty."

This identification with Christ seems to show the political leaders' extraordinary self-assertion, which brings me to the image and self-image of the leader in an aristocratic culture.

When leadership in such a culture is transferred by inheritance and/or ritual procedures, the *origin* of authority is removed to a *mythical distance,* and authority itself is supposed to be sanctified by godly revelation and grace, if not by long duration alone.

Where, as in Latin American independent countries, the selection of the caudillo precludes such godly sanctification, while on the other hand the aristocratic model of thought "demands" that it be an Election (with a capital E), there the mythical role of elector is allocated to history itself, as an autonomous instrument, uninfluenced by men in this respect.

The awareness of being elected by history makes it easier for the political leader to consider himself superior, also in character, to his adversaries.

"I have always been of the opinion," writes Heureaux, "that the special mission which destiny has charged me with, ought to provide a contrast to the haughty impatience of my opponents, and it is by obedience to this consideration, that I have been able to make myself superior to them."

I do not imply that thoughts such as these cannot be noted in other types of society than the Latin American; I do believe, however, that where "history" is the *only* legitimizing agent of the origin of authority, its role will be stressed more than elsewhere. In an ideal-typical construction it should therefore receive due attention. Luperón did when he refused to participate in a certain revolution "because I cannot justify myself in the face of the country or of history" (or as Fidel Castro did in his "History will absolve me"), there history is only a synonym of posterity and loses the connotation of active instrument of selection.

The emphasis by the political leader on the superiority of his own character, which I just hinted at, is really a striking phenomenon, because of its frequency and intensity.

President Heureaux often speaks of his "magnanimity, benevolence and generosity." Luperón writes of himself: "never has any man had more power over himself, more firmness of will, while being inspired by generous and grand ideas."

Nor is this self-glorification limited to leaders of a former century. Does not Juan Bosch say in his 1963 inaugural speech, that it is known to everybody that he cannot hate anybody?

And another present-day Dominican politician writes: "By natural predisposition and mental discipline, I am (...) an entity of love, of concord, of charity, who never, under any circumstance, could be poisoned by the virus of hate or of revenge. I only know to love, to serve and to forgive (...)"

It is obvious again that we deal here with a culture that permits an outspoken narcissistic individualism. I think we can detect one of its social functions by paying attention to the emphasis which altruistic qualities receive in most of these statements: when Heureaux writes that he always obeys an impulse of generous sympathy, which makes him "sought after by persons who are victims of miscalculations or bad luck," then we clearly see the protector-function come to the foreground; in the patronage-system of Ibero-american, he who wants to play the role of patron, is allowed to attract potential clients by referring to his charitative and generous inclinations.

This applies *a fortiori* to the greatest patron of all, the political leader, whose honorary titles, the Protector, the Benefactor, are mostly invented by flattering clients, partly in order to remind him continuously of his patronal obligations.

It is here the place to point out that in Mediterranean and Iberoamerican culture the role of patron (...) receives constant and authoritative validation from the (catholic) Church through the widespread cult of community and personal patron saints (...) "I think," writes Boissevain, "it is obvious that religious and political patronage reinforce each other, for each serves as a model for the other."

We might add that the patronage structure receives a similar reinforcement from the ritual kinship system.

Both the eager belief of being elected by History, as well as the awareness of being the patron or protector of the land, easily bring the leader to an identification of himself with the country and the people, which in its turn leads the caudillo to act as the somewhat arbitrary Director of a large private estate. In this way the psychological correlate is constructed of the patrimonial political structure.

6.
ZAPATA AND THE MEXICAN REVOLUTION

JOHN WOMACK, JR.

How did Emiliano Zapata become a caudillo? What was the
source of his appeal, the basis of his support? These and other
questions are skillfully handled by John Womack, Jr., Professor of History at Harvard University. Family networks and
personal qualities combined to make Zapata a chosen leader.
His power depended on his ability to continue to enjoy and
hold the trust of the dominant groups in his village; without
them he would have been just another combatant. Emiliano
shared the "honor" attached to the name Zapata, one of the
village's "revolutionary families," but he also had the personal
qualities and style that were attractive to the villagers and
other potential caudillos.

The old man was about to speak now, and the crowd of farmers
waiting under the arcades behind the village church quieted down to
hear him. They knew the meeting must be important. To make sure
everyone could come, the elders had called it for this evening, on
a Sunday. And to hide it from the hacienda foremen, they had passed
the word around in private instead of ringing the church bell. . . .

The four old men who composed the council began to take names
and prepare for the vote. They needed to offer no advice or ad-

From *Zapata and the Mexican Revolution,* by John Womack, Jr. Copyright © 1968 by John Womack, Jr. Reprinted by permission of Alfred A.
Knopf, Inc. and Thames and Hudson, Ltd.

monition: their presence alone guaranteed that the choice would be free, serious, and respected. For seven hundred years Anenecuilco had lived by the strength of will of men like them, and it had no better strength to trust in now. One of the elders, Carmen Quintero, had taken an active and independent part in local politics for twenty-five years, having started his career before some of the men at the meeting were born. Another, Eugenio Pérez, had loaded his rifle to defend village lands as early as 1887. As for the other two, Merino and Andrés Montes, they had been firm and faithful leaders for well over a decade. Nearly four hundred souls made up Anenecuilco, and probably every one of them could look on at least one of the four elders as uncle, great-uncle, cousin, brother, father, or grandfather.

. . . The Zapatas and the Salazars (his mother's people) had it bred into their bones what Mexican history was about.

. . . Exactly how Emiliano was related to this patriarch, who died three years before he was born, is still unclear, but José Zapata was probably a brother of his grandfather, a great-uncle. In any case his part in village history served to establish Zapata as an honoured name there.

Finally, the security of kinship was in the present meeting's very air: Emiliano was also a nephew of the incumbent chief, José Merino. The villagers knew they were in for trouble for the next few years. They had no better bet than Zapata to see them through. . . .

. . . A vote was called, and Zapata won easily.

It could not have been a surprise. Zapata was young, having just turned thirty a month before, but the men voting knew him and they knew his family; and they judged that if they wanted a young man to lead them, they would find no one else with a truer sense of what it meant to be responsible for the village. . . .

This was the man the villagers elected president of their council. But when they elected him, they were also laying bets that he would stay as they knew him. What convinced them that once in power he would not change and abuse their trust—what kept the question from rising in anyone's mind—was the reputation of his family. Zapata was an important name in Anenecuilco. . . .

Zapata spoke briefly. He said that he accepted the difficult responsibility conferred upon him, but that he expected everyone to back him. "We'll back you," Francisco Franco thirty years later remembered someone in the crowd calling out to Zapata: "We just want a man with pants on, to defend us.". . .

. . . though he was as tough as nails and no one fooled with him, he did look near tears. A quiet man, he drank less than most of the other men in the village and got quieter when he did. Once for several weeks he managed the ornate Mexico City stables of a Morelos sugar planter. It was a good chance to start climbing socially and economically—to feather his nest and wind up with his own stables and maybe even a little ranch. But toadying, wheedling petty obligations, maneuvering, operating, pulling deals—it sickened him, literally. . . .

. . . Some fifteen chiefs held commissions as colonels in the revolutionary forces. But none could legitimately give orders to the others. Retreating back into Puebla, one party of rebels (including Tepepa) solved the problem in form by electing Zapata "Supreme Chief of the Revolutionary Movement of the South." But in fact the problem remained. Other chiefs in other parties wanted the post, which looked increasingly important. When the revolution triumphed—and as March went by its triumph seemed ever more likely—the revolutionary boss in the state might then take over as provisional governor or state military or police commander. Now, with the official Maderista affiliation broken, whoever emerged as chief in charge would have to do so the hard way—by convincing his peers he deserved their backing.

This was a feat neither political ambition nor military ferocity would accomplish. The machinery to dragoon local followers did not exist. If a village resented a self-appointed chief, it simply kept its men home. The contest for revolutionary command in Morelos was therefore not a fight. It was a process of recognition by various neighbourhood chiefs that there was only one man in the state they all respected enough to cooperate with, and that they had a duty to bring their followers under his authority. The one man turned out to be Zapata, who was a singularly qualified candidate—both a sharecropping dirt farmer whom villagers would trust and a mule-driving horsedealer whom cowboys, peons, and bandits would look up to; both a responsible citizen and a determined warrior. But his elevation to leadership was not automatic, and never definitive. As he himself later wrote to Alfredo Robles Domínguez, he had to be very careful with his men: for they followed him, he said, not because they were ordered to but because they felt *cariño* for him—that is, they liked him, admired him, held him in high but tender regard, were devoted to him. It was because he was the kind of man who could arouse other eminently pragmatic men in this way that neither Tepepa, nor Merino, nor anyone else who cared about the movement ever tried to rival him. If he never bossed them, they never crossed him. But the process of taking command was nevertheless slow and erratic.

7.
BRAZIL AND THE MYTH OF FRANCISCO JULIÃO

ANTHONY LEEDS

University of Texas anthropologist Anthony Leeds dissects
the credentials of a once popular radical caudillo of Northeast
Brazil, Francisco Julião. Leeds finds that Julião's motives
were self-serving. Interestingly, however, Julião adopted the
style, including the open manipulation of symbols, which appealed to a new and potentially important electorate. Thus
the caudillo can shift his style according to the particular
sector he is appealing to.

It is not necessary to repeat here how often the Brazilian Northeast
has been alleged to constitute a "danger zone," a seat of "communist
revolutionary ferment," a fervid locus of *fidelismo,* or even the possible site of origin of "another progressive socialist revolution" in
Latin America. The Northeast is, in newspaper, journal, and magazine, virtually identified with Brazil, the axiom appearing to be, "As
goes the Northeast, so goes Brazil," and [Francisco] Julião is represented as the prophet and leader of this revolutionary activity, a man
who is likely to overthrow the stability of all Brazil. It is my purpose,
here, to present an interpretation of Brazilian socio-political conditions
that is at variance with these views. . . .

From Anthony Leeds, "Brazil and the Myth of Francisco Julião," *Politics
of Change in Latin America,* pp. 190–201, footnotes omitted. Edited by
Joseph Maier and Richard Weatherhead. Copyright © 1964 by Praeger
Publishers, Inc. Reprinted by permission of the publisher.

The Leagues

. . . In the first place, there are a variety of types of peasant leagues in various states of Brazil: Parana, São Paulo, Pernambuco, Paraíba, and elsewhere. . . .

. . . [T]he entire mass of rural workers concerned is being split into groupings of mutually antagonistic organizations whose formation is, in large part, being encouraged in a paternalistic manner by representatives of the controlling and more powerful mediatorial elites of the country.

. . . [A]s far as [Julião's] organizational roots are concerned, he is localized in a small, though influential, part of the Northeast, and has, according to informants from all other parts of Brazil, virtually no influence outside of the Pernambuco-Paraíba area. [It is in Pernambuco that he holds political office.] . . .

Second, as I have suggested above, the leadership comes from outside the "masses" who comprise the peasant leagues. I am aware of no instance in which a leader of a peasant league or even a syndicate has arisen from the masses themselves, and informants were unable to name one. Undoubtedly, there are such cases, but they are clearly in the minority in number and influence. The leaders and organizers, including Julião, as I shall show, have almost exclusively been representatives of urban-centered interests and politics, even when agricultural products and landholding have been involved. Their orienting interests have necessarily been urban-directed and industrial-commercial ones.

Julião as a Leader

. . . Julião's influence has neither the national scope usually attributed to him nor the total inclusiveness with respect to working-class interests usually pictured of him, even in his own Northeast. He is one of several paternalistic representatives, or ostensible representatives, of popular and semipopular social movements of great complexity in a small part of the very large Northeast, which is, itself, only a subordinate part of that vast, diverse and complex country, Brazil. . . .

First, it is quite necessary to know that Julião is a large plantation owner (*latifundista*). Second, all his "organizing" activities are done in territories physically separated from the location of his own *lati-*

fundium, which is *not* organized. Third, he is by profession a lawyer, and law is a highly regarded profession in Brazil and one that provides a crucial springboard (*trampolim*)[1] into political life. It is also largely an occupation of the higher classes.

Fourth, he was a state legislator and now has succeeded in getting himself elected as a federal deputy (for Pernambuco)—that is, he is sufficiently connected with, and not antipathetic to, the political machinery (i.e., the organs of the Brazilian controlling elites) to maintain himself in political positions that are of considerably greater importance than comparable positions in the United States. As a holder of political office, especially the higher one, he not only enjoys immunities but has access to an ostensibly national platform from which to expatiate. . . .

In passing, one may note that a careful reading of Julião's speech reveals a facile manipulation of a set of symbols that bear comparison with those of President Getúlio Vargas' speeches and his suicide note of 1954, as also, perhaps less neatly, with President Janio Quadros' letter of resignation of 1961. Their charismatic and inspirational Christian-nationalistic symbols, which help reinforce the paternalistic relationship of vertical dependence discussed below, occur throughout Julião's "redemption," "the patriotic" (to the state composed of members of Julião's own class?), "the kind and friendly '*campesino*' John XXIII," etc. Elsewhere, too, for example: "Thou givest the soldier to defend the Fatherland. And the Fatherland forgets thee," etc. . . .

Thus, Julião is distinctly a member of the controlling class even if he represents a somewhat aberrant individualistic but not, properly speaking, dissident faction of it. He has moved into the political power positions of interest to members of his class by means of attaching himself to, fostering, and controlling a social discontent already present among an aggregate—and potential electorate—of the landless and the impoverished. To stir these to true revolution would be to destroy himself; to use them is in his best interest. Among many others who use the masses, Julião has distinguished himself by uniqueness in

[1]"Trampolim": literally a "springboard," the point of departure for the creation of a career. For a full discussion of this see, Anthony Leeds, "Brazilian Careers and Social Structure, A Case History and Model," in Dwight B. Heath and Richard N. Adams (eds.), *Contemporary Cultures and Societies of Latin America.* (New York: Random House, 1965), 379–404.—APM

his method of manipulating them while operating in the political system of the elites. . . .

This situation can be properly interpreted, I believe, as one in which the masses concerned "organized," as I remarked above, from outside in a markedly paternalistic manner. This kind of organizing, along with appropriate ideological reinforcements, provides one of the best mechanisms for the management and maintenance of virtually impenetrable class boundaries and a practically nonrevolutionary lower mass—a mass of perhaps 60 per cent of the Brazilian population flowing around, beneath, and outside even the great, progressive, but largely "middle-class" labor unions. Virtually all peasant leagues—Julião's, the Catholic ones, or others—as well as the rural and urban unions and those other parts of the masses, organized or not, entering into relation with such large-scale socio-technical development agencies as SUDENE (Superintendencia do Desenvolvimento do Nordeste), are in just such paternalistic relationships. They guarantee a vertical dependence upward, ultimately to the president of the nation—the nodal center of political and economic power for the entire socio-political and economic system.

Whether consciously or not, what in fact Julião has done is to fashion his own myth, a self-mystifying myth, and create a political aggregate among the "masses" that serves as an electorate for the advance of his career as a politician within the body politic, i.e., the "classes," of Brazil.

It is a striking phenomenon that this sort of career procedure is relatively standardized in Brazil. A certain stance with a manifest meaning is adopted, usually early in the career. But the manifest meaning is merely an empty form. The latent and true meaning may be totally different from the apparent one. This true meaning, the careerist's private and, apparently, often unformulated set of goals, only appears once the foundations of the career are firmly established. . . .

One must infer that his aim is not revolution or insurrection among the masses at all, but rather the use of the masses (and the military, be it noted) against the great coastal sugar interests and the older class of coroneis ("colonels," i.e., local politico-economic caudillos). If this is a revolution at all, it is one pertaining to a newly rising segment of the controlling classes and it is firmly in the control of the

Julião's, the Brizzalas, the Goularts, the Furtados—all of whom are excellent examples of the career process I have spoken of. Though representatives of this type of men may be split among themselves, they are all ranged against the older entrenched interests. At the same time, they are all of them also firmly conservative, consciously or unconsciously acting to preserve the basic aspects of the system as they find it, making only such ameliorations (on whatever scale) as will foster that preservation. They all also enter into various paternalistic arrangements with large aggregates of the masses who contribute to their political ends.

These are exceedingly able and intelligent men, often of great vision, given their assumptions about the proper nature of Brazilian society. They are what we may call the "liberal-conservative" wing, or new guard, of the great controlling class of Brazil, the wing that is presently fighting the arch-conservative or strongly reactionary old-guard wing of the same class. . . .

In the context of total Brazilian political, social, economic, and geographical organization, Julião can be seen as only one of many elements constituting an exceedingly complex structure of various kinds and degrees of power and their manipulations.

8.
COLOMBIAN CONSTITUTIONALISM

LUIS CARLOS SÁCHICA

Virtually all Latin American constitutions call for an executive or presidential form of government. In such a system the
executive branch predominates over the other branches of
government. In Latin America this emphasis on the executive
is based, as Colombian constitutional lawyer Luis Carlos
Sáchica notes, on a "recognition of the exceptional leader."
Formal institutions, such as constitutions, have a definite
influence on social behavior. The fact that Latin Americans
early in their history adopted the presidential form of government—abandoned only during brief periods of experimentation with federalism—is crucial to an understanding of the
behavior of caudillos who become national executives.

In the presidential form of government the executive branch is the
center of all state activity, it takes the initiative, is the source of
impetus for governmental operations and is the locus of policy in
public administration. Within the executive branch the President of
the Republic who is its head, its chief, is at the same time the primary
figure, and his decisions are backed by near absolute power because
of the support he enjoys as leader of his party and political leader with
majorities in the representative chambers.

From Luis Carlos Sáchica, *Constitucionalismo colombiano* (Bogotá: Editorial el Voto Nacional, 1962), pp. 387–391, *passim*. Translated by Consuelo S. Maingot.

The parliamentary form of government, on the other hand, to be effective needs at all times substantial agreement between the executive and legislative branches on political questions, and experience has demonstrated how difficult this is to achieve, much less to maintain.

Rafael Núñez in a newspaper article explaining the political strength of the presidential form of government cited a phrase of Hamilton's which alludes to the importance that has been given the executive in political theory: "The quality of government is measured by the strength of the executive," an idea which is substantiated by the presidential form of government in North America.

Politically, the presidential form of government is the recognition of the exceptional leader as a man capable of giving rational and effective solutions to collective problems, of his gift for foreseeing conflicts and preventing them, of the charisma generated by the manner in which he presents policy and of his predisposition of service to the community. This recognition of outstanding personalities to whom the direction of the community is entrusted, seeking the advantages of the unity of opinion and command, carries implicitly in it the danger of personalist tyranny, if the leader feels himself unattached to the legal order and attempts to act above it.

In conclusion: the influence delegated to the President of the Republic in the political constitution of Colombia is such that each presidential term has defined profiles, a definite personal style, a result of the influence of the Head of State, of his intellectual attributes and even his temperament, giving the imprint of his temper to the whole administration. As Secretary of State Seward affirms; "We elect a king for four years and delegate to him such power that, within certain limits, he can define those limits for himself."

BIBLIOGRAPHIC SUGGESTIONS

The student seriously interested in pursuing the question of *caudillismo* in Latin America should immediately turn next to the complete works of John Womack, Jr., and Salvador de Madariaga only partially reproduced in this unit. Another work of importance is Robert L. Gilmore's *Caudillism and Militarism in Venezuela, 1810–1910* (Athens: Ohio University Press, 1964). Gilmore was the first to make the crucial distinction between caudillismo and militarism. Next the student should turn to the work edited by Hugh M. Hamill, Jr., *Dictatorship in Spanish America* (New York: Knopf, Borzoi Books, 1965). Well-selected reading, a truly provocative Introduction and an excellent Bibliographical Note make Hamill's a most useful work. Roger M. Haigh's *Martin Güemes: Tyrant or Tool* (Fort Worth: Texas Christian University Press, 1968) is more than just another study of an Argentine caudillo; Haigh documents the community and group basis of the caudillo's power. See also his essay "The Creation and Control of a Caudillo," *Hispanic American Historical Review, 44* (November 1964), 481–490.

Older but still useful studies which deal with individual caudillos or with the phenomenon in general include: A. Curtis Wilgus (ed.), *South American Dictators During the First Century of Independence,* 2nd. ed. (New York: Russell and Russell, 1963); George I. Blanksten, *Ecuador: Constitutions and Caudillos* (Berkeley: University of California Press, 1951); Harold E. Davis, *Latin American Leaders* (Washington, D.C.: Inter-American Bibliographic and Library Association, 1949). An interesting descriptive study of more recent Latin American caudillos is contained in Tad Szulc, *Twilight of the Tyrants* (New York: Holt, Rinehart and Winston, 1959). Robert J. Alexander, *Prophets of the Revolution: Profiles of Latin American Leaders* (New York: Macmillan, 1962), describes both civilian and military caudillos. A model of incisive and sensitive reporting on a Latin American leader is Lee Lockwood's *Castro's Cuba, Cuba's Fidel* (New York: Vintage Books, 1969). A dated but still useful bibliography is Charles E. Chapman, "List of Books Referring to Caudillos in Hispanic America," *Hispanic American Historical Review, 13* (1933), 143–146. More intensive bibliographical searches should turn to the *Handbook of Latin American Studies* published annually since 1935.

III.
Liberalism versus Conservatism in Nineteenth-Century Mexico:
Ideological Conflict or Factional Strife?

☫ CHARLES A. HALE

Since independence Mexico has experienced major periods of social upheaval, civil war, and foreign invasion—a heritage of conflict unique for its intensity in all of Latin America. In the nineteenth century this conflict reached a climax in the years 1854 to 1867, when the country was torn by civil war and by subsequent French occupation and the brief reign of a foreign monarch on a Mexican throne. The writing of history in Mexico has been inevitably affected by this unique heritage of conflict, and the political process since 1810 has been subject to two contrasting and equally nationalistic interpretations, the conservative and the liberal, which have held sway until recent years.

On the one side, the conservatives have seen the political process as a succession of senseless efforts to destroy Hispanic traditions, to substitute alien ideals and values, and by so doing to condemn the country to perpetual anarchy, dictatorship, and moral corruption. This line of argument, beginning with Lucas Alamán's great *Historia de Méjico* (1849–1852), identified the Mexican nation with the Spanish heritage, and revealed a nostalgia for the peace and apparent prosperity of New Spain, and particularly for the role played by the Catholic Church in colonial society. Such writers as José Vasconcelos, Mariano Cuevas, and José

Bravo Ugarte have perpetuated this interpretation in the twentieth century, identifying materialism, anticlericalism, and the influence of the United States as subversive and alien forces against which the nation must continually defend itself.

On the other side, the liberals have interpreted the political process as a continuing struggle for individual liberty and social democracy against the forces of political and clerical oppression, social injustice, and economic exploitation. Such evils have been seen as part of the legacy from colonial society which must be ultimately liquidated if Mexico is to become a modern nation. After Benito Juárez defeated the allied forces of Maximilian, the French army, and the native conservative party in 1867, the national destiny came to be officially associated with liberalism. The best summary of the liberal interpretation was presented by Justo Sierra in 1900 in his *Political Evolution of the Mexican People,* a book that has enjoyed wide popularity and continuing influence, despite the changes resulting from the great revolutionary upheaval after 1910. Our understanding of nineteenth-century politics in Mexico has been strongly affected by the dominance of partisan and oversimplified views of the past which have followed the dictates of ideology and nationalism.

This unit will provide an opportunity to examine the nineteenth-century political conflict through the eyes of the actors in the drama itself—the writers, the politicians, and the lawmakers of the postindependence years. The readings that follow are all from contemporary documents and through them it is possible to identify the arguments and the policy assumptions of the contending parties. The reader should look for key ideas, oftentimes frequently repeated, which when combined into a systematic program to solve the nation's ills or to change existing society and institutions, make up an ideology. The first problem, then, is to establish the elements of what could be termed ideological conflict.

Following "The Plan of Iguala," which sets the stage for the reader, the documents have been roughly arranged into major overlapping and interrelated areas—"Governmental

Organization and the Corporate Tradition," "Property," and "The Indian"—which constitute issues of great importance to nineteenth-century policy-makers. Because of this type of arrangement, the reader should be especially aware of the date of each document and he must place each in the proper context of events. The grouping of the documents by topics is designed to raise questions which are crucial to any analysis of the liberal-conservative conflict in the nineteenth century. One such question, for example, involves property, a central concept in all modern political and social thought. What distinctions were drawn by José María Luis Mora (document 6) between corporate property and individual property? What significance do these distinctions have in understanding the social as well as the political basis of the liberal reform program? How does Ponciano Arriaga's dissenting opinion in the constitutional congress on the right of property (document 7), differ from the majority opinion of his committee or from the relevant articles of the Constitution of 1857 (document 8)? Which of these later statements is closer to Mora's of 1833? What further insight into liberal policy can be gained by these comparisons?

Another kind of question to consider is whether there were points of agreement as well as points of obvious difference between liberals and conservatives, as revealed in these documents. In this regard, special attention might be directed to the documents which pertain particularly to the problem of the Indian. Did Mora (documents 9 and 11) regard the Indian population in terms that were markedly different from those expressed by *El Universal* (document 10)? Were Mora's general views of 1833 consistent with his policy recommendations of 1848–1849 in the face of massive Indian rebellion in Yucatan and the Huasteca? Mora, it should be said, was a Creole whose family fortune had been largely lost in the upheaval of 1810.

This unit is a frank effort to approach the turbulent and often baffling political history of nineteenth-century Mexico through ideas as a way of studying the assumptions that underlie or guide policy. Where possible, comparisons should be made with other analogous situations throughout the Western world—France, England, Spain, the United States, and Latin America. These comparisons can help clarify the nature of political conflict in Mexico and to establish its uniqueness or its similarity to that of other areas. For example, the reader might ask why Argentina and Chile had no civil war comparable to the era of the *Reforma* and the French Intervention in Mexico. Part of the answer might be found in a comparison of political ideas in the three countries, which in turn could lead to questions about institutional or social differences, for instance the position of the church or the character of the Indian population.

In seeking indications of the assumptions that underlie or guide policy, one should constantly ask how the various spokesmen were influenced by historic precedent. What precedents were evoked as inspiration and which were rejected? For example, what is the significance of Alamán's (document 3) or Zuloaga's (document 4) reference to the Plan of Iguala (document 1)? Did the attitude toward the Spanish colonial regime constitute a major point of difference between liberals and conservatives? What is the significance of Mora's references to the policies of Charles III (documents 2 and 6)? Besides seeking precedents, the reader should examine these documents from the perspective of more recent Mexican history, marked by contrasting periods of political calm (1876–1910 and 1940–1970) and of political and social upheaval (1910–1940). To what extent were the assumptions revealed in these documents perpetuated or revived in later years? What happened to conservatism after the victory of the liberal republic in 1867? Did it vanish from the Mexican scene? Did the fact that Mexico achieved political stability for so long under Porfirio Díaz imply that the earlier liberal-conservative conflict was limited to a few issues, which once "settled," resulted in a broad consensus among former combatants? Was the Revolution of 1910 a reenactment of the mid-nineteenth-century conflict, or was it based on completely new and different issues involving different social groups? Does a view from a later perspective suggest that possibly the liberal-conservative civil war was mere factional strife among what was a social and economic elite who shared many common assumptions? These are broad, far-reaching, and difficult problems to unravel, but they are ones for which the documents at hand provide some clues.

Finally, the reader should constantly try to see the limitations of the documents in answering these or related questions, and he should be prepared to test conclusions drawn from this unit against those drawn from Units I and II, which introduce other ways of viewing analogous political conflict. For instance, might one better understand the liberal-conservative conflict by a detailed knowledge of who in class and occupational terms supported the contending parties? How might such information, if obtainable, modify conclusions based on a study of political ideas, laws, and official government statements? In other words, might it be more effective to study political conflict through social analysis than through ideas, or must some combination of the two methods be achieved? Scholars have barely begun to study these questions, but they are ones worthy of consideration by the student of Latin American history at any level.

THE HERITAGE OF INDEPENDENCE—1821

Political conflict in nineteenth-century Mexico was affected by the confused and contradictory nature of the Revolution for Independence. Political leaders and publicists of the post-independence era could find in the events of 1808 to 1821 inspiration for several versions of national regeneration. The moderate Creole efforts of 1808–1810 to establish an autonomous New Spain were upset by the decision of the Creole parish priest Miguel Hidalgo to incite the Indian masses against Spanish injustice. As the cause of independence emerged by 1814 under Hidalgo's successor, José María Morelos, it became identified with popular insurgency, alienating most Creoles who flocked to the increasingly successful royalist cause. Yet in 1820, what had become a diminishing civil conflict within New Spain was suddenly transformed by events in the mother country into a remarkable, united effort for independence. An army revolt in Spain and the reinstitution there of the egalitarian and anticlerical Constitution of 1812 brought together in Mexico diverse colonial groups, liberal Creoles, insurgents, and conservative land-owners, church hierarchy, and Spanish merchants. The ensuing events were the model of irony. Agustín de Iturbide, a Creole royalist commander who had fought the insurgents since 1810, contradicted viceregal orders and met secretly in January 1821 with the insurgent commander Vicente Guerrero to discuss the "means of working together for the welfare of the kingdom." Soon thereafter, Iturbide formulated the following manifesto, proclaimed at the town of Iguala on February 24, 1821, presently the capital of the State of Guerrero. Symbolic of this confused heritage from the revolutionary era is the fact that while September 16 is Mexico's "Independence Day" in honor of Miguel Hidalgo, the tricolor of the Mexican flag represents the three guarantees of the Plan of Iguala.

1. The Plan of Iguala ❖ Agustín de Iturbide

Americans, and I include not only those born in America, but also Europeans, Africans, and Asians who reside in America, please hear me. . . . For three hundred years North America has been under the tutelage of the most Catholic and pious, heroic and magnanimous of nations. Spain raised it and made it prosper, creating these rich cities, these beautiful towns, these extensive provinces and realms which will come to occupy an important place in the history of the world. The population and culture of North America have grown, and its natural abundance from the soil, its mineral wealth, and its advantages of climate are well known. Also known are the disadvantages of North America's great distance from the mother country; in reality the branch is now equal to the trunk. It is the universal opinion that there should be complete independence from Spain and all other nations. This is what Europeans think, as well as Americans of every origin.

The very cry that resounded in the town of Dolores in 1810 and which caused such unfortunate disorder, debauchery, and other evils in our fair land, impressed upon people's minds that the general union of Europeans and Americans, Indians and Castes [*indios e indígenas*], is the only solid base on which our common happiness can rest. Can there be any doubt after the horrible experience of so many disasters, that anyone would fail to join the union to achieve such great things? European Spaniards: your country is America because you live in it.

From Lucas Alamán, *Historia de Méjico* (Mexico, 1852), 5, Appendix, pp. 8–11. My translation—CAH.

In it you have your beloved wives, your fond children, your haciendas, commerce, and possessions. Americans: who among you can say that he is not of Spanish descent? Behold the gentle tie that binds us. Add the other bonds of friendship, of mutual interests, of education, of language, and of similarity of feelings, and you will see that these bonds are so close and so powerful, that all men united in one opinion and one voice will of necessity promote the common welfare of the realm.

The moment has come for you to declare your uniformity of sentiment, and for our union to be the powerful hand that emancipates America without need of outside aid. At the head of a valiant and resolute army, I have declared the independence of North America. She is now free; she is now her own master; she no longer recognizes or depends on Spain, nor on any nation. Let all hail her as independent and let the hearts which uphold this serene expression be valiant and united with the troops that have resolved to die before quitting such a heroic enterprise.

The army is moved only by the desire to preserve the purity of the holy religion that we profess and to promote the common good. The solid bases on which its resolution is founded are as follows:

1. The Roman Catholic Apostolic religion, without toleration of any other.
2. The absolute independence of this kingdom.
3. Monarchical government, tempered by a constitution that is congenial with the country.
4. Ferdinand VII, and if necessary those of his dynasty or of another now reigning, shall be the emperor, so that we may have a ready monarch and thus prevent pernicious acts of ambition.
5. There shall be a junta, pending the meeting of a Cortes to put this plan into effect.
6. This junta shall call itself the Governing Junta and shall be made up of members already proposed to the Viceroy.
7. It shall govern by virtue of the oath it has given to the King, until he appears in Mexico to receive it personally, at which time all previous commandments shall be suspended.
8. If Ferdinand VII decides not to come to Mexico, the Junta or the Regency shall govern in the name of the nation, until it is determined who should be the crowned head.

9. This government shall be upheld by the Army of the Three Guarantees. . . .

12. All its inhabitants, with no distinctions between them save their merit and virtue, are citizens qualified to choose any occupation whatever.

13. Their persons and properties shall be respected and protected.

14. The property and privileges of the secular and regular clergy shall be preserved.

15. All government departments and all public employees shall remain as they are today. The only employees who shall be removed are those who oppose this plan, and they shall be replaced by those who are most outstanding for their steadfastness, virtue, and merit. . . .

Americans: Here you have the establishment and creation of a new empire. You have the oath sworn by the Army of the Three Guarantees, transmitted to you by him who has the honor of addressing you. You have the objective for which he is urging your collaboration. He asks of you only that which you should ask and desire for yourselves: union, fraternity, order, internal peace, abhorrence of and vigilance against any turbulence. . . . Having no enemies to combat, let us trust in the God of Armies who is also the God of Peace, that making up this combined force of Europeans and Americans, of dissidents and royalists, we serve as mere defenders, simple spectators of the great work that I have sketched for you today, to be finished and perfected by the founding fathers. . . . In your outburst of jubilation, proclaim: Long live the sacred religion that we profess! Long live North America, independent of all nations on the globe! Long live union, maker of the common happiness!

GOVERNMENTAL ORGANIZATION AND THE CORPORATE TRADITION

The spirit of social harmony and political optimism that accompanied the Plan of Iguala was short-lived. It was undermined in 1823 by the provincial rebellion against the "despot" Iturbide, led by General Antonio López de Santa Anna. The result of this rebellion was a congress which drafted the federalist Constitution of 1824. Despite President Guadalupe Victoria's attempt to return to political harmony after 1824, by 1827 the country was torn again by factional strife. By the early 1830s the optimism of the previous decade had vanished and along with it a faith in the "magic of constitutions," namely, the belief that the key to individual liberty and social progress lay in the properly conceived articles of a written code. The regime of Valentín Gómez Farías that came to power in 1833, again as the result of rebellion in the provinces against a "despotic" government, revealed a shift away from constitutionalism to a new examination of the social and institutional realities of the country which had made the written constitution unenforceable. José María Luis Mora, who became the chief theorist for the liberal reform regime, clearly reveals this shift. From 1824 to 1827 he had been the leader of the congress which drew up the constitution for the country's largest and most populous state, the State of Mexico, By 1833 he was still concerned with the "constitution," but he now meant by the term much more than a written document. Mora wrote the following selection in exile in Paris after the fall of the Gómez Farías regime.

2. The Corporate Spirit ❖ José María Luis Mora

. . . The men of 1833 resolved to preserve at all cost the representative system and the federal form of government, mindful of the difficulties they had to contend with, namely the habits created by the old constitution of the country. Principal among these is the *corporate spirit* diffused throughout all classes of society, which weakens or destroys *national spirit*. Whether by deliberate design or as the unforeseen result of unknown causes operating in the civil state of Old Spain, there was a notable tendency to create corporate entities, for them to amass privileges and exemptions from the common law [*fuero común*], to become enriched by donations from the living and by legacies from the dead, to accord them in short all that can lead to the formation of a corporate body, integral in spirit, complete in organization, and independent in its privileged jurisdiction [*fueros privilegiados*] and in the means of livelihood at its disposal. Not all corporate entities could reckon on equal privileges; and yet it was very rare for a corporation not to have enough to be sufficient unto itself. Not only did the clergy and the militia have general jurisdiction, subdivided into that of regular clergy in the first case, and in the second, artillery, engineers, and navy, but also the Inquisition, the University, the Mint, the Marquisate of the Valley (patrimony of Hernan Cortés), the entails from primogeniture [*mayorazgos*], the confraternities, and even the guilds, all had their privileges and their wealth, or in short their separate existence. The results of this complex situation were fatal to national spirit and prosperity, public morality and tranquillity, personal independence, and judicial and governmental order.

If independence had been carried out forty years ago, a man born or living in the country would have had little regard for the designation "Mexican," and would have considered himself isolated and alone

From José María Luis Mora, *Obras sueltas* (Paris, 1837), *1*, pp. xcvi–cxiv. My translation—CAH.

in the world, if he had had to depend solely on it. For such a man the designation "judge," "canon," or "guild-brother" would have been more esteemed and rightly so since each signified something positive. To discuss with him the subject of national interests would have been to speak to him in Hebrew. He did not nor could he know interests other than those of the corporate body or bodies to which he belonged. Moreover, he would have upheld these interests to the sacrifice of those of the rest of society, although the latter were more numerous and important. He would have done what the clergy and the army do today—that is, rebel against the government or against the laws which are not in harmony with the tendencies and interests of his class, however much this government or these laws are consonant with the interests of society.

If a congress had met at that time, can there be any doubt that deputies would have been named by the corporations and not by electoral juntas, that each deputy would have considered himself a corporate representative and not a national representative and that there would have been myriad disputes on privileges and jurisdictions, and that no one would have attended to the concerns of the mass of the people? Do we not see much of this happening today, despite the fact that elections are conducted otherwise, and despite incessant talk that deputies represent the nation? This is what I mean by corporate spirit destroying public spirit. . . .

There are several principles of social justice and of the representative system which are very difficult to combine with the corporate spirit, namely that all men are free to use their reason to examine questions and to form a judgment without fear of persecution, and that they can do this in all matters not injuring the rights of others or upsetting public order. The corporations exercise a kind of tyranny on the thoughts and actions of their members, and they tend strongly to monopolize influence and opinion by the creed they profess, the compromises they demand, and the obligations they impose. . . .

The existence and multiplicity of corporate bodies is a perpetual impediment to the progress of justice. The diversity of jurisdictions, their legal basis, and the individuals who enjoy them, all produce a multitude of artificial interests that society could well do without. . . . Jurisdictional rivalry, the ineffectiveness of criminal laws, and the lack of respect for common civil courts which are the fount of national justice, are all specific consequences of the corporate spirit. When this spirit is dominant, the last thing to be considered is the preservation and security of common rights. The principal concern is that the corporation come out ahead, and that it establish its exclusive jurisdiction at the expense of public authority. . . .

Similar and even greater obstacles, if this is possible, can be identified in the relation between the corporate spirit and the administrative order. There are interests which are difficult and often impossible to reconcile by law. What suits one corporate body is harmful to another; what one demands vociferously the other forcefully rejects. Nevertheless, if some one of the extremes in question were favorable to the mass of the people, this could be a factor determining the choice. But it usually happens that these conflicting internal demands are weaker than the corporate conflicts with society at large, resulting in ever mounting difficulties for a sickly and tumor ridden social organism which sees its own nutriments absorbed by other elements. With an absence of national laws and an excess of corporate laws, the government does not know what course to take. It has in its hands a constitution filled with declarations and principles favoring the mass of people; it has public officials and powers set up to obtain these objectives, yet it must observe laws and respect tendencies which are self-destroying. What results from all this?—protests, followed by discontent, and finally by bloody revolutions which are prompted, nurtured, and supported by the corporate spirit.

The greatest obstacle against which national prosperity has to struggle is the tendency toward perpetually monopolizing, accumulating, and reassembling land and capital. Since it is possible in society to increase indefinitely a given fortune without ever having to divide it, clearly in the course of a few centuries the means of subsistence can become very difficult or absolutely impossible for the mass of the people. . . .

The experience of fifty years of revolutions in Europe and the sorry disillusionment felt in Mexico during the period from independence [1821] to the end of 1836, make manifest that it is impossible for the two systems to operate together in harmony. This impossibility was clear in 1833 to all men of progress and the group among them to whom fell the direction of affairs. Finding themselves having to choose between the federal representative system established by the national constitution and the old regime based on the corporate spirit, they chose the former without hesitation, applying their full force and action to strengthening the one and dismantling the other.

The Spanish government had already experienced all of the obstacles that the privileged classes and political corporations throw up to social progress, and for over sixty years royal policies were calculated to diminish their number and weaken their force. Each day witnessed the disappearance of some corporation or the curtailment of the privileges of some class, yet up to 1812 enough of them still remained to complicate the course of affairs. The Constitution of 1812 abolished special jurisdictions except for the ecclesiastical and the military, a measure in full effect in Mexico after 1820 when the Constitution was proclaimed for the second time. . . . While it is true that the guilds, the Indian communities, the privileged professional associations of lawyers and merchants, the entails from primogeniture, and the multiplicity of legal privileges enjoyed by diverse individuals and groups all disappeared, there still remained the clergy and the militia with their special jurisdictions, and other entities which continued to maintain the design of their former organization, if not the specific privileges. . . .

[Let us first consider the clergy.] The clergy for the most part are made up of men who find themselves in society only materially and only accidentally in coexistence with the rest of the citizens. From their education, the clergy can regard as important only spiritual interests, which they construe to mean not merely religious beliefs and the practice of evangelical virtues, but also the supremacy and independence of their corporation, the possession of acquired wealth, and the resistance to having the civil and criminal suits of their members judged by the secular power, its laws, and its governmental and judicial authorities. . . . Because of celibacy the clergy are entirely free and isolated from family ties, the first and principal link of man with society. Finally, because of their kind of activities and their particular laws, they must renounce any lucrative undertaking, thus suppressing completely the love of work and the advances of fortune that always come from individual enterprise, and which establish the second link between man and society. The clergy abhor religious toleration and the freedom of thought and the press, since these principles and the institutions built upon them are such as to destroy or undermine their domination over the mind. The clergy detest legal equality which dissipates special jurisdictions and hierarchies, thus eliminating the power and respect these bring to the clergy as a class. They resist regulation of the civil status of citizens, for it takes from them their influence over the principal acts of life, birth, marriage, and death, and thus their influence over the fortunes of families. . . .

In summary, what power can the republic exert against a corporate entity in the country that is more ancient than it is, one governed by perpetual, absolute, and irresponsible superiors—the bishops—a corporate entity which counts on an income of from 15 to 120 thousand pesos and which has at its disposal a capital of about 180 million pesos, the productive portion of which yields 7½ million. Can a republic born yesterday, in which all branches of public administration are in disarray and patterns of authority lacking, a republic whose general resources yield only double that of the clergy and are far from meeting budgets, in short can such a republic, where all is weakness and confusion, hold its own against a corporate entity which has the will and the power to destroy its constitution, to undermine its laws, and to incite the masses to rebellion against it? The administration of 1833–1834 believed it could prevail and thus was determined to destroy the power of this political corporation, the single effective way of preserving the republic.

3. Monarchy in Mexico   ⋄   Lucas Alamán[?]

The years from 1835 to 1846 constitute a dismal decade of classic Latin American political turmoil, marked by numerous pronounciamentos, barracks revolts, and frequent changes in the presidency. Although there is evidence of important policy innovations and continuities during the period, intelligent political writing reached a low ebb. This condition changed markedly in 1846 when the threat of war with the United States over Texas brought on a new mood of crisis, provoking a disposition toward self-examination and a renewed search for remedies to Mexico's ills. The new mood can be seen clearly with the appearance on January 24, 1846, of

From Lucas Alamán(?), "Our Profession of Faith," *El Tiempo*, February 12, 1846.

El Tiempo, a daily newspaper which frankly called itself "conservative," a new term in the Mexican political vocabulary. The chief editor was Lucas Alamán, who most probably wrote the following unsigned article, entitled "Our Profession of Faith." Alamán had been chief minister in two previous administrations and had also been an active industrialist and promoter of national manufacturing. Alamán's call for monarchy in Mexico followed an earlier dramatic and sharply rejected open letter to President Anastasio Bustamante, written by José María Gutiérrez de Estrada in 1840. By 1846 Alamán hoped that President Mariano Paredes y Arrillaga would be more sympathetic to calling a foreign prince than had been Bustamante earlier. When this proved to be a false hope, *El Tiempo* protested and ceased publication on June 7, 1846. Nevertheless, monarchism remained alive in Mexico and finally came to fruition with the arrival of Archduke Ferdinand Maximilian of Austria in 1864.

We have promised a clear, explicit, and complete declaration of our political principles. We will now fulfill that promise. . . .

We believe that our independence was a great and glorious event and that it was necessary and inevitable. When kingdoms and provinces located so far from the metropolis reach a certain stage of development and growth, and when prosperity and enlightenment have created the necessary interests and qualifications for governing a country, then it is appropriate to loosen the bonds that tie young nations to those that are older and more advanced, which, as mother countries, gave them their upbringing and nourishment and initiated them to the ways of civilization. Thus, sooner or later, our independence was bound to come. Ten years of bitter wars could not bring it about, yet a military promenade of seven months in 1821 sufficed for the words of Iguala to become the country's banner. Why? Because the guarantees of that plan reconciled all spirits and united all sentiments, because the clergy, the army, and the people saw a sure future of glory and prosperity for the fatherland. For this reason, many Spanish clergymen, soldiers, and merchants continued their work and service in Mexico; for this reason, neither blood nor destruction was needed to carry through this important revolution. Independence brought together so many sentiments because it loosened and did not break the bonds which tied the past with the present and future.

The Plan of Iguala was not put into effect. Iturbide tried to found a dynasty for his own advantage, and this empire, without foundations, without legitimacy, without the respect that comes from time and tradition, fell into ruins with the first revolutionary tremor. The lamentable tragedy that took Iturbide's life, also robbed the fatherland of a faithful servant, who went astray because he was inexperienced and bedazzled by flattery. The United States then began to construct in Mexico another kind of empire. Fully trusting, we were enticed along new and dangerous ways by its books and ideas, by the promises of its representatives and by the deceptive spectacle of its prosperity. Republican ideas finally dominated the nation and took form in the government.

Then we began that ruinous road we still travel. We ignored the differences of origin, religion, and of history between Mexico and the United States. We did not take into consideration that our own social, political, and religious unity made a monarchical form of government advisable for us, just as their diversity of religions, peoples, and language made a republican federation advisable for them. We believed that the quickest way to achieve political liberty was to throw ourselves into the hands of the United States, to imitate slavishly its institutions, and to follow exactly its treacherous counsel. The absurd constitution of 1824 was then drawn up, and in the name of liberty the American representative [Joel R. Poinsett] established secret societies which tyrannized and devoured the country. The treasury was in disorder, the administration in ruins. When we should have had resources sufficient for all our obligations, public wealth was squandered and we began to contract increasingly ruinous loans. The nation was weakened by the expulsion of peaceful and hardworking Spaniards along with their Mexican families and their immense wealth. Civil liberty was smothered in continual revolts, and a tough and disciplined army became an instrument of ambition and anarchy. Presidents and congresses fell precipitously from bloody revolutions. Civil war in the countryside and disorder in the cities were from then on our almost normal state. Meanwhile, savage Indians boldly ravaged our land with impunity and the United States grabbed Texas and prepared the usurpation of California. . . .

How do we stand abroad? Our reputation in Europe is in shambles. . . . Our country, so rich in natural resources, no longer holds credit in any market. Our governmental instability discredits our institutions and blocks any political alliance we might draw up in Europe to resist North American invasions. No nation will enter into treaties with the unfortunate republics of Spanish America, condemned by fate to drag along in anarchy and upheaval. . . .

Thus we believe that republican institutions have brought us to a state of prostration and exhaustion, just as they would have done to Spain, England, or France. . . . Now, if asked what our desire is, we will state it frankly. We want a representative monarchy; we want national unity; we want order along with political and civil liberty; we want the integrity of Mexican territory; we want, in short, all the promises and guarantees of the Plan of Iguala, in order to secure our glorious independence on stable foundations. Indeed, the form of government that the most civilized and advanced countries of the world have adopted, after long upheaval, is the appropriate one for us. . . .

We want a regime in which justice is administered impartially, being free from politics; in which government has the stability and force to protect society and in which universally respected laws assure the individual freedoms of its citizens; in which the chambers are elective and royal power hereditary, so that political liberty and the existing order can be secured. We desire a type of organization that gives regularity to commerce and protection to industry; that allows national intellectual activity to develop; and that provides a place for all prominent men in its well-ordered hierarchy.

We want, as in all European representative monarchies, that there be an aristocracy based only on merit, capability, education, wealth, and on military and civil services; that a man is not asked who his ancestors were, but what he has done, the only relevant criterion for admitting him to any job and conferring him any honor.

We certainly want a strong and vigorous army which can cover itself with glory in noble defense of its country, in which the military hierarchy is respected out of regard for the worth of those who shed their blood for the fatherland; and we want victories abroad for that army. Moreover, the soldier must be assured a comfortable and stable retirement after his fatiguing career, not abandonment and misery which is how revolutions pay for his services.

We desire proper and dignified support for the Catholic faith of our ancestors, not that continuous threat to its properties brought about by anarchy. Born in the womb of the Catholic Church, we do not wish to see our cathedrals converted into temples of those sects which scandalize the world with their religious quarrels. Nor do we wish to see our national standard replaced on their towers by the abhorrent stars and stripes. . . .

There is room for all legal parties under our banner, all those who want to see the freedom and independence of their country made secure, all those who desire that our sorry and unfortunate country become the first nation of America. We have faith in its future, in its aggrandizement, and we do not believe that such a vast, rich, and privileged territory has to be the prisoner of disorder and anarchy.

But we do not want reaction of any kind. Conservatives by conviction and nature, we ask protection for all existing interests whatever their origin. It is madness to believe that a prince of royal blood coming to Mexico to establish a dynasty can be supported by foreigners. This could be done three centuries ago, but not today, especially in representative governments. We do not want a single office or a single military rank to be in other than Mexican hands; our army and our people should be bolstered only by those who claim permanent attachment to the country.

We have now concluded our profession of faith. It is at least complete and clear. Convinced that our ideas are the only ones that can save the nation, we will uphold them with civility, with moderation, but also with vigor and decisiveness. . . . What is sure is that we will never become the accomplices of foreign ambition and that in our newspaper the stars and stripes of the United States will never eclipse the colors of the national standard.

4. In Defense of Religion ✧ Félix Zuloaga

> The disastrous war with the United States occasioned a major debate in the press over the reasons for the defeat and the priorities to be followed in national rejuvenation. This

From Félix Zuloaga, *La Cruz*, 6 (January 28, 1858), pp. 584–589.

debate turned into civil conflict with the proclamation of the
Plan of Ayutla on March 1, 1854, which called for the overthrow of the dictator Santa Anna and the convening of a
new constitutional congress. Provincial chieftains, Mexico
City politicians, and opponents of Santa Anna of various
political persuasions flocked to the cause of Ayutla, and the
result was the government of Ignacio Comonfort, which pre-
sided over a series of reform measures and the formulation
of the Constitution of 1857 (document 8). Comonfort was
a moderate on the church issue and broke with the more
anticlerical members of his reform government, Benito
Juárez, Melchor Ocampo, and the brothers Sebastián and
Miguel Lerdo de Tejada. Comonfort's reluctance to enforce
the constitution provided an opening for the clerical and
military opposition, the leader of which was General Félix
Zuloaga. On December 17, 1857, Zuloaga issued the Plan of
Tacubaya, announcing the overthrow of the constitution, and
on January 28, 1858, the following manifesto and decrees.
Besides the constitution, Zuloaga's particular target was the
Lerdo Law of June 25, 1856, which had decreed the sale of
church real estate to those who were renting it, or to the
public at auction.

One of those terrible crises that God undoubtedly uses as a lesson
to peoples and governments is now threatening both the unity and
existence of the republic and the bases of its civilization. A violent
and unsettling upheaval is now leaving in its path widespread blood-
shed and destruction. . . . In such grievous circumstances, and now
that a victory unblemished by excesses or animosities has been won,
the victorious government hereby dedicates itself to and finds its
support in the glorious principles of 1821, the watchwords Religion,
Union, and Independence. . . . The church is under attack, our customs are in disregard, the most disrupting ideas are being sanctioned,
and property, family, and all of the social bonds are in jeopardy.
Nevertheless, the Constitution of 1857 has vanished, not because of
the work of its enemies or the powerful forces united against it, but
because of discord and disagreement among the established authorities themselves. It suited the designs of Providence that the edifice
which had been raised on such fragile foundations collapse by its own
weakness. . . .

The laws issued by the present government, to be circulated with this manifesto, make clear the necessities which must be immediately met and the measures which must be adopted in order to calm the public conscience and to reestablish harmony between civil and ecclesiastical powers. The church has come to regard its wealth as a legitimate and sacred patrimony, but it has not hesitated for a moment to risk this wealth in defense of its doctrine and the obedience it owes to the Almighty. The church has seen clerical jurisdiction attacked and its ministers deprived of the necessary means of subsistance. It has suffered a persecution that hardly seems believable in Mexico, and no one can excuse such persecution if he appeals to the impartial testimony of his conscience and the pure sentiments of his heart. What enlightened mind, what generous and judicious spirit can approve the laws which have been sanctioned? To remedy these evils, to calm spirits, and to present itself as an administration made up of faithful sons of the Catholic Church, eager to bequeath to the country and to posterity an example worthy of its forefathers, is our most pressing duty and one which cannot be thwarted even by the men who do not profess these principles. In the midst of this disaster, where all is in ruins and can only be regarded as a punishment from Heaven, why do we not invoke God's protection in redressing the wrongs that have been committed? . . .

It is quite appropriate to instill the idea, indeed it is a sacred obligation to do so, that only religious sentiment can free this unfortunate country from the many horrors of barbarism. There are those who want to throw over the moral and beneficent influence of the church and to establish a dictatorship of universal devastation and death. On this matter, then, the government will stand firm according to the principles it professes and according to the respect it owes to religion. . . .

The government will exhaust all possible measures to halt the armed conflict and to secure national unity through patriotism and conviction. Difficult as the situation in which we find ourselves is, with the factions resorting only to violence and force, the government pledges itself to avoid new misfortunes, and thus it declares from henceforth to the entire nation that the misfortunes which do ensue are not its responsibility. This it will make manifest to all the leaders and authorities that do not recognize it, opening the way for all to set their sights in the interest of the fatherland and, while there is still time, to stave off the impending ruin. . . .

With great satisfaction we include as follows the decrees published as separate edicts, by which the demogogic laws are annulled. . . .

[A.] Art. 1.   The measures contained in the law of June 25, 1856, and the regulation of July 30, 1856, which provided for the transfer of the landed property of ecclesiastical corporations, are hereby declared null and void. Consequently, the transfer of that property already carried out in execution of the above-mentioned law and regulation is also declared null and void. The above-mentioned corporations shall remain in full dominion and possession of the aforesaid properties, as they were prior to the enactment of the law.

Art. 2.   The governing council will advise all the measures it deems necessary which pertain to the restoration of sales taxes [*alcabalas*] and of transferred property belonging to civil corporations, to general resolutions on rents, and to other matters connected with the current law. . . .

[B.]   Military and ecclesiastical jurisdictions shall be reestablished to their full extent as of January 1, 1853. . . .

[C.]   The law of April 11, 1857 pertaining to parish fees is hereby annulled and the measures existing prior to that date shall continue in full force. . . .

[D.]   All officials and public employees, who by the mere fact of not having taken an oath to the Constitution of 1857 and for no other legal reason were deprived of their posts, shall return to the exercise of their respective functions. . . .

5. The Reform Program ✧ Benito Juárez, Melchor Ocampo, Manuel Ruíz, Miguel Lerdo de Tejada

> During the years 1858 to 1861, known in Mexico as the Three Years War, the country became divided between two rival parties and two armies, each calling itself the legitimate government. On the conservative side, Zuloaga's regime in

From Niceto de Zamacois, *Historia de Méjico* (Barcelona and Mexico, 1880), *15*, pp. 909–934.

Mexico City gave way to a group of younger officers, Miguel Miramón, Tomás Mejía, and Leonardo Márquez, superb military men who became zealous defenders of the prerogatives of church and army. On the liberal side, Benito Juárez, as chief justice prior to Zuloaga's coup, claimed the title of constitutional president and fashioned a reformist government which was forced to move from Guanajuato to Guadalajara, and finally by sea to Vera Cruz, where it became established on May 4, 1858. Vera Cruz, therefore, was the seat of government for the reformist cause until Juárez triumphed militarily and returned to Mexico City late in December 1860. The group around Juárez was divided on how rapidly to issue reform legislation, especially that pertaining to the nationalization of church property. Juárez tended toward moderation, but the radicals prevailed, particularly because extreme anticlerical measures had already been enacted by liberal state governors who thus threatened to assume *de facto* leadership of the national reform cause. The following manifesto, issued at Vera Cruz on July 7, 1859, stating the rationale and program of the Juárez regime, was followed over the next two years by a series of detailed decrees known as the Laws of Reform. Besides the part reproduced here, the manifesto dealt with other administrative and reform issues, but the emphasis was clearly on the church. A few days later, the conservative government of Miguel Miramón issued its own program from Mexico City in a similar manifesto.

In the difficult and compromising situation that the nation has found itself . . . the government, which by virtue of the Constitution of 1857 has the indispensable duty of preserving legal order in cases like the present one, judged it wise to withold its views on radically curing the evils afflicting society. Once armed struggle was initiated between the vast majority of the nation and those trying to oppress it, the government believed that the very superiority of a cause which has reason and justice on its side, in addition to the repeated frustration its adversaries experienced in their powerlessness to dominate it, would in themselves make these adversaries give up their criminal purpose, or soon succumb in the conflict.

But, whereas unfortunately this hope has not been fulfilled; whereas, despite the prolonged resistance which society has made against the triumph of that insurrection, its authors continue to persist in maintaining it (supported solely by the determined protection of the upper clergy and by the force of bayonets at their command); whereas, because of this disgraceful and criminal obstinacy, the republic seems condemned to continue suffering for some time yet the disasters and calamities which made up the awful history of such a shameful rebellion, the government would be failing in one of the primary obligations imposed upon it by the situation if it were to delay any longer the public declaration of its views, not only those relating to the serious matters now being aired on the battlefield, but also its views on the course to be followed in the various branches of public administration.

The nation finds itself today at a critical juncture because its future depends entirely on the result of a bloody struggle incited by the partisans of obscurantism and abuses against the clearest principles of liberty and social progress. At such a decisive moment, the government has the sacred obligation of going to the people and making the cry for cherished national rights and interests heard throughout the land, not only because public opinion will thus be increasingly mobilized for useful ends, but also because the people will better appreciate the reason for the great sacrifices it is making in combating its oppressors, and finally because we will thus succeed in bringing before all the civilized nations of the world the conflict which stirs the republic so profoundly.

In fulfilling this obligation today, the government need not express its thoughts on the political organization of the country. Since this government emanated from the Constitution of 1857 and considers itself furthermore as the legitimate representative of the liberal principles embodied in that constitution, it is naturally understood that the government aspires: to have all citizens enjoy equally, without distinction of class or condition, whatever rights and guarantees that are compatible with the good order of society; to make these rights and guarantees forever effective by the proper administration of justice; to have all authorities faithfully fulfill their roles and duties without exceeding the bounds set by the laws; and finally to have the states of the federation use the powers in their possession to administer their interests freely, as well as to do everything that will promote their prosperity, in so far as they do not oppose the rights and interests of the republic. . . .

In order to end definitively the bloody and fratricidal war that one portion of the clergy has been fomenting for so long solely for the purpose of preserving its interests and prerogatives, scandalously misusing the influence from its wealth and from its sacred ministry; and in order to strip this class immediately of the elements which serve to support its pernicious power, the government deems it essential to:

1. Adopt as an invariable general principle absolute independence between the affairs of the state and those which are purely ecclesiastical.

2. Suppress all corporations of the male regular clergy, without exception, secularizing the clergy that are presently in these corporations.

3. Extinguish likewise the confraternities, arch-confraternities, brotherhoods, and in general all the existing corporations or congregations of that type.

4. Close nunnery novitiates, but allow the present nuns to remain in the convents, along with the capital or dowries that each has contributed. An allowance is to be provided for the needs of worship in nunnery churches.

5. Declare all wealth now administered by the regular and secular clergy, under whatever heading, to have been and to be the property of the nation, including the surplus held by the nunneries after deducting the sum of the dowries. Alienate said wealth, accepting in payment for a portion of its value bonds of the public debt and bonds of the capitalization of diverse government pensions and annuities.

6. Declare, finally, that the payments by the faithful to the clergy, whether for administration of the sacraments or for any other clerical service, the annual product of which, if well distributed, is quite sufficient to cover the expenses of worship and of its ministers, is to be derived from open agreements between the faithful and the clergy, without any intervention whatever by civil authority. . . .

In short, such are the ideas of the present administration on the course to be followed, in order to secure peace and order in the republic, guiding it on the sure path of liberty and progress to its growth and prosperity. On formulating all its intentions in the manner here presented, the government believes it is doing no more than faithfully interpreting the sentiments, desires, and needs of the nation. . . .

PROPERTY

In December 1831 Mora was invited by the Governor of Zacatecas, a fellow opponent of the proclerical regime of Anastasio Bustamante, to enter a contest for the best essay on the nature of church wealth. The "contest," whether spurious or genuine, was won by Mora, and his essay marked an important departure from the moderate attitude toward the church that had prevailed since 1821. The anticlerical tone and the arguments used were reminiscent of those of the revolutionaries in France from 1789 to 1793 and of the Spanish liberals from 1810 to 1813. Mora's case for governmental limitation of church wealth, however, was explicitly based on much earlier precedents—namely the tradition of royal authority ("regalism") over "national" churches from the sixteenth to the eighteenth centuries. In these particular passages Mora distinguishes between corporate property and private property, a theoretical distinction which came to have important implications in the developing assumptions underlying the liberal reform program.

6. Corporate Property and Individual Property
~ José María Luis Mora

It has been proved that the wealth designated ecclesiastical is by its nature civil and temporal, both before and after it passed under the dominion of the church; that it cannot be spiritualized; that the church, considered as a mystical body, has no right to it; that neither governments nor individuals are obliged to give wealth to the church; that this same church, as the mystical body of Jesus Christ, can and has taken on *de facto* the character of a political community or corporation and that as such it can and has acquired wealth as legally permitted for communities of its type, that is—permitted by civil law and subject totally and exclusively to temporal authority; finally that in the nature, administration, and investment of its wealth there are abuses which ought to be remedied and that it is absolutely necessary to do so. Once proved that the church as a possessor of temporal wealth is a political community . . . it remains for us only to examine the right that civil authority has over the bodies it has created and over their wealth. It is very clear that this right is exclusive, or what is the same, that it can be exercised without the intervention of any outside authority. . . .

It is essential nevertheless not to confuse communities or moral bodies with associations of individuals to form commercial or industrial enterprises. The acquisitions of the former are never the property of their several members, totally or in part, nor are these acquisitions destined to benefit them individually, but rather to fulfill the publicly useful ends that the body is to pursue. These bodies then are, strictly speaking, simple administrators of the funds in their charge, funds which belong to the public and which are consequently subject to public authority. This is not the case with industrial and commercial companies; in them exists a common stock whose component parts

From José María Luis Mora, "Disertación sobre la naturaleza y aplicación de las rentas y bienes ecclesiásticas . . . . ," *El Indicador de la federación mejicana* (Mexico, 1833), 2, pp. 307–310, 317–319.

preserve the character of individual property that the stockholders recover upon the dissolution of the company, dividing the profits and paying the losses in proportion to the amounts they have invested. The stock of these companies, as has been said, preserves the character of individual property and has nothing in common with that of hospitals, schools, confraternities, monastic institutions, ecclesiastical chapters, municipal corporations, etc. No one will mistake these commercial companies for moral bodies, which is what we are referring to when we speak of the rights of corporations or communities.

There is no doubt that the church has a civil right to own its wealth, but this right is corporate, entirely different from an individual right in its origin, nature and extent. The laws have always distinguished personal wealth from corporate wealth, and they have accorded the former unlimited scope, the latter they have greatly restricted. The right of an individual to acquire wealth has never had limits. It has always been legal for him to increase his wealth by new acquisitions, even if these acquisitions devolve on an already excessively large fortune. The procedure with corporations has always been the opposite, for consistently they have been prohibited from exceeding certain limits placed on their acquisition of wealth. . . . An individual's right of acquisition is natural, prior to society; it belongs to him as a man and society can do no more than secure him in it. On the other hand, a community's right of acquisition is purely civil, subsequent to society, created by it and consequently subject to the limitations society wishes to put upon it. . . .

As we have stated, the rights of communities, as distinguished from those of individuals, can be enlarged, restricted, or revoked by the authority which granted them, without the intervention of any other, and since the church is only a community, its right of administration is subject to the authority to which it owes this right, none other than the civil authority.

In exercise of this authority belonging to the central government, the Laws of the Indies determined that in America the *mayordomos* or administrators of wealth belonging to church buildings be limited to secular clergy, and Charles III in his decree of September 11, 1764, ordered the regular clergy to retire to their cloisters and to entrust the administration of their haciendas to the secular clergy. Charles IV, in his decree of 1804 funding royal debts [*consolidación de vales reales*], took from the clergy the administration of all wealth of pious works which was now to be assigned to the sinking fund. His words were the following: "Since my sovereign authority to direct public institutions toward these and other ends of state is indisputable, I have resolved, after a full examination, that all landed property pertaining to hospitals, orphanages, almshouses, foundling homes, confraternities, monuments, pious works, and trusts for pious uses be disentailed." This measure was justly criticized as ruinous and impolitic, but no one dared to brand it illegal. All recognized the authority of the government as appropriate in the situation, and no one dared to attack the government as usurper of the rights of the church. Very much to the contrary, the landed properties which were sold in order that their capital pass to the sinking fund, have remained in the hands of the purchasers, without it occurring to anyone to dispute them. . . .

It is a principle recognized by all the economists and confirmed by repeated experience, that only direct and personal interest can make capital and landed property productive, and this applies to all types of wealth. This personal and direct interest can never exist in any corporation, which by its nature and constitution is deprived of unity of purpose, action, and will. Thus we see the immense difference between the wealth of a corporation and that of an individual. If this wealth consists of rural landed properties, fields are left uncultivated and uninhabited, and the appropriate shops and even farm implements are lacking. If it consists of urban properties, no repairs are made on them, leaving everything up to the tenant who often ignores them, with the result that in the course of a few years the property deteriorates, falls into ruin, and disappears, leaving only an abandoned structure of an unknown owner. Only in accidental circumstances, such as a long term lease on a rural property, or in the case of an urban property where there prevails the Mexican custom of not dislodging a tenant as long as he continues to pay the original rent . . . can rural properties be maintained or urban properties be spared a marked deterioration. But who cannot see that it is now really the tenant who manages the property and not the owner whose ownership becomes reduced to collecting a rent on it?

7. The Right of Property ⬦ Ponciano Arriaga

In the formulation of the constitution called for by the Plan of Ayutla (1854) one of the issues that stimulated debate and disagreement was the definition of the right of property. The rise of socialism in Europe and particularly the experience of the Revolution of 1848 in France had called into question the accepted liberal theory that property was one of the inalienable and natural rights of the individual. In Mexico, the "social question" was much in the minds of intellectuals and policy-makers, not only because of European events but also because of the recent Caste Wars of 1847–1850. One issue that arose was: What were the rights of the mass of the people in relation to the effective rights and powers of large landowners? The constitutional committee, of which Ponciano Arriaga was chairman, wrote into article 17 of the draft constitution a provision stating that the freedom to carry on honest and useful work, whatever it might be, "cannot be restricted by the law, nor by public authorities, nor by individuals as property holders." The final phrase was a reference to exploitation of peons and laborers by hacendados. This article in the draft version was transformed into article 4 of the final Constitution of 1857. Arriaga objected even to the draft article 17 on the grounds that it was too moderate. The following selection is from a speech he delivered to the convention on June 23, 1856, recording his dissent from the committee version of article 17.

One of the most deep-rooted evils from which our country suffers, and one which ought to merit the special attention of our constitution-makers, is the shocking distribution of landed property. At the same time that a few individuals possess immense uncultivated lands which could provide subsistence for many millions of men, a numerous population, the large majority of our citizens, groans under the

Reproduced from Francisco Zarco, *Historia del congreso extraordinario constituyente de 1856 y 1857* (Mexico, 1857), *1*, pp. 546–570. My translation—CAH.

burden of the most horrendous poverty, without property, without homes, without industry, and without work. Because of the absurd economic organization of society, such a people cannot be free nor republican, nor even less be happy, despite the fact that numerous constitutions and laws proclaim absolute rights which are fine in theory but impossible in practice.

There are proprietors in Mexico whose properties occupy (if one can call occupancy that which is unsubstantial and purely imaginary) a land surface greater than that of some of our states, and even greater than some European nations. Throughout this great expanse of territory, a large part of which lies idle, uninhabited, and abandoned, crying out for the efforts of man, are spread four or five million Mexicans who, having only agriculture to rely upon, lacking materials and tools for cultivation, lacking both the means and the place to make another type of honest living, either become lazy and inactive, if they do not turn to thievery and perdition, or they remain out of necessity under the yoke of the monopolist, which either condemns them to misery or imposes unreasonable conditions upon them. . . .

How and when will the grave problems presented by this situation be resolved? Are we to have popular government and yet have a hungry, naked, and miserable people? Are we to proclaim equality and the rights of man and leave the most numerous of our classes, the majority of those who make up the nation, in a condition worse than serfs or outcasts? Are we in our words to condemn and abhor slavery, while the conditions of the majority of our citizens is less happy than that of the Negroes in Cuba or in the United States? How and when will we consider the fate of the proletariat, of those we call Indians, of the servants and peons of the countryside, who drag with them the heavy chains of true servitude, that artful and peculiar variety established, not by colonial legislation, which was so often trampled and infringed upon, but by the arbitrary officials of the Spanish regime?

Wouldn't we have shown more logic and frankness by denying our four million poor all participation in political affairs, all access to public employment, all active and passive votes in elections, by declaring them things and not persons, and by founding a governmental system in which the aristocracy of wealth, or at best that of talent, would serve as the basis of institutions? One of two things is inevitable: either the element of *de facto* aristocracy is going to operate at long length in the bowels of our political regime, in defiance of our fundamental laws, and the man of title and rank, the veritable lord of the land, of a privileged caste that monopolizes territorial wealth, that profits from the sweat of their servants, is to have power and influence in all political and civil matters; or we must have reform without fail to shatter the bonds of feudal servitude, to destroy all monopolies and tyrannies, and to make all abuses perish. In this manner there can enter into the heart and veins of our political structure the fruitful element of democratic equality, the powerful element of popular sovereignty, the only legitimate and rightful authority. The nation wants it so, the people demand it. The struggle has begun and sooner or later that just authority will recover its ascendancy. The great word "reform" has been spoken and those who erect dikes against the torrent of light and truth do so in vain. . . .

At the present stage of history, we acknowledge the right of property and we recognize it as inviolable. If the form it takes in the country presents an infinite number of abuses, we would uproot them; but to destroy the right itself, to eliminate the idea of property, is not only imprudent but impossible. The idea of property carries with it inherently the idea of individuality, and "whatever human association becomes," says an illustrious author, "it will always contain two elements—society and the individual; the one cannot live without the other and vice versa, because they are two correllative existences which complement each other and mutually interact. Each element is so necessary by itself that neither can be sacrificed, and social progress consists simply of allowing each a simultaneous development, since everything that harms the individual also harms society, and what satisfies one satisfies the other. Any change which does not encompass these two conditions will be for this reason alone contrary to the law of progress. Precisely what we are criticizing in the present organization of property is that it does not heed the interests of a large portion of individuals, those who constitute a multitude of outcasts who are prevented from benefiting from the distribution of society's wealth." . . .

With very notable exceptions, which we are quick to acknowledge, a rich landowner of our country, who rarely knows his land intimately, or the administrator or overseer who represents him, is comparable to the feudal lord of the middle ages. On his feudal domain, he more or less formally sanctions laws and executes them, he administers justice, exercises civil authority, imposes taxes and fines, maintains jails, stocks, and implement sheds [*tlapixqueras*], aplies penalties and tortures, monopolizes commerce, and prohibits any trade or industry not specifically attached to the estate from being conducted without his consent. The judges or officials who exercise the powers of public authority on the hacienda are normally retainers or tenants, dependents of the proprietor, incapable of any freedom, impartiality, or justice, of any law other than the proprietor's absolute will.

The great variety of delicate means that are employed on the haciendas to exploit and victimize the hangers-on [*arrimados*], the peons, the retainers, and the tenants, by speculating and profiting shamelessly with the fruits of their toil, boggle the imagination. Unpaid tasks are imposed upon them even on the days reserved for rest. They are obliged to take rotten seeds or sick animals in part payment for their miserable wages. They are charged enormous parish fees out of all proportion to the agreement which the owner or overseer has made beforehand with the parish priest. They are obliged to buy everything within the hacienda, using I.O.U.'s or paper money that cannot be exchanged in any outside market. At certain times of the year, the dependents of the hacienda are provided with goods and materials of poor quality as regulated by the administrator or proprietor, which form the basis of an unredeemable debt. They are prevented from using hillsides and pasture lands, woods and waters, or any natural fruits of the field, without the express permission of the master. In sum, they are treated irresponsibly in a completely arbitrary manner, and with impunity. . . .

In practice, then, society is not based upon property as we would define it. Society is based on the privileges of the minority and the exploitation of the majority. Is this justice? . . . No, because society cannot rest on a principle that pertains only to a minority, but rather on an absolute principle which applies to everyone. As a consequence, it shall be necessary to adopt the theory that the fruits of labor become the property of the laborer. What must be done in order that the laborer become owner of the total fruits of his labor, and so that out of the present system of unreal property, which accords the right only to a minority, humanity may pass on to a real system of property, which will accord to the now exploited majority the fruit of their labor? Property must not be destroyed—this would be absurd; on the contrary, it must be made more general. . . .

I would not maintain that my proposals . . . will resolve all the problems that our system contains. I am not that presumptuous. All I say is that the grave economic conditions of our society should merit the attention and study of our legislators. . . . The proposals are as follows:

1. The right of property consists of occupation or possession, according to the requirements of law; but it cannot be determined, nor can it be confirmed or made integral except through work and productivity. The accumulation of great territorial possessions by a few persons without work, cultivation, or production is harmful to the common good and contrary to the nature of a republican and democratic government.

2. In order for the possessors of rural properties which are greater in extent than fifteen square leagues to be recognized legally as bona fide proprietors, they must survey and cultivate their properties, enclosing them at those points where they come in contact with the properties of others or with public roads. . . .

4. The lands of rural farms or estates that are more than fifteen square leagues in size and which in the judgment of the tribunals of the nation have not after two years been cultivated, surveyed, or enclosed, shall be considered vacant and shall be subject to renunciation and sale by the National Treasury, and auctioned off to the highest bidder. . . .

10. Rural inhabitants of the countryside not possessing a property whose value exceeds fifty pesos are free and exempt, for a period of ten years, of all forced levies, of the use of stamped paper in their contracts and negotiations, of court fees in their litigation, or labor in public works (even when sentenced by a court), of all parish and other clerical fees of whatever designation, and of any personal service or task against their will, except in the case of apprehended criminals. The wages of peons and day laborers cannot be considered legally paid or satisfied except by cash. . . .

8. Constitution of 1857

The Constitution was adopted on February 12. Articles 4 and 27 represent the majority view in the constitutional congress on the question of property.

Article 4.   Each man is free to follow the profession, industry, or labor that suits him, as long as it is useful and honest, and he is free to profit from the fruits of such work. These rights can be limited only by judicial sentence when he infringes on the rights of another individual, or by governmental decision, as specified by law, when he transgresses the rights of society.

Article 13.   In the Mexican Republic no one shall be judged according to private laws or special tribunals. No individual or corporation shall have privileged jurisdiction nor receive fees which are not in payment for a public service as established by law. Military jurisdiction shall be recognized only for the trial of criminal cases directly related to military discipline. The law shall clearly define the cases included in this exception.

Article 27.   Private property shall not be taken without the consent of the owner, except for reasons of public utility and by prior indemnification. The law shall determine which authority shall make the expropriation and the provisions by which it shall be carried out.

No civil or ecclesiastical corporation of whatever character, designation, or object, shall have the legal capacity to acquire ownership to, or administer in its own behalf, landed property, except for buildings immediately and directly related to the services or purposes of said corporations.

THE INDIAN

Educational reform was one of the principal concerns of liberal governments in the nineteenth century beginning with the regime of Valentín Gómez Farías in 1833. As adviser to the vice president, Mora was chief architect of a program which abolished the colonial university and attempted to establish instruction in the capital on a uniform and secular basis. As Mora reveals in the following passage, written in 1837, opposition to the reforms came from within the regime as well as from the military and clerical "defenders of *fueros.*" One of the dissenters was Juan Rodríguez Puebla, who, with the aid of a royal scholarship, had risen from an obscure background to become a legislator and director of the Colegio de San Gregorio, a former Jesuit school for Indians that was revived in 1824. The reasons for his dissent are clear in the selection below. The proclamations of the years 1810–1821 bequeathed to independent Mexico the principle of legal equality, abolishing the special tribute for Indians, as well as racial, caste, and class distinctions. In the early congresses there was a self-conscious but not always consistent effort to suppress the term "Indian" or at least to refer to the majority of the population as "those called Indians [*los llamados indios*]."

9. The 1833 Regime and the Indian
⋄ José María Luis Mora

The Gómez Farías administration necessarily and inevitably made many enemies, not only among those of the party of retrogression, but even among the men of progress themselves, who, without intending it, sparked the reaction which brought to the ground all that had been done. . . . The true impetus for this opposition arose from the new scheme of public education that was in open conflict with the desires and objectives of Juan Rodríguez Puebla concerning the fate of the remains of the Aztec race which still exist in Mexico. This man who claims to belong to said race is one of the notables of the country for his fine moral and political qualities. In his ideas he is a member of the party of progress and in his personal identification a member of the York rite [*Yorkino*] Masonic faction; but unlike the men who work harmoniously toward party objectives, Rodríguez Puebla does not limit his designs to obtaining liberty, but extends them to exalting the Aztec race. Consequently his principal objective is to uphold a separate existence for this race within society. To this end he has defended and continues to defend the former civil and religious privileges of the Indians, their communal property in its present state, the welfare establishments designed to aid them, and the Colegio [de San Gregorio] which is exclusively devoted to their education. In short, without admitting it explicitly, his principles and objectives tend visibly toward the establishment of a purely Indian system.

The Gómez Farías administration, in accord with all of its predecessors, thought differently. Persuaded that the existence of different races in a single society was and had to be forever a principle of discord, the administration not only failed to recognize these distinctions eliminated years before in the constitution, but it put all its efforts to hastening the fusion of the Aztec race with the general mass.

From José María Luis Mora, *Obras sueltas* (Paris, 1837), *1*, pp. cclxiii-cclxiv. My translation—CAH.

Thus it did not recognize in government acts the distinction of *Indians* and *non-Indians,* substituting instead that of *poor* and *rich,* extending to all the benefits of society. In the new scheme of public education, these principles were necessarily put into practice, developing schools, establishments, and a common educational endowment by consolidating the funds of primary and secondary schools and the fund for Indians. None of this conformed to the designs of Señor Rodríguez and to what he considered as his obligations. From that time on he was unfavorably disposed toward an administration which until then he had supported, and as always happens, his hostility increased when the question became personal and a matter of pride.

10. The Caste Wars   ⬦   *El Universal*

The "Caste Wars" was a term given to two large-scale and simultaneous Indian rebellions which broke out in Yucatan and in the Huasteca, a region northeast of Mexico City. Unlike the constant harassment of settlers by nomadic "savages" along the northern frontier, these rebellions involved traditionally sedentary Indian groups. The Yucatan uprising was the more serious of the two. It began in July 1847, just as the invading North American army was approaching Mexico City, and by the following May the Mayan rebels threatened the capital city of Mérida. Whites and mestizos in the peninsula feared virtual extermination in the midst of savage racial conflict. By mid 1849, however, the Mayan peasant soldiers began returning to their fields, the leadership of the revolt became divided, and the state government again regained the upper hand. While less severe, the war of the Sierra Gorda in the Huasteca was probably of greater concern in Mexico City, because it brought social turmoil and the specter of race war so close to home during the two years between January 1848 and December 1849. Thus the added issue of Indian upheaval formed part of the

From "The Caste Wars," *El Universal,* December 8–15, 1848.

great debate over the country's ills and the remedies for them that filled newspapers, pamphlets, and books in the wake of the disastrous war with the United States. The very survival of the nation seemed to be at stake. The following selection is from a series of five articles (December 8–15, 1848), appearing in the conservative newspaper *El Universal* which had just begun publication the month before. The articles were anonymous, but their author may have been Lucas Alamán, who as a boy of seventeen had experienced the siege of Guanajuato by Hidalgo's forces.

Not least among the great afflictions brought on our unfortunate country by governmental stupidity and even more by the destructive action of absurd systems are the present caste wars which have already ravaged a large part of the republic. . . . For more than a year the fields of Yucatan have been drenched continuously by the blood of thousands of victims sacrificed to the fury of the savages. It has been more than a year since the movement in the Sierra broke out, threatening to follow the same pattern as in the Yucatan peninsula. Yet until now we have seen no adequate steps taken to put an end to the horrors of Yucatan nor even to snuff out the incipient rebellion in the Sierra. . . . It is a struggle for life and death, and one that is a thousand times more dangerous than a war with a foreign nation. In a struggle between two nations, the vanquished acquires peace, to be sure at the cost of some painful sacrifices, but ones that do bring peace. But once a war of castes is begun, especially if one of them is uncivilized, the war has no end, nor can it have, short of the extermination of one or the other of the castes. When two races confront each other and the civilization which moderates brute instincts is lacking, there is no peace possible except the peace of death. . . .

The present situation is not new to our country, for this civil war is identical, with similar claims and similar methods, to the one which began in the year 1810, and it is bound to follow the same course. . . . Let us now examine the causes of this present war. . . . What immediately comes to mind is an extraordinary and extremely significant fact, to wit, the contentment, peace, and tranquillity of the Indian race in the era of Spanish regime. This contentment is the more extraordinary when compared to the discontent and hostile spirit that same race now displays, in as much as it would be more natural for the Indians to nurse a deep hatred toward the Spaniards who conquered and subjected them by armed force. Likewise it would be natural for the Indians to show gratitude toward the descendants of those same Spaniards for having brought about independence and having expelled the ones who had subdued the Indians and governed them for so long. . . .

Governments have only two ways of making people obey, by moral force or by physical force. . . . The Conquest had scarcely been completed when the Spanish government, with that customary good judgment and wisdom it pursued in colonial matters, directed all efforts toward the creation of a moral force in order to subject the numerous and warlike race which it had just dominated by force of arms. It used two methods to create this moral force. First, the Spanish government lent stimulus to the religious principle by emphasizing reverence for the grandeur of worship and establishing throughout the country numerous and well-staffed missions. It is an undeniable and accepted fact that those missionaries kept the Indians in submission with vastly more effectiveness and economy than would have been done by all the soldiers of the viceroyalty. Second, the Spanish government developed a profound respect for authority by utilizing the missionaries themselves, and then by bringing to bear upon the Indians the beneficent and paternal effect of royal power. . . . Authority was never degraded before the eyes of the Indians but was always endowed with lustre and majesty.

These methods resulted in a new element of order, indispensable for a people like ours, which was the considerable acquiescence and respect shown by the natives toward the man of our race as a being of superior intelligence. They designated the latter a man of reason [*gente de razón*] and he became an indispensable guide for the ignorant natives and the natural protector of their welfare. We would never contend that all individuals of the conquering race merited such an opinion; on the contrary, many abused this superiority to become oppressors and exploiters. Yet in general what we are referring to is an indisputable fact. By this wise combination of elements which constituted moral force, the Indians remained in peace and tranquillity for three hundred years without the need to resort to physical force. . . .

But the hour of the struggle for independence sounded and the *caudillos* of the movement, though themselves of European origin, tried to secure the support of the numerous Indian class. Thus instead of trying to unite the Indian race with the descendants of Spaniards in a common effort, they began with unpardonable lack of foresight to inspire in the Indians a hatred of and desire for vengeance against the conquering race, presenting the Spaniards in unceasing ridiculous harangues as their oppressors and mortal enemies. The caudillos represented the properties possessed by individual Spaniards as being usurped from the Indians and they incessantly invoked the memory of Moctezuma and the other heroes of the Indian race. The caudillos cursed the name of Hernán Cortés and the other conquistadors and denounced everyone who came from the mother country. They deplored the tyrannical oppression which, according to them, the whites had inflicted upon the Indians over three hundred years. Misguided by the ardor with which they had embraced the cause of independence, those caudillos denied their own race and condemned it to extermination.

This departure from reason, inexcusable even in the heat of combat, was even less pardonable after the victory [1821] when passions should have subsided. . . . We need only cite the multitude of speeches that annually mark the sixteenth of September, which with few exceptions serve only as a stimulus to this kind of caste war. . . . With the arrival of independence, policy came to be guided by men untutored in the science of government, who could find nothing better to guide the i.   nation than a slavish imitation of the [Spanish] Constitution of Cádiz [1812]. This constitution is a sublime model of legislation but one whose measures were extremely erroneous when applied to our country, as was proved later and is still being proved by painful experience. As prescribed by that constitution, the dogma of equality was adopted and consequently the Indians were declared equal to the Spaniards and their descendants, both in rights and in the duties of citizenship.

With the proclamation of the principle of equality, the wise Laws of the Indies were wiped out in a single stroke, laws which had effectively protected the Indians for so many years. . . . The equality proclaimed pertained not only to the rights, but also to duties and obligations. Rights, which came to be reduced to voting and perhaps being elected a member of some village council, hardly offered the Indians much advantage and consequently proved illusory. . . . Apart from the insignificant tribute they had been completely free of other military or civil services or obligations. Thus when the Indians were wrested from their fields and from the side of their families to be impressed into the army; when they found themselves encumbered with taxes like the other citizens; when they saw their animals seized in the name of the fatherland; and moreover, when they became convinced that the promised equality existed only in theory . . . then they began to feel the deception acutely. . . . What did it matter to the Indians when they were told with great solemnity that they were free and independent, that they were citizens of a great republic, that their rights were recorded in the constitution, if they saw all the positive benefits that they had previously enjoyed disappear, to be replaced only by the most insufferable tyranny? . . .

Now that the former sentiment which tied the natives to the conquering race was destroyed and the memory of promises made by some of the caudillos of independence was still fresh . . . the natives naturally came to reason as follows: (1) Sovereignty resides in the greatest number, we are the greatest number, thus sovereignty resides in us. (2) Legitimate authority rests on force, we constitute force, thus legitimate authority resides in us. (3) The Spanish conquistadors despoiled us of our properties, therefore we have the right to recover them from the descendants of those conquerors, the ones who presently possess them. The Indian has taken up arms to vindicate these principles, and the consequences fall upon the same people who proclaimed the principles.

The revolution of the Indians should not surprise us; it was bound to result from the course we have followed since independence. . . . Now our objective must be to apply the measures for suppressing it . . . that is, to reinstitute policies employed so successfully by the Spanish government, adapting them, of course, to our present circumstances. . . . Undoubtedly the first step to be taken is to ready ourselves to assert when absolutely necessary our superiority by force of arms in a rapid, decisive, and impressive way, at the same time trying to avoid as much as possible the resort to arms. . . . Once peace has been achieved by physical force . . . the government must proceed immediately to invest itself with the moral force to uphold peace and make it permanent. . . .

Following the example of Spanish policy, let the Indians be freed of military service, except for volunteers. Let them be freed of all taxes, establishing in their place a single personal tax like the former tribute, which they would doubtless be glad to pay and which in the last analysis would produce more revenue than the oppressive variety of taxes that have afflicted them since the suppression of the tribute. Let their animals never be seized, nor any personal service of any kind be imposed upon them. Let that beneficent law which designated them as minors and which effectively guaranteed the possession and preservation of their property be reestablished, for the abolition of this law has only benefited the rapacious and corrupt speculators who have despoiled the Indians of extensive and valuable lands for a pittance and a few bottles of brandy, so that large families, previously well off, are now in the greatest misery. Let the special funds or treasuries of the natives be reestablished along with their former administration. Let their former "republics" be reestablished, that is— their special way of administering justice among themselves through their own governors and magistrates, in conformity with their customs as wisely preserved by the Laws of the Indies. In short, let their former privileges and immunities be restored.

That fictitious equality which has deceived the Indians till now must no longer be preached to them. The protective influence of authority must be established and exercised exclusively in behalf of the Indians. To this end all governmental officials in contact with them should be chosen from individuals who enjoy prestige among the Indians, and they should be men endowed with the virtues and qualities necessary to conciliate spirits, calm passions, reestablish confidence, and solidify peace. These officials must be appointed by the central government and not be subject to removal by election. . . .

The religious sentiment has been the most powerful civilizing agent in modern societies. . . . It opened up the New World to civilization; it pacified and tamed the native and began to lead him gradually toward social perfection. . . . This sentiment has not been extinguished, it has not died out among the Indians . . . it can and must be revived. To do so it is necessary to proceed immediately to the reestablishment of the missions, both those that are permanent and those that are temporary or ambulatory, for they are absolutely indispensable institutions whose utility goes unrecognized only out of the grossest ignorance. . . .

It is also essential to increase the white race, so that its number balances the others. We will treat this matter extensively in our future articles on colonization.

11. The Caste Wars ⋄ José María Luis Mora

> The liberals returned to power in 1846 under the leadership
> of Valentín Gómez Farías. During these years of crisis, with
> the country threatened by foreign occupation and internal
> social dissolution, José María Luis Mora served as Mexican
> minister to England from 1846 until his death in 1850. Be-
> sides his formal diplomatic duties, he acted as an unofficial
> adviser to several Mexican governments and engaged in a
> lively private correspondence with two foreign ministers,
> Luis de la Rosa and Mariano Otero, who sought his advice
> on policy questions. The following three letters, the first
> private and the others official, record Mora's reactions to
> the Indian rebellions.

From Mora to de la Rosa, May 31, 1848*

If peace is drawn up as I expect and desire it will be, our most urgent necessity is to repress the colored classes, amassing throughout the whole republic as many settlers as can be discovered and brought in, without hesitating over conditions. It is equally necessary to always support this group in the continual struggle that it will inevitably have with the colored classes, and at the same time to restrain the latter by the most severe and forceful measures. If this is not done, everything is lost forever. However, we must first rely on

*Reproduced from Arturo Arnáiz y Freg, ed., *La Intervención francesca y el imperio de Maximiliano* (Mexico: Instituto Francés de América Latina, 1965), p. 39.

the mass of the white population which is closer, more available, and cheaper, for to await colonists that might come from Europe would entail a lengthy transaction in a matter of such great urgency. In the official correspondence you will find my ideas on this matter which I am proposing to the government; they seem to me clear and plain and above all practicable. I also think we should accept without hesitation the proposals you mentioned from American generals and volunteers that they serve in the interior of the republic, though service on the frontiers should be entrusted to other hands.

From Mora to Palmerston (British Foreign Secretary), June 26, 1848*

My second request is that Great Britain intervene in the present situation of Yucatan which is an integral part of the Mexican Republic. Your Majesty's Government cannot be ignorant of what is known to all the world, namely that the very numerous Indian class of that state has not only risen up against the existing government, but that it has avowed, and is now carrying out with unprecedented barbarity, a plan to exterminate the white class. With the great portion of its territory being occupied by American troops, and without an army or navy, ports or finances during the invasion, Mexico has been unable to take the immediate measures demanded by this most urgent matter. The accord reached between the Indian class and Governor Barbachano was the only one that the Mexican government was aware of (at the time of my most recent communications), and with this accord the government had hoped to be able in time to defend authority and the white class that the Indians are trying to eliminate. But this accord had only existed a few days before it was openly violated by a portion of the Indians who are perpetuating their system of devastation and their increasingly exaggerated barbaric conduct. Amid these urgent circumstances which do not allow for delay, I am, without instructions from my government, requesting that the government of your Majesty agree to providing direct aid and armed forces in order to check the ruthlessness of the Indians and to intervene in behalf of the security of the white class, at least until such time as the Mexican government is able to send

*Reproduced from Luis Chávez Orozco, ed., *La Gestión diplomática del Dr. Mora* (Mexico, 1931), pp. 78–79.

the force necessary to reestablish order and to secure life and property in that state. . . . The British government surely cannot view an uprising such as this with indifference, for it is one that also threatens the possessions of Your Majesty bordering on the State of Yucatan.

*From Mora to Mexican Foreign Ministry, July 31, 1849**

. . . I venture to call the attention of the Mexican government to the necessity of acting so that the caste rebellions not only come to an end, but that they become impossible in the future. The only way to achieve this is to merge all races and colors existing in the republic into one. We must attract into the already populated part of the republic any foreigners who are willing and able to come and settle, on any conditions whatever. There can be no hesitation over the means involved. Once settlement has been effected, it is equally essential for the government to favor the settlers in every way that does not constitute an open violation of justice. Ever since independence the supposed grievances of the colored classes against the white have been enumerated, repeated, and exaggerated *ad naseaum,* and sooner or later it all had to result in what we are now witnessing. We must stop this wretched adulation of a class that is only capable of turning adulation into irreconcilable hatred and ultimately into bloody revolutions. These revolutions only end up by undermining even the most solidly established social edifice, without bettering the situation of the rebels.

BIBLIOGRAPHIC SUGGESTIONS

BAZANT, JAN. *Alienation of Church Wealth in Mexico. Social and Economic Aspects of the Liberal Revolution, 1856–1875.* London: Cambridge University Press, 1971. A detailed and penetrating account of what happened to property taken from the church.

CALDERON DE LA BARCA, FRANCES E. *Life in Mexico: The Letters of Fanny Calderon de la Barca,* ed. Howard T. and Marion H. Fischer. Garden City, N. Y.: Doubleday, 1966. A definitive, il-

*Reproduced from Luis Chávez Orozco, ed., *La Gestión diplomática del Dr. Mora* (Mexico, 1931), pp. 151–152.

lustrated edition of the classic observations of Mexican society by the Scottish-American wife of Spain's first ambassador to independent Mexico. First published 1843.

CHEVALIER, FRANÇOIS. "Conservateurs et libéraux aux Mexique. Essai de sociologie et géographie politiques de l'indépendance a l'intervention française," *Cahiers d'histoire mondiale, 8* (1964), 457–474. A pioneering study of the social and regional bases of the liberal-conservative conflict.

COSTELOE, MICHAEL P. *Church Wealth in Mexico: A Study of the 'Juzgado de Capellanías' in the Archbishopric of Mexico, 1800–1861.* London: Cambridge University Press, 1967. A lucid discussion of the complicated matter of church wealth with some implications about the nature of the liberal-conservative conflict.

HALE, CHARLES A. *Mexican Liberalism in the Age of Mora, 1821–1853.* New Haven, Conn.: Yale University Press, 1968. Further discussion of issues raised in this unit.

O'GORMAN, EDMUNDO. *La Supervivencia política novo-hispana.* Mexico: Condumex, 1969. A brief interpretation of the liberal-conservative conflict by Mexico's most provocative historical thinker.

REED, NELSON. *The Caste War of Yucatan.* Stanford, Calif.: Stanford University Press, 1964. A fascinating account of the Indian upheaval, incorporating modern views of its causes.

REYES HEROLES, JESÚS. *El Liberalismo mexicano,* 3 vols. Mexico: UNAM, 1957–1961. The most recent and most elaborate liberal version of the nineteenth-century political conflict.

SCHOLES, WALTER V. *Mexican Politics During the Juárez Regime, 1855–1872.* Columbia: University of Missouri Press, 1957. Thorough narrative account of the *Reforma.*

SIERRA, JUSTO. *Political Evolution of the Mexican People.* Austin: University of Texas Press, 1969. Good but unfortunately abridged translation of the classic liberal interpretation of Mexican history. First published 1900.

VASCONCELOS, JOSÉ. *Breve historia de México.* México: Compañía Editorial Continental, 1956. Good example of the continuing conservative interpretation of the political conflict. First edition 1937.

IV.
The Growth of the Export Economies:
Latin America in the Second Half of the
Nineteenth Century

☙ ROBERTO CORTÉS-CONDE

I

Toward the middle of the nineteenth century, a number of
Latin American countries modestly entered world commerce, beginning a process whose dimensions were defined
clearly between the last decades of the century and the start
of World War I. In all cases, this phenomenon was based
on the extraction for export trade of previously untapped or
insufficiently exploited natural resources.[1] By beginning or
increasing the exploitation of those resources, each country
achieved a sharp rise in exports and, consequently, in revenues. (See Tables 1 through 4, which show how the exports
of some of these countries grew.)

Since all colonial economic activity had been devoted to
the appropriation of natural resources—principally silver
and gold—for the commerce of the mother countries, export trade and the extraction of resources were not new to
America. As they developed during the second half of the
nineteenth century, however, they took on features that
distinguished them from colonial exploitation.

---

[1]On the features of an economy based on exports, see the
important work of Douglas North, "Agriculture in Regional
Economic Growth," *Journal of Farm Economics*, XLI, No. 5
(December 1959), pp. 943–951.

Table 1.   Mexican Export Index
  Base: 1900 = 100

YEAR	VALUE IN SILVER
1877	51.2
1883	53.5
1887	65.9
1892	68.3
1897	82.1
1900	100.0

Source: *Estadísticas económicas del Porfiriato: Comercio exterior* (Mexico: El Colegio de México, 1960).

Table 2.   Argentine Exports

YEAR	VALUE IN MILLIONS OF GOLD PESOS
1864	22
1870	30
1877	45
1883	60
1887	84
1892	113
1897	101
1900	155

Source: Ernesto Tornquist y Cia., *The Economic Development of the Argentine Republic* (Buenos Aires, 1919).

Table 3.   Peruvian Exports

YEAR	VALUE IN MILLIONS OF PESOS	OF SOLES
1850	7.5	
1860	36.8	
1870		21.0
1878		25.0

Source: Jonathan Levin, *The Export Economies* (Cambridge, Mass.: Harvard University Press, 1960), republished from *Economista Peruano*, VI, No. 145 (July 1921).

Table 4. Chilean Exports, Including Silver and Gold

YEAR	VALUE IN MILLIONS OF GOLD PESOS 1 GOLD PESO = 18D.
1870	68.4
1877	69.4
1883	149.3
1887	125.7
1892	135.5
1897	136.7
1900	167.7

Source: Aníbal Pinto Santa Cruz, *Chile, un caso de desarrollo frustrado* (Santiago: Editorial Universitaria, 1962).

Whereas the resources of the colonies had been appropriated by the mother countries, which had monopolized colonial commerce, those of the nineteenth-century Latin American countries were offered for exchange, facilitated by the existence of free trade and by technological improvements which brought the markets of the industrial countries within the reach of Latin America. This access to industrial markets stresses a point which is rarely considered, but which was important in the development of export trade: that the resources in question had no outlets within their own regions—due to the level of development of these regions, their needs, and the characteristics of local demand—and thus were forced to find them elsewhere.[2]

Furthermore, nineteenth-century products differed in nature from colonial ones, for the needs of European countries had changed markedly since the seventeenth century. The

[2]Production is directed toward the export sector, not only because there is an external demand, but because there is no demand in the productive region. There is no choice of orienting it toward one market or another. If there is no external demand, there is no outlet for production. This is what differentiates the case of these countries from those taken into account by the classical theory of international commerce. See H. Mynt, "The Classical Theory of International Trade and the Underdeveloped Countries," *The Economic Journal*, LXVIII (1958).

ancien regime's desire for luxury items had given way to the demands of industry, a rising population, and a declining agriculture. Accordingly, in Latin America the extraction of gold and silver was supplanted by the production of industrial minerals, fertilizers, raw materials, and—much later in the century—foodstuffs.

Latin America's attempts to trade freely with the world had begun and were fairly widespread during the era of the revolutions for independence (1810–1820), but in the first decades of the century only Río de la Plata had experienced a rise in exports and revenues. For a variety of reasons, high costs of transport and the lack of technological conditions to permit the crossing of great distances kept a vast number of resources untapped. Except for the most limited commerce and the importation of manufactured goods from Europe, Latin America withdrew into itself. The first half of the century had been a period not only of war but, contrary to the optimistic expectations of the intellectuals of the Enlightenment, of isolation and economic backwardness as well.

The first successful attempts to establish export commerce were made by countries for which it was geographically and historically possible to have a non-European market. Chile, for instance, was able to sell its agricultural products in Peru, and in California during the gold boom. But what distinguished export trade after mid-century was that it was made possible by a strong flow of capital and labor from the old countries to the new ones.[3]

Flows of capital and labor did not always occur at the same time. In some cases, only the importation of capital was necessary to get production under way.[4] In others, natural resources could not be exploited without an increase in the labor force. The increases in production and exports

---

[3]Jonathan Levin, *The Export Economies.*

[4]Chile, which used less labor than the other countries, and Mexico, which boasted of a large labor force during the Porfiriato, did not experience migratory flows like those of Argentina, Brazil, Peru, and Cuba.

which resulted from the incorporation of large masses of capital and/or workers created supplementary demands which contributed to and in some cases extended the development begun by the external sector.

Between 1850 and the beginning of World War I, Latin America experienced remarkable growth, thanks to its introduction to overseas commerce. The difficult first decades of independence were followed by a golden age. Despite the fact that the different sectors of the population did not share equally in its profits, free trade, of which the *científicos,* liberals, and positivists of "order and progress" had dreamed, finally seemed to exist.

When this *belle époque* was ended dramatically by the crisis of 1929, the statesmen and the very populations of Latin American countries became less certain that a prolonged program of development based on the export of raw materials was possible. In their great disillusionment, as exports and revenues plummeted, as resources were exhausted before new products were found to take their place in the economy, they thought of the fickle nature of their wealth and of the need to become independent from the fluctuations of the merchandise and capital markets which their countries, as exporters of raw materials, could not control.

Industrialization that begins by substituting for imports that are restricted by a fall in exports is not only the necessary answer for a country that wants to base its level of economic activity on the internal market rather than on exports, but also a renewed cry of independence. Nevertheless, the countries which between 1930 and 1950 took serious steps toward industrialization, and which are convinced that industrialization is an irreversible process, still encourage export activities that offer comparative advantages. But they agree that the exploitation of a raw material for export involves some specific problems:

1. The rhythm and continuity of growth depend on the nature of the resources in question. Growth tapers off as the resource is exhausted, and often ends altogether.

2. Its commerce is at the mercy of fluctuations in the world markets of raw materials.[5] And to the extent that national income is based on the export sector, it fluctuates with the tendencies of the world markets.

3. If the export sector is supported by foreign capital, part of its revenue must leave the country as remittances of profits or interest.

4. If economic activity is highly concentrated and requires a large amount of capital, there will be a very uneven distribution of income.

These problems arise from a situation in which a modern export sector earning high profits exists side by side with a domestic sector characterized by bare subsistence. Although not all of these problems are found in all activities involving the export of raw materials, the history of the past century shows that they are common to most. And it is indisputable that wherever there is exploitation of a fixed resource, the rhythm of growth depends on its availability, which is—even in the case of the land—essentially fixed.[6]

Even the authors who in recent years have emphasized the possibilities for growth in an economy based on exports[7] point out that the export sector must facilitate growth in other sectors, and then allow a shift when the resource under exploitation, or its demand, diminishes or disappears.[8]

[5]H. W. Singer, "Comercio e inversión en países poco desarrollados," El Trimestre Económico (April–June, 1950).

[6]The hypothesis of the limited supply of land and its importance in the limiting of development has been advanced by the author in the case of Río de la Plata. See Roberto Cortés-Conde, "Algunos rasgos de la expansión territorial en Argentina en la segunda mitad del siglo XIX," Desarrollo Económico, VIII, No. 29 (April–June, 1968).

[7]Douglas North, "Agriculture in Regional Economic Growth," op. cit.

[8]Douglas North, "Location Theory and Regional Economic Growth," in Regional Development and Planning, ed. John Friedman and William Alonso (Cambridge, Mass.: The MIT Press, 1960); H. Mynt, "The Classical Theory of International Trade and the Underdeveloped Countries" op. cit.; Richard Cabes, " 'Vent for Surplus' Models of Trade and Growth," Trade, Growth and the Balance of Payments, ed. R. Baldwin et al. (Am-

They have written of the backward and forward linkages which promote the development of other sectors or activities,[9] and of the demand linkage,[10] through which the income generated by the export sector is distributed in a way which develops an internal market as an alternative to the external one and as a principal incentive for investment outside the export sector.

The most recent literature, which has distant antecedents in the study of the Canadian case,[11] generally maintains that economies based on the export of raw materials will develop differently according to the technological nature of production. The linkages which export activities might have, depend in each case on the nature of production, which also affects the distribution of income and, therefore, the formation of the domestic market.[12]

The so-called export-oriented models of growth, which for a time seemed to apply only to the historical experience of the nineteenth century, has a renewed, contemporary interest, since certain areas or regions undoubtedly should, could, or will stimulate their development by exporting raw materials. Knowledge of the characteristics of this kind of development, such as we have found in certain nineteenth-century Latin American cases, has a genuine historical interest, since many of these features have been concealed or confused because of the various prejudices with which their study was ap-

---

sterdam: North Holland Publishing Co., 1965); Melville H. Watkins, "A Staple Theory of Economic Growth," *The Canadian Journal of Economics and Political Science,* XXIX, No. 2 (May 1963).

[9]Albert O. Hirschman, *The Strategy of Economic Development* (New Haven: Yale University Press, 1958).

[10]Melville H. Watkins, "A Staple Theory of Economic Growth," op. cit.

[11]Harold Innis, *Essays on Canadian Economic History* (Toronto: University of Toronto Press, 1965).

[12]Melville H. Watkins, "A Staple Theory of Economic Growth," *op. cit.;* Robert E. Baldwin, "Patterns of Development in Newly Settled Regions," *Manchester School of Economics and Social Studies,* XXIV (May 1956).

proached.[13] It would also shed light on the study of situations in the new countries which the theoretical schema developed for the old countries did not foresee.[14]

II

The documents offered below do not cover the entire spectrum of factors related to this complex phenomenon. They have, however, an advantage which makes it advisable for students to analyze more carefully the primary sources for that earlier era, at least the less prejudiced ones, of which these are but a modest sample. They describe faithfully certain features and mechanisms which were not foreseen by any theoretical model. The knowledge of how the export economies functioned has generally been confused by special approaches and interpretations applied to them even by their contemporaries. Whereas those who pretended to interpret that reality using some known model have often given us a falsified image, those who merely recorded what they saw offier us some keys to understanding the essential processes.

[13]These failures can be attributed to both those who saw in international trade an undeniable means of increasing national wealth and those who in the twentieth century assumed that it was the way to exploit the wealth of countries which were not yet industrialized.

[14]Harold Innis, *Essays on Canadian Economic History*, op. cit.

1.
STATEMENT SUBMITTED TO THE SOVEREIGN CONGRESS BY DON FRANCISCO QUIROS AND DON AQUILES ALLIER, 1845

It is well known that guano produced a boom in the Peruvian economy from the end of the 1840s until 1880. It is also clear that this prosperity did not outlive the exhaustion of the guano deposits.[1] How did the exploitation of guano begin? How did its production and commercialization get under way?

The following document, the complaint of the first lessees of the guana deposits, vividly describes certain aspects of the exploitation of this previously unclaimed and untapped resource. It details the surprising discovery of the high profits guano could bring, and the subsequent actions of the government—its ultimate owner—and the consignees. It tells also how the fiscal authorities spend in advance the guano income to be forwarded by the consignees, and then brought against them all kinds of complaints and demands,[2] and relates this problem to the payment of the public debt.[3]

Exposición que Don Francisco Quiros y Don Aquiles Allier elevan al Soberano Congreso (Lima: Imprenta del Correo Peruano, 1845). Translated by Christopher Hunt.

[1] See Roberto Cortés-Conde, *The First Stages of Modernization* (in press).

[2] The Peruvian government and public charged on several occasions that they had been defrauded by the consignees. See *Documentos relativos al proyecto de venta directa del guano* (Lima: J. M. Noriega, 1867); also, *Documentos relativos a los cargos que hace el Fiscal D. D. José Aranibar a la casa de Dreyfus Hnos. y Cía. por diferencias de precios, utilidades en la manipulación del huano y mejor medio de venderlo* (Lima: Imprenta del Teatro Portas de San Agustin, 1878).

[3] W. M. Mathew, "The Imperialism of Free Trade: Peru, 1820–1870," *Economic History Review*, 2nd ser., XXI (1968).

All of these factors—bad administration, fraud, the foolish investment of guano revenues, or the failure to invest them at all—which for many years characterized the exploitation of guano under the consignatory system, first with Quiros and his English associates, the Meyers and Gibbs houses, and then with Dreyfus, can be blamed for the loss of considerable sums of money, and for the failure to accumulate capital, which delayed the development of Peru.[4]

We, Don Francisco Quiros and Don Aquiles Allier, both merchants of this Capital, present ourselves with due respect before Congress and declare: That the application of guano from the islands to European agriculture will unquestionably bring Peru incalculable profits, and that soon, thanks to this enterprise, the Republic will have at its disposal abundant resources, obtained exclusively from an area which has never before contributed to the public treasury.

His Excellency the President of the Republic served Peru with distinction by setting aside unreasonable worries and accepting the proposal of Don Francisco Quiros for the introduction of guano, which until then was unknown beyond our borders, to the commercial world. The popularity of this fertilizer in the countries which have tried it, and particularly in Great Britain, is only too well known; since Peru possesses it almost exclusively, the profits it will gain for the country cannot be estimated. . . .

If we adopt the prudent, well-calculated method of extraction which the English established for cinnamon in Ceylon, and General Santa Cruz used for Bolivian cascarilla, Peru's guano will undoubtedly command the highest prices farmers can afford. And if the Government extracts only a number of tons of the fertilizer, a small amount in comparison with the volume being taken to the market from Africa, it will accomplish the double objective of not wasting this rich resource—of making it inexhaustible—and of obtaining enough funds to pay for its expenses.

A look at the immediate future of the guano business shows that the men who initiated it have rendered the Nation a real and important service. They are Don Francisco Quiros and Don Aquiles Allier, and Congress deserves to know the consequences we have suffered for this service.

[4]Jonathan Levin, *The Export Economies*. See Table 3, Peruvian Exports on page 158.

First, one should note that when the contract for the lease of the guano deposits was agreed upon, neither we nor anyone else knew what prices guano could command in Europe. We had no idea that they would reach the level at which the first sales were made. Thus when we received a letter from Messrs. Wm. Jos. Meyers and Company of Liverpool, dated May of 1841 and stating that having observed the vegetation of a few plants fertilized with a small quantity of guano, they expected to sell the first shipment at twelve pounds sterling per ton, Don Aquiles Allier communicated the unexpected news to His Excellency the President, Don Agustin Gamarra, who was then in Lampa, and added that if those expectations were fulfilled, we intended to share the profits of the transaction with the Government. . . .

As soon as it became known in Lima, through correspondence which arrived from Liverpool on the English ship *Dyron,* that guano had been sold at as much as one hundred twenty pesos per ton, everyone became truly enraged. We were attacked most violently, and Mr. Colmenares, who held the position of Prosecutor for the Supreme Court, went to the extreme of calling for the seizure of the estate of Don Francisco Quiros for having defrauded the Government.

In the meantime, His Excellency Mr. Menendez had sent for Don Francisco Quiros in order to change the terms of the leasing contract, and a new one was drawn up with the President and Mr. Cano, the Minister of Finance, in which the lease continued under the condition that two-thirds of the net proceeds of guano would go to the Government, and one-third to the contractors.

Before the new contract was signed, His Excellency Mr. Menendez asked to see our correspondence. Since we had been led to believe that the agreement could be considered secure, and we thought it an insult to a President of the Republic and a gentleman to doubt his good faith and suspect him capable of going back on his word, we complied with the request.

Among the letters, Mr. Menendez and his Ministers saw an announcement from Messrs. Wm. Jos. Meyers and Co. stating that they would be able to sell seven thousand tons of guano: two thousand at eighteen pounds sterling per ton, and the rest at a floating and conditional price to be determined by its retailers.

This notice must have made a tremendous impression upon His Excellency Mr. Menendez, for instead of signing our recent agreement, which he himself had proclaimed secure, he called us to the palace within two days, and in the presence of his Ministers he told us that the public was convinced we had bought the contract with a gift of five hundred thousand pesos. Since his reputation was damaged by such rumors, he continued, he would not involve himself in the guano business; he would, however, alert the Supreme Court, which would pass judgment upon it. Upon saying this, he ordered our correspondence returned to us.

The Council of State seemed to suffer from the same temporary insanity; some of its members proposed that the Executive Power be authorized immediately to invest one or two million pesos in guano, and since this would require the annulment of our contract, the council passed a resolution opening the way to an act which might be unique in its class.

What we had anticipated both in words and in writing happened. Everyone had called for the annulment of the contract; before the annulment, they had all offered to make proposals which would be extremely profitable to the public treasury, but after it they all took one step backwards. Seeing that no one came forward with acceptable proposals, the Government asked for bidders in the official newspaper; disappointed here again, it recognized that its conduct with us had been unfair and imprudent. His Excellency Mr. Menendez sent for Don Francisco Quiros and General La Fuente contacted Don Aquiles Allier, and we were asked to take over the guano business again under the terms agreed upon before. We resisted at first, thinking that after what had happened, we could only be exposing ourselves to new troubles, but in the end we gave in; upon hearing Don Francisco Quiros agree to his proposal, His Excellency Mr. Menendez took his hands, pressed them in his, and told him that he would never forget the service we were rendering the Government, and him in particular, by taking the crushing burden from his shoulders.

In virtue of this reconciliation, we met that very night at the home of the Minister of Finance, Mr. Cano, and there we agreed on the terms of the new contract. We would give up thirty of the forty thousand pesos we had paid to lease the guano deposits for the first four years, of which only one had transpired, and advance the Government two hundred eighty-seven thousand pesos of its profits in the sales. In return, we received the right to export guano *anywhere abroad* for *five years*. Soon after this meeting we paid the first installment of eighty-seven thousand (87,000) pesos, having been assured by the Minister that His Excellency had signed the contract, and that a decree to that effect would appear in the next issue of the *Peruano*.

One can imagine our surprise when we saw that the contract which was published had been altered considerably without our knowledge, stipulating that our concession would last *one obligatory and four optional years* instead of five years, and would apply *only to Europe*.

The day after the publication of the decree of 8 December, 1841, three houses established in this Capital asked for permission to make proposals which would offer better conditions than ours, which the law allowed them nine days to do. Their case was heard in the Supreme Court, and in observance of the judgment of the Prosecutor the request of these houses was invalidated, but not before His Excellency Mr. Menendez had imposed a verbal condition, that we give the State uniforms and equipment for an entire regiment of cavalry, costing eight thousand pesos.

Despite the verbal assurances which his Excellency Mr. Menendez had repeatedly given us, a supplement to the *Peruano* of 29 December, the tenth day after our contract was signed and ratified, carried a proposal which offered to advance the Government 150,000 pesos for the four optional years of our export concession, extending it to all foreign areas. Thus we, whose hands had been so gratefully shaken, and whose services could not have been forgotten, were threatened with having paid for the privilege of exporting guano only to Europe, for only one year:

30,000 pesos in advance for a lease we had been forced to give up,
8,000 pesos for the uniforms and equipment demanded of us, and
287,000 pesos for a privilege which, for an advance of only 150,000 pesos, others might obtain for one year for all areas except
_____ Europe, and for four more years for all foreign areas, or
325,000 pesos in all.

The publication of this proposal—which seemed offensive to the honor and integrity of the Government—naturally alarmed us, for its mere appearance in the official journal showed that the Government considered it acceptable. Once again we went to the home of His Excellency Mr. Menendez, and once again he appeased us, saying that he had ordered the publication of the proposal because he did not want to conceal anything related to guano, but that he would not accept any offer which threatened our agreement, which he assured us would stay in effect.

After so many protestations from His Excellency Mr. Menendez, anyone could predict our surprise when a few days later, at a meeting to which we had been invited at his home, he declared in the presence of his Ministers that the Government had decided to dispose of the four optional years in our contract, and accordingly had called us together with the houses which wished to negotiate for them, in order to establish the bases for an agreement on the issue.

We were so shocked by this announcement that we left without awaiting the arrival of the other gentlemen, afraid that in our understandable excitement we might utter some expression which was disrespectful of the authority of the Government. Soon afterwards we registered a protest against such unexpected and extraordinary conduct.

Seeing at last that the Government had decided to dispose of our property against the express conditions of a signed and ratified contract on which the ink had barely had time to dry, we found that our only recourse was to join our competitors. We had already lost 38,000 pesos as an extorted gift, and 287,000 as an advance, and we were unable to match the 20,000 pesos with which the other gentlemen proposed to overcome the scruples of His Excellency Mr. Menendez and his Ministers. If we did not join them, we would inevitably be ruined; it would be impossible for us to extract enough guano to cover our advances in the one year in which we could export to Europe, particularly since our opponents would compete with us in the hiring of ships in order to deny us the means of supplying a market which would be theirs at the end of that year. As a result of this union a contract was approved on 19 February, 1842; it is still in effect.

While we were being stripped of the rights we had acquired so legitimately, the guano business was suffering a disastrous reaction in England. Feverish enthusiasm had given way to icy discouragement. Macdonald and Company had bought seven thousand tons, thinking, no doubt, that their name and the fact that they had introduced saltpeter from Tarapacá as a fertilizer would inspire farmers to use guano without first experimenting with it. When the retailing season—February, March and April—arrived, however, farmers bought only in small quantities for experimentation, and these speculators saw the folly of buying such large amounts of an unknown product, and at such high prices. This operation would undoubtedly have cost Macdonald and Company a great part of their fortune had England not opportunely received the news that the Government of Peru had annulled our contract and called for bidders to make new proposals for the extraction of guano.

Macdonald and Company informed Messrs. Wm. Jos. Meyers and Company that since our concession had been rescinded, they would not proceed with their purchases of guano. They claimed that they had agreed to the purchases with the understanding that the product could be obtained from only one party; now that it was in the hands of several parties, they would repudiate their contract and refuse to accept the fertilizer.

Messrs. Wm. Jos. Meyers and Company received this notice from Macdonald and Company along with a letter in which we informed them that we had made a new contract with the Government under which we were obligated to pay an advance of 287,000 pesos, which we proposed to obtain by drawing against the proceeds of the sales they had announced in their previous letters.

This coincidence of unexpected developments greatly discouraged Messrs. Wm. Jos. Meyers and Company. The Government of Peru's annulment of a contract to which they were a party seemed so foreign to the practice followed in other countries that they felt little confidence in the new agreement, and proceeded to protest all of our bills of exchange. Holders of the bills here went before the Court of Commerce, which went to the extreme of ordering the closing of our warehouses and offices—an affront which we did not deserve—reducing Quiros to suspending his business and mortgaging his farms, and Allier to trying to salvage his estate and his factory, forcing both of us to stop any form of business and causing us incalculable losses. . . .

If we have dwelled extensively on the importance of our service to the Nation; if we have shown Congress the great setbacks and damages we have suffered and still suffer because of the unjustifiable conduct of the Government of His Excellency Mr. Menendez; if we have tried to establish that justice and equity demand that the Nation give us some reward, both as payment for our services and compensation for damages caused by the clearly illegal acts of the Government, it is because there is a way in which such rewarding and indemnifying can be profitable to the country and the public treasury.

The Government is committed to applying a quarter of the proceeds from guano to the payment of the foreign debt. It seems to us that if after the number of tons allotted to the contractors has been extracted, Congress grants us as reward and indemnization the right to export a number of them which it will determine, this measure could profit the State, for we would agree to report the total proceeds of their sale, and to hand over three-quarters of them in cash and the other quarter in debentures.

In this way the Government would gain through our hands the entire proceeds from guano, regardless of the price at which it is sold and including the profits made by any speculator who might buy it here; the Treasury would receive the largest possible quantity of cash, and the part destined to the payment of the British debt, which under any other circumstances would be applied to the payment of interest, would be applied by us to the amortization of the principal of the debt.

The simple exposition of this plan shows the profit the Nation and the Government will gain through its adoption; they will get the greatest possible value from guano, as if they exported it themselves, paying only the customary expenses and commissions to the contracting houses.

British creditors will have no reason to oppose Congress in awarding us this privilege, for the service which it proposes to reward has been as useful to the Nation's creditors, particularly the British, as it has been to Peru. It is to our ideas and our sacrifices that they owe the privileged guaranty they enjoy today, for if the mercantile value of guano had continued to be ignored, the Government of Peru would not have such powerful and effective means of prompt amortization, which have caused the premium on Peruvian Bonds to rise from a nominal 16% to 33%.

Having detailed the enormous injustices and losses we have suffered, and explained how the Nation will profit if Congress grants us the reward and indemnization we seek, we feel it our duty to refrain from any further statement and leave the National Representation to determine the action it will take in the spirit of justice and magnanimity. In virtue of which,

Sir, we entreat you to look after our honor, granting us the reward you feel we deserve, which we seek under the present circumstances only because it not only does not draw on public funds, but to the contrary, affords the state evident and positive advantages.

2.

LABOR UTILIZATION: Brazil in 1889

M. F. Y. DE SANTA ANNA NERY

The system of labor utilization was one of the greatest problems in the economic exploitation of America.

Societies with ancient Indian populations were forced to
adapt to the changing circumstances produced by the demographic crisis of the seventeenth century and the resulting
shortage of labor. In the more sparsely populated areas of
the Atlantic coast, the importation of labor was essential to
the exploitation of the land. We know, for instance, that in
colonial Brazil the expansion of sugar culture depended on
the importation of slave labor.[1] In Rio, on the other hand,
and particularly in the new lands of São Paulo, the expansion of coffee culture was predicated upon by the availability
of labor.[2] This problem became more complex in the second
half of the nineteenth century as the slave labor force
diminished.[3]

While in Rio de la Plata the severe underpopulation of the
pampas area facilitated the entry of a great number of Euro-

M. F. Y. de Santa Anna Nery, *Le Brésil en 1889* (Paris, 1889). Translated
by Rita Pérez.

[1]Celso Furtado, *The Economic Growth of Brazil* (Berkeley and Los
Angeles: University of California Press, 1963).

[2]Pierre Denis, *Brazil* (London: Adelphi Terrace, 1911).

[3]Emilia Viotti da Costa, *Da senzala à colônia* (São Paulo: Difusão
Européia do Livro, 1966); Stanley Stein, *Vassouras; A Brazilian Coffee
County, 1850-1900* (New York: Atheneum, 1970).

pean immigrants, in Brazil there was a more interesting situation, for there a slave labor system was to be replaced by a free one.

Santa Anna Nery's document, *Brazil in 1889,* a report presented to European investors attending the International Exposition at Paris in 1889, describes certain aspects of this transition. We learn from it that the change to a free labor market did not ruin the producers, and that the system of colonization which was established represented very low investments. Given the fact that the government paid transportation costs, the investments were even lower than those represented by the importation and maintenance of slave labor.

This system of colonization, which took two diverse forms of tenancy—jobbing and leasing—and also existed in Rio de la Plata, can be understood only as a means of obtaining cheap labor in societies in which the abundant supply of labor permitted extensive exploitation. The land was limitless; one had only to occupy it, and if one did not, it would lie unused and unproductive. Its fruit was a function of labor, and since the jobber was paid in kind, production cost the owner nothing.

Slave Labor and Free Labor

The law no. 3553 of May 13, 1888 abolished slavery once and for all in the Brazilian empire. This law released from bondage all the Negroes who were still slaves and whose total number, according to official statistics issued on March 30, 1887, was 723,419. They were valued at approximately 485,225 *contos,* which at the rate of 400 *réis* to the franc were equivalent to more than 1,213,000 francs. In addition, the "golden law"—or *lei aurea,* as it was called at the time—severed all ties between the former slaveowners and the freedmen or *ingenuos*—Negroes who had been born free in accordance with the law of September 28, 1871, but who were forced to serve their mothers' masters until they reached the age of 21. Moreover, by liberating the last of the slaves and including the free-born blacks under the common law, the law of 1888 implicitly established both groups as Brazilian citizens by the very fact of their liberation.

The promulgation of this law was rightfully considered a victory by both pro-Negro and humanitarian groups. Brazil had done things well. Although it had been the last civilized Christian state to retain slavery, at least through this act of emancipation it raised the slaves to the level of their former masters; through a more liberal education of its citizens, it also managed to make a breach in the same kind of prejudices that in other countries had created an insurmountable barrier between the races. In Brazil the Negroes who had been set free were certain to share a perfect social equality with the other races.

But even if humanitarian and pro-Negro groups regard the law of 1883 as a mere act of justice, economists are forced to consider it a revolution in the conditions of labor throughout the nation. It would be interesting to study this revolution and its consequences. In the first place, because it shows us how a country that formerly sustained itself exclusively on agriculture and forest cultivation attempted a transition from forced, unpaid labor to free, remunerated work. Secondly, because coffee is one of the chief products of daily consumption in most countries, and Brazil is the largest coffee purveyor in the leading markets of the two worlds. Consequently, the size of the country's coffee output will determine the rise or fall of the product's value. And finally because we cannot remain indifferent to the economic development of a country that deals annually with more than one billion francs in foreign trade.

Let us examine then how Brazil sought—and still seeks—a way to replace the work that was done by the slaves, work that played such an important role in the country's international trade and to which Brazil was indebted for part of its economic production. For it cannot be denied that the liberation of almost two million slaves and half a million *ingenuos* in less than 17 years—from 1871 to 1888—could have caused the country's inevitable downfall if the imperial government had not taken certain measures to lessen the impact of such a radical economic disruption. These measures consisted mainly of a steady effort to draw to Brazil a large number of European immigrants to whom the country resorted in order to make up for the losses that the emancipation of the slaves had brought about. Thus, after a few years, the imperial government was able to conduct simultaneously the tasks of emancipation and immigration.

After 1871, the year of the promulgation of the "law of free birth,"[4] and up to 1888, more than 500,000 immigrants entered Brazil through the ports of Rio and Santos alone. These immigrants replaced the slaves in the plantations and brought to the country the benefits that accompany hired labor. The above figures do not correspond to all immigrants who came to Brazil; they apply only to the two big ports of Santos and Rio, and do not take into account other regions such as the Amazon. Anyone who has traveled from Europe to Pará or Manáos knows that the steamships of the Red Cross Line, leaving Liverpool for Pará, Parintins, Itacoatiára and Manáos, with a stop in Havre, are always packed with emigrants, mostly Portuguese, who seek their fortune in "the country of the caoutchouc."

It is mainly from Italy that emigrant farmers leave for Brazil today. This Italian exodus to the South American empire is rather recent. From 1855 to 1882, during a period of 28 years, only 11,000 immigrants of Italian descent entered Brazil. But from that date on Italian immigration has increased considerably.

From 1882 to 1885 the number of Italian immigrants who disembarked in Brazil came near 10,000. The plantation owners took advantage of this situation and asked for more workers from Liguria, Piedmont, Tuscany, Lombardy, and Tyrol. Thus in 1886 the number of Italian arrivals exceeded 14,000. As soon as they disembarked they were hired. The enthusiasm was contagious among plantation owners, and soon all wished to have Italian immigrants as their workers. In 1887 there were more than 40,000 of these; by 1888 more than 100,000.

Moreover, the number of immigrants of other nationalities equally increased, as stated with legitimate pride by the chancellor Rodrigo da Silva, minister of agriculture, in his report to Parliament in 1888. In *Brésil Méridional* appeared the total figures representing immigrants of all nationalities who had come to Brazil over a period of ten years. The figures are distributed as follows:

1878	22,423	1883	28,670
1879	22,189	1884	20,087
1880	29,729	1885	30,135
1881	11,034	1886	25,741
1882	27,197	1887	55,986
	1888	132,000	

[4]Literally, "Law of free womb." (Translator's note.)

While after ten years the average of the annual arrivals of all nationalities was 27,000, in 1888 Rio and Santos alone had admitted near 132,000.

In the meantime, there were pessimists who felt that Brazil would ultimately regret having achieved such a monumental reform without giving any indemnification to the slaveowners; and that the country would be the victim of the haste with which it pursued the final resolution of the conflict. Such view was understandable, since on March 9, 1888, the most radical of abolitionists could not have imagined in their wildest dreams that in only two months those very dreams would come true. . . .

From 1871 to 1887, and under the two emancipation laws promulgated on September 28 of 1871 and 1885 respectively, there was not a single infant brought into the world who was not born free; and one million slaves were liberated. Yet, as we shall see, the overall economic output did nothing but increase during this period of transition. A study of the coffee production figures—a predominant product in the country's present-day prosperity—would surprisingly reveal a continuous rise in production as the number of black workers diminished.

In fact, the volume of Brazil's total production was estimated in terms of coffee: from 1835 to 1840, during the slave trade, it was 40 million kilos; from 1855 to 1860, when the traffic came to a definite halt, 120 million kilos; from 1872 to 1877, during the first five years that followed the promulgation of the "law of free birth," it was 177 million; from 1877 to 1882, while the abolitionist campaign was being organized, 350 million; and finally from 1882 to 1887, during the last days of slavery, it came near 400 million.

It is almost impossible not to be impressed by the rapid and steady development that turned Brazil into the main provider for the big coffee markets of the two worlds. We cannot attribute Brazil's position to any other factors than those being examined in this chapter. For it is obvious that the increase in coffee production was due to the better care being given to the old plantations, as well as to the large quantity of land that was cultivated for the first time. Now, either this progress was effected by the work of the liberated slaves and *ingenuos* who had remained on the plantations—in which case their emancipation proved to be thoroughly beneficial, since it made their labor more productive; or such increasing prosperity was the result of the gradual intervention of the immigrants, who were paid for their services. It is thus evident that the national economy will be able to survive, without too much pain, the loss of servile labor.

To be sure, the radical emancipation of the last half million slaves was disastrous for a few private interests. In some cases a widow or an orphan whose only property was precisely their slaves were left in a precarious situation. In other instances, a well-to-do plantation owner, an "absentee" landlord who lived in a big city while his slaves raised coffee back in the *fazenda,* was forced to abide by the grand common law, "thou shalt earn your bread by the sweat of your brow." But none of these separate cases, worthy of consideration as they might be, could defer the urgent social reform that was taking place. Any structural transformation of this kind brings with it certain private catastrophes which are soon rectified by the individuals involved, and largely compensated by the resulting improvements made for the society in general. Thus, we can ascertain that the nation as a whole will not suffer from abolition, and that eventually it will benefit from it. This was also the opinion of many foreign investors at the time, as demonstrated by two main facts:

As soon as the administration of João-Alfredo Correia d'Oliveira came to power on March 10, 1888, it announced its plans to make slave emancipation effective immediately. At the same time, the President requested a large loan from the London market. This loan of 4½ percent to 100, issued at 96, was immediately covered without any apparent fear on the part of the English capitalists at a time in which the future of Brazil's popular ruler seemed uncertain. Moreover, the Paris market had not yet played an active role in Brazilian affairs, which had been financed so far almost exclusively by the English. In June of 1888, when the emancipation was already an accomplished fact, a trust company was created in Paris, headed by M. Fould and the viscount of Figueiredo, to invest capital of 100 million francs in Brazilian business.

Such confidence on the part of the foreign investors is easily explained. The European financiers knew that the Negro workers, as a labor force, were not very intelligent or very active, precisely because their labor was not remunerated. The experience derived from the provinces of Céará and the Amazon, which had been emancipated four years earlier, and from those of São Paulo, Rio Grande do Sul, Paraná, and Saint Catherine, where only a handful of slaves remained, testified to the fact that economic prosperity is not necessarily hampered by abolition.

In São Paulo the customs revenues (allotted to the state) and the revenues of the *mesa de rendas* (allotted to the province) were only 12 million francs in 1875–1876, but rose to almost 24 million in 1884–1885, while the coffee production, which was only 40 million kilos in 1873–1874, went up to 130 million in 1884–1885.

In the province of the Amazon, the official value of exported goods (especially caoutchouc [raw rubber]) went up in a proportion of 1 to 100 from 1873 to 1887.

In Céará the revenue doubled from one year to the next in spite of a terrible drought that 12 years before began to drive a large number of natives out of the provincial territory.

And we could go on giving similar examples.

One of the many disadvantages of slavery was that it discouraged immigrants from settling in Brazil, since they did not want to be associated with unpaid workers. Thus, from 1857 to 1871, during the 15 years that preceded the promulgation of the law of Rio Branco, only 170,000 immigrants came to Brazil. In contrast, from 1873 to 1887, the fifteen-year period during which the abolitionist movement was in operation, the number of immigrants was near 400,000. . . .

We can assert without chauvinism that the abolition of slavery in Brazil was indeed a splendid episode and an exemplary action. It was accomplished in six days (from the 8 to the 13 of May) by a remarkable man who publicly assumed the heavy responsibilities that this act entailed. By passing almost unanimously the emancipation law, the Brazilian Parliament did not only liberate the slaves from bondage, but also set free the conscience of the Brazilian patriots who were ashamed of the effrontery with which their country displayed its inhumanity to the world. . . .

Immigration

Ybicaba had a great influence on colonization, even if its organization was far from perfect. Its political system could only function smoothly under the paternalistic influence of the proprietor, who most of the time had to be willing to make concessions to the colonists. Whenever he demanded a strict fulfillment of contractual terms he would immediately encounter conflicts and troubles.

The crucial fact about the colony of Ybicaba and those modeled after it was the simultaneous existence of slavery and free labor. This fact, which ought to have been a source of all kinds of economic upheavals, was in reality what determined the manner in which Brazil was to abolish slavery. Even if the existence of slaves created an abnormal situation for the newcomers, the tremendous benefits that ultimately resulted outweighed the disadvantages, since the arrival of the European workers was the true cause of the extinction of slavery, as predicted by de Straten-Ponthoz:

The African of Brazil must first act as a pioneer worker on a land which the white man is also able to farm; once his mission is accomplished, the black man will be absorbed by the free population and emancipated from his bondage. In Brazil the existence of slavery paves the way for the emigrants, and the advantages of this situation should not be sacrificed for fear of making the Europeans victims of servile labor. The rising price of African slaves will steadily set them apart from the immigrants.

The convergence of the foreign population and the African race in Brazil ought to rehabilitate white labor, and at the same time be a significant step toward a peaceful and orderly extinction of human bondage. On the issue of slavery, Brazil and the United States follow opposite directions. For the Americans there is no possible compromise between the two races. The closer the black man comes to the white, the more rejection and antipathy he encounters. The cruelty of the white man's behavior surpasses the severity of the very laws that uphold slavery, and makes any attempt at emancipation illusory. In Brazil, on the other hand, emancipation is a social and political reality. The color of a man's skin does not repulse anyone; and the tolerance of our behavior exceeds the liberality of our laws. In the United States the abolition of slavery may only be accomplished through destruction and civil war; or through a gradual retreat into the South, in an attempt to find a solution by way of Texas or New Mexico. In Brazil, however, emancipation is being achieved in a more orderly fashion. The white race ought to regain numerical preponderance with the arrival of the European immigrants, and these in turn will favor the rehabilitation of the slaves. Our country should help abolish the unceasing traffic of African savages, an activity that right now takes precedence over the fostering of morality, the family unit, and other crucial principles of civilization. Next to the immigrant, every slave ought to become Brazilian in origin . . . the influx of immigrants will thus change the organization of the large plantations; it will substitute small-scale farming for the mechanical system that requires slavery as its center leverage. Agriculture will take the place of manufacture. Work done by families will accomplish the tasks formerly performed by the slaves. This is how the emigrant workers will reinstate white labor, labor motivated by the deep feelings experienced by man in his submission to divine law, instead of extracted by a whip, symbol of the degradation of human bondage. In Brazil neither custom, nor law, nor the physical environment constitute a barrier to the coming together of immigrants and slaves, a union that combines the means to achieve material prosperity with the means of emancipation.[5]

In order to confirm such predictions of the influence of immigration on abolition, we must add that during the last period of slavery the Brazilian abolitionists had the support of the foreign settlers, excepting a few Portuguese merchants from Rio and a small number of North Americans established in São Paulo. . . .

The small number of immigrants that arrived in Brazil between 1860 and 1870 were for the most part workers who settled in the cities; some of them were relatives of the colonists that the government had placed in the State's colonies, or small businessmen from Portugal. Very few of these settlers did agricultural work; this form of colonization was not developed at this time. In 1870 the consul of Portugal in Rio attributed this state of affairs to the conditions stipulated by the contracts under which the immigrants rendered their services:

I have seen from experience that freedom is the best system; everywhere it has been adopted the complaints of the colonists against the proprietors have ceased, and the proprietors have always paid the colonists according to the terms of their agreement, for they are certain that other plantation owners would hire immediately any worker who leaves a plantation out of dissatisfaction. I have thus abstained from making any service contracts for the colonists. I've always showed them how much they would gain by avoiding such agreements, since they probably would never lack employment in Brazil, and would always find a place to settle and work to their advantage.[6]

At that time the Portuguese government was in the process of making a detailed inquiry into emigration. The results of this investigation showed that working contracts had often been dictated in bad

[5]Gabriel Auguste van der Straten-Ponthoz, *Le budget du Brésil*, 3 vols., Bruxelles, C. Muquardt, 1854.

[6]*Primeiro inquerito parlamentar sôbre a Emigração Portuguesa, pela commissão da Câmara dos Senhores Deputados*, Lisboa, 1873, p. 467.

faith and carried loathsome conditions. The Portuguese Parliament was especially concerned with one contract that aroused its indignation more than any other. It involved two masons hired by a proprietor in São Paulo who imposed on them dreadful working conditions, took a lion's share of their meager wages, and legally bound them with a series of restrictive clauses. They were given 87 *centimes* a day at a time when any mason in Brazil would not have been paid less than five francs.[7] Undoubtedly, cases like this were the exception, but the mere fact of their existence was indicative of a state of affairs to which the government could not remain indifferent.

Towards the end of the war in Paraguay the condition of agriculture in Brazil seemed prosperous, especially that of coffee. This was a transitory prosperity, since it flourished in the midst of all the evils generated by slavery, and slavery itself was to be gradually extinguished for the sake of the social welfare of the country: Brazil could no longer sacrifice its well-being in the interest of a single industrial cultivation—that of coffee.

The Brazilian conservative party that was in power at the time (1871) undertook the abolition of slavery, but was not able to complete such radical social reform till 17 years later.

The reform began with the Rio-Branco law on September 28, 1871, and the sons of slave women were declared free. This law was passed thanks to the energy and eloquence with which the prime minister, the viscount of Rio-Branco, defended it against powerful opposition in the Brazilian parliament. Logically, the government must have been thinking of immigration at the time. In condemning slavery it had to organize hired labor and devote a considerable amount of money to immigration. . . .

In 1873 the imperial government began to allot a significant amount of money for colonization. Thanks to the support given to immigration by the ministry of Rio Branco, the colonists that the ministry had helped settle attracted others, and the flow of immigrants was set in motion in spite of the lack of continuity in the government's support of this cause. On the one hand, as the number of slaves diminished, the need for wage-earning workers increased, and the hope of better salaries attracted more immigrants. On the other hand, the Brazilians became more aware of the fact that it was in

[7]*Inquerito Parlamentar*, page 23. The proprietor's name is mentioned.

their best interest to multiply the number of workers in order to raise the value of the country's estate. Following the example of other countries, they devoted their efforts to promote immigration. For this purpose, and under the direction of the count-general Beaurepaire-Rohan and senator Excragnolle-Taunay, a society was formed in Rio that rendered extraordinary services. . . .

Brazil was very concerned with the need to make known to the European population the advantages that colonists would find in the Latin country. Today, however, we should not give to the so-called immigrationist propaganda the same importance that it received in the past. Experience has shown that men were encouraged to migrate in many different ways. Sometimes almost the entire youth population of a village migrated under the influence of a fellow countryman who had successfully settled in Brazil and managed to escape the poverty he would have suffered if he had remained in his own country. Other times an enthusiastic letter from a Trentino peasant established in São Paulo, or a migrant who returned to Italy with a few savings prompted hundreds of men to leave their native land. Many families that had been separated by emigration sought to be reunited, and often the sons who had migrated first sent their parents the necessary funds to get them to America.

As soon as a large number of emigrants settled in a country, they attracted others. This is what happened in Brazil, especially in the province of São Paulo, where more than 200,000 foreigners have settled in the last few years; in 1888, out of 131,268 immigrants who disembarked in Santos and Rio de Janeiro, near 92,000 settled in this province, making São Paulo one of the areas of the world with a large concentration of immigrants. The five large colonies of Australia do not have more than 64,000 annual arrivals.

We have seen when and how the influx of immigrants began. São Paulo's provincial assembly discontinued for a while the political and parliamentary verbiage that has always more or less characterized such assemblies in Brazil. It is precisely to the measures taken by the São Paulo assembly and to the law of September 28, 1885—a law that by accelerating slave emancipation indirectly made some tax revenues available for the purchase of tickets for immigrants—that we owe the sharp upsurge of immigration along the southern regions of Brazil in recent years.

It would be interesting to know what kind of jobs these immigrants found. Most of them went to work in the coffee plantations, and coffee production reached extraordinary proportions. The price of coffee remained high in the American and European markets, thus contradicting the predictions made by some economists, especially M. W. Scheffer who 20 years ago predicted a price drop that would put an end to coffee cultivation. And yet the increase in production was due, at least in São Paulo, to the European immigration. In December of 1888, the *Financial News* of London, a newspaper held in high regard by economists, studied this phenomenon and arrived at the following conclusions:

(1) in the rich province of São Paulo, where progress is rapidly being made, the coffee production grows considerably from day to day. (2) The price of 50 shillings for 100 kilos (approximately 100 francs for 50 kilos) still leaves a large profit for the plantation owners. (3) Only a small portion of the actual tillage is being done by Negro workers. (4) The climate and the type of cultivation done in the coffee districts are compatible with the work performed by the Europeans. (5) The number of immigrant workers from Italy living in São Paulo is large and continues to grow. Last year it was 92,000 and next year it will probably be 100,000. (6) With such influx of immigrants it is reasonable to expect that the cultivation of coffee will continue to expand, as long as prices hold up. (7) There is no reason to fear a decline in production. (8) Moreover, the United States showed us how the abolition of slavery (even if rapidly accomplished) coincided with a large increase in production. . . .

Most of the colonies in the province of São Paulo are prosperous. The Italians living there talk about it in the letters they write home, and every ship that arrives in Santos brings new groups of immigrants who have been claimed by their relatives. The French scholar Couty, who visited a large number of the colonies, gives a rather typical description of life in these settlements:

I will never forget the hearty welcome I received from those warm Italians. When they saw the proprietor and a group of visitors arrive, they rushed to offer us their home, as well as the few sweets, brandy, home-made beverages, cheese and dry fruit that they possessed. I nearly believed myself to be among those peasants from Limousin, my native land, whom I so love. It was the same candid hospitality, the same pride and love of their home, even the same comforts—in the restricted sense of the term. Strips of bacon and sausages were hanging from the joists of the ceilings; different vegetables and dry fruit were in storage in one of the rooms; there was a small plantation in the garden, and chickens and pigs behind the house; a humble bureau contained linens and sufficient plates and dishes of earthenware; in a corner of each of the two rooms was a bed that seemed large and adequate; and the men and women who planted in the fields were neatly dressed and wearing shoes; they also had a few savings kept in a drawer or in their landlord's safe.[8]

In 1884, when the price of coffee was very low in the foreign markets, the proprietors naturally lowered the colonists' salaries and the latter's profits diminished. Dr. Couty estimated that the average saving of a family of colonists who planted coffee was nearly 100 francs a year, which meant an average of 5 million francs in savings per year for all five thousand families who lived then in São Paulo under similar conditions. Today one could estimate those savings to be not less than 50 million francs, since the number of immigrants now is at least 10 times bigger.

[The laws governing the conditions of immigrant labor had many disadvantages.] The old legislation was modified in 1879, but many of the drawbacks of the preceding law were maintained. Under the new law many regrettable incidents occurred, but the economic situation greatly improved after a while, and many of the negative effects of the law were neutralized by the force of circumstances. In Brazil laws are not easily changed. One often accuses the Brazilian legislators of being slow, but many times, without altering the law, time and circumstances are the ones to bring out the changes. Thus, when the law of emancipation went into effect, public opinion had already forced the slave owners to set free such a large number of slaves that in a short time, and thanks also to the abolitionist campaign, all the slaves who were still in bondage would have been liberated without having to pass any laws. The law of contractual services, highly criticized in Brazil, still exists, but there is no need to apply it. There is a large number of jobs available. The arrival of European immigrants caused a significant increase in the labor force, but hardly enough to fulfill the needs of land cultivation completely. All this created an advantageous situation for the plantation owners, who

[8]Docteur Couty, *Étude de Biologie Industrielle sur le café,* Rio de Janeiro, 1883.

were always sure to find enough workers; and for the colonists, who were always certain to find a job. Edward de Grelle, minister of Belgium in Rio de Janeiro, visited the colonies in São Paulo and wrote on the subject:

The port of Santos is the point of landing for the emigrants. They have free transportation to São Paulo on the railroad that climbs up through the Serra-do-Mar and that, incidentally, offers the traveler a splendid view of this range of mountains and their virgin forests. The train leaves the newcomers near a big hotel that has been especially created to service the immigrants; it has excellent hygiene and sanitation. Admirably organized, the hotel can lodge more than a thousand people. The immigrants are housed there free for eight days while they wait for job offers; these usually arrive in no time. Ordinarily, all emigrant families are placed within three days, since as soon as they arrive they receive numerous proposals from the many proprietors searching for workers. *The contracts of services no longer exist. There is only a simple verbal agreement whose cancellation by either party is always optional.* The emigrants have a choice between the colonies created by the government and the ones that are privately operated. In the government colonies they may, if they have the means, purchase a house and ten acres of land for 1,250 francs in cash, or 1,500 francs on credit, payable in four years. They are allowed to raise in their concession any of the products mentioned earlier; they may have livestock, and they can work a few extra hours a day for the government as a salary of 1,000 *réis* (2.50 francs) per day. But there is no obligation in this respect. The sale of agriculture products is easily transacted, thanks to the rapid means of transportation and to the lines of communication that link the colony with the neighboring towns.

3.

MONETARY POLICIES OF LATIN AMERICAN REGIMES: The Silver Standard in Mexico

MATÍAS ROMERO

One of the themes which particularly excited economists of the late nineteenth century, especially outside America, was the monetary policy of the Latin American regimes. Those who assumed that a fixed standard of exchange—the gold standard—was necessary for a world economy in which merchandise and capital would flow freely over a base of financial security, looked suspiciously upon the covert but tenacious resistance of Americans to that mechanism and, implicitly, to the corrupt practices of the Creole governing classes, which found in emission a quick way to satisfy their thirst for wealth.

Thus, in the eyes of these economists, resistance to the gold standard would have been either the result of frivolous administrative practices or a means of controlling a larger share of the national wealth.[1] Although this might have been correct in some cases, resistance to the gold standard was used mainly to promote exports.

In Mexico as well as in Brazil and Argentina, the policy of flexible exchange, which meant the devaluation of the

From Matías Romero, *Mexico and the United States. A Study of Subjects Affecting Their Political, Commercial, and Social Relations, Made with a View to Their Promotion*, 4 vols. (New York: The Knickerbocker Press, 1898), vol. I, pp. 593–612. Footnotes omitted.

[1]Frank Whitson Fetter, *Monetary Inflation in Chile* (Princeton, N. J.: Princeton University Press, 1931).

national paper or silver currency, was used to promote exports, reducing their costs in international terms, and enabling them to reach world markets even, in a few cases, in a period of falling prices.[2]

Mexico experienced the devaluation of silver which spread throughout the world at this time. In the course of a few decades, Mexican silver lost 50 percent of its value in relation to gold: the silver/gold ratio fell from 16 to 1 to 32 to 1. Since Mexico's circulating currency was silver, this meant that Mexican money lost 50 percent of its value in international exchange.

Matías Romero, who represented the ideology of the economic scientists of the Porfiriato, was well aware, as the testimony below shows, of the role of this devaluationist policy in the promotion of exports, which would become the dynamic hub of Mexico's impressive growth during the age of Díaz.[3]

Reasons Why Mexico Has the Silver Standard

Mexico is legally a bimetallic country, because we have free coinage of both gold and silver at the ratio of 16 to 1; but practically we are a silver monometallic country, because under the operation of the Gresham Law all the gold bullion and the gold coin existing in Mexico is exported as merchandise, having a much greater market value than its legal value in Mexico, and silver is therefore the only metallic money used there in payment of debts or for any other purpose. The silver standard prevailing in Mexico was not adopted from choice. Mexico being the largest silver-producing country, over two thirds of the whole silver stock of the world having come out of its mines, silver has been our only currency for nearly four hundred years. We have kept so far our monetary standard, because, as will be seen farther on, it has not been an unmitigated evil for Mexico, because we have hoped that the commercial nations of the world

[2]See Fernando Rosenzweig, "El comercio exterior," in Daniel Cosío Villegas, *Historia moderna de México* (Mexico: Editorial Hermes, 1965); and Pierre Denis, *Brazil.* See also *Memoria presentada al Congreso Nacional de 1892 por el Ministro de Hacienda Emilio Hansen* (Buenos Aires: La Nueva Universidad, 1882).

[3]See Fernando Rosenzweig, "El desarrollo económico de México de 1877 a 1911," *El Trimestre Económico,* XXXII, No. 127 (July–September 1965).

would find it to their interest to rehabilitate silver in some way, and also because we have been anxious to avoid the derangements and disadvantages consequent to a change of monetary standard which would be also felt, although not in such a degree, by the United States, should they attempt to change their present gold standard for a silver one. A change from the silver to the gold standard would cause in Mexico general ruin, as we do not yet produce gold enough to base our currency on that metal, and as our exports of commodities are not yet sufficiently large to allow us to buy all the gold we need for that purpose. The high price of gold is a great incentive to gold-mining, and if gold continues at the present high price for some time, I am sure Mexico will before long be a large producer of that metal.

We never had any paper currency, either national, state, or issued by banks. Two or three banks, indeed, have now issued notes, but they are not legal tender. They are convertible into silver coin at the holder's pleasure, and while they circulate freely in the large cities and for convenience' sake are preferred to the hard dollar, they are almost unknown in the small towns and in the country. The bank issues special notes for each place, which are redeemable only in that place, thus keeping up in effect the old system of charging a high premium for the exchange of money from one place to another, the item of profit to the banks corresponding with what used to be the charge for transporting silver money.

Advantages of the Silver Standard to Mexico

The advantages to Mexico of the silver basis are the following, most of which could not be applicable to the United States on account of the different conditions prevailing in each country:

1st. The silver standard encourages very materially, so long as other leading commercial nations have the single gold standard, the increase of exports of domestic products, because the expenses of producing them, land, wages, rent, taxes, etc., are paid in silver, and therefore their cost, as compared with their market value, is considerably less than that of similar articles produced or raised in single gold standard countries. When sold in gold markets, therefore, they bring very profitable prices, as they are converted into silver, at a high rate of exchange. These conditions have caused a great development in the exportation of some of our agricultural products, because they yield very large profits; coffee, for instance, which costs on an average about ten cents a pound to produce it, all expenses included, has been sold at about twenty cents in gold in foreign markets. The export of other agricultural products which did not pay when gold and silver were at par, that is, at the ratio of one to sixteen, is now remunerative, because there is returned to us in exchange more than we lose in the gold price of the article.

The same is the result of some agricultural products that we could not export before because their price in foreign markets was not remunerative. Such is the case, for instance, with beans, which at eight cents would not pay when silver and gold were at par, but now that eight cents in gold make about sixteen cents in silver, it is a profitable price. Our exports for several years preceding 1869 were about a year $20,000,000.00

1872–73	31,594,005.14
1888–89	60,158,423.02
1891–92	75,467,714.95
1892–93	87,509,207.00

The Statistical Bureau of the Mexican Government quotes the price of our exports in silver, and therefore to find them in gold they have to be reduced to the market price of silver, but, even reduced to one-half, the increase is very remarkable.

Formerly we used to export only silver and gold; because of their small weight and bulk relatively to their value, they were the only articles that paid for transportation. But the proportion of other commodities has been increased recently to fifteen, twenty, thirty, and forty per cent of the export of our precious metals, and during the fiscal year ending June 30, 1896, the proportion was sixty-one per cent, as the exports of precious metals amounted to $64,838,596, and the exports of commodities to $40,178,306.

2d. The silver standard is a great stimulus to the development of home manufactures, because foreign commodities have to be paid for in gold, and, owing to the high rate of exchange, their prices are so high that it pays well to manufacture some of them at home, our low wages also contributing to this result.

For these reasons we are increasing considerably our manufacturing plants, especially our cotton mills, smelters, etc., and we begin now to manufacture several articles that formerly we used to buy from foreign countries, and all this, notwithstanding that the mountainous character of our country, the want of interior navigable watercourses, and the scarcity of fuel, make manufacturing very expensive in Mexico. But we are finding abundant coal deposits, and, when our railroads tap our coal-fields, that objection will be considerably diminished. One of our railroads, the International, built by Mr. C. P. Huntington and his associates, has already reached a very large coal-field at Salinas, near Piedras Negras, which is now supplying with coal a part of the country, and even some sections of the Southern Pacific system of this country, but of course it cannot supply the whole of Mexico. When that is satisfied, we shall have to contend only with the increased expenses of transporting the raw material to the factories and the manufactured goods to the place of consumption over a mountainous country with high grades and many sharp curves, unless some new means of transportation may be hereafter devised which shall overcome those obstacles. Eventually Mexico will utilize for manufacturing the many streams, almost torrents, which come down the steep mountains, and which constitute a very large water-power.

One of the leading directors of the Mexican Central Railroad has informed me that about ten years ago the supplies imported to operate that road amounted to sixty per cent of all the material used, and that to save the loss on exchange, the company has been following the system of manufacturing in Mexico all they possibly can, and that the proportion of foreign supplies imported during the last year has been reduced now to twenty per cent, and that they have decided to use Mexican rails, as soon as they can be manufactured in Mexico, which will still further considerably reduce that percentage.

As it is now, some manufacturing plants of the United States are being taken to Mexico, as appears in the following extract from the annual report of Mr. W. G. Raoul, President of the Mexican National Railroad Company, for the year 1894:

The most extensive and best equipped shops owned by the company are on the north side of the Rio Grande, in the United States, but the greater expense of operating them has caused the withdrawal of much of the work from them to the shops of Mexico. Our shops in Mexico are not adequate for the entire work of the road, and the removal of the Texas plant into Mexico becomes an economic necessity, if the peculiar trade and the industrial conditions now existing respectively in the two countries are to continue.

The development of manufacturers in Mexico has also brought about an increase in the production of raw materials consumed in our manufactories, and which before we used to buy from foreign countries, as is the case with cotton. The price of such articles in gold makes them so high that it is cheaper to raise them at home.

3d. While the fall of silver and free coinage in Mexico have not given to the Mexican silver coins, when converted into foreign exchange or sold for gold, any value other than that of the silver bullion contained in the same, nevertheless the purchasing power of the silver dollar is now, on the whole, as great as it ever was in Mexico, and it has only been reduced in the case of foreign articles, so that one can buy now almost the same amount of home commodities for the same number of dollars that they cost when gold and silver were at par, that is, at the ratio of 1 to 16, excepting such Mexican commodities as have their price fixed in foreign gold markets.

It is not a little puzzling to some travellers who go from this country to Mexico to see a United States silver dollar containing less silver bullion than a Mexican silver dollar, exchanged there for two Mexican silver dollars when silver is at about fifty-six cents an ounce but they do not bear in mind that in making such an exchange, the Mexican silver dollar is sold for the market price of the silver bullion it contains, just as if it was not coined, while the United States silver dollar is the representative of a gold dollar, received as such in this country, and is therefore an article of merchandise bought to pay debts in the United States or Europe; but notwithstanding that fact, the Mexican silver dollar has not lost any of its purchasing power in Mexico.

4th. The fact that foreign commodities have to be paid for in gold makes them so high that this operates as a protective duty against them, equal to the price of exchange, or the difference between the market value of the gold and silver bullion. Protectionists would count this as a very important advantage, although I myself do not attach much importance to it in that sense, as I believe in low duties, unless in certain cases and for certain reasons, high duties are rendered necessary.

5th. Our silver standard encourages the investment in Mexico of capital from rich countries having the gold standard, since every gold dollar when sent to Mexico is converted into two silver dollars, at the present rate of exchange, and, when invested in lands, wages, and other expenses for the raising of agricultural products which are sold for gold in foreign markets, like coffee, the proceeds are so large that they constitute a very great inducement for the investment of capital. Besides, if at any time in the future silver should be reinstated as a money metal by the leading commercial nations of the world, and rise in price, the capital invested in a silver country would be actually duplicated in gold.

6th. The development of the country has increased considerably the local traffic of our railroads, and that increase is very encouraging, and goes far to compensate the companies owning them for the losses which the depreciation of silver entailed on them in the payment of interest on their bonded debts.

7th. There is another very great advantage that Mexico has derived from the silver standard, although this may be peculiar to us. Before our railroads were built the only articles which we could export were silver and gold dollars—coinage being then made compulsory by law—because no other product could pay the very high expense of transportation. The result was that to pay for our imports we had to export almost all of our annual output of silver, so that very little was left for our home circulation. Thus we were almost constantly suffering from a contraction of currency; money became very dear, while the price of labor was very low. But now the conditions are reversed. The low price of silver abroad makes it unprofitable to export it, and its value at home makes it useful in all industries, and we send out our agricultural products to pay for our imports and for our gold obligations, keeping at home our silver and thus increasing our circulation, so that we now have an ample supply of money in our banks. That fact, of course, stimulates industry, keeps up prices, and increases the demand for labor.

8th. Most of our millionaires, and many rich Mexicans having large fixed incomes, preferred formerly to live in Europe, and used to spend their money there, but the higher rate of exchange has reduced their incomes so materially that a great many of them are returning home and now spend their incomes in Mexico.

[Romero then refers to the disadvantages that the silver standard can have, but concludes as follows.]

Conditions Resulting in Mexico from the Silver Standard

The disadvantages of the silver standard are considerably lessened in Mexico because of the fact that we have used coined silver for over three hundred years as our currency, and therefore we have not had to suffer the disturbances and drawbacks of changing the standard, but have continued with the same currency, regardless of the market price of silver bullion in foreign countries and this of course has prevented any serious derangement in business and in prices.

In consequence of these causes, we have had fewer business failures than other countries; our internal traffic has greatly increased, with much benefit to our railroads, which, with only one exception, have not gone into the hands of receivers, notwithstanding that they have to pay in gold the interest of their bonds and the increased price of the foreign commodities which they need to operate the roads.

We do not suffer in Mexico from one of the principal causes of the present (June, 1895) financial distress in other countries—the low prices of agricultural products. In fact, in some cases, the prices of domestic commodities have gone up considerably, when they are fixed by the value of the commodity in gold markets. This is the case with coffee, for instance. As the largest portion of our crop is exported and commands cash, its price is fixed by its value in gold markets, and in consequence of this its price in Mexico has been almost doubled, with great advantage to the producer.

We have greater stability of prices, wages, rents, etc. Although our wages are low, there has been in recent years a marked tendency to their increase. Our factories are not only in operation, but they are being greatly extended, and new plants and industries are being established. Instead of diminishing the demand for our laborers, we find occupation for them all, and we need to import them for the work to be done in some localities, and, as our laborers find occupation and increased wages, we have no strikes. Our silver mines have not stopped work, and we find them still quite profitable. We have more ready money with which to transact our increased business; we offer greater inducements to foreign investors than formerly; and the country is undoubtedly more prosperous than it has ever before been, although the silver standard is not the only cause of our prosperity. One of its principal causes is, undoubtedly the building of railroads, as already stated, but they could not have been as remunerative as they are without the production and coinage of silver.

Conclusion

Summing up the effects produced in Mexico by the silver standard, I can say, with perfect truth, that while it is a drawback, a great inconvenience, and a serious loss to the government and to the railroads to have our currency depreciated when we have to use it abroad, either to pay for foreign merchandise or the interest on our gold obligations, and while that depreciation increases our burdens to some extent, because our gold obligations and the price of foreign commodities are nearly doubled by it, the advantages we derive from the use of silver money in all our transactions are so great as, in my opinion, to fully compensate, if they do not outweigh, its disadvantages.

Notwithstanding the views of those who desire that the present depreciation of the Mexican money should continue in Mexico, I, for one, and I think that I express the views of a majority of my fellow-citizens, would like to see our silver commanding the same price as it had before it was demonetized in 1873, and we believe that the world will have to come back sooner or later to bimetallism, as the only way to have a common and a more stable level of values and to avoid most of the financial troubles from which the commercial nations of the world are now so keenly suffering.

4.

REPORT SUBMITTED TO THE NATIONAL CONGRESS OF 1892 BY ARGENTINE MINISTER OF FINANCE EMILIO HANSEN

The period of Argentina's incorporation into the world market began with a boom which, intensified by a strong influx of population and an even greater flow of capital, took on markedly speculative qualities, causing numerous imbalances and painful crises. The crisis of 1890, which took place amid a fever of speculation, is remembered as one of the most catastrophic; the banking house of Baring Brothers could not find buyers for the Argentine bonds it had agreed to negotiate in Europe, Baring failed, and the country went through one of its most difficult moments.

The nature of this speculative wave, its consequences, and the role of the foreign investor are described in the admirably economical pages of the report in which Minister of Finance Hansen informed the Congress of the dramatic situation.

The report also takes into account the way in which the remittance to the exterior of interest and profits—which formed a significant percentage of the value of the exports of those years—gravitated upon the balance of payments, and thus critically affected it when the influx of capital was cut off. Hansen conservatively estimates that 40 million pesos in gold left the country in the form of interest and

Memoria presentada al Congreso Nacional de 1892 por el Ministro de Hacienda (Buenos Aires, 1892), pp. 3–17. Translated by Christopher Hunt.

profits, while the exports of 1886 and 1887 were valued at 70 million and 80 million pesos in gold, respectively.[1]

Hansen also agrees with Romero that the devaluation of paper money, the Argentine currency, meant a fall in the cost of export products. Finally, the minister shows that this fiscal penury coincided with strong thrusts in production and exports, which ultimately characterized this period of rapid economic growth based on farming exports.

The year 1891 can be considered the decisive period in the economic crisis which has plagued our country since the middle of 1889, growing in intensity until its culmination in the failure of the official banks in June, and showing the first signs of reaction in the last days of the year.

In June and July of 1889, the government struggled to arrest the rapid depreciation of our currency, sacrificing the gold accumulated in the national coffers as backing for the fiat money under the Guaranteed Banks Law. The failure of this effort sounded the first alarm for those few men who had maintained the spiritual serenity necessary to understand the true meaning of the events unfolding before their eyes. . . .

Since 1880, the country had enjoyed a constantly increasing prosperity, and thus the transition from the great well-being of 1886–1887 to the enormous inflation of 1889 took place almost imperceptibly, worrying not even the most cautious souls.

Speculation and profiteering dominated all stocks, bonds and securities, and even the most fantastic projects seemed possible if they could be priced on the Stock Exchange. It was difficult to wake up to reality and see that we were living in a palace built on sand.

Once the Treasury had failed to prevent the appreciation of gold, paper fortunes began to disappear, and there was a general clamor for the government to collect new assets and resume the struggle.

European investors were so heavily committed to Argentine enterprises, and European bankers had previously been so solicitous that we expected them to come to our aid, if only to protect their own interests. We envisioned a new loan—70 or 80 million pesos in gold—with which we would face all problems, and resolve the monetary

[1]Alec G. Ford, *The Gold Standard, 1880–1914; Britain and Argentina* (Oxford: Oxford University Press, 1962).

crisis. This time, however, the bankers were afraid. The size of the request forced them to see the gravity of the situation, and they were unable to reconcile their great interest in averting a disaster with their deepening distrust of our markets. . . .

Negotiations for this loan were interrupted by the revolution of July, 1890. After the administration had been reorganized along lines which satisfied national aspirations and gained acceptance abroad, the talks were resumed, only to be ended by the fall of the Baring House of London, which forced the country to seek another way of saving the national credit.

The situation at the beginning of 1891, then, was roughly the following:

Argentine credit in Europe had disappeared completely. In London, a commission of bankers searched for a way in which the country could service its foreign debt, and thus avert the ruin of its creditors.

The flow of capital, which in previous years had entered the country, had been reversed with a violence which was limited only by the poverty of resources.

Foreign trade showed an unfavorable balance of 44 million pesos in gold.

Most provinces had suspended payment of their external debts, and the province of Buenos Aires was about to suspend payment of mortgage bonds.

Of the banks which had been established with so much work and sacrifice, only the National Bank and the Bank of the Province of Buenos Aires remained on effective footing.

Credit standing, the great motive force behind the late fictitious prosperity, had disappeared, depriving enterprise and initiative of their most active element.

The political situation, on the other hand, had improved remarkably. In national financing, order and economy in spending were practiced scrupulously. Congress, meeting in extraordinary sessions to deal with the economic situation, reformed the tax structure, drawing on previously untapped sources.

National production grew rapidly, stimulated by the same inflation which so hurt the nonproductive, consumer populations of the cities.

Commerce was recovering, confident that the country's productive capacity would overcome the problems that still plagued it. . . .

The key to the economic reconstruction of the country is undoubtedly the rapid development of production. Its surplus provides exports to cover the cost of the foreign goods we consume, and funds for the servicing of European capital, either as payment of the foreign debt or as remittance of commercial or industrial profits.

The following figures clearly establish the importance of borrowed gold to our economy:

I. Public Debt			
National		$205,692,404	
Provincial		143,315,533	
Municipal		24,596,423	
			$373,604,360
II. Railroads			
Guaranteed		$ 81,800,000	
Not guaranteed		230,700,000	
			$312,500,000
III. Industrial and Commercial Enterprises			
Guaranteed (Preserved meat factories, sugar refineries)		$ 6,700,000	
Not guaranteed:			
Banks	20,600,000		
Tramways	15,300,000		
Telephones	2,200,000		
Gas works	4,900,000		
		$ 43,000,000	
			$ 49,700,000
IV. Mortgage Bonds			
Gold, national		$ 15,000,000	
Paper:			
National	60,000,000		
Provincial	200,000,000		
Calculating gold at 300%		86,000,000	101,000,000
Total, in gold			$836,804,360

I have omitted European capital invested in other industrial and commercial enterprises because there is no certain way of determining its importance, and because I think the outflow it will generate in the remittance of profits to Europe will be offset by the annual arrival of new capital for the establishment of similar businesses or the expansion of existing ones.

Thus foreign capitalists have invested in the resources of the Republic more than 800 million pesos in gold, the servicing and profits of which must be taken into account when we consider the results of our foreign trade.

This sum will generate an outflow of a maximum of 5 percent of the total, or some 40 million pesos in gold per year, a figure chosen because it represents the annual cost of servicing mortgage bonds, guarantees, and the entire public debt. For reasons I will cite below, I think this percentage can also be applied to the capital invested in private businesses.

The effective outflow is actually much lower than the figure cited above, for the suspension of all national servicing, and some provincial servicing, such as that of debentures, reduces it to some 6 to 7 million, while the 270 million in unguaranteed capital probably does not yield more than an average of 2 to 2½ percent.

Furthermore, some of the most important railroads are engaged in programs of expansion, rebuilding, etc. with new capital raised in Europe, so that in effect they are not remitting funds; they use their net proceeds here, and pay dividends to European investors with money obtained in Europe.

However, this state of affairs is entirely abnormal, and we must begin to think of how it will be affected by the gradual recovery of the country.

As for the public debt, there is general agreement that the present arrangement, under which it is serviced at an annual interest rate of 6%, must be reviewed, for ultimately it will only add new and greater debts to existing ones, while it forces our creditors to sell the bonds they receive in payment at a very low rate. I think we can foresee an average annual rate of 2½ to 3 percent as a satisfactory solution, and that this rate could be applied to guarantees and debentures; in this way, there would be an annual reduction of some 12 to 15 million on these 500-odd million, cutting the total outflow to some 25 to 30 million, a figure which, if we allow the tragic experience of the past to guide and advise us, would be well within the economic capacity of the country. . . .

Thus if there is an equitable reduction of the rate of debt servicing, the maximum annual outflow will not exceed 25 to 30 million. Once this figure is reached, we will begin to feel a countercurrent of capital entering the country which will grow as the economic situation improves, until it covers in great part the remittance of profits on foreign investments.

The experience of the years before the crisis offers us a practical example of the role of this element in the balance of our foreign trade.

From 1886 through 1890, commercial statistics showed an unfavorable balance of no less than 170 million pesos in gold. I think this figure should be reduced by 10 percent to allow for statistical errors, and by an equivalent sum to allow for the inclusion of unpaid European debts. Approximately 140 million remain, which could only be paid with new capital entering the country, either through public stock or through private initiative.

In 1891, however, these sources dried up completely, the pressure of creditors demanding to be paid was constantly felt, and the unfavorable trade balance of 1890—42 million—abruptly became a favorable balance of 36 million. Imports fell from 142,240,812 pesos in gold to 67,207,780, or 53 percent, while exports rose by 2½ million, from 100,818,993 pesos in gold in 1890 to 103,219,000 pesos in 1891.

These figures clearly show the effort made by the country to reestablish its commercial balance. Once the sources of credit and new capital had been closed off, and a great demand for funds to cover oustanding debts had arisen, imports fell sharply, and production struggled to fill the vacuum in the internal market and simultaneously build a surplus with which to pay the debts.

I think such rapid and radical change should be studied carefully, for we should find in its motive factors the general tendencies of our foreign trade, and the influence which the monetary question has upon foreign trade and national production.

We have seen that the unfavorable balances of previous years were paid off in part with new capital entering the economic system, and that the remaining balance acted as a current debt owed by our industry and commerce to Europe's.

Once the crisis had begun, European markets found they had given us more credit than they wanted us to have, and they made their new distrust keenly felt in two ways: first, they stopped sending merchandise on credit, and second, they began to withdraw cash to settle old debts.

This outflow of cash naturally affected our currency, depreciating it more and more, and making imported goods increasingly expensive for the consumer, whose income was in paper money. The devaluation of paper money in turn stimulated production, which in some branches began to replace products which had once been imported, and in others helped increase the surplus available for export and created new lines of exportable products.

Thus one of the direct consequences of the crisis, insofar as it affected the value of our currency, has been the great stimulation of production and the establishment of innumerable industries which compete with their European counterparts.

Among the great branches of production, the pasturing industry seems least to have felt this influence, surely because by nature it does not allow a great expansion of exploitation from one year to the next. Agriculture, on other hand, has progressed remarkably, stimulated by the high prices it receives for its products, some of which it exports, and others—such as wines, sugars and alcohols—which now control domestic markets.

The manufacturing industry has also developed remarkably, favored by the cheapness of manual labor, which is paid in scrip, enabling it to undersell imported products.

BIBLIOGRAPHIC SUGGESTIONS

General

FOR THE COLONIAL ERA
STEIN, STANLEY, and BARBARA STEIN. *The Colonial Heritage of Latin America.* New York: Oxford University Press, 1970.

FOR THE ENTIRE PERIOD
HALPERÍN DONGHI, TULIO. *Historia contemporánea de América Latina.* Madrid: Alianza Editorial, 1969.

FOR AN ECONOMIC INTERPRETATION
SUNKEL, OSVALDO, and PEDRO PAZ. *El subdesarrllo latinoamericano y la teoría del desarrollo.* Mexico: Siglo XXI, 1970.

Brazil
COSTA, EMILIA VIOTTI DA. *De senzala à colônia.* São Paulo: Difusão Européia do Livro, 1966.
DENIS, PIERRE. *Brazil.* London: Adelphi Terrace, 1911.
ESCRAGNOLLE TAUNAY, AFFONSO DE. *Pequena história do café no Brasil (1727–1937).* Rio de Janeiro: Departmento Nacional do Café, 1945.
FURTADO, CELSO. *The Economic Growth of Brazil.* Los Angeles: University of California Press, 1963.
LUZ, NICIA VILELA. *A luta pela industrialização do Brasil, 1808 a 1930.* São Paulo: Difusão Européia do Livro, 1961.
MORSE, RICHARD. *From Community to Metropolis; A Biography of São Paulo, Brazil.* Gainesville: University of Florida Press, 1958.
PRADO JÚNIOR, CAIO. *Historia económica del Brasil.* Buenos Aires: Editorial Futura, 1960.
PRADO JÚNIOR, CAIO. *The Colonial Background of Modern Brazil.* Los Angeles: University of California Press, 1967.
STEIN, STANLEY. *Vassouras; A Brazilian Coffee County, 1850–1900.* New York: Atheneum, 1970.

Peru in the Guano Age
BASADRE, JORGE. *Historia de la República del Perú.* Lima: Editorial Cultura Antártica, S.A., 1946.
DUFFIELD, ALEXANDER J. *Peru in the Guano Age.* London: Richard, Bentley and Son, 1877.
LEVIN, JONATHAN. *The Export Economies.* Cambridge, Mass.: Harvard University Press, 1960.
MATHEW, W. M. "The Imperialism of Free Trade: Peru, 1820–1870." *The Economic History Review,* 2nd ser., XXI (1968).
ROMERO, EMILIO. *Historia económica del Perú.* 2nd ed. Lima: Editorial Universo, 1967.
UGARTE, CÉSAR A. *Bosquejo de historia económica del Perú.* Lima: Imprenta Cabieses, 1926.

Mexico Under the Porfiriato
BAZANT, JEAN. *Historia de la deuda exterior de México, 1823–1946.* Mexico: El Colegio de México, 1968.

BERNSTEIN, MARVIN. *The Mexican Mining Industry.* Albany: The State University of New York Press, 1965.

COSÍO VILLEGAS, DANIEL. "El Porfiriato." *Historia moderna de México.* Vols. VII, VIII. Edited by Daniel Cosío Villegas. Mexico: Editorial Hermes, 1965.

Estadísticas económicas del Porfiriato: Comercio exterior. Mexico: El Colegio de México, 1960.

Estadísticas sociales del Porfiriato, 1877–1910. Mexico: Dirección General de Estadística, 1956.

POWELL, FRED W. *The Railroads of Mexico.* Boston: The Stratford Co., 1921.

REYNOLDS, CLARK. *The Mexican Economy: Twentieth Century Structure and Growth.* New Haven: Yale University Press, 1970.

ROMERO, MATÍAS. *The Silver Standard in Mexico.* New York: The Knickerbocker Press, 1898.

ROSENZWEIG, FERNANDO. "El desarrollo económico de México de 1877 a 1911." *El Trimestre Económico.* XXXII, No. 127 (July–September, 1965).

TURLINGTON, EDGARD. *Mexico and her Foreign Creditors.* New York: Columbia University Press, 1930.

Argentina

ALVAREZ, JUAN. *Temas de historia económica argentina.* Buenos Aires: El Ateneo, 1929.

CORTÉS-CONDE, ROBERTO, and EZEQUIEL GALLO. *La formación de la Argentina moderna.* Buenos Aires: Paidós, 1967.

DÍAZ ALEJANDRO, CARLOS F. *Essays on the Economic History of the Argentine Republic.* New Haven: Yale University Press, 1970.

DI TELLA, GUIDO, and MANUEL ZYMELMAN. *Las etapas del desarrollo económico argentino.* Buenos Aires: Eudeba, 1967.

DORFMAN, ADOLFO. *Evolución de la industria argentina.* Buenos Aires: Losada, 1942.

FERRER, ALDO. *La economía argentina.* Buenos Aires: Fondo de Cultura Económica, 1963.

FORD, ALEC G. *The Gold Standard, 1880–1914; Britain and Argentina.* Oxford: Oxford University Press, 1962.

GIBERTI, HORACIO. *Historia económica de la ganadería argentina.* Buenos Aires: Raigal, 1954.

ORTIZ, RICARDO M. *Historia económica de la Argentina, 1850–1930.* 2 vols. Buenos Aires: Raigal, 1955.

WILLIAMS, JOHN. *Argentine International Trade under Inconvertible Paper Money.* Cambridge, Mass.: Harvard University Press, 1920.

V.
Slavery in Latin America

⚜ HERBERT KLEIN

Latin American intellectuals concerned themselves with the question of racial integration in their societies as early as this question was raised in the United States. But the initial reaction of these intellectuals was to accept the inevitability of an integrated society and the creation of a new "American" or Creole race. They held to the belief that the acculturation and homogenization were good and inevitable goals, although most Latin Americans understood integration to mean the progressive whitening of the black and mulatto populations to arrive at a "white" ideal phenotype.

As their nations seemed unable to break through the barriers of anarchy and underdevelopment many Latin American thinkers, especially in the nations with large Indian and black populations, began to doubt the wisdom of these goals. In seeking to understand the failure of development and the lack of stability in their societies many turned to the racism of Gobineau and the social Darwinism of Herbert Spencer. In these European doctrines they found the explanation for their problems, and intellectuals such as Nina Rodrigues in Brazil and Alcides Arguedas in Bolivia attacked the blacks, mulattoes, mestizos, and Indians as cancers in the social body of the nation. But even as the hostility to the Indian, black, and the mixed *castas* developed among some intellectuals, others rejected these extremist formulations. From Indianist writers such as Franz Tamayo to pro-black writers like Manuel Querino or José Marti came the belief that the very racial heterogeneity of their societies was their positive contribution to the development of mankind and the only true hope for their own national salvation. It was the voice of these few late nineteenth- and early twentieth-century intellectuals which finally broke through elite stereotypes and led to the great folklore movements in the post–World War I crisis period. It was in the context of these new Afro-Cuban and Afro-Brazilian movements of the 1920s and 1930s that the first systematic national and comparative studies of slavery and race relations began in Latin America. Under men like Gilberto Freyre and Fernando Ortiz, and a host of other scholars, the rich heritage of the Afro-American cultures was stressed and the positive aspects of Latin American racial integration were emphasized. All of this was written about with the full awareness of the separatist race relations experience of the United States.

The work of these Latin American scholars of the early twentieth century gave rise in the United States to the so-called comparative school of race relations studies. As North American writers finally began to deal with their own racism, they sought to understand the uniqueness of their race relations and in so doing began to investigate other societies. Starting with Donald Pierson and the work in English of such Brazilians as Gilberto Freye, Thales de Azevedo, and Arthur Ramos, by the early 1940s a new awareness was emerging in the United States that its current pattern of race relations differed markedly from those in the rest of the former slave societies of the Hemisphere.

In 1947, Frank Tannenbaum took this new viewpoint and made the first systematic attempt to account for this difference in his famous study *Slave and Citizen*. He stressed that the basic difference in the current status of blacks and mulattoes in Latin America was due to a different historical and cultural experience. He argued that the historical experience of slavery, the contact with both North Africa and black Africa prior to the conquest of America, and a Roman Catholic culture that stressed human rights and dignity, all worked to modify the impact of plantation slavery. He felt that the prime means by which this modification occurred was through a much higher incidence of manumission, and a recognition that the free persons of color represented an integral part of the social and economic order.

In elaborating on this theme, Stanley Elkins, in his major study of slavery in 1957, argued that it was essentially these cultural norms and social institutions, especially as reflected in the powerful institutions of the crown and the church, which prevented the dynamics of capitalism from reducing the black slave to chattel, a status that had occurred in the United States. Here the lack of an all-embracing church, a lack of imperial institutions which regulated slavery, and a lack of important pre-American contact with Africa left the dynamics of plantation agriculture as the only force to mold the role of the slave in society. This, plus a very strong racial prejudice, was sufficient to identify color with slavery and to condemn the freed men of color as outcasts and hostile to the very existence of a functioning American society.

While Tannenbaum and others who followed him were stressing a whole set of cultural, social, economic, and even ecological factors which made for difference in the Latin American and North American slave systems, a group of European and American sociologists and anthropologists attempted to analyze the cause for the current differences in race relations in terms of a different set of variables. Men like Marvin Harris argued that the slave systems were essentially identical in North and South America and that plantation agriculture molded all social relations into an identical form. The differences in current race relations were held to be accounted for by different causes than those proposed by Tannenbaum. For Harris, the key was in the demographic structure of the slave societies. In Brazil and the rest of Spanish America and the British West Indies, there were a very small number of whites in proportion to the black slave population. Unlike the continental United States, there was no massive poor white immigration to provide the planter elite with an intermediate group of persons who could control the slave masses. Thus the Latin Americans and West Indian planters had to rely on a free mulatto class to be the overseers, slave hunters, and control group who would manage their plantation regimes.

It was this demographic difference, more blacks than whites, which explained the differing attitudes toward the mulatto and free colored classes. After abolition, Harris argued, this pattern of relatively mild race relations was maintained because of the dominance of a rigid class structure. To Harris, as well as a major group of sociologists at São Paulo, the more rigid class system of Latin America was sufficient to guarantee relatively peaceful racial relations, since most blacks and mulattoes represented no serious threat to the white elite. The few really talented, successful, or lucky colored who did break into the upper elite could easily be absorbed as whites. The end result, as Harris graphically illustrated in his color perception studies on northeastern Brazilians, was a great fluidity in race definitions, while class distinctions remained sharp and clear. From this position, the more extreme proponents of the Harris school went on to predict that increasing industrialization of Latin America will lead to increased racial prejudice along the lines of the North American model, since to them race prejudice is simply a class defense mechanism. This whole school of thought, which sees the United States as the basic model for all multiracial societies, ignores the far more rapid social mobility already achieved by the blacks in Latin America, as well as the fact that the prejudice model was elaborated long before economic class competition developed in the United States, and in fact was a prime guarantee against that competition.

Not satisfied with a model of Western Hemisphere racial development which sees the United States as the primary model that all other states will eventually imitate, several sociologists have proposed alternative explanations. Two leading alternative theories are presented by Pierre Van der Berghe (*Race and Racism: A Comparative Perspective*) and H. Hoetink (*Two Variants of Caribbean Race Relations*), both of whom believe that the North American model is only one among several different approaches to race relations. Van der Berghe, in fact, sees some four major types of response to the slavery experience and postemancipation problem of integration. These go from the Mexican experience of complete integration of blacks, through the modified integration patterns of Brazil and Cuba, to the United States, and eventually South African patterns of alienation and exclusion. In attempting to explain why all these ex-slave societies, which had a common "paternalistic" race pattern, should have such divergent postemancipation societies, he returns to the position of Tannenbaum, with an even greater stress on the role of Catholic culture.

Hoetink, rather than seeing any evolution along different historical lines, especially after emancipation, instead sees the contemporary racial patterns frozen into the Latin American and North American societies from the time of first contact between the races. He argues that the Latins have a totally different perception of colored than the North European colonists. Their color perception (or "somatic norm image"), while stressing white as good and black as bad, nevertheless defines "white" so broadly as to include a large percentage of the mulatto class. Thus he finds the mulattoes in these societies operating as an integrative force, or just the opposite of the role that they play in the United States. In turn, he sees this different color perception as being due to a darker skin of the Mediterranean peoples.

It would thus seem that there are as many alternative explanations of the cause for the current differences in New World race relations as there are explanations of how many different patterns there are and the directions toward which they are all developing. Nevertheless, there is common accord on a surprisingly large number of facts about American racial relations. All scholars find that pejorative terminology and hostility to black skin are part of all former slave societies. However, they find that the intensity of such prejudice and its practical effects differ very markedly in Spanish and Portuguese America from the United States. They also find that in all societies but the United States, the mulattoes form a coherent and self-aware group which plays an important role as a third force in racial integration. There is disagreement, however, as to whether the mulattoes are more or less integrated or alienated in the British and French West Indies, as contrasted with Spanish and Portuguese America. Finally, many would agree that while blacks are found everywhere in the lower class in the majority, that in Spanish and Portuguese America, they, and above all the mulattoes, have achieved higher rates of social and economic mobility than they have achieved in the United States.

As to the cause for these current differences in race relations, scholars find themselves, as we have noted above, in sharp conflict, with no single school of thought yet achieving a common acceptance. There are nevertheless some areas of agreement, not only about current race conditions, but also about the slave experience as it differed in the several New World societies. Almost all serious scholars agree that the rates of manumission were very different in British North America and Spanish and Portuguese America. In 1860, for example, only 11 percent of the total black population in all states of the Union were freedmen, this compared to some 38 percent for Cuba in the same period, and over 70 percent for Brazil in the early 1870s. It is also evident that the freedmen in Latin America played a much more vital role in the economic and social life of the general society than they did in the United States. Also, urban slavery was much more fully developed in Latin America, and hiring out and self-employment of slaves more common than we experienced in the United States. What is not clear is to what extent the plantation experience was different in the North American and Latin American worlds, and here disagreement is strong among recent scholars. For this reason, I have selected the two best descriptions of the plantation regimes available in the literature. From these descriptions of a Brazilian coffee estate in the booming Paraiba Valley (Province of Rio de Janeiro) and of a sugar estate in Cuba, a rather clearly defined plantation culture begins to emerge. For the reader, a comparison with similar studies of North American plantation regimes (e.g., Philips and Stampp), should reveal both the similarities, and the sharp differences in these regimes. Because of space limitations I have been unable to provide sources on Afro-American religious cults, or studies of the major slave revolts. But it is hoped that these detailed descriptions, both of life as seen in the reconstruction of a social historian, and the reminiscences of an ex-field hand slave, will give the reader a basic feel for the Latin American slave experience. I have also sought, in the last two selections, to present the student with the essence of the argument about the significance of this slave experience as seen by the two leading representatives of the most current schools of thought, Frank Tannenbaum and Marvin Harris.

1.
VASSOURAS, A BRAZILIAN COFFEE COUNTY, 1850–1900

STANLEY J. STEIN

The following selection is taken from the work of Stanley Stein on the Vassouras Valley at the height of its coffee plantation period. The valley, which is located in the Province of Rio de Janeiro, was one of the first areas in Brazil to experience a major coffee boom. Stein's excellent social and economic history is the best single study available on a Latin American plantation community.

Slave life on the average Vassouras plantation of approximately eighty to one hundred slaves was regulated by the needs of coffee agriculture, the maintenance of sede and senzallas, and the processing of coffee and subsistence foodstuffs. Since the supply of slaves was never adequate for the needs of the plantation either in its period of growth, prosperity, or decline, the slaves' work day was a long one begun before dawn and often ending many hours after the abrupt sunset of the Parahyba plateau.

Cooks arose before sunup to light fires beneath iron cauldrons; soon the smell of coffee, molasses, and boiled corn meal floated from the outdoor shed. The sun had not yet appeared when the overseer or one of his Negro drivers strode to a corner of the terreiro and

Reprinted by permission of the publishers from Stanley J. Stein, *Vassouras, A Brazilian Coffee County, 1850–1900* (Cambridge, Mass.: Harvard University Press, 1957), pp. 161–173, footnotes omitted. Copyright 1957 by the President and Fellows of Harvard College.

reached for the tongue of a wide-mouthed bell. The tolling of the cast-iron bell, or sometimes a blast from a cowhorn or the beat of a drum, reverberated across the terreiro and entered the tiny cubicles of slave couples and the separated, crowded tarimbas, or dormitories, of unmarried slaves. Awakening from their five- to eight-hour slumber, they dragged themselves from beds of planks softened with woven fiber mats; field hands reached for hoes and bill-hooks lying under the eaves. At the large faucet near the senzallas, they splashed water over their heads and faces, moistening and rubbing arms, legs, and ankles. Tardy slaves might appear at the door of senzallas muttering the slave-composed jongo which mocked the overseer ringing the bell:

> That devil of a *bembo* taunted me
> No time to button my shirt, that devil of a bembo.

Now, as the terreiro slowly filled with slaves, some standing in line and others squatting, awaiting the morning *reza* or prayer, the senhor appeared on the veranda of the main house. "One slave recited the reza which the others repeated," recalled an ex-slave. Hats were removed and there was heard a "Praised-be-Our-Master-Jesus-Christ" to which some slaves repeated a blurred "Our-Master-Jesus-Christ," others an abbreviated "Kist." From the master on the veranda came the reply: "May-He-always-be-praised." The overseer called the roll; if a slave did not respond after two calls, the overseer hustled into the senzallas to get him or her. When orders for the day had been given, directing the various gangs to work on certain coffee-covered hills, slaves and drivers shuffled to the nearby slave kitchen for coffee and corn bread.

The first signs of dawn brightened the sky as slaves separated to their work. A few went into the main house; most merely placed the long hoe handles on their shoulders and, old and young, men and women, moved off to the almost year-round job of weeding with drivers following to check stragglers. Mothers bore nursing youngsters in small woven baskets (*jacás*) on their backs or carried them astraddle one hip. Those from four to seven trudged with their mothers, those from nine to fifteen close by. If coffee hills to be worked were far from the main buildings, food for the two meals furnished in the field went along—either in a two-team ox-cart which slaves called a *maxambomba,* or in iron kettles swinging on long sticks, or in wicker baskets or two-eared wooden pans (*gamellas*) on long boards carried on male slaves' shoulders. A few slaves carried their own supplementary articles of food in small cloth bags.

Scattered throughout the field were shelters of four posts and a grass roof. Here, at the foot of the hills where coffee trees marched up steep slopes, the field slaves split into smaller gangs. Old men and women formed a gang working close to the rancho; women formed another; the men or young bucks (*rapaziada nova*), a third. Leaving the moleques and little girls to play near the cook and assistants in the rancho, they began the day's work. As the sun grew stronger, men removed their shirts; hoes rose and fell slowly as slaves inched up the steep slopes. Under the gang labor system of *corte e beirada* used in weeding, the best hands were spread out on the flanks, *cortador* and *contra-cortador* on one, *beirador* and *contra-beirador* on the other. These four lead-row men were faster working pacesetters, serving as examples for slower workers sandwiched between them. When a coffee row (*carreira*) ended abruptly due to a fold in the slope, the slave now without a row shouted to his overseer "Throw another row for the middle" or "We need another row"; a feitor passed on the information to the flanking lead-row man who moved into the next row giving the slave who had first shouted a new row to hoe. Thus lead-row men always boxed-in the weeding gang.

Slave gangs often worked within singing distance of each other and to give rhythm to their hoe strokes and pass comment on the circumscribed world in which they lived and worked—their own foibles, and those of their master, overseers, and slave drivers—the master-singer (*mestre cantor*) of one gang would break into the first "verse" of a song in riddle form, a *jongo*. His gang would chorus the second line of the verse, then weed rhythmically while the master-singer of the nearby gang tried to decipher (*desafiar*) the riddle presented. An ex-slave, still known for his skill at making jongos, informed that "Mestre tapped the ground with his hoe, others listened while he sang. Then they replied." He added that if the singing was not good the day's work went badly. Jongos sung in African tongues were called *quimzumba;* those in Portuguese, more common as older Africans diminished in the labor force, *visaría.* Stopping here and there to "give a lick" (*lambada*) of the lash to slow slaves, two slave drivers usually supervised the gangs by criss-crossing the vertical coffee rows on the slope and shouting "Come on, come on"; but if surveillance slackened, gang laborers seized the chance to slow down while men and women slaves lighted pipes or leaned on their hoes momentarily to wipe sweat away. To rationalize their desire to resist the slave drivers' whips and shouts, a story developed that an older, slower slave should never be passed in his coffee row. For the aged slave could throw his belt ahead into the younger man's row and the youngster would be bitten by a snake when he reached the belt. The overseer or the master himself, in white clothes and riding boots, might ride through the groves for a quick look. Alert slaves, feigning to peer at the hot sun, "spiced their words" to comment in a loud voice "Look at that red-hot sun" or intermixed African words common to slave vocabulary with Portuguese as in "*Ngoma* is on the way" to warn their fellow slaves *(parceiros)*, who quickly set to work industriously. When the driver noted the approaching planter, he commanded the gang "Give praise," to which slaves stood erect, eager for the brief respite, removed their hats or touched hands to forehead, and responded "Vas Christo." Closing the ritual greeting, the senhor too removed his hat, spoke his "May He always be praised" and rode on. Immediately the industrious pace slackened.

To shouts of "lunch, lunch" or more horn blasts coming from the rancho around 10 A.M., slave parceiros and drivers descended. At the shaded rancho they filed past the cook and his assistants, extending bowls or *cuías* of gourds split in two. On more prosperous fazendas, slaves might have tin plates. Into these food was piled; drivers and a respected or favored slave would eat to one side while the rest sat or sprawled on the ground. Mothers used the rest to nurse their babies. A half hour later the turma was ordered back to the sun-baked hillsides. At one P.M. came a short break for coffee to which slaves often added the second half of the corn meal cake served at lunch. On cold or wet days, small cups of cachaça distilled from the plantation's sugar cane replaced coffee. Some ex-slaves reported that fazendeiros often ordered drivers to deliver the cachaça to the slaves in a cup while they worked, to eliminate a break. *Janta* or supper came at four P.M. and work was resumed until nightfall when to drivers' shouts of "Let's quit" (*vamos largar o serviço*) the slave gangs tramped back to the sede. Zaluar, the romantic Portuguese who visited Vassouras, wrote of the return from the fields: "The solemn evening hour. From afar, the fazenda's bell tolls Ave-Maria. (From hilltops fall the gray shadows of night while a few stars begin to flicker in the sky). . . From the hill descend the taciturn driver and in front, the slaves, as they return home." Once more the slaves lined up for rollcall on the terreiro where the field hands encountered their slave companions who worked at the plantation center (sede).

Despite the fact that the economy of the fazenda varied directly with the success of its coffee production, a high percentage of plantation slave labor, which some estimated at fully two-thirds, others at one-half of the labor force, was not engaged directly in field work. "On the plantation," Couty judged, "everything or almost everything is the product of the Black man: it is he who has built the houses; he has made the bricks, sawed the boards, channeled the water, etc.; the roads and most of the machines in the engenho are, along with the lands cultivated, the products of his industry. He also has raised cattle, pigs and other animals needed on the fazenda." Many were employed in relatively unproductive tasks around the sede as waiters and waitresses, stableboys and cooks, and body servants for the free men, women, and children.

Throughout the day in front of the house could be seen the activity of the terreiro. From his shaded veranda or from a window the fazendeiro watched his slaves clean the terreiro of sprouting weeds, or at harvest time revolve the drying coffee beans with wooden hoes. Until the hot sun of midday drove them to the shade, bare-bottomed black and mulatto youngsters played under the eye of an elderly "aunt" and often with them a small white child in the care of his male body servant (pagem) or female "dry nurse." In a corner slaves might butcher a pig for the day's consumption while some moleques threw stones at the black turkey buzzards which hovered nearby. Outside the senzalla a decrepit slave usually performed some minor task or merely warmed himself in the sun. From the engenho came the thumping sound of the pilões and the splash of water cascading from the large water-wheel. In the shade of the engenho an old slave wove strips of bamboo into mats and screens. Washerwomen, beating and spreading clothes to bleach in the sun, worked rhythmically "to the tune of mournful songs."

Behind the main house, the páteo enclosed on all sides offered a shelter from outsiders' eyes, a place to be at ease. Here and in the rooms around it the lives of the free and slave women blended together. Washerwomen chatted as they dipped their arms into the granite tank in the center of the páteo or stretched wet clothes to bleach on the ground, and through the door of the kitchen slaves occupied with the unending process of food preparation could be seen at long wooden work tables. From a small porch opening on the páteo, or from the dining-room window, the mistress of the house, *sinhá* (or more informally, *nhanhá*), in a dressing gown, leaned on the railing and watched, maintaining a flow of gossip with her slaves or reprimanding some. Yet, despite the close contact between free and slave, locks on the doors of pantries and cupboards and the barred windows of both gave mute testimony to the faith of the mistress in her slaves. Life for the female house slave often seemed easier in comparison with that of a field hand; indeed, many of the *mucamas* or household female slaves were chosen from the field gangs. Yet they felt they had less liberty than the field hands since they were constantly supervised. A former pagem put the case succinctly: "Of course life in the household was always better. But many a sinhá beat her mucamas with a quince switch.". . .

At evening roll call (*formatura*) slaves were checked and sent to evening tasks to begin what one Vassouras planter termed the "brutal system of night tasks" (*serão*), sometimes lasting to ten or eleven P.M. During winter months the principal evening task—the sorting of dried coffee beans on the floor of the engenho or on special tables— was continued in the light of castor-oil lamps or woven taquara torches. Preparation of food for humans and animals was the next most important job: manioc was skinned by hand, scraped on a huge grating wheel, dried, and then toasted for manioc flour. Corn cobs were thrown to pigs, while slaves beat other ears on tables (*debrulhadores*) with rods to remove kernels to be ground into corn meal. Women pounded rice in mortar and pestle to hull it. Coffee for the following day's consumption was toasted in wide pans, then ground. Slaves were sent out to gather firewood, and moleques walked to nearby abandoned groves to drive in the few foraging cows, oxen, mules, and goats. A light supper ended the serão.

In the dwelling house slaves cleared the supper tables and lit castor-oil lamps or candles. The planter's family retired soon to their rooms, followed by the mucama "whose job was to carry water to wash the feet of the person retiring." She departed immediately to return after a short wait, received a "God-bless-you" and blew out the light.

And now field hands straggled from the engenho to slave senzallas where they were locked in for the night. Household help too was locked in tiny rooms located in the rear of the house near the kitchen. For the slaves it was the end of a long day—unless a sudden storm blew up during the night while coffee was drying on the terreiros; then they were routed out once more by the jangling bell to pile and cover hurriedly the brown beans. Except for the patrollers, (*rondantes*) moving in groups on the roads and through the coffee groves to pick up slaves out without passes (*guías* or *escriptos*) to visit nearby plantations or taverns, activity ceased.

With the arrival of Saturday evening and Sunday—awaited with much the spirit of the American South's "Come day, go day, God send Sunday"—came the only interruption of the work routine of plantation life. On Saturday the evening stint was usually omitted to give the labor force an opportunity to live without close supervision. Near a fire on the drying terrace, to the beating of two or three drums, slaves—men, women, and children—led by one of their master-singers, danced and sang until the early morning hours.

Even Sunday too was partially devoted to work. In morning chores, lasting until nine or ten, field hands attended to the auxiliary tasks of the plantation; hauling firewood from clearings, preparing pasture by burning the grass cover, clearing brush from boundary ditches, repairing dams and roads, and killing ever-present saúva ants with fire and bellows. Sunday was the day for distribution of tobacco cut from a huge roll of twisted leaf smeared with honey, and of clean clothing for the following week's use. Chores completed, the master "gave permission"—permitted slaves to dispose of the remainder of the day until the line-up at nightfall. It was also common for planters to "give permission" on days other than Sunday to stagger the weekly day off and prevent slaves from meeting with friends from nearby plantations.

Many now scattered to small roças near the plantation center, where they raised coffee, corn, and beans. Planters gave them these plots for various reasons: they gave the slave cultivators a sense of property which, known or unknown to Brazilian masters, continued an African tradition and softened the harsh life of slavery; they provided subsistence foodstuffs which planters failed to raise in their emphasis on one-crop agriculture; and, by offering cash for the produce, planters put into slaves' hands small change for supplementary articles not provided by the plantation. Often planters insisted that slaves sell only to them the coffee they raised. Slaves obtained cash too when the custom became widespread among planters to pay for Sunday or saints'-day labor.

Where male and female slaves cohabited, men often were accompanied to the roças by their children, while women washed, mended, and cooked, bringing the noon meal to their mates in the field. The single men brought firewood for the cook to prepare their meal, returning at eating hours. Other slaves used the free time to weave sleeping mats or cut and sew clothing for sale. With cash or corn or beans, slaves went on Sundays to trade at nearby saloons (*tabernas*) or small country stores. On a visit to a fazenda of the province of Rio, the Swiss Pradez entered a fazenda-owned venda run by an aging slave "aunt" of the fazendeiro's confidence where he found the typical stock: tobacco and cachaça (particularly attractive to slaves), notions including mirrors, straw hats, and clothing cut from cotton cloth (*Petrope*) of a quality slightly better than the coarse cloth furnished by the plantation. Outside the confines of the fazenda, he found a white taberna proprietor who served Negroes with cachaça at a *vintem* per glass. In friendly fashion the white man, to Pradez's surprise, discussed with a slave the weather, the crops, and his master, as though the slave were a "client to be maintained."

More disturbing to coffee planters, and a very lucrative business to "their greatest enemies"—taberna owners—was the "large-scale clandestine commerce in stolen coffee" carried on "almost exclusively at night in places heavily populated with slaves." An ex-slave recounted how he used to obtain coffee for sale to a nearby taberna. After senzalla doors were locked, he climbed to the eave where tools were stored, and removed several roof tiles. Through the hole he crawled, then managed to get into the basement of the coffee storehouse. Here he drilled a hole in the floor and drained into a bag all the coffee he could carry. Then over the fazenda's outer wall and, avoiding the main road usually patrolled by rondantes, he arrived at the taberna. If the suspicious planter or his zealous overseer appeared at the door of the country bar, the taberneiro replied innocently that "No one is here." In return for the bag of coffee, the slave received a fraction of its worth in cachaça or tobacco. Not always, however, were planters put off with an innocuous "No one is here," as the following case reveals: "On the night of May 1st, Manoel, a slave belonging to the complainant, stole from the terreiro a bag of coffee and carried it away clandestinely to Ferreiros where he entered the doors of the store of Joaquim Teixeira Alves after ten o'clock." This was noted by the rondantes circulating in Ferreiros, and they sealed off Alves' store. On May 2nd after dawn, in the presence of witnesses, the store was searched. The slave was found without the coffee but with 1$400 reis and a piece of tobacco given to him as payment for the stolen coffee. "Alves and his brother, who acts as his clerk, confessed on the spot and begged and pleaded not to go to jail."

Fazendeiros tried to hinder the obvious collusion between their slaves and taberna-keepers, whose illegal intentions were blatant when they established tabernas on lonely roads, by demanding that the Câmara Municipal grant no licenses. They were not always successful, unless they moved against the exasperating tavern-keepers without waiting for municipal authorities. "In view of the repeated thefts of coffee on the complainant's plantation perpetrated by his slaves in collusion with several nearby taberneiros for the past three years, particularly so in the past month, the complainant, Joaquim José Furtado, reports that he sought carefully for the author of these thefts with absolutely no success. But he finally learned that Renovato Borges de Siqueira, who has an unlicensed taberna near the complainant's lands, is one of those who have been buying the coffee stolen by the complainant's slaves. For this purpose there exists a path from that taberna to the coffee lands of the complainant cleared by the offender and the slaves to carry on the illicit traffic in coffee as proven by the coffee berries scattered on the path as well as those which have already sprouted." Furtado learned from a female slave that "one Sunday she saw Hercules, a slave of the complainant who walks hobbled with ankle chains, sell the offender a bag of coffee . . . and not the first one." Some slaves were more indiscriminate in their choice of negotiable stolen goods as evinced by Manoel de Azevedo Barboza's report that a certain Luís bought from his slaves his treasured silver spoons and forks, pigs, turkeys, and chickens. More than the loss of coffee, however, was the continual drunkenness of slaves who stole; and in the repression of stealing and drunkenness there was fostered an "eternal, unequal, and inhuman struggle where the interests of the Senhor conflict with those of his slave, who suffers so many rigorous punishments and who flees to the forest to die by suicide, misery, eaten by worms."

2.

THE AUTOBIOGRAPHY OF A RUNAWAY SLAVE

ESTEBAN MONTEJO

The autobiography of the Cuban ex-slave Esteban Montejo is the best single slave narrative available for Latin America. This section describes life in the slave barracks (or barracoons) on the sugar plantation Flor de Sagua where he was a field hand carter. Particularly unusual about this narrative is its depiction of the culture and community of the field hand slaves. The internal stratifications, the living conditions, and the leisure time activities are all described in detail unavailable in any other source. Especially in terms of the availability of money, of the survival of African religious practice, and even of language, both here and in Vassouras should be compared by the reader with the slave narratives of the United States. Finally, the reader will note at the end of Montejo's narrative, his own declaration of rebellion, which prefaced his own flight from plantation slavery. As a runaway slave, he lived by himself in the woods of Cuba for over 10 years (between 1868 and 1878).

All the slaves lived in barracoons. These dwelling-places no longer exist, so one cannot see them. But I saw them and I never thought well of them. The masters, of course, said they were as clean as new

From *The Autobiography of a Runaway Slave,* by Esteban Montejo, edited by Miguel Barnet, translated by Jocasta Innes. Copyright © 1968 by The Bodley Head, Ltd. Reprinted by permission of Pantheon Books, A Division of Random House, Inc.

pins. The slaves disliked living under those conditions: being locked up stifled them. The barracoons were large, though some plantations had smaller ones; it depended on the number of slaves in the settlement. Around two hundred slaves of all colours lived in the Flor de Sagua barracoon. This was laid out in rows: two rows facing each other with a door in the middle and a massive padlock to shut the slaves in at night. There were barracoons of wood and barracoons of masonry with tiled roofs. Both types had mud floors and were as dirty as hell. And there was no modern ventilation there! Just a hole in the wall or a small barred window. The result was that the place swarmed with fleas and ticks, which made the inmates ill with infections and evil spells, for those ticks were witches. The only way to get rid of them was with hot wax, and sometimes even that did not work. The masters wanted the barracoons to look clean outside, so they were whitewashed. The job was given to the Negroes themselves. The master would say, 'Get some whitewash and spread it on evenly.' They prepared the whitewash in large pots inside the barracoons, in the central courtyard.

Horses and goats did not go inside the barracoons, but there was always some mongrel sniffing about the place for food. People stayed inside the rooms, which were small and hot. One says rooms, but they were really ovens. They had doors with latchkeys to prevent stealing. You had to be particularly wary of the *criollitos,* who were born thieving little rascals. They learned to steal like monkeys.

In the central patio the women washed their own, their husbands' and their children's clothes in tubs. Those tubs were not like the ones people use now, they were much cruder. And they had to be taken first to the river to swell the wood, because they were made out of fish-crates, the big ones. . . . As the rooms were so small the slaves relieved themselves in a so-called toilet standing in one corner of the barracoon. Everyone used it. And to wipe your arse afterwards you had to pick leaves and maize husks.

The bell was at the entrance to the mill. The deputy overseer used to ring it. At four-thirty in the morning they rang the Ave Maria—I think there were nine strokes of the bell—and one had to get up immediately. At six they rang another bell called the line-up bell, and everyone had to form up in a place just outside the barracoon, men one side, women the other. Then off to the canefields till eleven, when we ate jerked beef, vegetables and bread. Then, at sunset, came the prayer bell. At half-past eight they rang the last bell for everyone to go to sleep, the silence bell.

The deputy overseer slept inside the barracoon and kept watch. In the mill town there was a white watchman, a Spaniard, to keep an eye on things. Everything was based on watchfulness and the whip. When time passed and the *esquifación,* the slaves' issue of clothing, began to wear out, they would be given a new one. The men's clothes were made of Russian cloth, a coarse linen, sturdy and good for work in the fields—trousers which had large pockets and stood up stiff, a shirt, and a wool cap for the cold. The shoes were generally of rawhide, low-cut with little straps to keep them on. The old men wore sandals, flat-soled with a thong around the big toe. This has always been an African fashion, though white women wear them now and call them mules or slippers. The women were given blouses, skirts and petticoats, and if they owned plots of land they bought their own petticoats, white ones, which were prettier and smarter. They also wore gold rings and earrings. They bought these trophies from the Turks and Moors who sometimes came to the barracoons, carrying boxes slung from their shoulders by a wide leather strap. Lottery-ticket-sellers also came round, who cheated the Negroes and sold them all their most expensive tickets. If any of the tickets came up on the lottery you wouldn't see them for dust. The *guajíros,* or white countrymen, also came to barter milk for jerked beef, or sell it at four cents a bottle. The Negroes used to buy it because the owners did not provide milk, and it is necessary because it cures infections and cleans the system.

These plots of land were the salvation of many slaves, where they got their real nourishment from. Almost all of them had their little strips of land to be sown close to the barracoons, almost behind them. Everything grew there: sweet potatoes, gourds, okra, kidney beans, which were like lima beans, yucca and peanuts. They also raised pigs. And they sold all these products to the whites who came out from the villages. The Negroes were honest, it was natural for them to be honest, not knowing much about things. They sold their goods very cheap. Whole pigs fetched a doubloon, or a doubloon and a half, in gold coin, as the money was then, but the blacks didn't like selling their vegetables. I learned to eat vegetables from the elders, because they said they were very healthy food, but during slavery pigs were the mainstay. Pigs gave more lard then than now, and I think it's because they led a more natural life. A pig was left to wallow about in the piggeries. The lard cost ten pennies a pound, and the white countrymen came all week long to get their portion. . . .

The taverns were near the plantations. There were more taverns than ticks in the forest. They were a sort of store where one could buy everything. The slaves themselves used to trade in the taverns, selling the jerked beef which they accumulated in the barracoons. They were usually allowed to visit the taverns during the daylight hours and sometimes even in the evenings, but this was not the rule in all the plantations. There was always some master who forbade the slaves to go. The Negroes went to the taverns for brandy. They drank a lot of it to keep their strength up. A glass of good brandy costs half a peso. The owners drank a lot of brandy too, and the quarrels which brewed were no joke. Some of the tavern-keepers were old Spaniards, retired from the army on very little money, five or six pesos' pension.

The taverns were made of wood and palm-bark; no masonry like the modern stores. You had to sit on piled jute sacks or stand. They sold rice, jerked beef, lard and every variety of bean. I knew cases of unscrupulous owners cheating slaves by quoting the wrong prices, and I saw brawls in which a Negro came off worse and was forbidden to return. They noted down anything you bought in a book; when you spent half a peso they made one stroke in the book, and two for a peso. This was the system for buying everything else: round sweet biscuits, salt biscuits, sweets the size of a pea made of different-coloured flours, water-bread and lard. Water-bread cost five cents a stick. It was quite different from the sort you get now. I preferred it. I also remember that they sold sweet cakes, called 'caprices', made of peanut flour and sesame seed. The sesame seed was a Chinese thing; there were Chinese pedlars who went round the plantations selling it, old indentured labourers whose arms were too weak to cut cane and who had taken up peddling.

The taverns were stinking places. A strong smell came from all the goods hanging from the ceiling, sausages, smoked hams, red morta-dellas. In spite of this, people used to hold their games there. They spent half their lives at this foolishness. . . .

Sunday was the liveliest day in the plantations. I don't know where the slaves found the energy for it. Their biggest fiestas were held on that day. On some plantations the drumming started at midday or one o'clock. At Flor de Sagua it began very early. The excitement, the games, and children rushing about started at sunrise. The barracoon came to life in a flash; it was like the end of the world. And in spite of work and everything the people woke up cheerful. The overseer and deputy overseer came into the barracoon and started chatting up the black women. . . .

As soon as the drums started on Sunday the Negroes went down to the stream to bathe—there was always a little stream near every plantation. It sometimes happened that a woman lingered behind and met a man just as he was about to go into the water. Then they would go off together and get down to business. If not, they would go to the reservoirs, which were the pools they dug to store water. They also used to play hide-and-seek there, chasing the women and trying to catch them.

The women who were not involved in this little game stayed in the barracoons and washed themselves in a tub. These tubs were very big and there were one or two for the whole settlement.

Shaving and cutting hair was done by the slaves themselves. They took a long knife, and, like someone grooming a horse, they sliced off the woolly hair. There was always someone who liked to clip, and he became the expert. They cut hair the way they do now. And it never hurt, because hair is the most peculiar stuff; although you can see it growing and everything, it's dead. The women arranged their hair with curls and little partings. Their heads used to look like melon skins. They liked the excitement of fixing their hair one way one day and another way the next. One day it would have little partings, the next day ringlets, another day it would be combed flat. They cleaned their teeth with strips of soap-tree bark, and this made them very white. All this excitement was reserved for Sundays. . . .

I knew of two African religions in the barracoons: the Lucumi and the Congolese. The Congolese was the more important. It was well known at the Flor de Sagua because their magic-men used to put spells on people and get possession of them, and their practice of soothsaying won them the confidence of all the slaves. I got to know the elders of both religions after Abolition.

I remember the *Chicherekú*[1] at Flor de Sagua. The *Chicherekú* was a Congolese by birth who did not speak Spanish. He was a little man with a big head who used to run about the barracoons and jump upon you from behind. I often saw him and heard him squealing like a rat. This is true. Until recently in Porfuerza there was a man who ran about in the same way. People used to run away from him because they said he was the Devil himself and he was bound up with *mayombe* and death. You dared not play with the *Chicherekú* because it could be dangerous. Personally I don't much like talking of him, because I have never laid eyes on him again, and if by some chance. . . . Well, these things are the Devil's own!

The Congolese used the dead and snakes for their religious rites. They called the dead *nkise* and the snakes *emboba*. They prepared big pots called *ngangas* which would walk about and all, and that was where the secret of their spells lay. All the Congolese had these pots for *mayombe*. The *ngangas* had to work with the sun, because the sun has always been the strength and wisdom of men, as the moon is of women. But the sun is more important because it is he who gives life to the moon. The Congolese worked magic with the sun almost every day. When they had trouble with a particular person they would follow him along a path, collect up some of the dust he walked upon and put it in the *nganga* or in some little secret place. As the sun went down that person's life would begin to ebb away, and at sunset he would be dying. I mention this because it is something I often saw under slavery.

If you think about it, the Congolese were murderers, although they only killed people who were harming them. No one ever tried to put a spell on me because I have always kept apart and not meddled in other people's affairs.

The Congolese were more involved with witchcraft than the Lucumi, who had more to do with the saints and with God. The Lucumi liked rising early with the strength of the morning and looking up into the sky and saying prayers and sprinkling water on the ground. The Lucumi were at it when you least expected it. I have seen old Negroes kneel on the ground for more than three hours at a time, speaking in their own tongue and prophesying. The difference

---

[1]African word for bogey-man.

between the Congolese and the Lucumi was that the former solved problems while the latter told the future. This they did with *dilog-gunes,* which are round, white shells from Africa with mystery inside. The god Elegguá's[2] eyes are made from this shell.

The old Lucumis would shut themselves up in rooms in the barra-coon and they could rid you of even the wickedness you were doing. If a Negro lusted after a woman, the Lucumis would calm him. I think they did this with coconut shells, *obi,* which were sacred. They were the same as the coconuts today, which are still sacred and may not be touched. If a man defiled a coconut, a great punishment befell him. I knew when things went well, because the coconut said so. He would command *Alafia,*[3] to be said so that people would know that all was well. The saints spoke through the coconuts and the chief of these was Obatalá, who was an old man, they said, and only wore white. They also said it was Obatalá who made you and I don't know what else, but it is from Nature one comes, and this is true of Obatalá too.

The old Lucumis liked to have their wooden figures of the gods with them in the barracoon. All these figures had big heads and were called *oché.* Elegguá was made of cement, but Changó and Yemaya were of wood, made by the carpenters themselves.

They made the saints' marks on the walls of their rooms with charcoal and white chalk, long lines and circles, each one standing for a saint, but they said that they were secrets. These blacks made a secret of everything. They have changed a lot now, but in those days the hardest thing you could do was to try to win the confidence of one of them.

The other religion was the Catholic one. This was introduced by the priests, but nothing in the world would induce them to enter the slaves' quarters. They were fastidious people, with a solemn air which did not fit the barracoons—so solemn that there were Negroes who took everything they said literally. This had a bad effect on them. They read the catechism and read it to the others with all the words and prayers. Those Negroes who were household slaves came

[2]Elegguá, Obatalá, Changó, Yemaya: gods of the Yoruba, a Nigerian tribe, worshipped in Cuba by the followers of *santeria* . . .

[3]Lucumi expression meaning 'all goes well,' used particularly in the system of divination with sacred coconuts.

as messengers of the priests and got together with the others, the field slaves, in the sugar-mill towns. The fact is I never learned that doctrine because I did not understand a thing about it. I don't think the household slaves did either, although, being so refined and well-treated, they all made out they were Christian. The household slaves were given rewards by the masters, and I never saw one of them badly punished. When they were ordered to go to the fields to cut cane or tend the pigs, they would pretend to be ill so they needn't work. For this reason the field slaves could not stand the sight of them. The household slaves sometimes came to the barracoons to visit relations and used to take back fruit and vegetables for the master's house; I don't know whether the slaves made them presents from their plots of land or whether they just took them. They caused a lot of trouble in the barracoons. The men came and tried to take liberties with the women. That was the source of the worst tensions. I was about twelve then, and I saw the whole rumpus.

There were other tensions. For instance, there was no love lost between the Congolese magic-men and the Congolese Christians, each of whom thought they were good and the others wicked. This still goes on in Cuba. The Lucumi and Congolese did not get on either; it went back to the difference between saints and witchcraft. The only ones who had no problems were the old men born in Africa. They were special people and had to be treated differently because they knew all religious matters. . . .

All the plantations had an infirmary near the barracoon, a big wooden hut where they took the pregnant women. You were born there and stayed there till you were six or seven, when you went to live in the barracoons and began work, like the rest. There were Negro wet-nurses and cooks there to look after the *criollitos* and feed them. If anyone was injured in the fields or fell ill, these women would doctor him with herbs and brews. They could cure anything. Sometimes a *criollito* never saw his parents again because the boss moved them to another plantation, and so the wet-nurses would be in sole charge of the child. But who wants to bother with another person's child? They used to bathe the children and cut their hair in the infirmaries too. A child of good stock cost five hundred pesos, that is the child of strong, tall parents. Tall Negroes were privileged.

The masters picked them out to mate them with tall, healthy women and shut them up together in the barracoon and forced them to sleep together. The women had to produce healthy babies every year. I tell you, it was like breeding animals. Well, if the Negress didn't produce as expected, the couple were separated and she was sent to work in the fields again. Women who were barren were unlucky because they had to go back to being beasts of burden again, but they were allowed to choose their own husbands. It often happened that a woman would be chasing one man with twenty more after her. The magic-men would settle these problems with their potions. . . .

I saw many horrors in the way of punishment under slavery. That was why I didn't like the life. The stocks, which were in the boiler-house, were the cruellest. Some were for standing and others for lying down. They were made of thick planks with holes for the head, hands and feet. They would keep slaves fastened up like this for two or three months for some trivial offence. They whipped the pregnant women too, but lying face down with a hollow in the ground for their bellies. They whipped them hard, but they took good care not to damage the babies because they wanted as many of those as possible. The most common punishment was flogging; this was given by the overseer with a rawhide lash which made weals on the skin. They also had whips made of the fibres of some jungle plant which stung like the devil and flayed the skin off in strips. I saw many handsome big Negroes with raw backs. Afterwards the cuts were covered with compresses of tobacco leaves, urine and salt.

Life was hard and bodies wore out. Anyone who did not take to the hills as a runaway when he was young had to become a slave. It was preferable to be on your own on the loose than locked up in all that dirt and rottenness.

3.

SLAVE AND CITIZEN: The Negro in America

FRANK TANNENBAUM

> Frank Tannenbaum was a prolific historian, philosopher, and
> criminologist. His works in all areas are famous, and he is
> particularly well known in Latin American studies for his
> several books on the Mexican Revolution. This work on
> comparative slavery grew out of a seminar he held at Colum-
> bia University just after World War II.

This belief that equality among men is natural and reasonable is,
therefore, both pagan and Christian, and stems from the Stoics and
from the Christian fathers. The conception that man is free and
equal, especially equal in the sight of God, made slavery as such a
mundane and somewhat immaterial matter. The master had, in fact,
no greater moral status than the slave, and spiritually the slave
might be a better man than his master. *Las Siete Partidas* was framed
within this Christian doctrine, and the slave had a body of law, protective of him as a human being, which was already there when the
Negro arrived and had been elaborated long before he came upon
the scene. And when he did come, the Spaniard may not have
known him as a Negro, but the Spanish law and *mores* knew him

as a slave and made him the beneficiary of the ancient legal heritage. . . .

Spanish law, custom, and tradition were transferred to America and came to govern the position of the Negro slave. It is interesting to note that a large body of new law was developed for the treatment of the Indians in America, whereas the Negro's position was covered by isolated *cedulas* dealing with special problems. It was not until 1789 that a formal code dealing with the Negro slave was promulgated. But this new code, as recognized by the preamble itself, is merely a summary of the ancient and traditional law. Saco says of it that it merely repeats in amplified form "our ancient laws," and the practice recommended is "very usual in our dominions of the Indies."

This body of law, containing the legal tradition of the Spanish people and also influenced by the Catholic doctrine of the equality of all men in the sight of God, was biased in favor of freedom and opened the gates to manumission when slavery was transferred to the New World. The law in Spanish and Portuguese America facilitated manumission, the tax-gatherer did not oppose it, and the church ranked it among the works singularly agreeable to God. A hundred social devices narrowed the gap between bondage and liberty, encouraged the master to release his slave, and the bondsman to achieve freedom on his own account. From the sixteenth to the nineteenth century, slaves in Brazil, by reimbursing the original purchase price, could compel their masters to free them. In Cuba and in Mexico the price might be fixed at the request of the Negro, and the slave was freed even if he cost "triple of the sum." The right to have his price declared aided the Negro in seeking a new master, and the owner was required to transfer him to another.

The law further permitted the slave to free himself by installments, and this became a widely spread custom, especially in Cuba. A slave worth six hundred dollars could buy himself out in twenty-four installments of twenty-five dollars each, and with every payment he acquired one twenty-fourth of his own freedom. Thus, when he had paid fifty dollars, he owned one twelfth of himself. On delivering his first installment, he could move from his master's house, and thereafter pay interest on the remaining sum, thus acquiring a position not materially different in effect from that of a man in debt who had specific monetary obligations. There seem to have been many instances of slaves paying out all of the installments due on their purchase price except the last fifty or one hundred dollars, and on these paying one half a real per day for every fifty pesos. The advantage in this arrangement apparently lay in the fact that a Negro, thus partially a slave, could escape the payment of taxes on his property and be free from military service.

In effect, slavery under both law and custom had, for all practical purposes, become a contractual arrangement between the master and his bondsman. There may have been no written contract between the two parties, but the state behaved, in effect, as if such a contract did exist, and used its powers to enforce it. This presumed contract was of a strictly limited liability on the part of the slave, and the state, by employing the officially provided protector of slaves, could and did define the financial obligation of the slave to his master in each specific instance as it arose. Slavery had thus from a very early date, at least insofar as the practice was concerned, moved from a "status," or "caste," "by law of nature," or because of "innate inferiority," or because of the "just judgment and provision of holy script," to become a mere matter of an available sum of money for redemption. Slavery had become a matter of financial competence on the part of the slave, and by that fact lost a great part of the degrading imputation that attached to slavery where it was looked upon as evidence of moral or biological inferiority. Slavery could be wiped out by a fixed purchase price, and therefore the taint of slavery proved neither very deep nor indelible.

In addition to making freedom something obtainable for money, which the slave had the right to acquire and possess, the state made manumission possible for a number of other reasons. A Negro could be freed if unduly punished by his master. He was at liberty to marry a free non-slave (and the master could not legally interfere), and as under the law the children followed the mother, a slave's children born of a free mother were also free. Slaves in Brazil who joined the army to fight in the Paraguayan war were freed by decree on November 6, 1866, and some twenty thousand Negroes were thus liberated.

In the wars of independence many thousands of slaves in Venezuela and Colombia were freed by Bolívar and enlisted in the army of liberation. In Argentina perhaps as many as a third of San Martín's host that crossed the Andes was composed of freed Negroes. And, finally, as early as 1733, by a special *cedula* repeated twice later, slaves escaping to Cuba from other West Indian islands because they wished to embrace the Catholic religion could be neither returned to their masters, nor sold, nor given in slavery to any other person.

But significant and varied as were these provisions of the law in the Spanish and Portuguese colonies, they were less important in the long run than the social arrangements and expectancies that prevailed. It was permissible for a slave child in Brazil to be freed at the baptismal font by an offer of twenty milreis, and in Cuba for twenty-five dollars. A female slave could seek a godfather for her baby in some respectable person, hoping that the moral obligation imposed upon the godfather would lead to freeing the child. It was both a meritorious and a pious deed to accept such a responsibility and to fulfill its implicit commitments, and it bestowed distinction upon him who accepted them. In the mining regions of Minas Geraes a slave who found a seventeen and a half carat diamond was crowned with a floral wreath, dressed in a white suit, carried on the shoulders of fellow slaves to the presence of his master, and freed and allowed to work for himself. A parent having ten children could claim freedom, whether male or female.

The freeing of one's slaves was an honorific tradition, and men fulfilled it on numerous occasions. Favorite wet nurses were often freed; slaves were manumitted on happy occasions in the family—a birth of a first son, or the marriage of one of the master's children. In fact, the excuses and the occasions were numerous—the passing of an examination in school by the young master, a family festival, a national holiday, and, of course, by will upon the death of the master. A cataloguing of the occasions for manumission in such a country as Brazil might almost lead to wonder at the persistence of slavery; but as I have pointed out above, the importations of slaves were large and continuous in Brazil all through the colonial period and late into the nineteenth century.

Opportunities for escape from slavery were further facilitated by the system of labor that prevailed in many places, particularly in cities. Slaves were often encouraged to hire themselves out and bring their masters a fixed part of their wages, keeping the rest.

Skilled artisans, masons, carpenters, blacksmiths, wheelwrights, tailors, and musicians were special gainers from the arrangement. But even ordinary laborers were allowed to organize themselves in gangs, *gente de Ganho,* as they were called. . . .

With all its cruelty, abuse, hardship, and inhumanity, the atmosphere in Brazil and in the Spanish-American countries made for manumission. Even in the rural regions individuals were allowed to sell the products from their own plots, given them to work for themselves, and to save their money toward the day of freedom. In Cuba, one writer notes, the raising of pigs by slaves provided a ready source of the sums accumulated for such a purpose. It should be further noticed that, in addition to their Sundays, the Negroes in Brazil had many holidays, amounting all together to eighty-four days a year, which they could use for their own purposes, and for garnering such funds as their immediate skill and opportunities made possible. The purchase of one's freedom was so accepted a tradition among the Negroes that many a Negro bought the freedom of his wife and children while he himself continued laboring as a slave, and among the freed Negroes societies were organized for pooling resources and collecting funds for the freeing of their brethren still in bondage.

These many provisions favoring manumission were strongly influenced by the church. Without interfering with the institution of slavery where the domestic law accepted it, the church early condemned the slave trade and prohibited Catholics from taking part in it. The prohibition was not effective, though it in some measure may have influenced the Spaniards to a rather limited participation in the trade as such. . . . More important in the long run than the condemnation of the slave trade proved the church's insistence that slave and master were equal in the sight of God. Whatever the formal relations between slave and master, they must both recognize their relationship to each other as moral human beings and as brothers in Christ. The master had an obligation to protect the spiritual integrity of the slave, to teach him the Christian religion, to help him achieve the privileges of the sacraments, to guide him into living a good life, and to protect him from mortal sin. The slave had a right to become a Christian, to be baptized, and to be considered a member of the Christian community. Baptism was considered his entrance into the community, and until he was sufficiently instructed to be able to receive it, he was looked upon as out of the community and as something less than human.

From the very beginning the Catholic churches in America insisted that masters bring their slaves to church to learn the doctrine and participate in the communion. The assembled bishops in Mexico in the year 1555 urged all Spaniards to send the Indians, and especially the Negroes, to church; similarly in Cuba in 1680.

In fact, Negroes were baptized in Angola before leaving for their Atlantic journey to Brazil. Upon arrival they were instructed in the doctrine, and as evidence of their baptism carried about their necks a mark of the royal crown. As a Catholic the slave was married in the church, and the banns were regularly published. It gave the slave's family a moral and religious character unknown in other American slave systems. It became part of the ordinary routine on the slave plantations for the master and slaves to attend church on Sundays, and regularly before retiring at night the slaves gathered before the master's house to receive his blessings. If married by the church, they could not be separated by the master. Religious fraternities sprang up among the slaves. These were often influential and honorific institutions, with regularly elected officers, and funds for the celebration of religious holidays subscribed to by the slaves out of their own meager savings. In Brazil the slaves adopted the Lady of the Rosary as their own special patroness, sometimes painting her black. In a measure these religious fraternities emulated those of the whites, if they did not compete with them, and the slaves found a source of pride in becoming members, and honor in serving one of these religious fraternities as an official.

4.
PATTERNS OF RACE IN THE AMERICAS

MARVIN HARRIS

> Marvin Harris is a leading cultural anthropologist who has
> done a series of important studies on race and economic
> class in the Brazilian northeast. Along with Charles Wagley
> and other anthropologists he engaged in a major UNESCO
> study on class and caste in rural Brazil. This selection comes
> from his important general summary book, which was writ-
> ten in the early 1960s.

At one point, and one point only, is there a demonstrable correlation between the laws and behavior, the ideal and the actual, in
Tannenbaum's theory; the Spanish and Portuguese codes ideally drew
no distinction between the ex-slave and the citizen, and actual behavior followed suit. The large hybrid populations of Latin America
were not discriminated against *solely* because they were descended
from slaves; it is definitely verifiable that all hybrids were not and
are not forced back into a sharply separated Negro group by application of a rule of descent. This was true during slavery and it
was true after slavery. With abolition, because a continuous color
spectrum of free men had already existed for at least 200 years, ex-
slaves and descendants of slaves were not pitted against whites in the
bitter struggle which marks the career of our own Jim Crow.

However, to argue that it was the Spanish and Portuguese slave codes and slave traditions which gave rise to these real and substantial differences in the treatment of the free Negro and mulatto is to miss the essential point about the evolution of the New World plantation systems. If traditional laws and values were alone necessary to get the planters to manumit their slaves, and treat free colored people like human beings, the precedents among the English colonists were surely greater than among the Latins.

If anything, the laws and traditions of England conspired to make its colonists abhor anything that smacked of slavery. And so it was in England that in 1705 Chief Justice Holt could say, "As soon as a Negro comes into England he becomes free." Let it not be forgotten that five of the original thirteen states—New Hampshire, Massachusetts, Connecticut, Rhode Island and Pennsylvania, plus the independent state of Vermont—began programs of complete emancipation before the federal Constitutional Convention met in 1787. Partial anti-slavery measures were enacted by New York in 1788, and total emancipation in 1799, while New Jersey began to pass anti-slavery legislation in 1786. Furthermore, all of the original states which abolished slavery lived up to the declared principles of the Declaration of Independence and the Constitution to a remarkable degree in their treatment of emancipated slaves. . . .

We see, therefore, that if past laws and values had a significant role to play in the treatment of Negroes and mulattoes, the hounding persecution of the free Negroes and mulattoes should never have occurred in the English colonies. For contrary to the oft-repeated assertion that there was no matrix of English law or tradition into which the slave could fit, it is quite obvious that very specific laws and traditions existed to guide the Anglo-Saxon colonists. These laws and traditions held that all men had natural rights, that the Negroes were men and that slaves ought to become citizens. That the Constitution asserts "all men are created equal" is not some monstrous hypocrisy perpetrated by the founding fathers. It was an expression of a general Northern and enlightened Southern belief that slavery was an institution which was incompatible with the laws and traditions of civilized Englishmen. That the American versions of these laws were later subverted by court decisions and that the Constitution's guarantee of freedom and equality became a grim joke is surely ample testimony to the futility of trying to understand socio-cultural evolution in terms of such factors.

Understanding of the differences in the status of free "non-whites" in the plantation world can only emerge when one forthrightly inquires why a system which blurred the distinction between Negro and white was materially advantageous to one set of planters, while it was the opposite to another. One can be certain that if it had been materially disadvantageous to the Latin colonists, it would never have been tolerated—Romans, *Siete Partidas* and the Catholic Church notwithstanding. For one thing is clear, the slavocracy in both the Latin and Anglo-Saxon colonies held the whip hand not only over the slaves but over the agents of civil and ecclesiastical authority. To make second-class citizens out of all descendants of slaves was surely no greater task, given sufficient material reason, than to make slaves out of men and brutes out of slaves.

Although the slave plantation per se was remarkably similar in its effects regardless of the cultural background of the slaves or slave-owners, the natural, demographic and institutional environment with which slavery articulated and interacted was by no means uniform. It is the obligation of all those who wish to explain the difference between United States and Latin American race relations to examine these material conditions first, before concluding that it was the mystique of the Portuguese or Spanish soul that made the difference.

The first important consideration is demographic. Latin America and the United States experienced totally different patterns of settlement. When Spain and Portugal began their occupation of the New World, they were harassed by severe domestic manpower shortages, which made it extremely difficult for them to find colonists for their far-flung empires. Furthermore, in the New World the conditions under which such colonists were to settle were themselves antithetical to large-scale emigration. In the highlands a dense aboriginal population was already utilizing most of the arable land under the tutelage of the *encomenderos* and *hacendados*. In the lowlands large-scale emigration, supposing there had been a sufficient number of potential settlers, was obstructed by the monopolization of the best coastal lands by the slave-owning sugar planters. Only a handful of Portuguese migrated to Brazil during the sixteenth century. In the seventeenth century, a deliberate policy of *restricting* emigration to Brazil was pursued, out of fear that Portugal was being depopulated. Cried the Jesuit father Antonio Vieira, "Where are our men? Upon every alarm in Alentejo it is necessary to take students from the university, tradesmen from their shops, laborers from the plough!"

The migrations of Englishmen and Britishers to the New World followed an entirely different rhythm. Although the movement began almost a century later, it quickly achieved a magnitude that was to have no parallel in Latin America until the end of the nineteenth century. Between 1509 and 1709 only 150,000 people emigrated from Spain to the entire New World, but between 1600 and 1700, 500,000 English and Britishers moved to the North American territories. . . .

For almost one hundred years, white indentured servants were the principal source of manpower in the Anglo-Saxon colonies. Black slave manpower was a relatively late introduction. The case of Virginia would seem to be the most important and most instructive. In 1624, there were only 22 Negroes in Virginia (at a time when several thousand a year were already pouring into Recife and Bahia). In 1640, they had not increased to more than 150. Nine years later, when Virginia was inhabited by 15,000 whites, there were still only 300 Negroes. It was not until 1670 that Negroes reached 5 per cent of the population. After 1680 slaves began to arrive in increasing numbers, yet it was not until the second quarter of the eighteenth century that they exceeded 25 per cent of the population.

In 1715 the population of all the colonies with the exception of South Carolina was overwhelmingly composed of a white yeomanry, ex-indentured servants and wage earners. . . . Against a total white population of 375,000, there were less than 60,000 slaves in all of the colonies. If we consider the four Southern colonies—Maryland, Virginia, North Carolina and South Carolina—the ratio was still almost 3 to 1 in favor of the whites.

At about the same time, the total population of Brazil is estimated to have been 300,000, of whom only 100,000 were of European origin. In other words, the ratio of whites to non-whites was the exact opposite of what it was in the United States. A century later (1819) in Brazil, this ratio in favor of non-whites had climbed even higher, for out of an estimated total of 3,618,000 Brazilians, only 834,000 or less than 20 per cent were white. At approximately the same time in the United States (1820), 7,866,797, or more than 80 per cent of the people, out of a total population of 9,638,453 were whites. Although the Negro population was at this time overwhelmingly concentrated in the South, Negroes at no point constituted more than 38 per cent of the population of the Southern states. The high point was reached in 1840; thereafter, the proportion declined steadily until by 1940 it had fallen below 25 per cent in the South and below 10 per cent for the country as a whole.

Clearly, one of the reasons why the colonial population of Brazil shows such a preponderance of non-whites during colonial times is that a large part of the population increase resulted not from inmigration but from miscegenation and the natural increase of the European-Negroid-Amerindian crosses. Thus, in 1819, there were almost as many mestizos, free and slave, as there were whites, and by 1870, there were more "mixed bloods" than whites. This situation reversed itself toward the end of the nineteenth century after the first great wave of European immigrants had begun to flood São Paulo and the Brazilian south. According to the 1890 census, there were 6,302,198 whites, 4,638,495 mixed types and 2,097,426 Negroes. This "whitening" trend has continued until the present day, when whites number about 62 per cent of the population, mixed types 27 per cent and Negroes 11 per cent. These figures, of course, should be read with an understanding that many persons classed as "whites" are actually "mixed" in conformity with what has previously been said about the inherent ambiguity of racial classification in Brazil. . . .

But the ratio of whites to free colored is indeed astonishing, especially if one admits that many of the "whites" quite probably had non-white grandparents. The central question, therefore, is, why did the Brazilian whites permit themselves to become outnumbered by free half-castes? Several factors, none of them related to alleged special features of the Portuguese national character, readily present themselves.

In the first instance, given the chronic labor shortage in sixteenth-century Portugal and the small number of people who migrated to Brazil, the white slave-owners had no choice but to create a class of free half-castes. The reason for this is not that there was a shortage of white women, nor that Portuguese men were fatally attracted to dark females. These hoary sex fantasies explain nothing, since there is no reason why the sexual exploitation of Amerindian and Negro females had necessarily to lead to a *free* class of hybrids. The most probable explanation is that the whites had no choice in the matter. They were compelled to create an intermediate free group of half-castes to stand between them and the slaves because there were certain essential economic and military functions for which slave labor was useless, and for which no whites were available.

One of these functions was that of clearing the Indians from the sugar coast; another was the capture of Indian slaves; a third was the overseeing of Negro slaves; and a fourth was the tracking down of fugitives. The half-caste nature of most of the Indian-fighters and slave-catchers is an indubitable fact of Brazilian history. Indian-Portuguese *mamelucos* were called upon to defend Bahia and other cities against the Indians, and the hordes of people who were constantly engaged in destroying the *quilombos,* including Palmares, were also half-castes. . . .

Who then were the food growers of colonial Brazil? Who supplied Bahia, Recife and Rio with food? Although documentary proof is lacking, it would be most surprising if the bulk of the small farmer class did not consist of aged and infirm manumitted slaves, and favorite Negro concubines who with their mulatto offspring had been set up with a bit of marginal land. There was no one to object in Brazil, if after eight years of lash-driven labor, a broken slave was set free and permitted to squat on some fringe of the plantation.

All those interstitial types of military and economic activities which in Brazil could only be initially filled by half-caste free men were performed in the United States by the Southern yeomanry. Because the influx of Africans and the appearance of mulattoes in the United States occurred only *after* a large, intermediate class of whites had already been established, there was in effect no place for the freed slave, be he mulatto or Negro, to go.

BIBLIOGRAPHIC SUGGESTIONS

Aside from the books from which the readings were selected, other major works on slavery and race relations in Latin America include:

DÍAZ SOLER, L. M. *Historia de la esclavitud negra en Puerto Rico, 1493–1890* (Madrid, 1953). This is the best study on Puerto Rican slavery, which contrasted in many important ways from the experience in neighboring Cuba.

FERNANDES, FLORESTAN. *The Negro in Brazilian Society* (New York: Columbia University Press, 1969). The major summary statement by the leader of the so-called São Paulo group of sociologists on race relations in southern Brazil. It forms a sharp contrast to the studies on the Northeast.

FREYRE, GILBERTO. *The Masters and the Slaves* (New York: Knopf, 1946) and *The Mansions and the Shanties* (New York: Knopf, 1963). The two masterpieces of the Brazilian social historian, they represent an important statement about the social, and above all cultural, history of slavery in the Northeast of Brazil.

KLEIN, HERBERT S. *Slavery in the Americas: A Comparative Study of Cuba and Virginia* (Chicago: Quadrangle Books, 1970). This is a detailed comparative analysis of two major centers of plantation slavery.

MÖRNER, MAGNUS. *Race Mixture in the History of Latin America* (Boston, 1967). An important survey of the whole problem of the mulatto and mestizo in colonial Latin American society.

ORTIZ, FERNANDO. *Hampa afro-cubana: los negros esclavos* (Havana, 1916) A classic study of Cuban slavery by the leading authority on the subject.

PIERSON, DONALD. *Negroes in Brazil, A Study of Race Contact at Bahia,* 2d ed. (Carbondale: Southern Illinois University Press, 1967). This is the classic 1930s study by a North American sociologist on the history and development of race relations in the northeastern city of Bahia.

WAGLEY, CHARLES, and MARVIN HARRIS. *Race and Class in Rural Brazil* (Paris, 1952). This is a major study on attitudes toward race relations in the interior towns of Brazil carried out under the auspices of UNESCO.

VI.
Getúlio Vargas and the Estado Nôvo, 1937-1945:
What Kind of Regime?

⚜ THOMAS SKIDMORE

The Revolution of 1930 marked a watershed in Brazilian history. An armed conspiracy in the wake of a presidential election placed a defeated candidate in the presidential palace. This break in constitutional succession resulted more from regional and factional rivalries than from any profound social pressures. During the subsequent five years, however, Brazil did undergo significant political change, veering sharply in the direction of a more activist and centralized regime. The power of local states was reduced as the economic, political, and military power of the federal government grew. The transformation was carried out in the name of economic necessity, although clothed in the promise of a return to a more authentic political liberalism. A new constitution was finally approved in 1934, thereby replacing the first Republican Constitution of 1891. Getúlio Vargas, the nondescript southern politician who had lost the presidential election of 1930 but had taken over the presidency in a coup, had subtly maneuvered himself into being elected (by the Constituent Assembly of 1933–1934) as the first president of the new constitutional government. His term was to expire in 1938, when a successor would be elected in a direct national election.

As Provisional President from 1930 to 1934, Vargas used

his decree power liberally to remold government institutions. He negotiated skillfully with leaders of state political machines, assembling a network of loyalties to his federal government. Ultimately, however, his power rested on the army, which had placed him in power in 1930. The new president proved attentive to the military's urgent demands for increased budgets and greater support against the state militias, whom the generals saw as a serious threat to federal power. It was the army that quelled the São Paulo revolt of 1932 and put down the Communist rebellion of 1935. By 1937 the state militias had been successfully neutralized by the buildup of federal forces.

In the economic sphere the Vargas government faced well-nigh insoluble problems, as did every other export-oriented economy during the Depression. Coffee continued to be the principal foreign exchange earner, but plummeting prices kept export earnings far below the levels needed to pay for Brazil's imports and foreign debt service. Expanded cotton exports took up some slack, but neither the "blocked mark" bilateral trade agreements with Nazi Germany nor aggressive marketing policies in North America could stop the slide toward unilateral suspension of dept payments in 1937.

This economic crisis was in part responsible for the coup staged by Vargas and the army in November 1937. Disturbed by the mounting tension generated by the campaign for the presidential election of January 1938, Vargas and his generals decided to end the pretense of liberal democracy and opt for authoritarian rule. Yet the change was not really abrupt. Civil liberties had been suspended almost continuously since the abortive Communist uprising of November 1935, and left-wing politicians had been constantly harassed and imprisoned. This growing suppression had been to the direct benefit of the right-wing *Integralistas,* whose colored uniforms, street parades, and paramilitary tactics strongly resembled European fascism. But soon after the coup Vargas turned against the *Integralistas* as well, disbanding their paramilitary "sporting clubs." Out of desperation they attempted a putsch in May 1938, but failed. In the ensuing repression the movement collapsed and its Führer, Plínio Salgado, fled into exile.

The ideologues of the new regime gave it the name of *Estado Nôvo* (or "New State"), borrowing the language of Portugal's Salazar. It was legitimized by a new constitution, arbitrarily issued by Vargas on the night of the coup. What was the nature of this new government? Was it a dictatorship? Was it Fascist? Whom did it favor? What did it accomplish? Was it a personalistic aberration or a logical development of historical forces?

The *Estado Nôvo* lasted eight years (1937–1945). Its legal justification, never very impeccable, disappeared before the regime's actual demise. Vargas and his cabinet justified the coup on the basis of their reading of the "emergency" facing the country. Yet the new constitution did set a six-year deadline for a plebiscite to decide on the fate of the government and the president. The deadline came and went in 1943, with Vargas declaring that special conditions of wartime made such a vote impractical. Thus the last two years of the *Estado Nôvo* were *de facto* extralegal by the government's own definition.

This dubious legal basis did not cause much concern. The open political system of the mid-1930s had resulted in such fierce battles, including street fighting and armed revolt, that the propertied classes (including both landowners and the urban middle sectors) appeared ready to accept authoritarian rule if it would protect them from popular mobilization on the left. Vargas furnished that protection.

The *Estado Nôvo* was not, however, a simple reactionary regime. Vargas represented that part of the elite which believed it necessary to "preempt" the potentially unpleasant consequences of modernization by creating a strong state capable of controlling social conflict while preserving the essential patterns of landownership and commercial privilege. The model chosen for this "preemptive" social policy was corporatism, then popular among European right-wing authoritarian governments. The essence of corporatism was the creation of a state-supervised network of associations to represent every profession and industry, with parallel organizations of employers and employees. The existence of these economically based associations thereby eliminated the need for direct elections on the liberal democratic model.

The creation of such a corporatist structure had begun earlier (the Constituent Assembly of 1933 included representatives of professions) but was greatly accelerated during the *Estado Nôvo*. Urban employees were almost fully organized under the aegis of the labor law codification of 1943, which specified compulsory dues payment, a minimum wage, and exclusive representation rights for the government-recognized union. It also outlawed strikes, requiring that all disputes be subject to compulsory arbitration of government-supervised labor tribunals. Employers' associations were also created, but they lacked the comprehensiveness of the workers' syndicates. They also competed with the previously founded commercial associations, which continued a parallel existence, whereas the old labor unions, often dominated by the Communists or anarchists, had already been transformed at the hands of Vargas's Labor Ministry soon after the Revolution of 1930.

The government of the *Estado Nôvo* also undertook an expansion of the ambitious social welfare system begun by the federal government in the early 1930s. Government-sponsored pension funds were established for virtually every sector of urban worker, often extending to other benefits such as medical care, housing, and recreational facilities. Although financed by deductions from the workers' paychecks, these services helped to undercut the rationale for any independent labor movement. Benefits came from government initiative, rather than from the painful struggles of a mobilized movement.

State intervention also benefited the employers. They were relieved of the fear of strikes, while compulsory arbitration usually worked to their advantage. Equally important, the *Estado Nôvo* moved to protect landowners and industrialists from the vicissitudes of the market. Surplus coffee harvests were purchased with federal funds, and government-sponsored marketing agreements guaranteed profits for pine and sugar producers. Industrialists such as Roberto Simonsen complained that the government did too little to promote industrialization, but the war-induced shortages soon gave Brazilian industry a protected market. A large stride toward industrialization was made when Vargas's diplomacy extracted a U.S. loan for a mixed public-private steel plant in return for American use of the strategically important air and naval bases on the northeastern coast.

The *Estado Nôvo* was directly affected by Brazil's response to the widening world war. Before 1941 the army high command had shown sympathy for Germany. Generals Dutra and Góes Monteiro made no secret of their admiration for Nazi military prowess, while the Germans had looked upon Brazil as an important trading partner in the mid-1930s, when the operation of the "blocked mark" system boosted German-Brazilian commerce sharply. When Vargas sought foreign financing for Brazil's first steel plant, he was approached by Krupp before finally opting for a U.S. Export-Import Bank loan in 1941. In 1942, however, Brazil joined the Allies, from whom it had far more to gain than from the Axis.

By opting for the Allies, Brazil was repeating its policy in World War I, when it was the only major Latin American country to contribute combat forces. A squadron of fighter planes and a division of infantry went to Europe, where they fought alongside American forces. This experience greatly influenced the Brazilian military, who developed a strong tie with their North American counterparts. American influence, direct and indirect, grew within the Brazilian officer ranks, forming the basis for the intimate liaison of the postwar era.

The fate of the *Estado Nôvo* was closely linked to the progress of the war. Vargas had postponed the constitutionally required plebiscite of 1943 because of the wartime emergency. As the Allies moved toward final victory in early 1945, that excuse grew weaker. In February the press censorship began to lift, and in late May the censorship bureau

(DIP) was closed and a December date was set for general elections, including the direct election of a new president. At this point the president's intentions became the center of intense speculation. Getúlio endorsed a swing to the left in policy just as the political system was reopening. In August 1945 his justice minister, Agamemnon Magalhães, issued an antitrust decree aimed at controlling large economic interests, especially foreign. It produced angry cries of protest from foreign capitalists and the American Embassy. Furthermore, Getúlio tacitly encouraged a popular movement demanding that he cancel the presidential election and preside over a constituent assembly. The movement was closely linked to the Brazilian Communist party, then emerging from ten years of suppression. Speculation about Vargas's sympathy toward the left was reinforced by his release of Communist leader Luís Carlos Prestes, who had been jailed since 1936.

In the midst of wild rumors about the government's intentions, old-style liberal politicians grew certain that their archenemy was planning another coup. Once again, as in the 1937 presidential campaign, they would lose their chance at power. Now, however, they had the military on their side. Vargas could no longer count on the conservative generals to underwrite his maneuvers, especially as he veered toward a left nationalist policy and tacitly encouraged a mass mobilization movement. When Vargas appointed his brother as police chief of Rio de Janeiro, the senior military commanders decided to heed the warnings of the alarmists. The president was preemptorily informed by the military that he must abdicate the presidency. After a brief play for time, he acceded on October 29, 1945.

The elections were held in early December, signaling an apparent return to the liberal, pluralistic, constitutional federal system that had preceded the *Estado Nôvo*. Regular elections became the norm at every level. The new Constitution of 1946 dispersed powers within the federal sphere, while returning some power to the states. Yet the corporatist structure was hardly touched. The labor syndicates and employers' associations remained the backbone of representation in the economic sector. And the inheritors of the newly democratized regime showed the lasting influence of the *Estado Nôvo*. Two of the new parties that emerged in 1945 were direct products of the dictatorship—the PSD (*Partido Social Democrático*), controlled largely by the regional political bosses, and the PTB (*Partido Trabalhista Brasileiro*), which was Vargas's first step toward organizing the urban workers into a separate party. The third principal party, the UDN (*União Democrático Nacional*), was led by Vargas's longtime enemies of the right and center, who represented the liberal constitutional traditions snuffed out by the coup of 1937. The new president was General Dutra, a colorless officer of strong anti-Communist persuasion who had helped guarantee military support to Vargas throughout the dictatorship.

The political face-lifting of 1945–1946 left much of the *Estado Nôvo* intact. Within a new liberal democratic framework, the corporatist administrative state continued. While preserving many of the institutions created by the "preemptive" social policy, Brazil was ready for an experiment in democracy, which later included Vargas's return as an elected president (1951–1954).

VARGAS DEFENDS THE *ESTADO NÔVO*

On the night of the coup of November 10, 1937, Vargas broadcast an explanation to the Brazilian people (document 1). It was an uncompromising defense of the need for "emergency" measures to defend the nation against extremist ideological movements and divisive regionalist politicians. By the former were meant the remnants of the left-wing *Aliança Nacional Libertadora* (outlawed since July 1935) and, on the right, the burgeoning *Integralista* movement. By the threat of regional "caudillos," Vargas meant powerful state leaders such as Flores da Cunha of Rio Grande do Sul, who had backed the candidacy of Armando de Salles of São Paulo in the presidential campaign then under way. The coup of November 10 was only possible because of support from the military, as Vargas makes clear in document 2, which is taken from one of his speeches in mid-1938. The president is also remarkably frank in describing what the military was getting in return for its support.

1. Radio Broadcast of November 10, 1937

❖ Getúlio Vargas

During its legal phase, the Government, which grew out of a national revolutionary movement and was maintained by the legitimate power of the nation, continued its task of economic and financial reconstruction. Faithful to the rules of the established system, it sought to avoid political rivalries and to create a calm and confident atmosphere which would aid the development of democratic institutions.

While following that policy in the strictly political realm, it labored to pursue social justice, a goal to which it had been committed from the beginning. Without controversy it launched a program capable of satisfying the justifiable claims of the working classes, laying stress on the elementary guarantees of stability and economic security, without which the individual cannot become useful to society nor share in the benefits of civilization.

In contrast to the Government's actions, always inspired by the constructive impulse that underlays all its activities, the political groups continued to rely on mere electoral promises.

Both the old and the new parties, the latter being the old parties reorganized with new labels, lacked any ideological significance. They lived in the shadow of personal ambition and local domination, serving groups engrossed in dividing up the spoils and making opportunistic alliances for petty ends. . . .

Universal suffrage has thus become an instrument for the audacious and a mask barely disguising a conspiracy to satisfy personal and collective appetites. As a result, Government decisions are influenced not by an organized national economy, but by private economic forces that have insinuated their way into power which they then exploit to the detriment of society's legitimate interests.

From Getúlio Vargas, *A Nova Política do Brasil* (Rio de Janeiro: José Olympio, 1938), V, pp. 19–32. My translation—TS.

When parties use the extension of constitutional liberties and similar demands to pursue merely political objectives, their agitation touches only the surface of social life without disrupting the activities of labor or production. Today, however, when the state's influence and control over the economy is increasing, political competition is directed toward the control of economic forces. The threat of civil war, which constantly confronts governments dependent upon party alignments, is replaced by the incomparably graver threat of class warfare.

In such circumstances the Government loses its capacity to resist and the peaceful battle of the ballot box moves to the arena of aggressive confrontation and armed conflict.

We are approaching that perilous situation. The failure of the traditional political system to respond and the parties' degeneration into feuding classes are factors that inevitably pose the political problem in terms of violence and social warfare, not in terms of democracy.

In some states electoral preparations have been replaced by military preparations, raising for the nation the cost of the uncertainty and instability produced by divisive agitation. Regional caudillism, disguised as party organization, has been preparing to impose its will on the nation, thereby creating an obvious threat to national unity.

Meanwhile, all over the world there have emerged new party forms which by their very nature are inconsistent with democratic procedures. They present an immediate danger to our institutions and urgently require that the central authority be strengthened in proportion to the intensity of the conflicts. This was already evident at the time of the extremist coup of 1935, when the legislative authorities were compelled to amend the Constitution and institute a state of war. Continuing in force for more than a year, the state of war had to be reinstituted on request of the armed forces because of a Communist resurgence, which had been encouraged by the turbulent atmosphere of rallies and electoral competition.

An awareness of our responsibilities makes unmistakably clear our duty to restore national authority by ending this anomalous political existence which could lead to our disintegration as the final result of domination by local particularisms and the clash of irreconcilable forces.

The nation is caught between the menace of caudillos and the threats of deliberately aggressive parties. Although the nation can count on the patriotism of an absolute majority of Brazilians and the decisive and vigilant support of the armed forces, it does not have any effective legal means of defending itself. Normally it must resort to the exceptional measures that characterize a state of immediate risk to national sovereignty or from external aggression. Such is the truth, and it must be stated above any fears and evasions. . . .

If the political organism was to be readjusted to the country's economic requirements and if the indicated measures were definitely to be carried out, then there was no alternative to the steps which created a strong regime of peace, justice and work. When the instruments of government no longer correspond to a people's actual life conditions, there is no other solution than to change those instruments and establish other guidelines for action. . . .

Honored by the confidence of the armed forces and responding to the widespread appeals of my fellow citizens, I only agreed to forego my well-deserved rest and occupy my present position with the avowed purpose of continuing to serve the nation. . . .

When political rivalries threaten to degenerate into civil war, it indicates that the constitutional system has lost its practical value and become a mere abstraction. The country had arrived at exactly that point. Its complicated machinery of government no longer functioned. There were no appropriate organs that could transmit the nation's thoughts or carry out its wishes.

We shall restore the nation to its authority and freedom of action—restoring its authority by giving it the instruments of real and effective power which will enable it to overcome divisive influences, whether internal or external; restoring its freedom by opening a court of national judgment on the means and ends of the Government and allowing the nation to work out freely its history and destiny.

2. Getúlio Vargas Speaks to the Military on the Estado Nôvo and the Armed Forces

When I tell you that the [new] Military School is one of the most significant and characteristic accomplishments of the *Estado Nôvo,* I must also remind you that in little more than half a year the regime created last November 10 has been able to record a large number of accomplishments.

The *Estado Nôvo* reorganized the structure of Brazilian life. In the case of the Army, it promulgated all the basic laws and supplementary regulations that govern its existence. Throughout the country old barracks are being modernized and new ones constructed. Everywhere there is a maximum effort to meet the needs of the armed forces. Defense industries have been enlarged. Soon we shall be able to produce almost everything the Army needs to equip itself and to update its facilities. Anything not yet being produced by Brazilian industry has already been ordered abroad. Soon the Army will be prepared to meet every eventuality for the country's defense.

Our naval combat fleet is being equipped and modernized through orders placed abroad as part of the same national defense plan. In the meantime our shipyards and arsenals, with admirable enthusiasm, are producing and launching naval units which will help the Navy maintain its superb traditions and efficiently meet modern needs.

In the civilian realm the government has never neglected the continuous and productive task of restoring public finances, stimulating economic forces, and making plans for the construction of our basic industries. . . .

The armed forces have been and continue to be the only organized national force. In their profound civic consciousness and sense of patriotic resistance, they felt that the country could be saved only by resorting to the extreme recourse of reacting against a state of affairs that was leading us precipitously toward the loss of our national life, our independence, and our sovereignty.

From Getúlio Vargas, *A Nova Política do Brasil* (Rio de Janeiro: José Olympio, 1938), V, pp. 241–245. My translation—TS.

The *Estado Nôvo* was set up by you and your commitment has assured its continuation. A movement that enjoyed broad support among national public opinion and popular sectors created this government. It has sensed constantly growing support among the armed forces and has adopted as its highest priority their reequipment so that they can fulfill their great civic and moral mission.

A HOSTILE FOREIGN VIEW OF THE *ESTADO NÔVO*

> Foreign observers often disagreed about the nature of the *Estado Nôvo*. As might be expected, their interpretation usually reflected their own political views. Samuel Putnam was one of the most hostile critics. A literary historian and skilled translator who knew Brazil well, Putnam was at this time (1941) deeply influenced by the political position of the Communist party.

3. The Vargas Dictatorship in Brazil ⋄ Samuel Putnam

The question may now be put: what, precisely, is the character of the Vargas regime? Is it, or is it not, a fascist regime?

It would seem, to begin with, that there could be no doubt in anyone's mind on one point: that it is not, in any sense of the word, a "democracy," or even a constitutional "republic," but a dictatorship established and maintained by force. Yet, strangely enough, there are those who would make it appear that this dictatorship is itself the

From Samuel Putnam, "The Vargas Dictatorship in Brazil," *Science and Society,* V (Winter 1941), pp. 97–116, footnotes omitted. Reprinted by permission of the publisher.

form which Latin American democracy, frequently at least, assumes. . . .

The truth is, Vargas's supporters are not agreed among themselves as to the exact "ideological content" of the "New State," as is indicated by the numerous treatises on the subject with their conflicting points of view. Some see the *Estado Nôvo* as "authoritarian," others as a "corporate state" patterned after Mussolini's; but none would assert that it is a democracy, save in that sense which we have heard expounded by Vargas and Campos—and it is for North Americans to say if that is what democracy means to them.

The recent biography of Vargas by Andre Carrazzoni throws additional light on the dictator's views. As far back as 1919, in the provincial legislature of Rio Grande do Sul, he had declared: ". . . the European war demonstrates the ineptitude of parliaments, when it comes to resolving conflicts. In a period of great crises, superior individuals know how to give their imprint to the course of events, by dominating the anarchy of parliaments in place of being directed by them."

This might almost be described as a fascism before Mussolini. Even at this early date, Vargas seems to have had a contempt for what his biographer terms "the decrepit forms of parliamentary government" and for "the feline that sleeps in the collective soul." As Sr. Carrazzoni puts it, his subject "detests the idolatry of certain abstract expressions—People, Liberty, Democracy." The principles of liberalism are outmoded, not worth discussing, and the parliamentary state is an "amorphous entity."

So much for the political principles, or lack of principles, of Getúlio Vargas. At bottom it is clear that he is animated by one "principle": personal power; the seizure, maintenance, and consolidation of that power. His is an "anti-Machiavellism" that delights his doting biographer, as witness: "His policy: the shortest distance between two points is the careful suppression of all obstacles." Again, with reference to the events at the end of 1935: "Following the November uprising, he legally armed the state. After that he was in a position to speak softly, for the reason that, as old Theodore Roosevelt used to say, he carried a big stick."

If the early utterances of Vargas are carefully studied, it will be seen that, while he is in a way the typical Latin American "strong man" looking for a "revolution" to bring him to power, at the same time he exhibits certain attitudes which are distinctly of his era, the era which followed the first World War and which saw the rise of fascism in Europe. What those who would make him out to be an "old-fashioned dictator" fail to realize is that the character of his regime is not a matter of personal temperament or choice with the dictator, but is determined for him by the socio-economic and political forces of his age. In the age of imperialism, at an advanced stage of the general crisis of capitalism, the "old-fashioned strong man" dictatorship is not merely an anomaly, it is an impossibility in a semicolonial country with the vast wealth of Brazil. Such a dictatorship once set up, as that of Vargas was in 1930, must inevitably, amid the intense play of imperialist forces, find a finance-capital base and must eventually become a dictatorship of finance capital. The history of the Vargas regime surely goes to prove this. And what is the dictatorship of finance capital—the "open, terrorist dictatorship"—but *fascism?*

The difference between fascism in a country like Brazil and fascism in Germany, Italy, or Japan is that in the case of the semicolonial nation the finance capital which in reality exercises the dictatorship is not native but foreign. This leads to certain dissimilar features; and indeed . . . fascism is never the same in any two countries, anymore than democracy is, but takes on specific characteristics and exhibits local variations which are due to the concrete historical situation existing in the country in question. It is above all affected by the history and traditions of the people, their national aspirations and frustrations, and must take account of these in creating those "myths" or illusions by which it establishes and maintains itself in power.

In Latin America, ever since the days of Simón Bolívar, the Great Liberator, there has existed a constitutional-republican tradition, even though constitutions may have meant little enough in the past, even though they may have been, too often, little more than ornate bits of parchment; and it is worth noting that few "strong men," or dictators, have felt themselves sufficiently strong to be able to flout this tradition, but rather they have played upon these *constitutional illusions,* just as Hitler played upon the post-Versailles illusions of his people. We have seen Vargas doing this in his constitutions of 1934 and 1937, having his term "constitutionally" extended, as he all the time gathered more and more power into his own hands. And may it not be that we in the United States have something to learn in this regard from the coming of fascism to Brazil?

Another characteristic of semicolonial fascism, distinguishing it from that in a finance-capital country, is its essential instability. This is to be explained by the continuing conflict of rival imperialisms and the constant changes in their relative strength and strategic positions, in accordance with the law of the uneven development of capitalism. Such a fascism is that represented by the Vargas dictatorship. For the Vargas regime is fascism. It is an unstable and as yet unconsolidated fascism, but it is fascism, nonetheless. It is, moreover, a fascism that has been in good part established and supported by our own country, the United States.

A MODERATE FOREIGN VIEW

Another observer from the United States, Professor Karl Loewenstein, was less disturbed by the ideological character of the *Estado Nôvo*. Loewenstein was a refugee from central Europe who had seen continental fascism firsthand. This experience may in part explain his conclusion that the Vargas regime was a pragmatic and relatively mild authoritarian system.

4. Brazil Under Vargas ⟡ Karl Loewenstein

The regime has evolved no political theory of its own; as a matter of fact this is conspicuous by its absence. Even the most painstaking scrutiny of the many addresses and speeches of Vargas—under the wholly unwarranted assumption that they were not composed by "ghost" writers—will not yield a consistent political theory. They are pragmatic, opportunist, and in many parts, thoroughly sound. But Francisco Campos himself published in 1940 a volume *O Estado Nacional* which was widely advertised abroad as the Fascist credo of the regime. People in this country who have not read it denounced it as the Brazilian version of *Mein Kampf;* Brazilians who have read it, with their inborn sense of humor, shrug their shoulders; another literary prank of their versatile "Chico" Campos. On closer inspection, the volume, written with an unobtrusive though rather superficial erudition, is neither diabolic nor more Machiavellian than Brazilian political opportunism in general. It envisages implicitly the *Estado Nôvo* as the realization of the Brazilian application of Hegel's *Weltgeist.* Campos harbors admiration for the Italian "Hegelians" Federzoni and Gentile. Undeniably the book adopted a considerable number of Fascist slogans. It is thoroughly antiliberal and to a large degree also antidemocratic. But far from being an ideological blueprint for the future it is more an apology of sorts on behalf of the existing constitution, and an *ex post facto* commentary on his work; opportunistically it justifies all deviations from the customary rule of law under the constitutional state. In its violently sophistic diatribes against what is described as the "aberrations and perversions" of the *"democracia dos partidos"* and the inherent defects of the "Legislative State" it is an example of brilliant dialectics—and the Brazilians, by temperament and education, excel in that art. But the solutions are less Fascist than authoritarian; it does not extol violence nor does it indulge in state mysticism. Moreover, it is so legalistic in its entire approach that one easily understands why the volume completely failed to serve the purposes of a persuasive and dynamic ideology. Today it is rarely quoted and seems to be forgotten by intellectuals. Nor should the time of its publication—shortly after the outbreak of the war—be overlooked. Vargas himself, under the impression of the impending collapse of France, came out bluntly for Fascism in June 1940. This has not precluded him from being today our staunchest ally in South America. South of the Rio Grande politics are a merry-go-round.

Likewise the Fuehrer principle has not been introduced in Brazil. With its regimentation and automatism—both wholly alien to the liberal and individualistic temperament of the Brazilians—it is as much ridiculed as in this country. Nor have corporative ideas made much headway, though they may be congenial to the frame of mind of a Catholic land. The social philosophy of the Church in the Encyclicals *Quadragesimo anno* (1931) and *Divini Redemptoris*

(1937) are much referred to; but the regime evidently soft-pedals corporativism in the wise recognition of how unprepared the country is for its adoption. To build an "ideology" on racialism would be suicidal even for the Luso-Brazilian ruling class. If there is a country in the world to which the criteria of a "pure" race are inapplicable, it is Brazil. A reason why so many marriages on the highest social level remain childless, this writer was told, is the fear that some black or brown or otherwise colored grandmother would unexpectedly make her appearance.

The truth in the matter of "ideology" is that Brazil since 1930 has not gone through a genuine social revolution. What has happened and still is happening is accelerated social reform in the course of which political institutions are adjusting to changing economics. The process did not call for a new "ideology." And there is another aspect of which the foreigner may be wholly unaware unless Brazilian friends tell him who know. What emotional outlets a realistic and mature nation like the Brazilians may need—beyond expression in rather innocuous dialectics—takes refuge in the mystical undercurrents of social life, reflected in and serviced by Christian mythology as well as the half-pagan, African traditions. Under the surface of Westernized rationalism deep layers of folkloristic superstitions are submerged. Where they cannot be satisfied by what the Church has to offer they institutionalize themselves in the religious-mystical groups and societies of the *Macumba* to which even intellectuals pay dues as a matter of precaution. For the masses Catholicism has been blended with the aboriginal cults. They need no soporific in the form of an artificial political ideology. The men who lead Brazil, with their feet on the rich and mysterious Brazilian earth, know well enough that no spurious indoctrination would take root in it.

THE CREATION OF CORPORATIST INSTITUTIONS

One of the most permanent creations of the *Estado Nôvo* was the corporatist associational structure. Government-sponsored associations were set up for both employers and employees. The first selection that follows (document 5) is by Professor Philippe Schmitter, who has conducted extensive field research in Brazil. His study of the contemporary operation of this corporatist system included an examination of the origins of the system. Document 6, by the Brazilian scholar Lourdes Sola, explains the political effects of the labor union system, and document 7 is taken from one of Vargas's speeches explaining to the workers the rationale of corporatist social policy.

5. The Rationale of Corporatist Organization
⋄ Philippe C. Schmitter

From 1930 to 1937, the pattern of policy toward interest representation in particular and toward "the social question" in general went

Reprinted from *Interest Conflict and Political Change in Brazil* by Philippe C. Schmitter, pp. 111–112, 114–115, 124–126 (footnotes omitted), with the permission of the publishers, Stanford University Press. © 1971 by the Board of Trustees of the Leland Stanford Junior University.

through a period of experimental innovation and modification. From the *Estado Nôvo* coup of 1937 until 1943, it became increasingly consistent, culminating in the promulgation of the Consolidation of the Brazilian Labor Laws (CLT), the provisions of which continue to control the system of semiofficial interest representation. The corporatist ideologues of this period loudly insisted that all this innovation in welfare legislation was purely the paternalistic personal gift of a benevolent leader to whom all should be duly thankful. Recently, the truth of these claims has been increasingly questioned. Everardo Dias, a working-class militant of this early period, argues that almost all the so-called gifts of the Labor Code had already been won in earlier class struggles. Evaristo de Moraes Filho, Brazil's foremost contemporary labor lawyer, in reviewing the parliamentary debates and the work of the Parliamentary Commission on Social Legislation, concludes that it would be a historical injustice to accept the official line that the Revolution of 1930 entered an institutional vacuum. There was a tradition both of organized worker protest and of legislative concern. The new authoritarian regime merely continued, at first hesitantly, along preestablished lines.

There was, however, an important difference. Authority groups began self-consciously to implement a policy that might be called "preemptive co-optation." . . . This policy is an almost perfect example of . . . "artificial corporatism." The state sponsors, creates, and supports the emergence of representative associations before they can emerge by themselves, for the reason that structural differentiation has not yet proceeded far enough. Out of gratitude for this gesture of preemptive co-optation, "instead of acting as a negative force hostile to public authority [they] should become [in the words of Vargas] useful elements of cooperation with the ruling mechanism of the state." Artificial corporatism by means of preemptive co-optation requires: the creation of a set of legal norms governing the formation of representative associations; a set of rewards and punishments to reinforce the norms; sufficient authority to administer the rewards and punishments; and a set of institutionalized channels of representation that will provide at least a simulacrum of access ability. It took some years for artificial corporatism to become fully established, but its success is evidenced by its subsequent resistance to further modification. . . .

The *coup d'état* of 1937 and its "graciously granted" Constitution erased all ambiguity about future policy. Corporatism and unitary, controlled syndicalism were rigorously reinstated: "Professional and syndical association is free. However, only the syndicate regularly recognized by the state has the right to legally represent those who participate in any given category of production, to defend their rights before the state and other professional associations, to make collective contracts binding on all their members, to impose contributions and exercise functions delegated by public authority" [Article 138 of the Constitution]. In addition to a wide variety of other social provisions (including an article prohibiting strikes as "an antisocial recourse . . . contrary to the superior interests of national production"), the document outlined a vast scheme for professional and functional representation in policymaking through the syndicates, culminating in a Council of National Economy. This, like many of the Constitution's provisions, went unimplemented. In the succeeding years of direct authoritarian rule (the Constitution had abolished all parties and suspended the legislature), a veritable avalanche of decrees and administrative rules were promulgated concerning social and syndical matters. In 1943, these were consolidated in a Labor Code proudly proclaimed as the most advanced in the world. Although since 1943 the Labor Code has been enriched by an extensive jurisprudence and a considerable number of executive decrees and ministerial instructions, and although the application of its rules has been inconsistent, its major legal dispositions continue to be valid. . . .

It would seem . . . that the pattern of Vargas's interest group sponsorship was exclusively that of artificial corporation—that he sought to eliminate or chose to ignore preexisting, spontaneously created associations. For a short period, an attempt was made to eliminate nonconforming groups. . . . [A law was issued] in 1939 that would have fragmented or bypassed the Federation of Industries of the State of São Paulo. This same law also stated that "No act of professional defense will be permitted to an association not registered in the form laid out in this article, and none of its demands or representations will be recognized." In the declaration of intent prefacing the law, the motives of the Labor Ministry técnicos were clear: "With the institution of this registry, the entire life of the professional associations will gravitate around the Ministry of Labor; in it they will be born; with it they will grow; beside it they will develop; within it they will be extinguished." The private entities apparently reacted, and one year later, another decree was passed, this one allowing the President of the Republic to grant "to civic associations constituted for the defense and coordination of economic and occupational interests" the status of "consultative and technical organs." The first group to be so privileged was the Commercial Association of Rio. Many others followed. As a result of this policy of natural corporatism, a number of pro-Vargas leaders were elected to posts in these associations, and several of them gained permanent access to important government councils. It is also perhaps interesting to note than many of these private entities, such as the Commercial Association of Rio, the Brazilian Press Association, the Club of Engineers, and the Association of Commercial Employees, built their impressive *sêdes,* or headquarters, during this period. It was not always necessary to be a syndicate to benefit from the regime's largess.

The partisans of "authoritarian democracy," with their preoccupation with organizing the people (before, I might add, the people could organize themselves) and for integrating them into the state, admitted that "in Brazil, there is no climate for a single-party system." With "the multiple-party system dissolved and the single-party system not recommendable, there was only one alternative possible for the authoritarian state: to search for the sources of democracy in organized classes." This search for legitimation and information involved . . . tactics of both "artificial" and "natural" corporatism. But these efforts had to be supplemented by an attempt to link the co-opted entities to the state apparatus through which Vargas ruled. They had to be given at least a semblance of participation in decision-making. For this reason, "a considerable number of prelegislative, administrative, juridicial, and consultative institutions" were created with functional interest representatives from both semiofficial and private associations. In the Ministry of Labor, Industry, and Commerce, a vast number of permanent commissions, such as those governing *enquadramento* [the system of membership categories], the *impôsto sindical* [compulsory union dues], the *salário mínimo* [minimum wage], and social welfare, as well as ad hoc working groups, were established, usually with equal representation of workers and employers. The Labor Court system . . . was organized on a similar principle, as were the special Maritime Labor Delegations. The autarchic Retirement and Social Welfare Institutes for various categories of workers (IAPI, IAPM, IAPB, etc.) presently are governed by such tripartite councils.

Outside the Labor Ministry, a number of councils were established largely to treat economic problems generated by war conditions. These included the Coordination of Economic Mobilization, the Central Price Commission, the National Council of Industrial and Commercial Policy, the Textile Executive Commission, and many others. The most important of these was the Federal Council of Foreign Trade *(Conselho Federal de Comércio Exterior),* because it was instrumental in setting the guidelines of general economic policy. At the end of the war a National Economic Planning Commission was created with a very wide mandate to review and coordinate the adaptation of the economy to peacetime conditions. On all these councils sat representatives of interest associations, though in most cases the representatives were from employers' groups only. . . .

Another distinctive product of this period was the creation of autarchic institutes for the control of specific commodities. These include the Brazilian Coffee Institute (IBC), the National Institute of Pinewood (INP), the National Institute of Maté (INM), the Institute of Alcohol and Sugar (IAA), and the Brazilian Institute of Salt (IBS). Individual states also began to maintain functional institutes for such commodities as tobacco, cacao, lard, wine, rice, and meat. Other commodities like wheat, rubber, cotton, fish, and even manioc, have been regulated by administrative agencies that never developed into full-blown institutes. The provisions for interest representation to these bodies have varied. Some have only producers' representatives; others have workers' representatives as well. The more important (IBC, IAA, INP, for example) have, in addition to these, representatives from the governments of the states where the commodities are produced. They usually have virtually autonomous powers to set prices, wages, and quotas, distribute credit, and regulate foreign trade. Their respective revenues are also virtually autonomous, resting on an obligatory tax on production or exports. The producers accepted this degree of state penetration into their economic freedom partly because of the collapse of markets in the 1930's and partly out of fear of official reprisal; but they continued to cooperate mainly because they were granted ample subsidies and have been able to control policy-making in these autarchies. "At heart, our autarchic institutes . . . are really cartels, or obligatory employer organizations," [as described by Oliveira Vianna, one of Vargas's key advisers]. Thus it seems that Vargas, unable to co-opt the rural sector voluntarily through syndicalism, co-opted its more specialized employer elements through institutes and commissions. These became de jure administrative agencies, but remained de facto representative associations. The full impact of this policy of granting decisional and financial autonomy would be felt later, when, in the interests of industrialization, other authority groups would attempt to force these commodity clienteles, these feudalities, to conform to their more general objectives.

6. How Labor Was Organized   ⬦   Lourdes Sola

During this period legislation was passed placing relations between urban workers and laborers and employers under state control. The new regime also implemented an earlier policy initiated with the creation of the Ministry of Labor in 1931, headed by Lindolfo Collor. The difference was that now this system would be perfected and extended to include all occupational groups, and a new bureaucratic apparatus would be established, subordinate to that Ministry, and responsible for executing the measures written into law. Many of these provisions would actually be carried out only some time after their creation; such was the case of the minimum wage law, which first appeared in the 1937 Constitution, but did not become effective until 1940.

From Lourdes Sola, "O golpe de '37 e o Estado Nôvo," pp. 302–305, in *Brasil em perspective,* edited by Carlos Guilherme Mota. Copyright 1968 by Difusão Européia do Livro, São Paulo. My translation—TS. Used by permission of the publisher.

. . . The working class and business employees gained the following benefits during the Vargas regime: eight-hour workday; paid vacations; employment tenure; severance pay; collective labor contracts; labor regulations for women and minors; and the establishment of the Institutes of Pensions and Retirement Funds, which guaranteed assistance to those groups.

Continuing the trends of the previous period, the judicial system was consolidated in 1939; four new institutional cadres emerged, tied to the judiciary, hierarchically structured . . . and given the job of deciding conflicts between employers and employees. . . .

All of these legislative and administrative measures undoubtedly represented a certain degree of progress in the treatment of the "social question," since they did grant hitherto unheard of benefits to the workers.

This additional State intervention—which broke with the privatism until then characteristic of contracts and labor disputes—implied a greater control of the workers' political activity as well. This was not incidental; even before the *Estado Nôvo,* the government had sought to discipline and unite under its control the entire syndical movement. By making use of new methods, the new regime was able to fortify this position.

According to the Constitution of 1937, strikes and lockouts were declared illegal, as they were said to be "antisocial actions detrimental to work and capital, and incompatible with superior national interests." All ideological considerations were banned because they were "alien to the professional and economic interests of the workers."

The *Estado Nôvo* eliminated syndical autonomy once and for all in 1939 when the regime prohibited the existence of associations not integrated into the official system which basically provided for recognition of only one syndicate per profession on a district, municipal, state, and interstate basis. Only in exceptional cases, and with the express authorization of the Ministry of Labor, could there be national associations.

This corporative structure was strengthened by the introduction of the syndical tax which was the compulsory deduction of a sum equal to one day's wage per year, from all employees. These fees, channeled through the Ministry of Labor, were distributed among the syndicates. Now given a bureaucratic apparatus and a paid staff, the syndicates legally combined all the services of credit and consumer cooperatives, including legal aid and hospitalization benefits.

The syndical tax also served, however, to make the syndicates and their affiliates politically dependent upon the state. In order for labor leaders to obtain favors, they were forced to influence their constituents to follow the directives issuing from official policy.

The "benevolent despotism" of this entire structure made relations between workers and government rather paternalistic. The workers identified Getúlio Vargas with the government. In the first few years of the *Estado Nôvo,* this system had as its primary political goal the conquest—and simultaneously, control and discipline, of the working-class organizations. Only later, toward the end of the regime, was it used to mobilize "the masses," leading them to intervene actively in political struggles in favor of Vargas, and against the opposition.

The efficiency of these resources may be partly explained by the composition of the proletariat: a social "class" continually absorbing an influx of rural migrants, for whom urban life was synonymous with rising status and benefits acquired from labor legislation. But even more, the social and cultural differences between urban and rural life demanded of them and their families difficult adjustments which drained a good deal of their energies. There was neither the time nor the necessary political conditions for them to formulate autonomous demands and begin organizing on their own.

7. Vargas Speaks to the Workers

My government's labor policy has consistently sought to establish harmony among the factors of production, which is a basis for social equilibrium and is fundamental to human progress. We have avoided the errors of the liberal-individualist regime which legalized the strike as a conflict-solving device; we have also avoided the pitfalls of totalitarian states which institute slave labor.

From *Cultura Política,* Año II, No. 15 (May 1942), p. 100. My translation —TS. Used by permission of the publisher.

In our system, the State carries out the role of judge in relations between employees and employers. It sees that . . . clashes are avoided, excesses are corrected, and benefits are equitably distributed. Because of this, the government in turn has the right to expect your full support and cooperation. In this emergency situation, every man must do his job; at supreme moments, risks can't be considered, because it is "preferable to lose one's life than to lose one's reason for living."

WORKERS!

Before our regime, the date of May 1 meant anxiety, fear, and apprehension. Police squads were reinforced, troops were withdrawn to the barracks in anticipation of trouble. It was feared that the workers would take advantage of the day devoted to them to demand their rights.

But the National State attended to these just aspirations, and this date came to be celebrated with joy and brotherhood. . . . Soldiers of the armed forces, whose sacred mission is to maintain order and national harmony, joined with workers, soldiers of the constructive forces of our progress and grandeur.

After all, we are all soldiers in the service of Brazil, and it is our duty to face the challenge of the moment so that future generations will proudly remember us for never doubting for an instant the immortal destiny of the Brazilian Fatherland.

A NEWSPAPER EDITOR ATTACKS
CENSORSHIP

One feature of the *Estado Nôvo* was unmistakably authoritarian-press manipulation and censorship. A special federal agency (*Departmento da Imprensa e Propaganda,* or DIP) was charged with the responsibility of handling press relations and enforcing the government's strict press rules. In February 1945 government policy suddenly loosened, as Vargas began the apparent transition to constitutional processes. A flood of bitter criticism soon filled the press. Among the most outspoken critics was Costa Rego, editor of *Correio da Manhã,* a prestigious Rio de Janeiro daily. These editorials (selections 8, 9, and 10) by Costa Rego appeared in early March 1945, in the immediate wake of the relaxation of censorship.

8. DIP ⋄ Costa Rego

Although I've known many a style of censorship in my 39 years as editor, I've never gathered as many noteworthy memories as I have of the Fascist-inspired DIP. . . .

From *Correio da Manhã,* March 1, 1945. My translation—TS. Used by permission of the publisher.

. . . DIP, unabashedly a system of propaganda for propaganda's sake . . . subjected the press to many abuses, although it provided one service: it . . . showed the public for the first time . . . that the press could not be free; it could not even be accurate, because not only was its role as critic curtailed or distorted, and its publication of news items tightly controlled, but it was also obliged to insert tendentious material prepared at DIP.

According to Article 122, Paragraph 15, of the Constitution of 1934, no paper can refuse to insert government communiques. . . . At first we thought that this dictum referred to written communiques, or simple notes. But—it wasn't so . . . DIP would send us (and send us abundantly!) opinionated material which had to be published under the guise of editorials. Thoughts were expressed compulsorily. Pure Fascist methodology.

All of us working on newspapers had to stand for this humiliation. This explains why the press has forsaken the government today. But only the publishers, editors-in-chief, and editorial assistants know the full moral (or immoral) extent of DIP's role in what was called the New State, since they were the ones forced to receive daily (and verbally, since DIP never gave written orders) the dicta of Censorship. I have an awesome collection stored up in my memory, and I don't intend to keep them to myself for very long. . . .

When the DIP began operations in 1939, it wrote on certain doctrines of the Constitution decreed a short while before. These articles were, as a rule, poorly written. In all fairness to the honor of the Brazilian intelligentsia, let it be pointed out that the good writers never placed themselves at the service of DIP. But, aside from being badly written, these articles sinned from a kind of intentional ignorance.

One day, I had a rather daring article on hand, which praised the *Estado Nôvo* for having eliminated Parliament. I asked for a telephone connection with Dr. Lourival Fontes [head of DIP].

"Fontes," I said, "turn to Articles 38 to 63 of the Constitution of 1937. As you will note, all make references to the Legislative Power whose chambers are to be called 'National Parliament.' The *Estado Nôvo* did not do away with Parliament!" Dr. Fontes gave me the order not to have the article published.

When compared to other cases, this episode is inconsequential.

However, I have always considered it to be most representative of my extensive dealings with the Censorship of the *Estado Nôvo*.

I was vividly aware of the sheer nonsense of the propaganda flowing from the DIP; the insincerity and disinterest of its writers reduced to the level of mere advertising agents who were interpreting a regime with such indifference that they might just as well have been discussing the virtues of an ointment for corns.

Seven years of practicing these tricks did not kill the press; but it certainly poisoned and weakened the government. . . .

9. Plaster Cast ⋄ Costa Rego

. . . The public really knows nothing about the hardships wrought by Censorship; they think the only thing involved was the arrest of journalists and the closing of some papers. While these standard methods were sometimes used, a real gag was placed upon the press through the use of decree-laws.

Such was the case in the distribution of newsprint to the Press. Not only was this subject to tariff regulations, as determined by DIP, but the Department would also decide the amount of newsprint to be imported, and could suspend tax exemptions on imports at any moment. Without this latter benefit, the price of newsprint would be exorbitant for newspaper establishments; most papers could not survive beyond two or three months. Thus, journalists were even deprived of the ability to show courage through disobedience, for this would have been the death toll for their paper.

Not only was this a standard Fascist technique, but the practice was downright immoral and unfair. DIP would suspend exemptions only for those newspapers that displeased the government. The *Correio da Manhã* suffered this outrage eight years ago for 26 days because it had reported the appointment of Dr. Coriolano de Gois as Chief of Police in an "original" way, placing the official announce-

From *Correio da Manhã*, March 2, 1945. My translation—TS. Used by permission of the publisher.

ment directly beneath a commentary on the hardships of life. Other papers received the same punishment for reasons equally as valid. . . .

10. Rights of the Press ⟡ Costa Rego

DIP ceased to exist as a propaganda agency when censorship was added to its functions, because propaganda seeks to seduce and persuade while censorship cuts and repels. These two functions are mutually exclusive, and DIP absurdly sought to unite them. . . . Anticensorship, or the Press, emerged victorious from this conflict. . . .

. . . Getúlio Vargas's errors were compounded by censorship, because it kept him from finding out the state of public opinion. His good deeds were also hurt by propaganda, which, by exaggerating their proportions, made them subject to criticism and cynicism.

In the last analysis, censorship was irksome to the press, but it did not manage to strip away its authority, while propaganda, boundlessly praising a given man, wound up snuffing out his popularity. We may conclude that DIP actually had an abrasive effect within the government, and the government itself had to take precautions against it on occasion. . . .

Ever since President Epitácio Pessôa's regime [1919–1922], press laws have been generally useless, and will continue to be so, if the aura of censorship remains. . . . The Constitution of 1937 imposed the most radical limitations on the press; prior censorship was required of actions or facts which would "endanger peace, order and public security." DIP subjected literally everything to censorship.

. . . But men of good will are wont to change their minds according to their mood of the moment. Now even Góes Monteiro seems opposed to limitations on the press. . . .

From *Correio da Manhã,* March 7, 1945. My translation—TS. Used by permission of the publisher.

BUILDING THE DICTATOR'S IMAGE

Much of the propaganda issued during the *Estado Nôvo* was intended to glorify President Getúlio Vargas. The techniques could be varied, as the following examples make clear. Selection 11 is a radio broadcast praising Vargas's accomplishments on the occasion of his birthday. Selection 12 is an apology for press censorship published by the censorship agency, and selection 13 is a "human interest" story about the dictator's generosity which was undoubtedly planted by DIP in a Rio de Janeiro newspaper.

11. Getúlio Vargas and His Concept of Government
• Almir de Andrade

President Getúlio Vargas's government developed a form of political democracy which Brazilians have long cherished—not a liberal democracy, nor one which was merely on paper, but a democracy of work and action, of justice for all. . . .

From Almir de Andrade, "Getúlio Vargas and the Brazilian Doctrine of Government," *Cultura Política,* Año II, No. 15 (May 1942), pp. 8–9. My translation—TS. Used by permission of the publisher.

The current President showed us that it is possible and necessary to change the task of government from that of command and domination to that of serving the nation and its best interests. . . . The government is a public service, and like all others, should serve the people in the interest of their well-being, progress, and happiness.

This idea eliminates the former duality between the governors and the governed, and destroys the clash of interests between them. There are no longer any "ruled" or "governing" classes, because the people themselves serve as the government to express and fulfill their needs and aspirations. The government no longer imposes upon society the ideals and interests of the parties that elected it; it merely interprets and satisfies the objective interests which society dictates. Consequently, the government has no need for great shows of strength or elaborate fantasies to capture the sympathy of the public; its strength lies in the masses themselves. . . .

If the government is indeed a public service, which demands self-lessness, ability, and energy, group interests and privileges no longer influence the selection of members of the administration; government workers are chosen on their own merits. . . .

. . . A perfect example in this case comes from high up—the supreme ruler of the country. Our President is outstanding for his statesmanship, his tireless energy, conscientiousness, and constant concern for the common good. He is a living example of democracy —that democracy which characterizes the Brazilian political mind of today: democracy based on work and action, one in which everyone, from the Head of State down to the most humble clerk, cares only about the ways of best serving the nation for the prosperity, order, and social development of Brazil.

This is why this celebration of the birthday of President Getúlio Vargas is so important for all of us. When we celebrate it, we are actually celebrating a system of government and administration, inspired by a statesman and a shining example of personal conduct in the execution of public service—the most arduous and complex public service of them all: guiding the nation in the fulfillment of its objective needs, popular aspirations, and its place on the international scene.

12. How Vargas Interprets the Popular Will

Joracy Camargo

Getúlio Vargas became the most perfect Executive Power Brazil has ever had, for His Excellency learned how to orient national politics toward the popular will. . . .

. . . In his efforts to stimulate the growth of cultural and artistic groups by granting new benefits and means of support, Vargas actually brought about the development of the national intelligentsia. He opened new horizons and helped enable intellectuals to exercise their social and 'civilizing' functions. . . .

. . . The Press had traditionally been used by parties and individuals for their own private interests. Although always intelligent, the journalists were not always aware of their duties and responsibilities. Consequently, a free press came to disturb national life, exciting hatred and passions, and defending ambitious minorities and indefensible causes. Without control, irresponsibility was the rule, and disorder resulted to such a degree that censorship was actually requested.

. . . With the interests of the masses at heart, Vargas showed journalists what their true mission was. Aside from extensive state support to papers, which are, after all, the representatives of public opinion, he had the National Press Council join in improving living conditions for journalists. In addition, he enjoys personal contact with journalists in daily group meetings, and individuals visit his study every day. To him, journalists are the legitimate representatives of the popular will. . . . The journalists, in turn, go along with everything to make Brazil great. . . .

From Joracy Camargo, *Getúlio Vargas e a Inteligência Nacional,* p. 18. Copyright 1940 by DIP, Rio de Janeiro. My translation—TS. Used by permission of the author.

13. Getúlio Vargas Takes a Walk in Petropolis

While Getúlio Vargas was strolling through Petropolis one day, he was approached by a poor cripple who explained that his physical handicap had been caused by an accident at the textile factory where he formerly worked. [He added that] the small pension he received as compensation barely covered the costs of supporting his four children. He made an appeal to the head of state, in whose heart he placed all his hopes. His appeal was for a small wagon like those commonly used by cripples.

Comforting him with words of courage and faith, President Getúlio Vargas instructed him to go to Rio Negro Palace, where one of his secretaries would assist him; he would get the cart.

Antonio Raeshi, expressing his gratitude, prayed to God to protect and grant health to the head of the nation, from whom, he emphasized, the working classes and needy people had always received the greatest of favors. . . .

From *Correio da Manhã,* February 16, 1945. My translation—TS. Used by permission of the publisher.

BRAZIL AND CENSORSHIP

In late May 1945 the government abolished DIP and created a new Information Department that was instructed to avoid any censorship. Just before this important change, Frederico del Villar, the Italian-born Brazilian correspondent of the *Inter-American,* wrote a caustic article surveying DIP's operations.

14. Brazil and the Gag Men ✧ Frederico del Villar

If there is one quality the Brazilian DIP *(Departamento da Imprensa e Propaganda)* lacks above all others, it is a sense of humor. One of its first acts following its birth in the dreary days of November, 1939, was to clamp down on the gay and pointed wit so typical of Brazilians. Senator Macedo Soares' *Diário Carioca* commented that DIP was a good name for a French poodle, but not so good for a government agency. The paper was closed for twenty-four hours.

As DIP grew out of its swaddling clothes it became evident that

From Frederico del Villar, "Brazil and the Gag Men," *The Inter-American,* IV, No. 7 (July 1945), pp. 16–17; 44–45. Reprinted by permission of the publisher.

this hated agency, which for five years kept Brazil and the world from knowing the truth about the Vargas dictatorship, was to grow in power, self-importance, and fear of a good joke.

Conceived along the lines of Goebbels' organization in Germany, the agency was born out of wedlock from the union of the Police Censorship Division and the President's Secretariat of Propaganda. The head of the latter, Lourival Fontes, present Ambassador to Mexico, was appointed Chief of the new Department. The Army, which already controlled the Ministry of Transportation, the Post and Telegraph Department, the autonomous Central of Brazil Railways, the Police of the Federal District, and other key positions, strangely enough got nothing on the DIP deal.

Apparently Fontes was the DIP and the DIP was Fontes. At any rate, nothing new was created after Fontes was finally ousted by the Army. As long as it exists (early this year Vargas promised to disband it), the DIP machine will run on the well-oiled wheels and cogs so deftly assembled by its first director.

An obscure journalist until 1930, Fontes is a warm and open admirer of Mussolini's political theories and a devoted friend of Vargas'. "I am with the President until death," he told me recently. Having fought hard for Vargas' triumph in 1930, he was appointed presidential press secretary.

One of Fontes' first acts as DIP Director General was the suppression of all foreign language papers, a step directed exclusively against the few English language publications. The subsidized German and Japanese papers went on printing their stuff in Portuguese, keeping their readers, subscribers, and advertisers. Faced with the alternative of having to appear in Portuguese with strict censorship on pro-Allied news, Ralph B. Ross' unsubsidized, brilliant English language daily *News,* folded. With the *News* died the *Times of Brazil,* the *Brazilian American,* and a few others in Rio and São Paulo. . . .

A number of divisions help keep the DIP stranglehold on the country's thoughts and words. These are the divisions of Press, Radio, Theater and Motion Pictures, Propaganda, and Tourism. Every division except Press has its own director. All are under the supervision of the DIP's Director General, now Army Major Amilcar Dutra de Menezes.

Because the DIP was born in wartime, the activities of Tourism have been nil. Those of Propaganda are limited to distribution of a few posters of Vargas' "New State" and pictures of Vargas, "The Leader of the Nation." The other divisions are active, although the word "censorship" is carefully avoided.

By far the most important is the Press Division, which operates under the direct and personal control of Director General Dutra. It is divided into the "press control" (censorship) department, the *Agência Nacional,* and two official publications, the quarterly *Revista de Cultura Política* and the monthly *Brasil Reportagens.* The last is a picture magazine printing virtually nothing but photos of Vargas and the DIP's Director. It would be surprising if more than a thousand people in Brazil ever heard of these magazines.

The press control is run by a former Associated Press man, Sampaio Mitke. In older days his name was simply Sampaio. But after Germany's smashing victories of 1939–1940, he took to using the "Mitke," his mother's surname. . . .

Sampaio is the "grey eminence" of the DIP. Directors come and go, but he stays. Until lately one of his jobs was to call up newspapers and news agencies every day and issue verbal instructions. Nothing is ever put in writing at the DIP. Officially there is no such thing as censorship in Vargas' Brazil. Instructions usually were to ignore certain happenings, or comment on certain events from a certain angle, to praise Government measures and decisions, to give or not to give front page display to this or that development.

One permanent directive was never to headline news, military or otherwise, about Russia. This has probably gone overboard since establishment of relations between Brazil and the Soviet Union. For many months no news or editorial comment on Argentina could be printed without previous consultation with Sampaio. Of course any criticism of the Government or Government men was strictly forbidden.

The following episode is typical of DIP censorship. The 1937 Constitution creating Vargas' new State promised Brazil that a plebiscite would be held "as soon as possible" to accept or reject both Vargas and the new charter. The promise was never kept, and one of the DIP's first instructions was to forbid the use of the words "elections" and "plebiscite." About the same time Vargas finally found the courage to pay his first visit to São Paulo since the city's revolution of 1932. The usual "spontaneous" demonstrations took place, and on Vargas' return to Rio de Janeiro, São Paulo Interventor Adhemar de Barros declared to the press that the "reception given Vargas in São Paulo was more significant than any plebiscite."

At the time I was working for a French news agency which also supplied a domestic service. The dispatch with the Interventor's statement came across my desk. After some hesitation, as it wasn't my organization's policy to give Vargas unnecessary plugs, I put the thing out, quoting the Interventor.

That afternoon I was summoned to the telephone by Arnaldo Fabregas, Sampaio's predecessor as DIP censor, who asked me what I thought I was doing "disregarding the DIP's instructions." *Correio da Noite,* out earlier than the other evening papers, had front-paged the Interventor's statement. I told Fabregas that I didn't understand what it was all about, pointing out that the Interventor's statement was quite a compliment to Vargas.

"But the word 'plebiscite'," Fabregas yelled. "You cannot use the word 'plebiscite.' It may make people remember and give them ideas. . . ." The issue of *Correio da Noite* was seized. No other paper carried Adhemar de Barros' statement.

Brazilian papers had to obey or die. The first time a paper failed to comply with the DIP's directives, the editor would be summoned to Sampaio's office. If personally important, he would be called to the Director General's presence. He would be told in barrack-like terms where he stood, and usually ordered to print one of the DIP's tailor-made "editorials," generally expressing a viewpoint diametrically opposite to the paper's previous comment.

Second or more serious offenses would cause "previous censorship" on the paper or on one of its writers. That is, all material had to be okayed by DIP before publication. Writers subjected to previous censorship in the early part of 1945 included ex-Senator J. E. de Macedo Soares, publisher of *Diário Carioca;* ex-Senator Costa Rego, editor of *Correio da Manhã;* Ruben Braga, *Diário Carioca* columnist and now a war correspondent in Italy; Aparício Torelly, better known as the "Baron of Itararé," a columnist for *Diário de Notícias;* and several others. Previous censorship was imposed on Samuel Wainer's liberal weekly *Diretrizes* before the magazine was finally closed down. . . .

A more severe punishment was the appointment by the DIP of an interventor to take charge of the editorial staff of the paper. An interventor was placed in charge of all departments of *O Radical*—a labor paper which later joined the Vargas bandwagon—when it criticized a book by DIP Director Dutra.

A still more drastic punishment was cancellation of the privilege to import newsprint free of duty. This was a death sentence, since no Brazilian paper can survive for more than a few days or weeks without this privilege. One paper which survived forty days of this ban was Rio de Janeiro's leading morning paper, *Correio da Manhã*. Publisher Paulo Bettencourt had refused to express official indignation against Britain when a Brazilian ship was detained at Lisbon with a cargo of German-purchased weapons in 1941.

Outright suppression rarely occurred in the case of big dailies, but such fine papers as São Paulo's *O Estado* and *Correio Paulistano* were taken over by the Government and "incorporated in the National Patrimony." All of these measures were supplemented by a sword of Damocles ever hanging over a newspaperman's head in Brazil: arrest by Army or police authorities, prison for local journalists, deportation for foreign correspondents. War emergency laws—issued in 1942 and retroactive for two years—against anyone "spreading news harmful to the state," gave the DIP practically unlimited powers.

Some of the North American correspondents in Rio grew famous for their struggles with the DIP. Among them is fearless U. P. Bureau Manager James Allen Coogan, whose only concern is whether or not he can get the news out. Another is tough-talking, hard-drinking *Time* correspondent Jane Braga, whose frequent trips to Buenos Aires so far have kept her out of jail. Less fortunate was Mexican born A. P. correspondent Ray Ordorica, thrown out of the country several years ago after a severe beating at police headquarters. . . .

The *Agência Nacional* is the Government's official news agency. It passes out the publicity of all Government departments and supplies the papers with reams of "news," both domestic and foreign. Its domestic service includes a report of all of Vargas' activities ad infinitum. . . .

A subdivision of the *Agência Nacional* is the so-called "copywrite department," where half a dozen writers laboriously pen eulogies of Vargas. These are distributed to newspapers all over Brazil, which must print them as their own editorial stuff. Writers are paid an average of $100 a month, but they must write at least three "editorials" a day. . . .

The script of every play produced in any Brazilian theater must first be submitted to the DIP's Theater and Motion Picture Division, one of whose officials supervises both rehearsals and performance. Every picture and newsreel must have the DIP's approval before public showing. . . .

The Radio Division runs along the same lines. The script of every program must be submitted for approval with a DIP official supervising rehearsals as well as actual broadcasts. The propaganda is covered by the daily *Hora do Brasil,* which must be carried by every station from eight to nine P.M. The *Hora do Brasil* faithfully reports the President's day, the decrees he signed, the interviews he gave, as well as the activities of every one of the Ministries and Government departments. It includes a short musical and news program, limited to official communiques. No one in Rio ever listens to it, but cafes and restaurants throughout Brazil having radio sets must keep them switched on during the *Hora do Brasil.*

The DIP costs the nation around a million dollars a year. It figures on the budget for $350,000, to which must be added a sum twice as large paid by other Government departments for handling and distributing their publicity.

DIP's present Director General, Major Dutra, is as keen to stay away from the barracks as his predecessor, Coelho dos Reis, was eager to return to them. Repeatedly summoned by the Ministry of War for medical examination, so far Dutra has consistently ignored the summons. His continued presence at DIP is perhaps the only indication that the outfit is to be disbanded soon, as Vargas has promised.

1945: ACCOMPLISHMENTS AND PROSPECTS

By 1945 it was possible to see that during the *Estado Nôvo* Brazil had achieved significant economic progress, especially under the stimulus of the war mobilization effort. Samuel Wainer reviewed this record while also arguing for political liberalization and long-term American support for Brazilian industrialization. Wainer was a European immigrant to Brazil and later became a leading newspaper publisher (the *Ultima Hora* chain) of left-wing nationalist views.

15. Brazil—Now and Tomorrow ⋄ Samuel Wainer

Brazil, enormous country of enormous problems, is beset by a two-headed politico-economic monster which, if not brought under control, may rob the country of its leading position among the Latin American nations.

Both the political and economic puzzles give plenty to work on, and they are so interwoven that no Brazilian can talk about one without digging into the other. But unlike most of Latin America, the

From Samuel Wainer, "Brazil—Now and Tomorrow" (illustrations omitted), *The Inter-American*, IV, No. 3 (March 1945), pp. 20–23. Reprinted by permission of the publisher.

country looks toward the future with more hope than worry. There are two reasons for this attitude. First, Brazilians are incurable optimists. Second, despite enormous unsolved problems, the country already has a working foundation for the industries which will maintain her new claim to the title of the most powerful nation in South America.

The Brazil which took up the sword against Germany in August 1942 was a far different nation from that which declared war in 1917. Then, she produced practically no iron, steel, coal, or cement. There was no metallurgical industry.

In 1942, the country's small network of steel factories turned out about 350,000 tons of iron and steel, coal mines yielded 1,600,000 tons, 700,000 tons of cement were produced, as well as a certain amount of manufactured articles of iron, steel, aluminum, and other metals. Industrial production had far outstripped the value of the agricultural yield. While this production satisfied only a fraction of the country's needs, it was progress of a high order to a land which only a few years before had been officially described as "essentially an agricultural country."

However rapid industrial progress had been up to 1942, it was as nothing compared to the rate of development after the country took up arms. Factories sprang up like mushrooms, mostly under the supervision of U.S. technicians. Brazil found herself producing important quantities of chemical and pharmaceutical products, machine tools and motors. Production of foodstuffs, wood, leather, ceramic, and metal articles shot upward. A new steel industry was planned around Volta Redonda, a modern plant which when completed will produce as much as all the other Brazilian mills put together. The once-agricultural country now has 76,000 factories employing 2,000,000 workers who turn out a billion dollars worth of goods a year.

But if the war boosted the industrial program, it also cruelly exposed the country's great weaknesses. As submarine sinkings reached their height, the flow of supplies from the United States dwindled, and Brazil's proud young industrial giant turned out to have the feet of a child.

Industry slowed down, limped along, and in some cases stopped dead. For without fuel, industry cannot function, and Brazil needs

800,000 tons of coal a year more than she produces. She produces no petroleum at all. The country's oldest and most important single industry, textiles, needed almost 100 percent new machinery for replacements alone. New machinery came in the smallest dribbles, and the engineers were hard pressed to keep the mills rolling. Serious shortages of caustic soda, salt-wort, and other essential industrial chemicals cut production still further.

But these troubles were less serious than the calamitous state of the country's never-adequate system of land transportation. In normal times, the needs of the almost-foodless northeast were served by coast-wise ships scalloping from port to port. Virtually the only railways are those running from the port cities inland a few miles. As more ships were torpedoed, some almost within sight of shore, fewer brought dried meat and rice from the rolling lands of Rio Grande do Sul, or coffee, corn, rice, and beans from the rich fields of São Paulo and Minas Gerais.

The entire burden of supplying the sprawling northeast, where nearly half the country's 43,000,000 live, fell on the pathetic land transportation from south to north.

Look at a [map of Brazil]. Brazil's coastline wanders more than 5,000 miles from north to south, across thirty-eight degrees of latitude. (If the great country were tipped up on its northern edge and flipped over like a playing card, the southernmost point would just about hit Boston's latitude.) Brazil's arid, sprawling northeastern states are traditionally cursed with the one-crop economies of cotton and sugar. Practically all the country's food is produced from Minas Gerais southward, and all her industries are concentrated in the south, with São Paulo as the axis. This region has 88 percent of the manufactured goods, 89 percent of the factories, 85 percent of the agricultural production, 74 percent of the railroads, 60 percent of the roads, and 90 percent of the electric power.

There is a rail connection of sorts with the extreme southern part of the country. But from the mesh of railways covering São Paulo, Rio, and part of Minas, a single tenuous feeler wavers northward to Pirapora, on the São Francisco River. From Pirapora slow and clumsy river boats must carry all the northbound cargo 700 sandbar-beset miles before finding another railway. There, from Joazeiro on the southern bank, a venerable single-track line wanders south to important coastal cities by-passed by the São Francisco. From Petrolina on the opposite bank a similar line ventures northward about ninety miles, expiring at Mafrense.

A hundred miles farther down the São Francisco, at Cabrobó, cargo may be trans-shipped by mule-cart across 85 inhospitable miles to be trans-shipped again to another single-track, woodburning line which eventually reaches Fortaleza. Brazil's third city, Recife, about the size of New Orleans, had to depend on the same rail-riverboat-muletrain express for much of its food, as well as many other necessities.

The mules and the river held up pretty well under the strain, but the rickety old railways literally collapsed. The northeast was stranded except for an occasional ship which managed to run the blockade. Local prices zoomed upward. Each day long lines of sturdy, calico-dressed peasant women formed before the shops.

Inflation also affected the rest of the country. Money poured in from U.S. contracts. The Government, unable to maintain price control, left the country at the mercy of a small group of industrialists and speculators. These, taking prompt advantage of the complete absence of foreign competition, virtually monopolized national production and cleaned up in a big way.

The cost of living reached unbelievable heights, while the value of money fell 60 percent from 1939 to 1943, as revealed by the April, 1944 reports of the City Bank of New York, and those of the Brazilian Coordinator of Economic Mobilization published in the *Diário Official* of May 19, 1944. In 1940, 4,815,000,000 cruzeiros circulated in the country; in June, 1943, 9,634,286,000 cruzeiros; in September, 1944, 13,815,061,000 cruzeiros, according to the statistics published by the Caixa de Amortização of Brazil.

Speculation in real estate reached such a point that a Bolsa dos Imóveis, an exchange for trading only in real estate, was created, with offices in São Paulo and Rio. Parasitical banks, which existed only to lend money at exorbitant rates for more speculation, multiplied.

Here politics comes into the picture. The little group close to the Administration of President Getúlio Vargas has controlled the nation's financial dealings for years. These, favored by the Vargas Government, went in for behind-the-scenes manipulation on a grand scale.

The flood of U.S. money and the wartime controls made it laughably easy. Men in official positions became multi-millionaires.

There are specific examples of how abuses of privilege have affected the country's economy. The all-important Volta Redonda steel mills were originally scheduled to begin production in December, 1943. But personal friends of Government officials wanted U.S.-built equipment for their own profit-making enterprises. Priority and the limited shipping space were often requested for importation of nonessential equipment while sixty million Export-Import Bank dollars and important Brazilian and North American technical skills were kept marking time at Volta Redonda. To date these mills have not produced a single ton.

Politics also had much to do with the transportation crisis. Before the going got tough, railway experts submitted a much-needed plan for renovation of the rail system, and urgently recommended prompt action. Nothing was done. It is now estimated that $300,000,000 will be needed to refurbish the remains of the existing system, without laying any of the additional thousands of miles of track necessary to make a unified nation of Brazil.

Another vital need for which no postwar program has been planned is the mechanization of agriculture. Today farming is mechanized in varying degrees in the southern states of Rio Grande do Sul, Santa Catarina, Paraná, São Paulo, and Minas Gerais. In the rest of the country, primitive farming tools are used. Only with modern farming machinery can sufficient food be raised cheaply enough to balance the miserably inadequate diet of the average Brazilian. This deficient diet, incidentally, is largely responsible for the high infant mortality rate of 145 per 1,000.

The Brazilian people are convinced that one of the main causes of the entire situation is the utter lack of civil liberties under the Vargas Administration. It is difficult for a North American to realize the type of government which exists today in Brazil. In his efforts to keep absolute control of the country, President Vargas allows men to be arrested and held indefinitely for no more than speaking against the Government. If a newspaper dare print anything with which the Government disagrees, it may be closed down permanently. Last fall, for example, the old and highly respected medical journal *Mundo Médico* was folded for its articles favoring medical cooperatives. "Spreading Socialist propaganda," said the reactionary rulers of the country. My own weekly magazine, the eight-year-old *Diretrizes*, was padlocked with even less explanation. The Department of Information and Propaganda order which arrived at my office said simply:. "From now on *Diretrizes* is suspended."

Growing discontent with such arbitrary measures is met by increased oppression. Such a condition obviously cannot continue indefinitely without an explosion. Vargas, who has been in power since 1930, has promised elections after the war, but most Brazilians believe that the results will be well arranged beforehand.

Thus, the road to economic emancipation is dependent at least to some extent on the solution of the political impasse. For the rest, most Brazilians feel that the country's future development will find rough going without continued cooperation from the United States. They believe, moreover, that if cooperation has been effective in wartime, it can become broader and more permanent in peace. They realize that they will have to conjure with trusts and international groups, some of which are still unconvinced that international trade can be more profitable between two prosperous nations than between a rich nation and a poor one.

However, Brazilians are certain that in the government and private enterprises of the United States, there are many who believe that Brazil's industrialization will be a factor in the economic progress of the entire hemisphere, and that in peace, rather than in war, the Good Neighbor Policy will be decisively tested.

BIBLIOGRAPHIC SUGGESTIONS

BELLO, JOSÉ MARIA. *A History of Modern Brazil, 1889–1964*. Stanford, Calif.: Stanford University Press, 1968.

COUTINHO, LOURIVAL. *O General Góes Depõe*. Rio de Janeiro: Coelho Branco, 1955.

DULLES, JOHN W. F. *Vargas of Brazil: A Political Biography*. Austin: University of Texas Press, 1967.

LEVINE, ROBERT L. *The Vargas Regime: The Critical Years, 1934–1938*. New York: Columbia University Press, 1970.

LOEWENSTEIN, KARL. *Brazil Under Vargas*. New York: Macmillan, 1942.

PEIXOTO, ALIZIRA VARGAS DO AMARAL. *Getúlio Vargas, meu Pai.* Pôrto Alegre: Editorial Globo, 1960.

SKIDMORE, THOMAS E. *Politics in Brazil, 1930–1964: An Experiment in Democracy.* New York: Oxford University Press, 1967.

VARGAS, GETÚLIO. *A Nova Política do Brasil.* 10 vols. Rio de Janeiro: J. Olympio, 1938–1944.

WIRTH, JOHN D. *The Politics of Brazilian Development, 1930–1954.* Stanford, Calif.: Stanford University Press, 1970.

WYTHE, G., R. A. WIGHT, and H. M. MIDKIFF. *Brazil: An Expanding Economy.* New York: Twentieth Century Fund, 1949.

VII.
Peronism:
Argentina's Experiment with Populism

✠ ELDON KENWORTHY

Theorists of national development tell us that the crises that developed nations faced sequentially often hit Third World countries simultaneously. Mass participation arrives while rules of political competition are still being ironed out; state-fostered industrialization is launched before governments have the resources to play such a role; urban populations expand faster than industrial employment; nationalism precedes national unity. There are shortcomings to this view, one being the implication that the developed nations have safely put behind them the crises that afflict the rest. Yet if one knew nothing more about Peronism than that it addressed simultaneously several unresolved questions of Argentina's development, he probably would have grasped its significance. Peronism was an ambitious, even courageous, *tour de force* which, in the face of this challenge, only partly succeeded.

This introduction reviews the crises confronting Argentina in the post-Depression years and then summarizes Perón's attempts to resolve them through populism. Its purpose is to underscore the interdependence of these problems and to describe the cleavages they generated in Argentine society. The selections that follow treat some of the individual problem/policy areas in greater detail. Behind this format lies the assumption that it is no longer useful to argue the pros and cons of Peronism *in toto*. The Peronist experience must be disaggregated to be understood—as long as the trade offs between its component parts are not forgotten. Perón succeeded in some areas while he failed in others, these successes and failures often being related. By Peronism, let it be clear, we mean Juan Perón's years at the head of the Argentine government, 1945–1955, not the subsequent experience of his supporters.

The economic question inescapably posed by the Depression, but probably unavoidable in any case, was how and to what extent Argentina should industrialize. By World War I Argentina had developed into a leading exporter of meat and grains through the modern exploitation of its major natural resource, vast plains of good topsoil (the *pampas*). One estimate, for around 1930, claimed that Argentina was the sixth wealthiest nation per capita in the world. None of this could have happened, however, without large infusions of British capital and of Spanish and Italian immigrants, and the country remained dependent on overseas markets for its continued growth. All of this, of course, was called into question by the Depression, which disrupted these links to the rest of the world.

The conservative governments of the 1930s confronted the economic problem by jettisoning cherished beliefs in free trade and laissez-faire. In fact, several of the "statist" measures usually associated with Perón had their inception in Agustín Justo's conservative administration (1932–1938). In responding to the Depression, Justo's government stimulated the first sustained industrialization in Argentine history. Since the policies that encouraged import-substituting industries also protected the leading agricultural sector, namely the chilled beef interests of Buenos Aires Province, the *intentions* of the conservatives remain less clear than the effects of their policies. Between 1935 and 1943 the number of manufacturing establishments increased 60 percent, the industrial labor force 80 percent, while value added in manufacturing doubled.

The social question deals with the incorporation into the

nation's public life of that large portion of the population which elites call masses. It has obvious implications for economic and cultural issues and can hardly be separated from politics. Many a stable set of political institutions has crumbled in the face of expanded popular participation, if only because the loyalty of elites to those rules was conditional on the outcomes they produced. This was the case in Argentina.

By the turn of the century the rise of labor unions, socialist and anarchist movements, and most important a mass political party (the Radical Civic Union) indicated that the days of elite rule were numbered. As with the economic question, however, an accumulating crisis crystallized around 1930. The analog to the Depression was the reelection in 1928 of the Radical leader Hipólito Yrigoyen and his overthrow two years later. Up to this point the liberal social and economic elite centered in Buenos Aires (what many Argentines call the Oligarchy) had contained its political rivals through exclusion, then co-optation, with some sharing of power added to the mix after 1912. The 1928 election was won, however, by that faction of the Radical Party which no longer was willing to collaborate with the Oligarchy, as seen in Yrigoyen's use of presidential powers to drive the elite out of its remaining political redoubts. Add to this the inadequate response of this old and headstrong leader to the cresting economic crisis, and one understands why the Oligarchy struck back, allied with army officers who had their own reasons to distrust Yrigoyen. The coup that deposed the Radicals in 1930 rang down the curtain on a half-century of constitutional succession and nearly two decades of liberal democracy.

Force continued to dominate public life throughout the 1930s, although frequently in the subtler form of intimidation and fraud. Labor unions were kept at bay while electoral machinations prevented Yrigoyen's followers from recapturing the presidency. The social question, however, did not go away. In fact, in the cities a largely apolitical generation of immigrants gave way to native sons and daughters who felt more closely identified with Argentina, more desirous of participating in its public life. They were joined by rural peons who abandoned the stagnant countryside for the burgeoning industrial suburbs of the *litoral* (the coast).

This growing national consciousness among the lower classes was not transformed into effective political action, however. For one thing, the continual replenishing of the urban labor force, coupled with government repression and differences between the new and old workers, undercut union organization. Despite stagnant real wages in the late 1930s and early 1940s, and appalling conditions in several industries, there was a drop-off in strikes and a growing gap between the size of the industrial labor force and union membership. So the social question could be postponed, it seemed, but only at the hidden cost of dissipating what legitimacy the Oligarchy retained and of sowing a near-revolutionary situation in the 1940s.

The cultural question is best described as a dualism running through nearly all classes and institutions of Argentine society, linked to the country's two heritages: southern European-Catholic-traditional and North Atlantic-secular-liberal. Significantly, *two* factions of army officers had plotted against Yrigoyen. Momentarily dominant was the group led by General Uriburu, an aloof patriarch who espoused an authoritarianism distinguishable from fascism by its disdain for a mass base. Uriburu's civilian support was linked to the once-dominant, now-displaced elite of Argentina's interior. The center of power, however, lay on the coast, and there a different constellation of values held sway: the liberal, capitalist propensities that had transformed Buenos Aires into a cousin of London and Paris by tapping the resources of the *pampas* for world trade, and the cosmopolitanism which was its natural accompaniment. The Buenos Aires Oligarchy seemed more conversant with London clubs and French theater than with Argentine reality, particularly the reality of the forgotten provinces of the interior.

Unable to consolidate his revolution in the face of opposition from this liberal elite, General Uriburu stepped aside for General Justo, an engineer by training and a scion of the Buenos Aires Oligarchy. This inaugurated the *Concordancia,* an upper- and middle-class coalition led by this more progressive, liberal elite. The 1930s are called the "infamous decade" in Argentina because liberalism was *not* dethroned but merely abrogated in practice, thus opening a gap between appearance and reality which many Argentines found suffocating.

The coming of World War II aggravated this dualism. Within the army, the Uriburu tendency grew at the expense of the Justo tendency. Outside the army, both rightists and leftists discredited the liberal elite by portraying its members as cosmopolitan *vendepatrias* who would sell out their country for private gain. The import-substitution of the 1930s came largely at the expense of U.S. goods and of those Argentines selling to the United States; little was done to undercut trade with England, on which this elite depended. In fact the Justo government signed an agreement favoring British manufactures in exchange for London's promise not to cut its imports of Argentine beef. Given the "colonial" dependence perceived in this arrangement, given scandals implicating cabinet members and foreign investors, and given the *Concordancia*'s unwillingness to commit itself publicly to all-out industrialization, the *vendepatria* accusation stuck. The next coup (1943) was a replay of 1930, only this time the aloof hispanophiles had the broad support of nationalists from other strata, including most army officers.

The rightists never could form a viable government, however. The governments of Uriburu (1930–1931), Castillo (1940–1943), and Ramírez (1943–1944) not only labored under the critical eye of the Buenos Aires elite—which is to say, the nation's economic power—but were unpopular with most of the lower and much of the middle class as well. Thus they remained vulnerable to the machinations of their military supporters. All three presidents, significantly, were forced out by generals they themselves had appointed to high posts. What kept the rightist governments isolated was their hard line on the social question. In a society experiencing continuous expansion in the urban working class, no elite could acquire popular legitimacy—the legitimacy needed to escape dependence on the army—if it continued to deny ordinary citizens more than marginal participation in the nation's wealth, status, and decision-making.

The natural allies of the rightists probably were the new workers streaming into the cities from the countryside. Scarcely literate, these migrants were rebuffed by the urban middle and upper classes and rarely integrated into working-class unions and parties. For, in their fashion, many working-class leaders also were liberal and cosmopolitan, attributing great importance to events in Europe (e.g., the Spanish Civil War) and to abstract ideological formulations. The new worker looked for a patron to protect him and for familiar symbols to make him feel at home. As patrons, however, the rightists leaders could not project—as Juan and Eva Perón later did—a warm "personal" relationship to large numbers of people through rallies and radio. More important, they would not deliver on the social question.

To summarize: the unresolved issues of Argentine life created vertical and horizontal cleavages which made it increasingly difficult for *any* government to attend to these same issues. Elites were divided on the cultural question writ large, including a split over foreign policy provoked by different reference groups abroad. Elite-mass alliances were frustrated by opposing positions on the social question, positions which, in a pattern of circular causation, grew further apart. In 1940–1944, for instance, the rightists' social policy alienated labor leaders, who responded by trying to form a popular front, which frightened the rightist governments into adopting even harsher measures, and so on.

These were the pieces of the puzzle which Perón had to assemble—which brings us to *the political question* or questions, for in reality there were two. By the early 1940s Argentine politics had lost whatever it once possessed by way of a stable structure. For one thing, the loyalty of the army to the government was no longer assured. From May 1940 through October 1945 there was not just one successful coup but three other instances of military pressure successfully used to depose top government personnel and eleven additional conspiracies or uprisings seeking the same end! The only way an administration could avoid perpetual vulnerability to its critics would be by possessing overwhelming might and/or overwhelming popularity. (The two are related inasmuch as officers are as reluctant to confront a vastly popular president as they are to continue supporting a wholly unpopular one.) Argentine politics was modern in the sense that a plurality of self-conscious groups vied for power, but still primitive in that little agreement existed on the rules needed to keep this competition within bounds so that administrations could go about the nation's business with some assurance of tenure and compliance.

In an atmosphere of near-Byzantine intrigue, the *primary* political question is how to form a coalition capable of ruling. This, Machiavelli tells us—for he wrote about a similarly chaotic situation—requires a leader who possesses versatility with courage and luck (*virtù* and *fortuna*). Perón was that person. The *second* political question is, of course, how to overcome this very dependence on leadership. Truly functional are those political systems that need not rely on leaders with exceptional charisma and cunning, being routinized to the point where more ordinary mortals are able to serve society reasonably well.

Peronism represents one of Latin America's earliest cases of populism, which one might define as the politics of incorporating the lower classes into national life, rather suddenly and belatedly, without a social revolution. It means, in terms of our previous discussion, giving policy priority to the social question.

Throughout much of Latin America, the resistance of oligarchies to the gradual growth of popular participation has foreclosed the more incremental and institutionalized solution to the social question found, say, in English history. Admission of the lower classes to arenas of power and prestige has posed as much a problem as the admission of the blacks has in the United States. (In several Latin American countries the differences *do* go beyond class to include differences in culture and race. Argentina, however, has very few Indians and virtually no blacks. Like the United States, Argentina largely exterminated its Indians in the process of "civilizing" its great plains.)

Initially each of the region's armies tended to support its local oligarchy in the attempt to keep decision-making within the upper strata. As this proved hopeless, officers often intervened to prevent a revolutionary resolution of the social question. With incrementalism and revolution ruled out, populism was almost the only path open, although in recent years—partly out of dissatisfaction with the policy outcomes of populism—some military governments have sought a technological-bureaucratic mode of controlled incorporation of the masses into national life (e.g., Peru after 1968).

Available evidence suggests that Perón shared the rightist views, widespread in the Argentine army officer corps in the early 1940s, that the country was being slackly run by civilians, that industrialization was necessary to equip the army and to make the country less dependent on foreign powers, and that the left threatened social dissolution. Perón differed from almost all his military colleagues, however, in seeing that this last tenet did not require a wholly negative response to the social question. In effect he tried to convert the army to the view that "communism" could best be forestalled by adopting a sympathetic attitude toward labor—a position, incidentally, that U.S. officials would echo in later reaching their rapprochement with Perón. No doubt Perón's study tour in Fascist Italy played a role in this analysis. In any case he was prepared to form the rightist elite–mass alliance which previous leaders, military and civilian, had been unwilling or unable to pull off.

Before and after the 1943 coup, Perón was in contact with union leaders and politicians. He preferred an alliance with Intransigent Radicals, Yrigoyen's nationalistic heirs, but he could only attract second-echelon leaders of this key group. This forced him to concentrate more on organized labor, which was led by Socialists, Communists, and a few Syndicalists. To win support in this sector, however, Perón was forced to veer to the left on the social question. If in early 1944 he pictured the military government's Labor Department, which he headed, as mediating between labor and management in the interests of social order, by mid-1945 he identified his efforts almost exclusively with labor and even employed some Marxist rhetoric.

The more Perón veered to the left on the social question in the formative months of his coalition, the more he alienated not only civilian elites (e.g., business and professional associations) but the army as well. To solidify support among the officers, Perón used the resources of the government to attend to their personal and institutional needs, including expanded enlistment, faster promotions, and the creation of military factories producing the latest matériel, at least in quantities sufficient for a good military parade. This Perón was able to do through having acquired a hold on the War Ministry from the early days of the 1943 military government, thanks to his *hombre de confianza* relationship with General Farrell.

Thus in mid-1945, when the crunch came—that is, when it was apparent to all that Perón had ambitions for the presidency and was in league with labor leaders (Socialists! and *that* woman Eva!)—he had his fellow officers over the barrel. Many of them would happily have dumped Perón. But the civilian opposition to him, stimulated by Allied victory in the war, threatened a precipitous end to military government *per se*. Not only did this imply that the army was unfit to rule and that its "Revolution of 1943" had been a mistake—stiff blows to military pride—but revocation of the privileges recently acquired by the officers as well. Cross-pressured, key army commanders several times failed to take decisive action against Perón. Finally on October 17, 1945, Perón's working-class allies stormed the streets in a massive general strike which raised the ante beyond the point where most army opponents wished to play.

Thus, through use of government policy-making to deliver

tangible and symbolic rewards to his supporters, Perón succeeded in locking labor and the army into a coalition neither would have chosen. This solved the first "political question": how to get sufficient popular and coercive support to rule. October 1945 represents the showdown with regard to coercion. Massive working-class support for Perón meant that, to be rid of him, his military opponents would have to risk civil war and, as just indicated, they weren't *that* single-minded about Perón's defects. The irrefutable demonstration of popular support came the following February, when Perón won a bitterly fought but essentially honest election by the clear margin of 54 percent. This achievement required an appeal extending well beyond the workers, an appeal Perón fashioned by striking a nationalistic stance and by projecting a general ebullience regarding Argentina's future. The clumsy intervention of the U.S. State Department on behalf of Perón's opponents cast him in the enviable role of protector of Argentine sovereignty, thereby pulling many Radical voters out from under their own confused leadership.

A nonrevolutionary solution to the social question probably requires immediate and tangible benefits to the working class. Where revolutionaries can offer symbolic rewards, the populist leader must deliver. To truly satisfy, symbolic rewards usually must be baptized in blood and sustained by the conviction of its being "us" versus "them." Although Perón did utilize symbolic rewards, he hesitated to travel too far down this road. He seemed to function best when Evita stoked the fires of working-class militancy while he, more powerful than she, reassured the pillars of society that everything was under control.

Tangible benefits to labor meant, however, less investment and more consumption; a tendency to skew the sizable investment controlled by the government toward social rather than strictly productive ends (e.g., housing instead of petroleum); as well as the protection of jobs in existing industries regardless of their efficiency. Real remuneration of labor (wages plus fringe benefits) rose 80 percent between

1943 and 1949, the years in which Perón consolidated his rule. In 1943, 500,000 Argentines were covered by social security; by 1946 the total had passed 2 million and was still rising. A common Perónist slogan was "Perón cumple" (Perón delivers).

Much of the foreign exchange Argentina earned during and immediately after the war through the sale of agricultural products to a ravaged Europe was spent nationalizing existing facilities, such as the British-owned railroads, not in generating new productive capital. Once more, one sees the logic of populism at work, among other things. To keep class antagonisms within bounds, thereby avoiding a revolutionary confrontation, Perón had to project a confident and expansive future in which every Argentine might participate, save the cosmopolitan, "gilded" Buenos Aires elite. Cannot a great nation run its own railroad? Can it not pay cash on the barrelhead? To prove it, Perón spent precious pounds and dollars on the immensely popular but, in terms of opportunity costs, highly expensive nationalizations.

Thus the economic question came in a poor fourth, after the social, cultural, and at least the first of the two political questions. If in retrospect it seems that populism required this, it also should be remembered that the exceptional economic boom of the late 1940s encouraged Perón to treat the economy as (in his words) "elastic." The deleterious effects of this attitude are set out by Díaz Alejandro (document 4). Here it is enough to note that when the "negative feedback" was inescapably clear, Perón acted on it.

Solidly installed in power, Perón began reversing priorities in the early 1950s. Labor's benefits were cut back, the right to strike curtailed, and the country reopened to foreign investment (by now the United States had supplanted Britain in this role). By 1949 real per capita product and real wages had peaked, and as the economy floundered and Perón revamped policy, both fell until, by 1952, they were back to 1943 levels. (Total payments to labor did not fall quite so precipitously, but this index includes money a worker doesn't see until he retires, if then.) Washington agreed, through the Export-Import Bank, to finance part of the San Nicolás steel project; Kaiser came in to manufacture automobiles; and at the time he was overthrown, Perón was waiting for a reluctant Argentine Congress to approve a contract with Standard Oil of California for the development of petroleum deposits. This retreat on both social and cultural fronts (culture referring to the self-confident, nationalist stance Perón had assumed) cost him popular support.

In 1954 Perón turned against the Church, a move whose reverberations led to his overthrow the following year. This may have been provoked by the modest inroads Catholic lay groups were making in the electorate and in the labor movement, but most likely it was an attempt to refurbish Perón's tarnished leftist image—and by so doing rekindle sufficient working-class enthusiasm to offset his growing dependence on the army—through attacks on the one elite whose collaboration seemed dispensable. Whatever his motives, Perón's imbroglio with the Church had a polarizing effect: his supporters, now fewer, became more militant while his opponents, now numerous, became more incensed *and* more linked to military officers who shared the Church's penchant for order, hierarchy, and public piety. Perón was creating a revolutionary situation. True populist to the end, he abandoned the fight not when he was licked—a majority of the army and probably of the public still responded to him—but when it appeared that the conflict would not quickly and bloodlessly be terminated.

The way Perón's government ended provides a clue to Argentina's enduring political problems. Had the last years of Peronism been less embittering to its opponents—had the churches not been burned, opposition spokesmen not imprisoned, the arming of workers not suggested—the essential nature of Perón's populism might have been clearer. As it was, a counterrevolution set in where, in reality, no revolution had occurred! On balance, Argentina's elites (military no less than civilian) were lucky to have had an adroit populist to lead the country through its participatory crisis without unleashing the revolution whose preconditions these same elites had sown in 1930–1944. The corruption and repression of Perón's later years, however—much of it gratuitous—elicited a counter-Peronist repression which left Argentina in shambles. In the years following Perón's overthrow, his followers were rejected by, and in turn rejected, other political groups to the point where no governmental institutions could be called national (because all respected them) or effective (because their controversial rulings were obeyed). The political role of the masses, therefore, was not institutionalized, assuming that this word connotes uninterrupted participation in policy-making and leadership-selection at all levels, in proportion to a group's size and organization.

Most people agree that Perón's contribution to the institutionalization of Argentine politics was negative. This, however, should neither surprise us nor cause us to gainsay his considerable political skills. Rare is the leader who both builds a viable government under Argentine conditions and then goes on to create impersonal institutions. In the recent history of Latin America probably only Mexico's Lázaro Cárdenas achieved both. After all, even Machiavelli's model of the Prince, Cesar Borgia, failed to solidify his regime.

1.
POINT OF DEPARTURE: The Army in 1943

JUAN V. ORONA

It is commonly thought that the following manifesto was written by Perón and circulated among his army colleagues in the weeks preceding the June 1943 *coup d'état*. Authenticity is not beyond doubt, however, and Robert Potash (who has written the most detailed study of the Argentine Army of this era) thinks the manifesto was circulated after the coup, if at all. Whereas early students of Peronism found in this document proof of the Fascist, repressive, and imperialistic character of Perón's goals, it should be viewed more as a tactical ploy. It probably was used by the GOU, a secret Army lodge of which Perón was chief ideologue, to recruit new members among the more nationalistic officers, and/or used in an attempt to impose the GOU on the post-coup government as the embodiment of the Army's conscience. In both respects the GOU experienced far from total success, and we now know that Perón was saying quite different things to politicians and labor leaders at virtually the same time.

The manifesto is valuable for what it reveals about those to whom it was addressed. First of all, it indicates the

This version of the GOU manifesto was translated by EK, the editor of this unit, from what is reputed to be the original version, reproduced by Colonel (ret.) Juan V. Orona in his *La logia militar que derrocó a Castillo* (Buenos Aires, 1966), pp. 110–111. Used by permission of Colonel Orona. Substantially the same text has been published by at least four other Argentines.

geopolitical thinking and pro-Axis sympathies of many Army officers whose training was based on German military texts. Second, it indicates the foreign policy horizons of the Argentine military. While denying military equipment to Argentina after 1941, Washington poured large amounts of Lend-Lease aid into Brazil, a country that met Washington's expectations regarding hemispheric cooperation. This disparity accentuated the rivalry Argentina felt for Brazil as well as contributed to the former's coolness toward the United States, sentiments discernible in this document. Finally, the manifesto reveals that keen sense of manifest destiny which long has characterized Army officers' thinking (among others') and has fed their disdain for "inept" civilian rule. For the 350-odd colonels of 1943, all of whom had invested a minimum of 25 years in their military career, the manifesto held an obvious appeal. They, who had little hope of earning glory on the battlefield, were being called upon to lead their nation toward its destined place among the world's powers.

Comrades: The war has clearly shown that by themselves nations no longer are defensible; thus the insecure game of building alliances, which mitigate but do not correct this serious problem. The era of the nation is slowly giving way to the era of the continent. Yesterday duchies united to form nations. Today nations must unite to form regimes. This will be the outcome of the present war.

Germany is making a titanic effort to unite the European continent. The greatest and best-equipped nations will rule the destinies of the continents now taking form. In North America the guiding nation will be, for a while, the United States. But in the south there is no nation so indisputably strong that its tutelage would be accepted without dissent. Only two nations could assume this role: Argentina and Brazil. Our mission is to make our hegemony possible and undeniable.

The task is immense and full of sacrifices. But one doesn't create a nation without sacrifices. The giants of our independence era gave their lives and fortunes. In our time Germany has imparted a sense of heroism to life. These will serve as our examples.

To take the first step along the difficult road leading to a great and powerful Argentina, we must assume power. Civilians never will comprehend the grandeur of our goal. Therefore, they must be removed from the government and given the only mission appropriate to them: work and obedience.

Once in power, our sole mission will be to grow strong, stronger than all the other countries combined. We will have to arm ourselves and remain armed, overcoming difficulties, fighting against external and internal circumstances. Hitler's struggle in peace and war will be our guide. The first step is to make alliances. We have Paraguay, Bolivia, and Chile. With Argentina, Paraguay, Boliva, and Chile, it will be easy to bring pressure to bear on Uruguay. Then the five united nations easily will attract Brazil, owing to its form of government [the Vargas dictatorship?—EK] and its large concentrations of Germans. Once Brazil has fallen, the [South?] American continent will be ours. Our tutelage will be fact, a great and unprecedented deed achieved by the political genius of the Argentine Army.

Mirages, utopias, some will say. However, let us look at Germany again. Defeated, in 1919 she was forced to sign the Treaty of Versailles, which sought to keep her a second-rate power under Allied domination for at least fifty years. In less than twenty years she has traveled her fantastic course. Before 1939 she already had armed more than any other nation, and while still at peace she annexed Austria and Czechoslovakia. Later, during the war, she bent all of Europe to her will. But this was not done without great sacrifice. An iron dictatorship was necessary to impose on her people the sacrifices required for this great program.

So it will be with Argentina. Our government will be an inflexible dictatorship, although initially it will make the concessions necessary to consolidate power. Public support will be attracted, but inescapably the people will have to work, make sacrifices, and obey. They will work harder and deny themselves more than any other people. Only in this way can the crucial armament program be carried out.

Following Germany's example, using radio, controlled press, movies, books, the church, and the schools, the people will be inculcated with the spirit required to embark on the heroic path they must travel. Only in this way will they come to renounce the comfortable life they now lead.

Ours will be a generation sacrificed on the altar of the highest good, that of the Argentine nation, which later will shine with unparalleled brilliance for the greater good of the continent and of all humanity.

¡Viva la Patria! ¡Arriba los corazones!

2.
EN ROUTE: The Election of 1946

PETER SMITH

In fair balloting following a bitterly fought campaign, Perón received 54 percent of the valid votes in an election which stands as a watershed in Argentine history. Nine-tenths of the Congressmen elected that year never had served before, and for the first time a significant portion of those elected came from the working class.

At *this* time, Perón's political machine was a jerry-built affair, resting on a newly created Labor Party staffed by union leaders, and a "reformed" faction of Radicals staffed by old political pros. The two groups bickered constantly. Thus, while Perón had the resources of the government behind him—his opponents were backed by the business community and the prestigious newspapers—his victory was not the contrived result of a powerful political organization. Thus the election of 1946 stands as a fairly good indicator of public opinion at the time. As such, it has been analyzed by historian Peter Smith in an attempt to discover "the social base of Peronism."

Counties (*partidos*), not individuals, are the units of Smith's study for the simple reason that relevant data on individuals do not exist. Smith's conclusions, therefore, are

From Peter Smith, "The Social Base of Peronism," *Hispanic American Historical Review* (February 1972), pp. 55–73. Copyright 1972 by the Duke University Press. Reprinted by permission of the author and the publisher.

Space limitations permit only the reproduction of Smith's conclusions. For the evidence and qualifications accompanying Smith's interpretations, the reader should consult the original article.

"ecological": while he can tell us that counties with a large number of Peronist voters also had a large number of industrial workers, he cannot say that the two groups of individuals were the same, although this inference can be drawn when such a relationship is found across many counties. Strong relationships did not emerge on a *national* scale, suggesting that Argentines in different places supported Perón for different reasons. Only when counties were divided into three groups according to their degree of urbanization did significant relationships appear, Perón receiving the largest and most consistent support in counties having at least one city of 50,000 inhabitants or more. (Smith's term for these counties is "Big Cities"; "Countryside" denotes counties having no town larger than 2,000 inhabitants, while "Townships" fall in between.)

In summary, statistical analysis of the 1946 election returns leads to several conclusions about the social base of the early Peronist movement. Since my findings are "ecological" they cannot be conclusive, but they have a demonstrable factual basis and, at the very least, they offer some promising hypotheses for future research. Other investigators might well test these propositions by non-statistical methods; ultimately, of course, a comprehensive understanding of Peronism will have to depend upon qualitative criteria as well as purely quantitative ones.

1. No single socioeconomic variable explains Perón's electoral popularity to any large degree. Facile generalizations about urbanization, internal migration, young voters and other such factors do not stand up to empirical analysis.

2. In the Big Cities, Perón drew greatest support in large, economically developed areas containing both industrial workers and internal migrants. This much generally agrees with standard literature on the subject. But electoral statistics yield two additional refinements: Perón did well among specifically *industrial* districts, not in all working-class neighborhoods; and the "old" laboring groups played a more crucial political role than did internal migrants.

3. In the Townships, Perón attracted votes from both urban and rural lower-class groups.

4. Socioeconomic issues played relatively little political role in the

Countryside, though Perón won numerous votes in underdeveloped areas whose constituents might have been eager for modernization. In rural counties traditional allegiance or local strongmen seem to have determined electoral outcomes; incidentally, one possible reason that internal migrants did not exert more positive impact on the Peronist vote in urban areas might be that they retained their customary loyalties for some time after moving to the city.

5. To the extent that socioeconomic factors can provide an explanation, Peronism began as a protest movement against Argentina's pattern of modernization, a process which made many people feel exploited or abandoned and thus exerted a differential political impact.

6. Partly for this reason, Peronism began as a loose and potentially unstable coalition of differing social groups. What was good for Big City workers would not always be good for commercial employees in Townships or agricultural entrepreneurs in the Countryside. The unexplained portions of variance in all three urban-rural categories also imply that many people followed Perón for non-economic reasons. Perón was leading a fragile alliance, not a monolithic class or mass movement.

7. In pursuit of the previous point, these interpretations combine to produce some provocative speculation about the subsequent development of the Peronist movement. *El Líder's* rural following would probably remain secure as long as he could keep up friendly relationships with local leaders, though he could withstand some loss in districts containing fairly small proportions of the population. For Perón, as for most other politicians, the key to power lay in urban areas. It seems likely, and history appears to show, that the self-identity and sectoral solidarity of the industrial work force could survive any crisis and maintain Perón's base in Big Cities.

One cannot be so sure about the Townships. If a loose class-wide coalition of Peronist supporters found unity in socioeconomic awareness, as implied by variables about unemployment, wage scales, and land distribution, political allegiance in those areas would probably depend upon tangible gratification. Job-seeking, wage-conscious laborers and land-hungry farmers would be likely to react to the *performance* of the Perón regime, rather than to political bargains or ideological affinity. This reasoning leads to the hypothesis that, in the Townships, (a) inflation and other economic difficulties after

1950 alienated urban workers, (b) governmental deemphasis of agrarian reform disappointed small farmers and rural laborers, and (c) consequent weakening of the lower-class alliance undermined an essential portion of Perón's political base and helped make possible his downfall in 1955.

3.
POINT OF ARRIVAL: Leader of the *Descamisados*

EVA PERÓN

The following speech was delivered by Eva Perón at the traditional Labor Day rally held on May 1, 1952, scarcely three months before she died of cancer at the age of 33. Its themes are characteristic of Peronism in its heyday, although they are stated more baldly by Eva than Juan would have stated them. But this too is characteristic, for Evita (as she preferred to be called by workers) tended to exaggerate what was populist and personalist in the Peronist regime: its fanaticism *and* its charity, its "cult of the personality," *and* its genuine identification with the poor.

Evita's relationship to Perón seemed to mirror that of the lower classes to them both. At times the voice from below (and Evita's) was full of steel and anger. At other moments the voices were subservient, asking only to be led, pledging "Our lives for Perón."

Lower class and a woman, Evita had not accepted the narrow, deferential roles which both implied in the Argentina of the 1930s. Like many of her class contemporaries, she fled to the big city in hopes of finding something better. There she moved from being a bit-part actress into her own radio series, and into liaisons with army officers. As Perón's

Speech by Eva Perón, reproduced in *Perón y Eva Perón hablan en el día de los trabajadores* (Buenos Aires: Argentine Republic, Presidencia de la Nación, Subsecretaría de Informaciones, 1952). My translation—EK.

cohort, then wife, Evita played the contrasting roles of the workers' comrade (*compañera*) and their fairy godmother, ruthless politician and innocent "true believer," feminist and stereotypical First Lady. Characteristically, her illness (anemia followed by cancer) was attributed both to long hours working for the cause and to the punishing diet she followed to keep her actress figure.

Seven months prior to this speech (September 28, 1951) a group of dissident officers tried to overthrow Perón. While the uprising easily was put down by the army, it signaled an end to the truce which Perón's military opponents had observed since October 1945. During this crisis workers demonstrated on Perón's behalf without, however, actually engaging the rebel troops. Remembering this incident, and aware that this could be her valedictory, Evita stresses in this speech the importance of Peronists being prepared to defend their leader against his "oligarchical" opponents. Beyond this emphasis, the speech contains such recurrent Peronist themes as: Peronism as a third position between the "two imperialisms" of capitalism and communism; the local oligarchy as subservient to foreign interests (and hence *vendepatria*); and the revolutionary role played on October 17, 1945, by the *descamisados* (literally "the shirtless ones"), the label Perón's genteel opponents applied to the workers who turned out that day to reclaim their leader.[1] As happened with *sansculotte* in the French Revolution, the intended "put down" was adopted by the victorous Peronists as a term of pride. The reader should remember that this was a *speech,* not an exercise in logic.

My beloved *descamisados:*

Once more we come together here, workers and women of the people; once more we *descamisados* gather in this historic square

---

[1]Some writers apparently believe that the term *descamisado* literally arose from the attire of Perón's supporters on that unseasonably warm October 17. Photographs of the crowds belie this, however. The term appeared in Spain as early as the liberal uprising of 1820–1823, perhaps as a corruption of *sansculotte*. By the time it came to be applied to the Peronists, *descamisado* had become a figure of speech denoting the rabble, or what Marxists would call the lumpen proletariat. I am indebted to José Napolitano for philological advice on this and other points.

where October 17, 1945, occurred, in order to give our reply to the Leader of the people who this morning, on concluding his speech, said: "Those who would hear, let them hear; those who would follow, let them follow." Here is your reply, my General: it is the working people, the little people of the nation, who here and throughout the country are on their feet, ready to follow Perón, the Leader of the people, the Leader of humanity, because he has raised high the banner of salvation and justice for the masses; ready to follow him against the oppression of traitors within and without, traitors who in the darkness of the night would like to inject their snake venom into the soul and body of Perón, which is the soul and body of the Nation. But they won't succeed, any more than toads in their jealousy can succeed in silencing the nightingale's song or snakes succeed in halting the flight of the condor. They won't succeed, my General, because we—the men and women of the People—we are here to guard your dreams and to watch over your life, since yours is the life of the Nation, the life of future generations, and we would never forgive ourselves if we hadn't protected a man as fine as General Perón, who nurtured the dreams of all Argentines, particularly the dreams of the working people.

I pray to God that He won't permit those fools to raise a hand against Perón, because if that day comes, my General, I will take to the streets with the working people, I will take to the streets with the women of the People, I will take to the streets with the *descamisados* of the nation, and not a single brick that isn't Peronist will be left standing. Because we are not about to let ourselves be ground under the oligarchical and traitorous heel of the *vendepatrias* who have exploited the working class; because we are not going to let ourselves be exploited by those who, having sold themselves for four pieces of silver, now serve bosses from foreign centers and sell out the people of their own Nation with the same calm with which they sold out the country and its conscience; because we are going to care for Perón more than for our own lives, since in so doing we protect a cause that is the cause of the Nation, the cause of the People, the cause of those ideals which we have carried in our hearts for so many years. Today, thanks to Perón, we stand on our feet like men. Men feel more like men, and we women feel greater dignity, because from the frailty of some [of us] and the strength of others there arises the spirit and the courage of Argentines to serve as a shield defending the life of Perón.

I, after a long time of not being in contact with the people as I am today, I want to say these things to my *descamisados,* to the humble people I carry in my heart, to whom in moments of happiness and moments of pain and moments of uncertainty I always raise my eyes, because they are pure and being pure see with the eyes of the soul and know how to value such an extraordinary man as General Perón. I want to talk today, although General Perón asked me to be brief, because I want my people to know that we are ready to die for Perón and because I want the traitors to know that from now on we will not come here [merely] to say "present" to Perón [i.e., as one says "present" in a roll call, a response common to mass rallies in Argentina] as we did September 28, but that henceforth we are going to take justice into our own hands.

There is much pain to be alleviated and many wounds to be bound, because there still are many who are sick and many who suffer. We need you, my General, just as we need air or the sun or life itself. Our children and our country need you in these uncertain times for mankind, in which men debate between two imperialisms, one of the right and one of the left, that would carry us toward death and destruction. We, a handful of Argentines, are fighting with Perón for mankind's happiness by bringing justice and dignity to our people. This is where Perón's greatness lies. The greatness of a country cannot be founded on the suffering of its people, only on the happiness of the working people.

Compañeras, compañeros: once more I am in the fight, once more I stand with you, as it was yesterday, is today, and will be tomorrow. I am with you in order to be a rainbow of love between the people and Perón. I am with you to be this bridge of happiness and love which I always have tried to be between the Leader and the workers.

Once more I am with you, like a friend and sister. I must work night and day to bring happiness to the *descamisados,* because in this way I know I am fulfilling my duty to the Nation and to Perón. I must work night and day alleviating pain and binding wounds, because I know I am meeting my obligations to that legion of Argentines who are carving a brilliant page in the history of the fatherland. And just as on this glorious May first, my General, we want to come back many, many years, and over the centuries we want future generations to come so that we can tell them, in the splendor of their lives, that we were here, present, my General, with you![1]

Before finishing, *compañeros,* I want to leave you with a message: be alert. The enemy waits in ambush; he will never tolerate the fact that an Argentine, a good man, General Perón, is working for the well-being of his people and for the greatness of the Nation. The *vendepatrias* from within, those who sell themselves for four pieces of silver, they too lie in ambush ready to strike at any moment. But we are the People, and I know that if the People remain alert we will be invincible, for we are the very Nation itself.

[1]The published version of this speech may contain a typographical error substituting *decirles* for *decirle.* If so, the meaning of this sentence is altered to: "we want to return and we want others to come over the centuries in order to say to you [Perón], in the bronze [strength, stature?] of your life or in the life of your bronze [your statue], that we . . ." etc.

4.
THE ECONOMIC QUESTION

CARLOS F. DÍAZ ALEJANDRO

Franklin Roosevelt's policies toward World War II and the world organization to follow were influenced, some claim, by a desire to avoid the problems Woodrow Wilson encountered a quarter-century earlier. The following selection argues that Perón's economic policies were a belated and out-of-phase response to the shock Argentina experienced during the Depression.

In the preface to the book from which this selection is taken, the author remarks that friends find his analysis "reactionary." Try as he might, it seems doubtful that any economist working close to the facts could avoid coming down hard on Perón, or avoid the invidious comparison with the socially short-sighted but economically savvy administrations of the 1930s. Allowances can be made and the author makes several: the primitive state of economic planning at the moment Perón embarked on his first Five Year Plan, the uncertainties inherent in the postwar situation, even the vagaries of nature (e.g., a severe drought in the early 1950s). Indeed, the explanation of Perón's policy-making as overcompensation for the trauma of the Depression seems intended to soften retrospective criticism.

Still, Perón must pay his dues. He used public policy for

From Carlos F. Díaz Alejandro, *Essays on the Economic History of the Argentine Republic*, pp. 107–117, 126 (with excisions). Copyright © 1970 by Yale University. Reprinted by permission of the publisher.

short-term political ends—and, given *this* goal, used it effectively—at the expense of sustained economic development. Political payoffs and economic policy are obverse sides of the same coin, and Perón spent his politically. When he reversed priorities, later in his administration, he found that many of his options had disappeared.

In excerpting this selection from a richly documented study of the Argentine economy, footnotes and tables had to be omitted. Interested readers should consult the original. One explanation of terminology may prove helpful. *Importable* goods are those *consumed* in Argentina that could be purchased abroad or made at home. Likewise, *exportables* are goods *produced* in Argentina that could be sold abroad or at home. Both are *tradables*. *Home goods* are those that cannot be traded, in some cases due to their very nature (e.g., services), in others due to government measures which artificially isolate them from foreign competition. Thus many Argentine manufactures were "importables" in the 1930s but, under Perón, became "home goods"—too expensive to be sold abroad and too protected to be undersold at home by foreign-made goods.

. . . Until 1929 the system, on the whole, had worked, and prosperity smoothed tensions. But the depression discredited the liberal system and brought to the surface latent frictions. The manner in which Argentina was treated by her trade partners, especially the United Kingdom, increased nationalistic feelings and reduced the influence of Argentines who advocated encouragement of foreign trade and investment. The climate of corruption and repression dominating the political life of the 1930s extended, in the mind of the public, to the dealings between the government and foreign investors and traders; major scandals involving foreign investors reinforced this feeling.

The conservative regimes of the 1930s, in spite of their flirtations with fascist reformism, brought to a halt the modest momentum for political and social reform started by the Radical governments. Their failure to buttress the relatively healthy economic structure with social and political arrangements allowing for growing security and political participation for rural and urban masses contributed to the creation of revolutionary possibilities.

The expansion of manufacturing, coupled with rural stagnation, stimulated internal migration toward the urban centers, especially Greater Buenos Aires. The growing urban labor force appeared to be a passive mass without leadership or organization; it will be recalled that members of labor unions amounted to 473,000 in 1940, at a time when the total urban labor force was about 3.5 million. The traditional parties, including Radicals and Socialists, showed a curious sluggishness in providing leadership for this group. By 1943 most of the urban workers were either children of immigrants or had come from rural and small urban communities of the interior and were of older Argentine stock. The Socialist Party leadership, on the other hand, came from immigrants or was closely identified with foreign ideologies, which often did not fit popular nationalistic feelings. Finally, the wage share in national income declined between 1935–36 and 1940–42 (under mildly inflationary conditions) while the social security system remained grossly underdeveloped.

Under these circumstances, and also taking advantage of new pressures created by the war, a gifted leader, General Perón, was able to build up massive support for himself and for a program of higher wages and social reform, accompanied by extreme nationalism. Favoring domestic consumption over exports pleased the urban masses, and strengthening import restrictions pleased urban entrepreneurs. All who would lose, it appeared, were foreigners who had to do without Argentine wheat and beef and could not sell manufactures to Argentina, and the oligarchs who had previously profited from the export-import trade and their association with foreign investors. Favorable foreign prices and demand conditions, which lasted until 1949, plus the foreign exchange accumulated during the war, temporarily hid the balance of payments consequences of these policies. These conditions also permitted not only the launching of expensive programs favoring the urban masses, but also the purchase of several major foreign-owned assets such as railroads, thus pleasing nationalists without requiring radical alteration of property rights.

Policies against foreign trade and investment were motivated not only by frictions generated during earlier periods, and by the frustrations and humiliations of the 1930s, but also by the outlook for world commerce in 1945. A person making decisions in 1945 could not be at all sure about the future of international trade. The previous fifteen years had been disastrous and many were forecasting a major postwar depression or another war between the United States and the USSR. (When Korean hostilities broke out, some thought this expectation was being realized.) Traditional markets for Argentine exports in Western Europe were under the gun of the Red Army and faced enormous tasks of reconstruction, which precluded an early return to free trade and convertibility. Inconvertibility caused Argentina real losses, not only during the 1930s but also during the war, when sterling balances piled up while increases in the British and world price levels reduced their value. . . .

The decision to neglect foreign trade and shun foreign investors had, therefore, deep roots in history and, in particular, can be viewed as a delayed response to the Great Depression.

In spite of relatively favorable external conditions provided by a world economy that after all did not experience a major postwar depression nor a third world war, the average annual growth rate in real GDP between 1941–43 and 1953–55 was around 3 percent. Commodity-producing sectors grew substantially less than services. While government services (or more accurately, government employment) expanded at about 6 percent per year, the rural sector grew at a rate variously estimated at 1.1 or 0.2 percent per annum. The growth of government services, as well as of transport and financial services, was also higher than the highest estimate for the manufacturing growth rate. . . .

Most of the expansion taking place between 1941–43 and 1953–55 was packed into a three-year interval between 1945 and 1948 when GDP expanded by nearly 29 percent (CONADE), or by 25 percent (BCRA). From 1948 to 1955 aggregate output expanded only by an additional 16 percent (CONADE), or by an additional 12 percent (BCRA). Between 1948 and 1955 population grew by a total of 16 percent; the peak reached in per capita product during 1948 was not surpassed during the rest of the Perón years. Once the favorable external conditions of 1945–48 and the reserves accumulated until 1946 had disappeared, and in spite of the brief Korean commodity boom, the economy was not capable of sustaining a growth rate superior to that of population. . . .

. . . [T]he net effect of public policy was to twist further the domestic terms of trade against the rural sector and to discriminate in favor of nontraded goods. These policies were implemented using a variety of tools—overvalued and multiple exchange rates, government controls over marketing of rural produce, a policy of absolute protection for many, but not all, manufactured products, etc. The discrimination against rural expansion was worse than that implied by relative prices; this sector found it very difficult to obtain, either domestically or abroad, certain inputs (fertilizers, tractors, etc.) that could conceivably have allowed it to react to the price decline by increasing productivity. This lack of modern inputs, not fully reflected in price data, was also accompanied by weak public efforts in agricultural research and extension services, and labor shortages in the countryside.

. . . [T]he export quantum declined sharply during 1945–54; by 1950–54 it was 37 percent below the levels for the depression years of 1930–39. Lack of foreign demand could hardly be blamed for this shrinkage; the Argentine share in world trade of her traditional export commodities fell substantially, and in 1952 the country even had to import wheat. The main explanation for the export performance was that rural output increased between 1935–39 and 1950–54 by only 14 percent (and output of the traditional exportable goods *declined* by 10 percent), while domestic absorption of rural goods increased by more than 40 percent. Part of the stagnation in rural output may be blamed on poor weather, especially during 1950–54, but government policy toward rural exportables (of which price policy was only a part) must bear the principal blame. Vulnerability to bad breaks was greatly increased by public policies. Exports of manufactured goods, which had expanded during the war and the immediate postwar period, shrank to insignificant levels after 1946. Argentina turned her back on the worldwide expansion of trade, while Canada and Australia profited from it.

Although the sharp fall in the export quantum may not have been foreseen by the authorities, part of their overall strategy was not to bother much with exports. Their main interest centered on some aspects of import-substituting industrialization, and on the provision of health, education, recreation, and other mass services. Besides pleasing nationalistic and reformist sentiment, this policy had the additional advantage of generating employment and security for the urban working class, a political pillar of the regime. Light manufacturing, construction, government, and the nationalized railroads came to be viewed more as sources of jobs than as activities producing goods and services. The migration from rural to urban areas which had been taking place since the 1930s was accelerated by this policy, even though it was extremely doubtful that the social value of the marginal product of labor in, say, the nationalized railroads, was higher than in rural activities producing exportables.

The policy of import substituting for some industrial products was not an integrated and thought-out plan. Rather, it proceeded from one improvisation to another, reacting to short-run economic and political pressures. Toward the end of the war and during the early postwar years, the main preoccupation was defending industries that had arisen and expanded during the war, regardless of their efficiency. This attitude had an important implication; as the protection granted existing activities included not only the shutting out of foreign competition . . . but also the importation of their inputs at an increasingly overvalued exchange rate, some branches of industry (the potential producers of imported inputs) often suffered, not only relative to the favored activities, but also in comparison with a situation of free trade and equilibrium exchange rates. Oil extraction is one example of an activity discriminated against by that system of protection. Some types of machinery and equipment were also relatively neglected. The policy of stimulating light industries rather than more capital-intensive ones could conceivably be defended on efficiency grounds, but this would imply that either (1) exports were expanded to finance the importation of goods produced by the lagging heavy industries, or (2) the foreign exchange saved by the expansion of light industries was sufficient to finance the required imports. A combination of (1) and (2) could, of course, be sufficient. During the euphoria of 1945–48 little thought was given to these matters and when exports contracted in 1949 the country faced an exchange bottleneck, because import substitution had not released enough exchange to finance imports required by a 5 percent growth rate. First priority was given then to raw materials and intermediate goods imports needed to maintain existing capacity in operation. Machinery and equipment for new capacity could neither be imported nor produced domestically (at least in the short run). A sharp decrease in the rate of real capital formation in new machinery and equipment followed.

The impact of the exchange bottleneck on nonconstruction capital formation worsened the economy's capacity to transform, which in turn made the bottleneck more intractable. Expansion of import-substituting activities, or even export activities, required investments in new machinery and equipment with high import components. Hostility toward foreign capital, which could have provided a way out of this difficulty, aggravated the 1948–53 crisis.

Protection and credit policies gave rise to a constellation of costs and prices that increased the profitability of investment in some branches of manufacturing, while decreasing it not only for the rural sector producing exportables, but also in several potentially import-competing industrial branches. Even when prices reflected, on average, social opportunity costs, their erratic movements induced by policy changes and by inflationary conditions increased uncertainty and deprived such signals of a great deal of their usefulness. A situation developed where neither coherent planning nor the price mechanism were used to allocate resources rationally. Minor disequilibria were allowed to turn into major structural imbalances for lack of an adjustment mechanism.

In summary, it may be useful to distinguish between the different types of economic inefficiencies that government policies created. One major type, which could be called "macro" inefficiencies, includes (1) those arising from the unnecessary closing of the economy (discouragement of exports) and (2) once the closing of the economy is granted, those arising from the failure to have a balanced expansion of industry that would create a productive structure capable of meeting demands generated by a 5 percent growth. But even taking these "macro" inefficiencies as given, the tools used by the government to promote its aims (import prohibitions for some goods, credit rationing with negative or very low real rates of interest, etc.), by curtailing competitive pressures and creating quasi-monopolistic conditions in the domestic market, led to further "micro" inefficiencies as the favored industries were not pressed to improve efficiency and minimize costs in their operations. Micro-inefficiencies arose within most sectors also as a result of deficiencies in public services and changes in labor legislation and work-rules.

The policies followed during 1943–55 were, in many ways, more extreme forms of those followed during 1930–43. They continued trends in allocation of resources which, although justifiable during the depression, were out of line with the more favorable world conditions of 1943–55. . . .

Peronist policies present a picture of a government interested not so much in industrialization as in a nationalistic and populist policy of increasing the real consumption, employment, and economic security of the masses—and of the new entrepreneurs. It chose these goals even at the expense of capital formation and of the economy's capacity to transform. The favorable external conditions of 1946–48 helped to mask the conflict between nationalist and populist goals and long-run economic development, a conflict that became clearer after 1948.

A final irony is that greater attention to exportables during 1943–55 would have resulted in more, rather than less, industrialization, as the examples of Canada and Australia suggest. Modestly expanding exports, by making feasible a higher overall growth rate, could have resulted in manufacturing expansion greater than that observed. Also, a different attitude toward foreign investment would have encouraged industrialization, especially in key sectors, in the same way as such investment encouraged manufacturing during the 1930s. Bitter memories of the Great Depression, as well as dimmer memories of the years immediately after World War I, led economic authorities to neglect the long-run economies of growth for the sake of short-run economic security.

5.
THE SOCIAL QUESTION

GERMÁN N. ROZENMACHER

Just as the economist's verdict on Peronism is bound to be negative, the assessment of one who focuses on the social question is likely to be positive. Whatever his motives, Perón succeeded in bringing the lower classes into the life of the nation, imparting to them a new sense of dignity and a new consciousness of their power. This did not "solve" all social questions. Indeed, class conflict was exacerbated, as more priviliged strata reacted to this challenge to their relative status. Still, it seems clear that Argentina's future as a nation depended on its facing up to the inequities in its social and political life, and equally clear that Perón was the leader who forced the country to face that fact. Argentina in 1940, one should remember, was one of the wealthiest nations of Latin America, yet quite backward with regard to social services; one of the most politicized populations, yet saddled with a plutocracy posing as a democracy.

According to Gino Germani's estimates, nearly 40 percent of the net growth in the population of the rest of the country migrated to Greater Buenos Aires in the years 1936–1947, changing the complexion of the city demographically (provincials outnumbering the foreign born for the first time) as well as changing its complexion quite literally. For the mi-

"Cabecita Negra," by Germán N. Rozenmacher. From the collection of short stories by the same name, published by Jorge Alvarez, Buenos Aires, 1962. Translated and slightly abridged by the editor of this unit. Reproduced by permission of the author.

grant from the interior was a *mestizo*, bearing the darker skin and traces of Indian features which were less common on the coast, due to prior waves of European immigration. To express disdain for the poor, scarcely literate migrant, the the good burghers of Buenos Aires used such terms as *negro* ("black"), *cabecita negra* ("little black-headed one"), and the shortened and even more derisive *cabeza* ("head"). A black-headed Argentine goldfinch is also called *cabecita negra*, thus imparting to the term a certain rural and sub-human cast while principally calling attention to racial characteristics.

While many, perhaps most, of these rural-to-urban migrants became Peronists, they were numerically and organizationally a less significant source of popular support for Perón than the older working class, which consisted primarily of immigrant stock. For Perón's opponents, however, the *cabecitas negras* became the symbol of all that they despised in Peronism: its leveling, demagogy, its "ignorant masses." Indeed, the term came to embrace all whom the middle and upper classes viewed in this light, dark-skinned or not. (This upper-class-inspired interpretation of Peronism later received some scholarly accreditation from those who embraced social mobilization theories, which tend to view all noninstitutionalized political behavior of the "masses" as unconscious and politically pathological.)

The following story captures, better than any scholarly treatment might, the shape of the "social question" under Perón. The image the storyteller employs, that of the house being occupied (in the military sense), also occurs in a story by the older and better-known Argentine writer, Julio Cortázar. In "Casa Tomada" Cortázar remains wholly metaphorical, whereas here Rozenmacher is more explicit: the house (nation) is invaded by social underdogs who achieved some power (symbolized by the policeman's role) under Perón. Whereas the owners of Cortázar's house are fading remnants of the aristocracy, Rozenmacher's are *nouveau riche*. Prophetically, in this story the take-over is reversible, although "things will never be quite the same again."

Mr. Lanari couldn't sleep. It was three-thirty in the morning and he smoked, angry, cold, leaning on the third-floor balcony overlooking the empty street, shivering inside an overcoat with its lapels turned up. After tossing and turning in bed, taking some pills, and roaming through the house frantic as a caged lion, he had gotten dressed as if to go out, even to the point of shining his shoes.

And so there he was, wide awake and tense, crouched over the balcony listening to the invisible pounding of some horse pulling a vendor's cart, while a taxi circled the block, its headlights slicing the fog, waiting its turn to enter the Cangallo Street garage. A Number 63 streetcar, its windows opaque from the cold, passed from time to time, dragging itself between the one-, two-, seven-story buildings, between the few bright hotel signs shining wet, scarcely visible, in the street below.

This insomnia was terrible. Tomorrow he would have a cold and walk around like a sleepwalker all day. Worse, never before had he committed the stupidity of getting up in the middle of the night and dressing, only to stand there, smoking on the balcony. Who would think of doing such a thing? He shrugged his shoulders, feeling miserable. Night was meant for sleeping and he was living in reverse. Yet he felt full awake in the midst of the enormous silence of the sleeping city. A silence which caused him to move with a certain caution, even secrecy, as if he might awaken someone.

He wouldn't tell his partner at the hardware store about it or he'd never hear the end of it, especially his having shined his shoes in the middle of the night. In this country where everybody took advantage of each opportunity to look good at someone else's expense, you had to be careful to preserve your dignity. If you got careless, you'd be squashed like a roach. He sneezed. If his wife had been there she would have made him one of her herb teas and he'd have been cured already. He sighed, feeling forlorn. His wife and son were spending the weekend at the country place at Paso del Rey. They took the maid with them, leaving him alone in the house.

Still, on reflection, things weren't going all that badly for him. He couldn't complain. His father had been a bill collector for the light company, an immigrant who had eked out a living without amounting to much. He himself had worked like a dog, but now he owned this flat on the third floor, near the Congress, and a few months before he had purchased the small Renault that stood downstairs in the garage, not to mention spending a small fortune installing those stained-glass windows in the entranceway. His hardware business on Avenida de

Mayo was doing well, so now he also owned a country place where he spent vacations. He couldn't complain; he had satisfied his needs. Soon his son would be a lawyer and would marry, surely, into some distinguished family. Of course he had had to make sacrifices. In times like these, where political disorder is routine, it was normal to have been on the verge of bankruptcy several times. (Bankruptcy! that terrible word which meant scandal and ruin, the loss of everything.) Sure, he had had to squash some people to survive, but if he hadn't, they would have done the same to him. That's life. And he had come out on top.

As a young man he had played the violin and there was nothing in the world he liked better. But his future had looked doubtful, full of poverty and humiliation, and this had frightened him. After all, one is responsible to others, especially to one's family; one can't just do whatever he likes. Subsequently everything he had done in life was done so that one day he would be called "sir." Out there, in the streets—why, they could be killing themselves. But he had his home, his refuge, this place where he was master and where he could live in peace, a place where he was respected. The only thing troubling him was insomnia. It was now four o'clock. The fog was getting thicker. A heavy silence had fallen over Buenos Aires. Not a sound. Everything still, down to Mr. Lanari who was trying to keep from waking anyone else as he smoked, waiting for sleep to come.

Suddenly a woman screamed. All at once this woman cried out with everything she had, like some wild animal wordlessly begging for help, her screams slicing through the fog, calling to someone, anyone. Mr. Lanari grunted, startled, then he trembled. Her cries seemed to beat against him like fists. He wanted to make her stop. After all, it was the middle of the night and she could wake somebody up; one really ought to be less noisy. There was silence. Then the woman screamed again, ripping the calm and order, creating a scandal by pleading for help with this visceral howl from deep within her body, sounds prior to words, like the sobbing of a little girl desperate and alone.

The wind kept blowing. No one woke up. No one seemed aware. So Mr. Lanari went down to the street and, in the fog, groped his way to the corner. There he saw her, nothing more than a *cabecita negra* sitting on the stoop of a hotel which carried a lighted sign

"Rooms for Ladies" over the door. Hardly yet a woman, she was sprawled out there, drunk, her hands plopped down on her skirt, beaten and alone and lost. Her legs were spread beneath a dirty skirt that had garish red flowers on it, her head was on her chest, a beer bottle in her hand. "I want to come home, Mother," she cried. "I want a hundred pesos to take a train home." This girl sitting there on the narrow wooden steps in that shaft of yellow light, why, she could have been his maid.

Mr. Lanari felt a hesitant tenderness, an unformed pity. He told himself, "Well, this is how these *negros* are. What is one to do; life is hard." And so, smiling, he took out a hundred pesos and, rolling them up, stuffed them in the neck of the beer bottle, feeling vaguely charitable. In fact, he felt good. Hands in his pockets, he stood watching her, eyeing her condescendingly.

"What are you two up to?" The voice was hard. Even before turning he felt the hand on his shoulder. "Okay, you two, you're under arrest. Disturbing the peace." Mr. Lanari, frightened and perplexed, gave the policeman a consenting smile. "Just look at these *negros,* Officer, they spend half their lives getting drunk and afterwards they get happy and make so much ruckus nobody can sleep."

When he realized the policeman was also quite dark-complexioned it was too late. He wanted to explain what had happened. "You foul old man," interrupted the policeman, his eyes full of hate at the puffed-up little man before him, "Let's get moving." The order struck Mr. Lanari like a blow. "Come on, single file, move!" Mr. Lanari blinked out of confusion. Then he reacted, suddenly shouting at the policeman, "You'd better be careful, sir, very careful. This could cost you dearly. Do you know with whom you are speaking?" Mr. Lanari said it like someone firing wildly in the dark, for in fact he had no friends who were influential with the police.

"Come on, you lewd old man, get moving. And don't think that I don't know you belted her one. And now you'd like to wash your hands of it." The officer grabbed him by the collar, while also pulling up the girl who had stopped crying by now and was passively taking it all in, tired, absent, and quiet. Mr. Lanari shuddered. Was everybody crazy? What did all this have to do with *him?* But what if after going to the police station and explaining everything he found they didn't believe him. . . . Things could get even more complicated. He'd never been inside a police station before. All his life he had done everything so as not to have to set foot inside a police station. He was a decent man. (This damn insomnia, it's to blame!) No, there was no assurance the police would clear everything up. Lately, strange things were happening. One couldn't even trust the police anymore. No, going to the police station would just be a useless embarrassment.

"Look, Officer, I had nothing to do with this woman." He could sense that the policeman didn't believe him. He wanted to say that here there were the two of them on the side of the law, while there stood that stupid *negra*—who, to make things worse, said nothing— *she* was the one to blame. Suddenly he turned to the cop, who was a head taller than he, and who was watching him with cold scorn through eyes that seemed right out of the jungle, which along with his thick mustache made him seem an animal, another damn *cabecita negra*. "Officer, sir," he said in a low, confidential tone so that the woman wouldn't hear—the woman standing there holding her empty bottle like a doll, head swaying, vacant, as if she had been so crushed that nothing mattered anymore. "Officer, sir, look, why not come over to my place. I have some good cognac. You'll see that everything I'm telling you is true." And he gave the policeman his card and showed him his documents. "I live just next door." Whining and meek, Mr. Lanari was almost crying. He knew he was in the other man's hands since he didn't know anyone, not even a Congressman, who could bail him out. Yes, it was best to pacify the cop, even bribe him, plead with him, do anything to make him leave one alone.

The policeman looked at his watch and then suddenly, cheerfully, almost as if Mr. Lanari had come up with a great idea, took him by one arm and the woman by the other and started walking, just as if they were old friends. When they arrived at the flat, Mr. Lanari turned on the lights and showed his guests the apartment. The woman took one look at the master bedroom and threw herself on the bed, falling into a deep sleep. How awful, he thought, if someone should come in just now, his son, some relative, or just anyone, they would see him here with these *negros,* caught on the fringes of society, as if he were their partner in some dark, dirty mess. It would be a scandal—the worst thing imaginable—and who would believe his explanation? He would be repudiated, guilty of some nameless deed, when in reality what had he done? He hadn't done anything! Yet what was he doing here, at four in the morning, at a time when people should be asleep, with these *negros?* Here he was, an upright citizen, trapped by this madness in his own home, as if he were common trash.

"Get me some coffee," said the policeman. Mr. Lanari knew he was being humiliated. All his life he had worked so as not to be put in a position where others would push him around, and now, all of a sudden, this man, this nobody, this worthless cop, was treating him familiarly, ordering him around, offending him. And what was worse, he could see in the policeman's eyes a hatred so cold, so inhuman, that he didn't know how to react. Perhaps the best thing would have been to go to the police station, since this guy could be a murderer disguised as a policeman, intending to rob and kill him, to take away everything he had acquired over years of hard work, and on top of that to humiliate him. The woman may have been bait for the trap. He shrugged his shoulders. Nothing made sense anymore.

He served coffee to the policeman and showed him the library. He felt something ominous in the air, something about to happen, some terrifying thing that would fall on him at any moment. But without knowing why, Mr. Lanari showed the policeman his library stacked high with the finest books. He had never found time to read them, of course, but there they were. Mr. Lanari had culture. He had finished school and he owned the whole set of Mitre's *History* bound in leather. And although he hadn't been able to study violin, he had a good record player which permitted him, whenever he wanted, to listen to the finest music the world had produced.

He would have liked to sit down with that man and, in a friendly manner, talk about books. But what books do you talk about with a *negro?* With that one sleeping in his bed and the other here in front of him, ridiculing him, he felt a suffocating sickness. The policeman took off his shoes, flung his cap aside, opened his shirt, and started drinking, slowly.

Mr. Lanari remembered that time when he saw *negros* wash their feet in the fountains in front of the Congress. Feelings from that moment came back to him now; he felt incensed and angry. If only his son were here, not so much to defend him against these *negros* who were now squatters in his house, but just to have another human being there, another civilized person to help him make some sense out of the situation. It was as if his home had been invaded by savages. He felt dizzy, at loose ends. He felt as if his head were about to burst. He was sweating. Everything was crazy. That girl, who could easily have been his maid, sleeping in his bed! And this man, who he couldn't even be sure was a policeman, sitting here drinking his cognac. The house had been taken over, occupied.

Finally the policeman said, "What did you do to her?" "Sir, watch what you say. I've treated you with the utmost consideration, so please show me the courtesy of . . ." The policeman (or whoever he was) grabbed him by the collar and struck him across the face. Mr. Lanari could feel the blood running down his lip. He lowered his eyes, stunned; he was crying. Why were they doing this to him? What did they want him to say? Two strangers enter his home in the middle of the night and ask him to explain something he knows nothing about.

"She's my sister. And you ruined her. You brought her here to work as a maid, and then you thought you could do whatever you wanted with her. Whenever you felt like having a piece, eh? But today I showed up, you bastard, I showed up and I'm going to make you pay for this. You, a real gentleman . . ."

Saying nothing, Mr. Lanari ran to the bedroom and desperately began shaking the girl. She opened her eyes, shrugged her shoulders, turned over and went back to sleep. Now the policeman began beating him, kicking him in the pit of the stomach. Mr. Lanari shook his head to say No, but numbed, just let it happen. Finally the girl awoke, looked at him, then said to her brother, "That's not him, José." She said it with a dry, tired, expressionless voice but said it clearly. Mr. Lanari took in the stunned face of the man, suddenly frightened; saw that he stopped abruptly; and registered that the woman was getting up, slowly. Finally something inside him said, stupidly, "At last this damn insomnia is going away," and he fell asleep.

When he woke up, the sun was in his eyes, blinding him. The room was in shambles with everything strewn all over. There was an awful ache in the pit of his stomach. He felt dizzy, as if he was losing his mind. He closed his eyes to stop the spinning. Then suddenly he rushed to inspect the drawers, the pockets of his pants, rushed down to the garage to see if the car was still there. He was panting, desperate, looking to see that nothing was missing.

What should he do? Who should he turn to? He could go the the police station and report everything, but . . . report what? "Take it easy," he told himself, "Nothing's happened." But it was useless. His stomach ached, everything in the flat was turned upside down, and the door to the street stood open. He swallowed hard. Something basic had been violated. "These people must be crushed," he said, trying to get a grip on himself. "This rabble must be put in its place. Public opinion is behind us, we have the forces of law and order. . . ." He felt hatred. Then all at once Mr. Lanari realized that he would never again feel secure; he could never be sure of anything anymore.

Having read this story, it is possible that some readers will conclude that Peronism was but another episode in the struggle of poor people around the globe for the justice and respect denied them. The human (let alone moral) meaning of history is rarely that simple, however, as may be witnessed in the fact that thousands of students, workers, intellectuals, Argentines of all classes, suffered imprisonment, torture, and in several cases, death for their opposition to the Peronist regime. The anti-Peronists, in other words, were not simply a collection of Mr. Lanaris. Insight into that opposition— and into its fascinating blend of principled and self-interested people—may be found in Beatriz Guido's novel *El incendio y las vísperas,* which has been translated into English as *End of a Day* (Scribner's, 1969). As an attempt to portray the human meaning of Peronism, it is a necessary complement to the Rozenmacher story reproduced here.

6.
ON THE OUTSIDE LOOKING IN

DAVID GREEN

Americans have interpreted Peronism less in terms of Argentina's historical evolution than in terms of international events salient to the United States. This has been true of the U.S. public generally, whose image of Perón still remains that of a pro-Axis dictator, a view that owes much to the negative publicity U.S. newspapers gave Argentina's neutrality during World War II. A subsequent drop-off in attention has left this distorted and dated view behind in the popular mind. An equally extrinsic though less static image is held by U.S. academics, who first described Peronism as a species of fascism and then switched the genus to Nasserism as interest in the Third World supplanted preoccupation with totalitarian-democratic contrasts.

Of no group, however, is the subordination of Argentine reality to global patterns more true than of U.S. policymakers. One sees this in the radical change Washington's position toward Perón underwent once Washington's preoccupation shifted from defeating the Axis to containing the Communists. Indeed, as the following selection suggests, the change was so abrupt that the Truman administration found it difficult to bring public opinion along with it. One might

Reprinted, with excisions, by permission of the author and Quadrangle Books from *The Containment of Latin America* by David Green, pp. 112, 234, 238–254. Copyright © 1971 by David Green. Footnotes have been omitted here; see the original for Professor Green's citations.

even say, somewhat exaggerating the point, that Peronism was our Molotov-Ribbentrop Pact.

This selection was chosen, then, not solely for its portrayal of U.S.-Argentine relations during the critical months of Perón's consolidation of power, but also because it recaptures several of the "frames of reference" through which U.S. citizens viewed—and some still view—Peronism. The selection, of course, has *its* frame of reference, but this, at least, is based on what was happening *in Latin America* at the time. The author sees Peronism as an example of the "militant nationalism" growing in this region since the 1930s.

In tracing the evolution of Washington's policy toward Perón, David Green says relatively little about the corresponding movement inside Argentina. The reader should know that, while the State Department overestimated the importance of pro-Axis activities in Argentina during the war, these were not wholly figments of its imagination. Particularly in the final quarter of 1943, the Argentine government laced its neutral foreign policy with several pro-Axis activities, including unsuccessful negotiations to buy arms from Germany. Subsequently the Argentine government moved away from its pro-Axis position, although in fits and starts inasmuch as—thanks to Cordull Hull's pressuring—this had become a matter of honor for many army officers. How could Buenos Aires adjust to the coming Allied victory without seeming to knuckle under to Washington's ill-disguised threats? The adjustment came, although it involved sacrificing one president (Ramírez) and three foreign ministers—and subjecting Perón to several close calls. It came, in large measure, because Perón was moving his government behind the scenes in much the same direction as Nelson Rockefeller was moving his. In 1945 neither man was interested, any longer, in World War II, and while they had different visions of the postwar world, their maneuvering coincided.

As the war drew to a close in Europe and Asia, amid mounting economic distress in the rest of Latin America, the Good Neighbors south of the Rio Grande might well have begun to wonder who had had the best of the bargain. Was it they, having of necessity fitted their economies to the war machine of the northern metropolis? Or was it the Bad Neighbor to the deep south, who, having an independent base of national prosperity, could afford to thumb her nose at the United States and leave the fight for freedom and democracy to others? It would soon become clear that the rest of Latin America was developing grave doubts about "multilateral economic cooperation," North American style, as a more productive approach for Latin America than the militant economic nationalism of Argentina. . . .

. . . If the United States could somehow overcome the dangerously disruptive and challenging force of Peronist nationalism, and check the possibility of a trend toward nationalism and statism in Latin America, thus assuring a totally Open Hemisphere for American private enterprise, the United States would be on the high road to the construction of an American Century in Latin America—and perhaps elsewhere as well. Indeed, as Nelson Rockefeller had remarked at the San Francisco Conference, unless the United States "operated with a solid group in this hemisphere," it "could not do what we wanted to do on the world front." With a "solid group," the world-wide task would much more easily fall into place. Creation of a "solid group," however, demanded neutralization of the threat of revolutionary nationalism in Latin America. The chief embodiment of revolutionary nationalism was the Peronist movement in Argentina. Therefore the policy-making logic of the Truman administration demanded an all-out effort to deal effectively with the Peronist threat. . . .

A primary aspect of the problem was Argentina's position in the growing East-West conflict which threatened to undermine chances for lasting peace in the postwar world. In the spring of 1945, with the wartime Big Three alliance showing signs of breakdown, Western Hemisphere unity seemed more important than ever. This was certainly no time to permit it to founder on the rocks of traditional Argentine-American rivalry. As long as great-power cooperation remained intact, the Argentine-American conflict could be treated within the context of Western Hemisphere relations. United States policymakers could concentrate upon the threat to hemispheric security posed by what State Department Political Adviser Laurence Duggan called "the totalitarian character of the Argentine Government itself." But a breakdown in great-power unity put Argentine-American rivalry into a new context. If Soviet Russia were really determined to employ all available means to weaken the United States, it could seize upon such a rivalry and exploit it for Soviet purposes. Argentine anti-Americanism might become more important than Argentine "totalitarianism." The policy signficance of such a situation was clear. All during the war, the Roosevelt administration had been calling attention not merely to the Argentine government's pro-Axis foreign policy, but also to its anti-democratic internal structure. Hull in particular had done much to convince the American public that Argentine "fascism" had to go. Yet if continued United States opposition to Argentine policies tended to increase Argentine anti-Americanism, the United States could no longer afford to take such a militant stand. This was one reason for the State Department's dilemma.

The other reason concerned Argentina's role in Western Hemisphere economic relations. By any standard, Argentina was at the close of the war among the richest and most powerful of all the Latin American nations. In terms of financial independence, Argentina was the only Latin America republic (with the one exception of Panama, described by an IADC official as a "boom town living off the Canal Zone payroll") which had emerged from the war with no outstanding indebtedness to the Export-Import Bank of Washington; Brazil and Mexico, her closest rivals for Latin American leadership, were in debt to the Bank to the extent of $84.9 million and $60.3 million, respectively. . . .

The most important reason why Argentina was a pivotal country in inter-American relations, however, was neither a function of extra-hemispheric politics nor merely a question of short-term comparative prosperity. Argentina was of crucial importance because of its emergence into the ranks of the industralized "mass-participation societies" of the postwar era. The social revolution taking place in Argentina in 1945, was a clear portent of the dawning of a new day in Latin American political economy and socio-economic relationships. . . .

Peronism, by 1945 the leading political and economic force in Argentine life, was a complex phenomenon; it seemed to contain elements of both fascism and communism in its bases of support and political techniques. How the United States would respond to it depended on how American foreign policy architects perceived this fascist-communist dualism, particularly in the context of hemispheric relationships and the developing East-West conflict. To those who still saw fascism as the major postwar threat to the Americas, Peronism would have to be divested of its fascist overtones to make it accept-able in the hemisphere. But if communism seemed to be the major threat, then the prime task was to make sure that Peronism did not become allied with Soviet communism, or travel too far to the left in its domestic programs. The main question, then, was not *whether* Peronism was a potential danger to the United States; it was rather *what kind* of danger Peronism was, and how best to meet it. This was the operational dilemma that faced United States policy-planners in the spring of 1945.

On August 25, 1945, Nelson Rockefeller was fired as Assistant Secretary of State for Latin American Affairs. State Department official Carl Spaeth privately told a member of the United States Embassy staff in Buenos Aires that Rockefeller had been "blown through the roof" of the State Department by the public attacks of two major newspapers, the *New York Times* and the *Washington Post*. The *Times* and the *Post*, Spaeth said, felt that Rockefeller had aided the forces of Argentine fascism by his overenthusiatic support of the Farrell-Perón regime at the San Francisco Conference of the United Nations. The two newspapers had continually attacked both Perón and Rockefeller, and had finally succeeded in forcing Rockefel-ler's dismissal from the State Department. The *Times* particularly had noted that as a result of United States sponsorship of Argentine ad-mission to the conference, for which it held Rockefeller directly responsible, the United States had "detracted from its ability to argue for moral principles in the forthcoming negotiations with the Russians on the Dumbarton Oaks amendments." The *Times* feared that by backing Argentine fascism the United States would only strengthen the prestige of Russian communism. Therefore, the *Times,* in alliance with the like-minded *Washington Post,* had put pressure on the State Department and had forced Rockefeller's removal.

The logic of these newspapers was a curious one. In the first place, they assumed that Peronism was primarily a fascist movement. But they also argued that indirectly Peronism held a communist danger, in that United States support for a fascist regime would inevitably cause a public reaction in favor of the Russian position and thus strengthen the Soviet Union's standing vis-à-vis the United States. In a curious way, the *Time*'s position synthesized two forms of anti-Peronism; but its root assumption, namely that Peronism itself was mainly a right-wing threat, was still only one way of looking at the problem.

The other side of the coin was seen by Ambassador Spruille Braden, the State Department's representative in Argentina. Braden arrived in Buenos Aires in May 1945, just as Perón was beginning his flirtation with the Argentine communists, who up to that time had vigorously opposed him. Braden was impressed (though in a negative way) by Perón's militantly nationalist, pro-labor policies. Perón had already stopped issuing new charters to foreign banks. He had not yet nationalized the Argentine banking system, but the threat was in the air. Perón was already playing off the industrial countries against each other as they bid for the Argentine markets. . . .

Most important, Perón seemed to be leaning heavily on the support of militant organized labor. . . . He was talking threateningly about "profit-sharing" schemes; and when 862 of 937 local Argentine business, industrial, and banking associations signed a manifesto against the military government and against Perón in particular, Perón retorted that he now had enough forces in the regular army and "in that other Army of labor" to put down any insurrection. Sir David Kelly, the British Ambassador in Buenos Aires, wanted to take a conciliatory approach to Perón, hoping thereby to extract an Argentine commitment to protect British investments. Braden did not trust Perón; he did not feel the risk was a good one.

Sir David [Braden told reporters] keeps coming back to the point that British investments are so much more important than American. My reply has been No matter—[sic] if this guy keeps on your investments will be worth nothing either through him or by a reaction to communism.

Braden was taking the inverse approach from that of the *New York Times*. Perón was a gangster, no doubt, and in the simplified political rhetoric of the time he was therefore in some sense a "fascist." But Perón's revolutionary nationalism was the real threat; it could lead to communism "by a reaction" set off through its unleashing the political power of labor. Moreover, Argentina had been a fascist gateway to the hemisphere during the war; there was no reason to rule out the possibility that she might as easily become a communist gateway after the war.

The main point was that Peronism might lead to an internal upheaval which would undercut the security of all external capital investments in Argentina. The Argentine example might also prove uncommonly dangerous as a precedent for other Latin American countries. The *New York Times* worried about the external forces of communism which would be strengthened by United States support for Perón; Braden feared that support for Perón would lead to internal revolution, followed by communism. Between them, they covered most of the spectrum of anti-Peronism.

Somewhere in the middle of this spectrum stood Nelson Rockefeller, the man who had so largely influenced actual formation of United States policy toward Argentina until the newspapers had undercut him. Rockefeller fundamentally agreed with both positions; he wanted to avoid strengthening Soviet communism as an external threat to the Americas, and he wanted to avoid a buildup of Argentine revolutionary nationalism which might lead to an internal communist threat. But he differed from both positions, too, in that his tactical assumptions were different. He felt that the best hope of undercutting both these communist threats was by working through Perón, rather than against him.

It is not entirely clear just when Rockefeller first decided that the United States could work with the Peronist regime. As early as January 1945, Rockefeller had received word through Under Secretary of State Grew that the Argentine government might be ready to talk about a rapprochement, "owing to the pressure to which they were being subjected." At the opening of the Chapultepec Conference in late February, Rockefeller began moving to bring about such a rapprochement. In the meantime, he worked to consolidate his control over aspects of Latin American policy formulation in the State Department. . . .

By the time the San Francisco Conference ended in June 1945, the basic American policy decision regarding Argentina had been worked out to its logical regional conclusion. Argentina had been started on the path to reintegration into the hemispheric system, while the system itself had achieved the sought-for juridical and political autonomy as well as a strong dose of built-in anti-communism.

Rockefeller's views on the internal political and economic situation in Argentina were perfectly consistent with his views on the larger hemispheric and world-wide significance of the Argentine problem.

While liberal-labor groups in the United States such as the CIO were actively supporting Ambassador Braden and attacking the "fascist" regime in Buenos Aires, Rockefeller had already discounted the seriousness of Peronism as a threat from the extreme right. He sponsored Argentine admission to the United Nations Conference knowing of her actual performance in regard to her Chapultepec commitments. He was ready to go along with State Department aide Avra Warren's recommendation to give military supplies to Perón, and was dissuaded only by the pressure exerted from Buenos Aires by Ambassador Braden.

Rockefeller could afford to take this indulgent view of Peronism. All through 1944, it had been clear from Ambassador Norman Armour's reports that Perón himself was not in fact a representative of the most nationalistic elements in the Argentine military. In January 1945, Rockefeller had had indications that the Argentine government was ready to seek a rapprochement with the United States. After the Chapultepec Conference, Perón had acted unusually fast, if somewhat halfheartedly, in declaring war on the Axis. Argentina had also made an ostentatious gift of five million bushels of wheat to UNRRA. Most important, in the course of Avra Warren's visit to Buenos Aires with General Brett in early April, Warren had had encouraging discussions with Argentine business leaders about the reopening of Argentine markets to United States industrial exports. The Argentines were as anxious as were American businessmen to unclog trade and investment channels and normalize Argentine-American business relations. Close business relations, as Rockefeller well knew, were the surest way to undercut a dangerously anti-American nationalism in Argentina. Rockefeller therefore moved to eliminate the remaining diplomatic obstacles to an Argentine-American rapprochement.

By the end of the San Francisco Conference, the foundation of the rapprochement was secure. Rockefeller had unwittingly undercut his own position, but his policy had been accepted by the State Department. In an interview years later, a former ranking State Department official stated categorically that Rockefeller's dismissal from the Department in August 1945 was a gesture to public opinion in the United States and nothing more; in no way did it denote a substantive change in United States policy toward Argentina. By August

1945, Rockefeller, who was a Republican anyway, was becoming a political liability to the State Department; it was easy enough to dispense with his policy approach. The selection of Ambassador Braden to replace Rockefeller as Assistant Secretary of State for Latin American Affairs was merely the other side of the coin in this public relations move. Braden was considered by the influential newspapers to be a firm anti-Peronist; putting him in to replace Rockefeller was the obvious gesture to satisfy the anti-Peronists in the United States. Again, this move indicated no change in policy.

Braden's fundamental strategic position on Argentina was not really different from Rockefeller's anyway. Both men accepted the strategic premise that Argentine political and economic nationalism must be undercut. They differed only with respect to tactics. Rockefeller was convinced by late April 1945 that Perón could be used as the means to an Argentine-American rapprochement. He decided to work through Perón. Braden, more frightened by Perón's labor support and by his political flirtation with the Argentine communists in the late summer of 1945, decided it was necessary to work *against* Perón. . . .

All through 1946, however, Braden, with public opinion in the United States still largely favorable to his anti-"fascist" position, continued to take his "promotion" seriously and issued numerous broadsides aimed at the "neurotic nationalism" of the Perón regime in Argentina. Meanwhile, his replacement in Buenos Aires, George Messersmith, was by order of Secretary Byrnes and President Truman quietly working at cross-purposes with Braden, trying desperately to re-establish friendly relations between the United States and Argentina so that the Rio Conference [on hemispheric defense] could proceed. . . .

When it came to actual policy execution, Braden's tenure in Washington ultimately was no more than a delaying action. By January 1947, Senator Vandenberg was calling publicly for convening of the Rio Conference, in a speech which included a virtual demand for Braden's resignation. At first the new Secretary of State, General of the Army George C. Marshall, was preoccupied with European problems. But by the late spring of that year, the Secretary, along with President Truman, had decided that the conference had been postponed long enough. Braden was quietly informed that his services would no longer be needed. . . . Perón was to be wooed—and won. The fly-swatter approach had not worked; there was nothing left but to try the flypaper.

BIBLIOGRAPHIC SUGGESTIONS

This bibliography is confined to two dozen works in English that are available in most university libraries, excluding works from which selections were taken. Those who read Spanish may augment this list by consulting the publications of, among others, the Argentine government, Darío Canton, Gonzálo Cárdenas, Alberto Ciria, Dardo Cúneo, Torcuato S. DiTella, Carlos S. Fayt, Alfredo Galletti, Rogelio García Lupo, Gino Germani, Félix Luna, Alejandro Magnet, Juan and Eva Perón, as well as the United Nations Economic Commission for Latin America.

ALEXANDER, ROBERT J. *The Perón Era*. New York: Columbia University Press, 1951. The first book-length analysis of Peronism, written while Perón was still riding high. Emphasis on Perón's relations with labor and his economic policy.

BAILY, SAMUEL L. *Labor, Nationalism, and Politics in Argentina*. New Brunswick, N.J.: Rutgers University Press, 1967. Most complete study of Argentine labor; develops the notion of a cultural difference between the old and new workers of the 1940s.

BARAGER, JOSEPH R. *Why Perón Came to Power*. New York: Knopf, 1968. Collection of writings by Argentines and others on the conditions and consequences of Peronism.

BLANKSTEN, GEORGE I. *Perón's Argentina*. Chicago: University of Chicago Press, 1953. Along with Alexander's book, an early and occasionally flawed description of Perón's rule. Focus on politics and ideology.

COCHRAN, THOMAS, and RUBEN REINA. *Entrepreneurship in Argentine Culture*. Philadelphia: University of Pennsylvania Press, 1962. The history of SIAM DiTella, an industrial firm which achieved prominence during the Peronist period, with insights into businessmen's attitudes toward labor and the government.

FERNS, H. S. *Argentina*. New York: Praeger, 1969. One-volume history of Argentina by a British scholar. The chapter on Peronism emphasizes the interaction between political payoffs and economic errors.

FERRER, ALDO. *The Argentine Economy.* Translation by Marjory Urquidi. Berkeley: University of California Press, 1967. Economic history by a well-known Argentine economist (and later Economics Minister), written in nontechnical language.

GERMANI, GINO. "Fascism and Class," *The Nature of Fascism,* ed. S. J. Woolf. New York: Vintage Books, 1969. Analysis of how Peronism differed from Italian Fascism, by a leading Italo-Argentine sociologist now teaching at Harvard.

GERMANI, GINO. "The Transition to a Mass Democracy in Argentina," *Contemporary Cultures and Societies of Latin America,* ed. Dwight Heath and Richard Adams. New York: Random House, 1965. One of several articles by Germani on social mobilization in the decades preceding and accompanying Peronism.

IMAZ, JOSÉ LUIS DE. *Los que mandan.* Translated by Carlos Astiz. Albany: State University of New York, 1970. Analysis of recruitment and career ladders within several Argentine elites (political, military, economic, etc.) and how they changed between 1936 and 1961.

KENNEDY, JOHN J. *Catholicism, Nationalism and Democracy in Argentina.* South Bend, Ind.: University of Notre Dame, 1958. History of the Argentine Church's involvement in politics.

KIRKPATRICK, JEANE. *Leader and Vanguard in Mass Society: A Study of Peronist Argentina.* Cambridge, Mass.: The MIT Press, 1971. Despite the subtitle, this is essentially a study of post-Peronist Argentina, focusing on the attitudes of rank-and-file Peronists.

PENDLE, GEORGE. *Argentina,* Third edition. London: Oxford University Press, 1963. Another one-volume history by an Englishman. Contains a chapter on Perón which is more sympathetic than are most accounts written in English.

PETERSON, HAROLD P. *Argentina and the United States, 1810–1960.* New York: State University of New York, 1964. History of diplomatic relations between the two countries.

POTASH, ROBERT A. *The Army and Politics in Argentina, 1928–1945.* Stanford, Calif.: Stanford University Press, 1969. Most complete study of civil–military relations in the years when Perón rose to power (as well as previous decades).

ROMERO, JOSÉ LUIS. *A History of Argentine Political Thought.* Translated by Thomas F. McGann. Stanford, Calif.: Stanford University Press, 1963. Political/intellectual history written by a distinguished

Argentine historian. The analysis of Peronism takes too seriously
Perón's early speeches.

SCOBIE, JAMES. *Argentina: A City and a Nation,* Second edition.
New York: Oxford University Press, 1971. The best history of
modern Argentina written in English. Particularly adept at weaving
social and economic developments into the historical narrative.

SILVERMAN, BERTRAM. *Labor Ideology and Economic Development in
the Peronist Epoch.* Studies in Comparative International Development, IV: 11. St. Louis: Washington University Press, 1969.
Analysis of the costs to Argentine economic development of Perón's
populism.

SILVERT, KALMAN H. "The Costs of Anti-Nationalism: Argentina,"
Expectant Peoples. Edited by Silvert for the American Universities
Field Staff. New York: Vintage Books, 1967. One of several
articles on Argentina by one who views Peronism as a manifestation of a southern European-Latin American penchant for corporatist solutions to social change.

SMITH, PETER H. *Politics and Beef in Argentina.* New York: Columbia University Press, 1969. Primarily an analysis of Argentina's
economic elite in the years preceding Peronism. Contains an analysis
of why labor forsook liberal democracy for Perón.

SNOW, PETER G. *Argentine Radicalism.* Iowa City: University of
Iowa Press, 1965. Brief history of Argentina's once leading political
party including the responses Perón elicited from its various
factions.

WALTER, RICHARD. *Student Politics in Argentina.* New York: Basic
Books, 1968. History of student involvement in politics, including
student-worker conflicts under Perón.

WHITAKER, ARTHUR P. *Argentine Upheaval.* New York: Praeger,
1956. Description of the final months of Perón's administration,
written shortly after his fall. One of several books on Argentina
by this U.S. historian.

WHITAKER, ARTHUR P., and DAVID JORDAN. *Nationalism in Contemporary Latin America.* New York: Free Press, 1966. Contains
chapter on the distinct nationalisms of the Argentine left and
right.

Finally, the attempt to relate Peronism to worldwide patterns of
societal change has produced several interesting and contrasting interpretations—frequently as sweeping in their central thesis as they are
careless in factual detail. Representative of this genre are A. F. K.

Organski, *The Stages of Political Development,* "Syncratic Politics"; John H. Kautsky, *Political Change in Underdeveloped Countries,* "The Role of the Intellectuals" and "The Totalitarianism of the Intellectuals"; Seymour Martin Lipset, *Political Man,* "The 'Fascism' of the Lower Class"; and Samuel Huntington, *Political Order in Changing Societies,* "Mass Praetorianism."

VIII.
Civil-Military Relations in the Twentieth Century:
Fundamental Reform or Strategic Shifts?

♆ ANTHONY P. MAINGOT

Military intervention in the politics of Latin American nations is widely regarded as one of the most typical and continuous characteristics of the politics of that Hemisphere.

Until recently many scholars advanced the interpretation that this intervention was an expression of continued *caudillismo* and were satisfied that that behavior was generally a departure from the otherwise democratic tendencies of the other sectors in the political arena. A quick moral judgment and a wistful expression of hope for a civilian future was generally the extent of their concluding thoughts. More sophisticated studies avoided the moralizing overtones but hitched the civilian-democratic future to the rising star of the middle class. Only this class could break the pattern of aristocratic recruitment and reactionary interventionist politics in the armed institutions of the Hemisphere.

The documents in this unit provide a more sociologically accurate picture of the military as an integral part of these societies and of the very complex patterns of interaction between the society and the military, both as corporate groups with their own internal dynamics and as individual professionals with class and institutional loyalties.

Not that there is fundamental agreement to be found

among these interpretations. At a minimum level these
documents do address themselves to three critical areas of
analysis in the field of civil–military relations:

1. *Recruitment* of the officer corps. Specifically, how do
   the upper classes regard the military as a profession
   and career, and to what extent do they enter military
   service?
2. *Socialization* while in the military academy and in the
   specialized training courses and schools.
3. The *corporate interests* of the military as an institution
   as reflected in their actions as an interest group.

Any history of civil–military relations must obviously
trace changes in both the military as well as the civilian
sectors of society. If military men and institutions have become more professional and technically competent, so have
the civilian political-administrative structures. Civil–military
relations differ from country to country but, in general, one
can divide that history into two major periods: the pre-
professional and the postprofessional. The crucial event serving as dividing line would be the institutionalization of
military education—the establishment and functioning of the
formal military school or academy. Formal education necessarily brought a change to the haphazard recruiting of officers, the erratic and nonprofessional socialization process,
and consequently to the institution's sense of corporate
identity. Beginning in Chile in the 1880s, the professionalization of the armies of the large Latin American countries,
trained largely by Prussian missions, had established an
identifiable pattern by World War I. Professional and ade-
quately equipped navies and air forces were a later development and play generally, with the exception of Argentina,
a secondary role in Latin American politics.

It should be emphasized, however, that besides this formal
professionalization many Latin American countries have had
very idiosyncratic national experiences which represent crucial stages in the development of their military institutions
and consequently in their civil–military relations. Chile's

military victories during the War of the Pacific (1879–1883), which increased its land size and mineral wealth, doing just the reverse to Peru and Bolivia, put the military in a strong position to demand a Prussian military training mission. It was defeat and humiliation in the Chaco War (1932–1935) rather than victory which led the Bolivian military to reconsider their recruiting patterns and political orientations. The victorious Paraguayan military also expanded their political role following this war, a role that continues to this writing.

World War II generally meant some new North American weapons and training missions, but to the Brazilian officers who fought with the Allies in Italy it had deeper significance. It provided them with a pro-American orientation which had a profound influence on post–World War II politics. Similarly, the officers of the Colombian "Batallón Colombia," the only Latin American unit to fight in Korea, played a crucial role in shaping military attitudes during the 1957–1962 period.

No two Latin American nations show exactly the same pattern of civil–military relations. No single Latin American country has a socially homogeneous and ideologically united military institution. But even within the variety there are broad overarching generalizations about Latin American military behavior which are useful for analysis. Note, for instance, the similar tone and direction of the new questions which characterize much of the discussion in more than one Latin American country concerning the "proper" role and function of the armed forces in developing societies in general and theirs in particular. With professionalization—in the sense of military expertise—an accomplished fact, a new phase of Latin American civil–military relations might be in its preliminary stage. In document 1 Jacques Lambert highlights the most salient features of contemporary civil–military relations: the new modernizing attitudes of the officer corps. Lambert attributes this change of orientation in part to the professionalization which has changed military socialization but, more important, to the social class origins of these modernizing officers. Their middle-class allegiances militate against continued aristocratic domination, especially since this latter class disdained entry into the military.

Alfred Stepan (document 8) similarly has found a strong new attitude among the Brazilian military. But he minimizes the importance of social class origins and stresses the corporate interests of the military institutions; these, he claims, transcend class allegiances. These interests make the military a *situational* rather than a *class* elite. This difference of interpretation and approach is also to be found in the rest of the documents and serves to emphasize the great complexity of the subject. No facile moralisms will explain away that complexity.

One critical sociological aspect to bear in mind is that one cannot attribute new causes to phenomena which, as it turns out, are quite old. Antiaristocratic sentiments among the military are clearly tied up with the pattern of recruitment. Virtually all evidence available demonstrates that the supposed recruitment of the military from the traditional elite was and is a myth. Where aristocrats did enter the military they tended to be "bad children of good families," a saying or expression which is used throughout Latin America. Similarly, professionalization *per se* is not new, as José Luis de Imaz shows in document 5. It is the ideological context of that professionalization which has shifted.

Many of the fundamental issues are hardly new ones. Don Manuel V. Villarán (document 2) describes the fluctuations in the social status of the military career in Peru. The fluctuations in popularity were found in other countries. General Carlos Sáez M., in document 3, addresses himself to the discrimination *within* the Chilean army, an extension of the general pattern existing in the broader society. Thus, the antiaristocratic sentiment of many officers was already present; it was a necessary condition for the new brand of military politics being witnessed in Latin America. But the will and capacity to move directly against the traditional groups required other conditions before they could be actualized. A partial explanation of what these conditions are is found in document 3. General Sáez corroborates what Lambert and

José Luis de Imaz document: the ever-present civilian support and pressure for military political action. That civilians have encouraged military participation to the detriment of the armed forces is true, but it also appears to have been to their own detriment as well since a "habit" of intervention was early developed in the military.

The increased complexity of national and international politics and administration has shown the traditional elites to be substantially less than the competent administrators they have been widely held to be. The military no longer act as temporary guardians of power, salvaging the ship of state for others; rather they intend to move the society themselves. Not all observers, however, believe the military intend to carry these new notions to the extent of bringing about fundamental change. In document 4 Peruvian Colonel and authority on civil–military relations, Victor Villanueva, openly questions the motives behind these new moves. Villanueva reflects a minority view when he states that there is no fundamental change in military thinking. Most observers would cite the views expressed by General Morales Bermudez of Peru (document 6) and General Ruiz Novoa of Colombia (document 7) as reflecting those of the "new wave."

Changes in recruitment, changes in the educational content of military training, or realistic and strategic shifts in "style" to suit changes in the socioeconomic milieu—all these interpretations have their advocates. More basic research is needed to establish which one, or combination of them, best describes reality. The student does well to remember, however, that even if Latin America does count itself, and is counted by the "experts," as part of the Third World, these are not "new" societies. To study Latin American civil–military relations utilizing frames of reference designed to study civil–military relations in truly new states, such as those in Tropical Africa, might be misleading. Civil–military relations in Latin America, no matter what pattern they show today, are not post–World War II developments; they reach back to the early days of Independence. No student will claim that the pattern of the 1970s is the culmination of a process. No social pattern is ever static; civil-military relations will continue to evolve with the rest of society.

What has been established and documented here are three fundamental aspects of civil–military relations in Latin America:

1. The military are not, and probably never were, a consistently homogeneous group either in terms of recruitment, institutional social status, socialization, or institutional policy.

2. Civilian sectors have always regarded the military as integral parts of the political system and, on that assumption, have made appeals to it to intervene politically.

3. There is today a widespread sentiment among the military against the traditional elites and their handling of affairs of state. There is no single model of development, however, which the military in Latin America generally, or even within one country, regard as ideal.

To be sure, Latin America is a multisociety continent with great varieties in civil–military relationships. One should not minimize the similarities in military behavor, however, for these reflect the similarities of societal and ideological currents presently flowing through many of these nations and through the Hemisphere.

1.

LATIN AMERICA: Social Structures and Political Institutions

JACQUES LAMBERT

In this work, first published in France in 1963, French political scientist Jacques Lambert deals with some of the crucial questions of Latin America civil–military relations: Is there a new attitude among the military? How do civilians regard a political role on the part of the military? Is education, military socialization, more important than social background in shaping military attitudes? From which sector is the military recruited? His answers are clearly not unanimously accepted in the ·field, but they do form an incisive and well-informed argument, a good introduction to the subject.

It may seem paradoxical to describe the political role of the military as one aspect of the role of the middle classes and to interpret it as an expression of political forces in the advanced or developing society. Resort to arms to seize power occurred in the very first days of independence, and therefore its recurrence appears to many observers as an anachronism. The proliferation of military dictatorships outside Latin America today suggests, however, that they are a feature of the first stage of development, rather than of true underdevelopment.

From Jacques Lambert, *Latin America: Social Structures and Political Institutions,* pp. 228–242. Translated by Helen Katel. Originally published by the University of California Press. Copyright © 1967 by the University of California Press; reprinted by permission of the Regents of the University of California.

Military interventions in politics are tied to political, economic, and social immaturity, but also to the weakening of archaic economic and social structures and to attempts to modernize them.

It is true that generals, colonels, and even lieutenants never stopped meddling in politics in Latin America and using their men to seize power or control the government. But these are not the same officers or the same army as formerly, and their intentions in politics have taken on different characteristics. . . .

. . . The military are now led by officer cadres trained in military colleges. The officer corps is too well organized to enable one man to use an army for strictly personal motives. Interventions must express the collective will of the officer corps or a large segment of it and correspond to their ideology or interests. . . .

. . . [It] was in Chile that [this] new attitude emerged and reforms were carried out, leading to the formation of a corps of officers conscious of their professional role in the nation. Chile took the initiative of reorganizing the armed services with the help of European professionals. Her successes in the War of the Pacific (1879–1883), which enabled her to wrest from Peru and Bolivia the nitrate-rich northern deserts, moved her to maintain a modern army. In 1885 the government asked Germany to send a military mission and granted very broad powers to its head, General Koerner, who was appointed Chief of the Chilean General Staff. A military college was organized to train young officers, and a military academy to train higher officers. Their instruction was carried out by German officers and was supplemented by additional training in the German army. Koerner also prevailed upon Chile to enact the first Latin American conscription law, which deeply changed the nature of the services by bringing in other elements than the most backward and least integrated in the nation. Koerner's reforms gave the military profession a technical character and a dignity it had not had since independence.

Chile's example spread rapidly to a large number of countries. . . .

The influence of the military missions, the training geared to national defense, the technical nature of the training required by modern equipment, all have contributed to give Latin American military men a new idea of their social function. This, however, has not stopped or substantially lessened the frequency of political interventions by the military, because they result primarily from a deep concern for internal security. The international situation combined with political instability places the burden of maintaining domestic peace upon the armed services. . . .

The role of the armed services lends itself to much misinterpretation because the military are constantly being asked to intervene in politics. All of Latin America complains about the excessive role of the military in political life, but it should be said in all fairness that all social classes and all parties try to provoke these interventions whenever they are displeased with their government. All too often under the Latin American regime of presidential dominance, presidential succession breeds political crises, either because a president whose term is about to expire tries to cling to office illegally, or because he tries to impose a successor of his own choosing. This flaw of Latin American political regimes is called continuism. When it occurs, the advocates of legality request the military to restore the rule of law by ousting the dictator or would-be dictator. Also, the losers in an election, who are not accustomed to accept defeat, claim that the elections were fraudulent and ask the military to seize power in order to hold better ones. This is a convenient excuse, and the military do not always need prodding. Seizure of power by a junta that promises to hold proper elections is quite customary. A large segment of public opinion invariably support the military in such a case. . . .

It is widely believed that most military interventions in Latin America have been reactionary, or at least have aimed at preventing popular forces from reforming an archaic society. Such a belief, however, stems from seemingly logical reasoning rather than from actual observation of facts. Even a specialist on Latin American affairs as knowledgeable as (A. Curtis) Wilgus wrote: "The officer class was composed chiefly of older sons of the aristocracy who entered the military service for the social prestige it gave them. With control of military forces, it was not difficult for the aristocracy to control the government."

This comes from equating Latin America with Europe. Such reasoning, as a matter of fact, would be invalid almost anywhere outside Europe. Military interventions in Latin America would be impossible to understand if their instigators were elder sons of aristocrats. Although these interventions have usually (but not always) been aimed at governments whose form was democratic, this does not make them politically conservative. This is because in the countries involved, compliance with the forms of democracy has often led to the hegemony of the most archaic political forces. . . .

. . . On the whole, at any rate until the rise of Communism and Castroism in Latin America, political interventions by the military had aimed at change rather than at maintaining the status quo. Military interventions did much to prevent a return to caudillismo and to hasten the decline of government by the upper class.

One of the reasons for this is the officers' social background. Despite the European traditions of Latin America, the officers were recruited (at least in the nineteenth century) from other social strata than in Europe. Since most of them came from the middle classes, they usually wished to reform societies that had remained very aristocratic.

Stereotyped thinking valid only for Europe usually pictures the military profession as traditionally tied to the conservative ruling classes because respect for hierarchy is one of its basic values and because its influential members belong to those ruling classes. . . .

In Latin America, however, military traditions are altogether different. This modern military profession only started to emerge in the nineteenth century as the product of revolutionary armies instead of traditionalist royal armies. The landed aristocracy had not yet lost its wealth or its political power. Far from it, Creole aristocracy, freed from the tutelage of the Peninsulares, was at its height in the nineteenth century. Only exceptionally were members of a wealthy ruling aristocracy attracted by the military profession. On the other hand, the masses were too ignorant and despised to be admitted to military colleges. With few isolated exceptions, they could join the services only as enlisted men.

Hence the officers were usually recrited from the middle classes. The armed forces in Latin America, far from being a haven for men barred from power by social evolution, were the stepping stone for a class on the rise and aspiring to wrest power from the aristocracy. Within the static societies with a rigid hierarchy based on *latifundio* ownership, there were very few ways to improve one's social status. The liberal professions provided some opportunities but were largely monopolized by the aristocracy. Industry was scarcely developed and many of the large enterprises, notably trading concerns, were in the hands of foreigners or recent immigrants. Military colleges, on the contrary, provided openings for young men of little wealth, particularly if they already had some connection with the military.

Since lower-class people, whether white or colored, were barred *de facto* through subtle discrimination, it is not true that the officer corps in Latin America was democratically recruited. It would be even less accurate to say that its background ties it to the traditional ruling classes and that it tends to be used as a tool for the preservation of the status quo. If any generalizations are in order, the most legitimate would be that within the very diversified middle-class group which has gained power in the years since World War I, the officers have tended to form a caste equally remote from the aristocracy and from the people. The very great opportunities for advancement that the political power of the Latin American armed forces have provided, coupled with the ease with which officer's sons are admitted to military schools, have tended to make recruitment hereditary. . . .

Naturally, any generalization that becomes too systematic is bound to be erroneous. The officer corps cannot be the same either in its composition or in its outlook in twenty countries as different from one another as Haiti and Argentina, and it has not remained unchanged throughout one and a half centuries. Since it plays a political role, the officer corps must necessarily represent different opinions. The different services are not recruited in the same way and do not have the same outlook. Neither do higher officers after they have become generals share the opinions of second lieutenants.

2.
DISCURSO (The Military)

DON MANUEL V. VILLARÁN

The Peruvian scholar Don Manuel V. Villaran notes a crucial characteristic of Peruvian military history: the oscillating character of their image in the eyes of the public, from high status to low status to moderate status. This lack of a homogeneous and consistent institutional image and status characterizes much of Latin America's military history. In hierarchical, steeply stratified societies there tends to develop a vicious circle between recruitment and prestige or status. Recruitment from a lower socioeconomic sector tends to debase the institution's prestige; low status further affects the institution's ability to recruit from a higher status group. Often a deliberate Executive Act, or a state of war broke the circle and set the institution on a different path.

If the ecclesiastical career today has extremely few candidates recruited from people of a certain social position, perhaps there are even fewer of these who aspire to the military profession. In 1826, with the War of Independence already over, the national army reached 9,000 men and their maintenance cost 1,500,000 pesos a year. The number of officers and commanders [*jefes*] was excessive. It made good sense that those self-denying servants of their country

From Don Manuel V. Villarán, "Discurso," *Anales de la Universidad Mayor de San Marcos,* vol. 27 (Lima, 1900), pp. 13–16. Translated by Consuelo S. Maingot.

be compensated generously; a few should have been retained and the others retired totally. But they chose to assure them of a pension in an indefinite future and so forced them, on the threat of losing it, to continue as military men. That is how an interminable army list was formed, a list which grew after each revolution. In 1874 there were 2,833 commanders and officers without counting 206 invalids and retired ones. . . .

What is happening in Peru occurs more or less in all the republics of our race. . . . Spain . . . has given us in this, and in many other things, a very bad example. The Spanish army recently had 540 generals; France with an army nearly three times as large has 300.

The military, besides being numerous have not in general been enlightened and noteworthy people. "Domestic disturbances," states a report from the Ministry of War, "have brought to the army a multitude of individuals who would have been of much better use in another profession." Paz-Soldan observes that "upon initiating our independent life the military career was subject to ordinary and routine practices and its commanders and officers represented, but with rare exceptions, the most ignorant part of the society."

Despite that the social and political power of the military was immense: the admiration for them uncontainable. They retained that great ascendency for a long time, and the career of arms attracted . . . a multitude of persons who were distinguished by reason of their position and birth. The military were the absolute owners of the government. Without exception they governed the departments and provinces. The most lucrative positions in the public offices nearly always were theirs. As the well known saying goes, the presidency of the Republic was the natural culmination of their career.

The excess of power held by the military is today, as we know, an historical fact. The army, wiser today, understands that it has to limit itself to its proper mission, which to be sure does not involve governing, but rather the defense of the State. Unfortunately, we have to observe with regret that public opinion, because of a reaction which is as unjust as it is irremediable, has lost all the appreciation it once had for the military career. Today there is no career less solicited than the career of arms, just as there is no other, aside from industrial careers, in which we have a greater interest to foment and ennoble. Who knows of any distinguished and rich young men who are stimulated or even authorized by their families to enter the army? In England, in Germany, a young son of princes feels it an honor to be a cadet. The militia is a profession for the rich and noble. Here many parents would lose esteem for a son who felt a vocation for the military.

Despite the fact that there are commanders and officers in the army who are irreproachable, it is necessary to admit that our military men are not generally well received by society. Many people, especially ladies, have a revulsion to the insignias. They believe that the uniform stands precisely for ignorance, a dissipated life, a lack of manners and lowly origins. The burden of this social anathema has led the youth of our army into a state of disorientation. That is why they withdraw, isolate themselves and stay to one side. Only in very rare cases do you see uniformed officers in clubs, or in theatres, or in discussion meetings [tertulias], or in any of the centers frequented by enlightened people. How profound must be the bitterness of our officers who have to experience this sort of atonement which persecutes the military class! But they are duty-bound to open a way for themselves in society; to erase through public recognition of their talents and conduct that general predisposition which for the time being unjustly denies the Peruvian military man of his just share of honor and respect.

3.
RECUERDOS DE UN SOLDADO

GENERAL CARLOS SÁEZ M.

General Carlos Sáez M. was born in 1881 in Chillán, Chile, to relatively poor parents. As an officer he participated in many of the conspiracies of the early twentieth century; was a member of the *Liga Militar* of 1912 which lobbied for laws and legislation favorable to the military institution. Sáez headed the military training mission to Colombia, 1914–1916; participated in the *coup* attempts of 1924 and 1925 in Chile; and in July 1931 after the overthrow of Carlos Ibañez was made minister of war. A new conspiracy in August 1931 forced him to retire from the army. General Sáez claimed that he was writing his memoirs to help his two young officer sons and all the other young members of that institution.

[In Europe great men are proud of their past poverty and hard work.] We [Chileans] generally proceed in a different fashion. Here we have an abundance of individuals who mortify themselves seeking a lineage. The desire to rise socially tends to make men belittle themselves. That is a miserable affair and I am confident that my children will know how to avoid it.

I hope to demonstrate that those who attempted to heap oppro-

From General Carlos Sáez M., *Recuerdos de un soldado,* 3 vols., 2nd ed. (Santiago: Biblioteca Sucilla, 1934), I, pp. 8–46, *passim.* Translated by Consuelo S. Maingot.

briums on the military institutions because of their intervention in affairs foreign to their natural activities have acted unjustly; they have forgotten that [the military] have merely been the toy of high-powered politicians, and, what is more, the victims of the environment in which they have had to act.

[To the member of poor background] the army is an eminently democratic institution. Sometimes men with prominent family names rise, but true merit always ends up by imposing itself, that merit which is the product of a life of permanent efforts. [This was not so at one time.] We lived, unfortunately, under a regime of favoritisms which continually created irritating injustices. A good recommendation was enough to annul the best service record. Those officers who belonged to high society had their careers assured. [Even the study trips to Germany were not due to merit] . . . the favored ones owed that reward in the most cases to recommendations from outside the army. For every one distinguished officer sent to Germany there were several officers with only excellent social connections.

[This regime of favoritism led to an established tactic.] Impelled by self-interest, some officers soon began to understand the need to solicit the friendship of people who were in a position to lend them an opportune hand, and no help could be more effective in those days than the aid of politicians. A command, a change of garrisons, or a trip to Europe often depended on the intervention of a deputy, or a senator. Politicians are practical men, alien to certain scruples of conscience. Their friendship during that period of acute parliamentarianism was of extraordinary value. (This was prejudicial to the military institution. It threatened to destroy the institution.) . . .

A Chilean aristocrat is generally a *gran señor,* proud of his old parchments; he lives on a higher plane from which he looks with quite natural disagreeableness upon the mass of his fellow citizens. . . . Between a gentleman of great lineage [*rancios abolengos*] and a man with no other titles than his own merits there exists a distance which the former can shorten through expressions of benevolence but which he can never abolish except in very special cases.

4.

NUEVA MENTALIDAD MILITAR EN EL PERU?

VICTOR VILLANUEVA

It is revealing that the Brazilian edition of this book by
Peruvian retired Colonel Victor Villanueva carried the title
The Coup of '68 in Peru, From Caudillismo to Nationalism?
Villanueva, a man intimately acquainted with the nature of
conspiracy and the *coup d'état* in Peru, has consistently
argued that there has been no overriding ideology to Peruvian military politics, merely personal and corporate self-
interest. In 1963 he published the satirical *Manual for the
Conspirator* (Lima, 1963) to dramatize his general interpretation of military behavior. In this, his most recent work,
Villanueva is more cautious, yet still refuses to accept the
Peruvian military as the modernizers they are presently
widely held to be. His skepticism is worth serious attention
if only because of his great personal proximity to and
knowledge of the situation.

The Aristocratic Tendency of the Military

It is frequently said that the army is a democratic institution in
which every soldier, as in the Napoleonic Epoch, carries a Field
Marshal's staff in his knapsack. And today, in defense of that theory
it is said that the present President [of Peru], General Velasco Alvar-

From Colonel Victor Villenueva, *Nueva mentalidad militar en el Peru?*
(Lima: Editorial Juan Mejía Baca, 1969), pp. 250–259. Translated by
Consuelo S. Maingot.

ado, began his career as a simple soldier. Mere words without any basis in fact. . . .

The Peruvian army, like all permanent armies, and similar naval and air force institutions, has an aristocratic tendency. Its stratification into classes is a continuing demonstration not only of its origin but also principally of its tendency. . . .

The officer corps and the troops in the armed forces constitute two fundamentally and socially different groups. An officer cannot sit at the same table with a soldier, nor sit in the same section at public events, nor travel in the same coaches of a train. In the Chilean army, because of its Prussian tradition, the differences are even more marked. Officers travel in Pullman, noncommissioned officers first class, and the troops second class. Officers cannot walk in the street carrying packages by hand because such an act affects the "dignity of the uniform . . ." a soldier may not remain seated if there is an officer present . . . [all] prescriptions which are undoubtedly legacies of the etiquette of nobility and of monarchical societies.

In Peru, the aristocratic tendency of the military and their emulation of the upper classes of the bourgeoisie is manifested in a thousand ways. The Círculo Militar of Peru is located on the plaza San Martín, the most central location in Lima . . . equipped with English-made furniture, French porcelain, etc. It is considered one of the best social centers of the capital. . . .

But this has not been enough to satisfy the military's desire to excel. The government has just built another club on a central avenue, even more spacious and luxurious. The "Club Nacional" . . . is the social club of Lima's "aristocracy," the most exclusive club of the capital. That explains [the military's] pride in the fact that the "Círculo Militar" is more luxurious. The aristocratic tendency of the military and their emulation of the upper classes are fully confirmed in this case.

But the difference between officers and troops are not merely formal and external. They go even deeper. Entry to the Escuela de Oficiales is governed by a double standard of discrimination, one socioeconomic, the other racial. Officers are recruited from bourgeois sectors, the troops fundamentally from the peasantry, [and] in minor proportions from urban sectors. . . . In terms of origin, thus, officers and troops belong to two different social classes.

. . . In Peru, a minimum height of 1.65 meters [5'4"] is required to be an Army officer. Apparently this is a reasonable condition, very much in keeping with the arrogance which officers are supposed to have. But as it turns out, Peru is a country whose racial conglomerate is of low stature. Only 16 percent of the troops reach 1.65 m. in stature, and of the soldiers of Indian race, who constitute the majority, only 11 percent have the height required to be an officer. . . . It is no exaggeration to say that 90 percent of the Indian race, which predominates in Peru, is impeded by this circumstance from belonging to the officer corps of the armed forces. . . . It is possible that the discrimination against the Indian race . . . will be more drastic in the future. The Indian peasantry constitutes today a powerful pressure group, inclined toward subversion. They will have to be stopped from reaching command positions in the Armed Forces. . . . If this interpretation is correct one would have to agree that the discrimination against Indians becoming officers is not based on racial prejudice but rather on political necessity.

Social Background

Of the thirteen generals and admirals who initially composed the government . . . close to 50 percent are descendants of military men or have direct family links with military men. One of the members of the new regime is the son of a general who had been President of the Republic on three occasions, not once by popular vote. Two of the new ministers are sons of generals who had occupied political offices during *de facto* military regimes, one is a son of a colonel and another two are blood relatives of two generals. . . . This constitutes nearly a norm in the Latin American context: the hereditary recruitment of officers. . . . At least seven members of the military government have fathers who belong to the well-to-do strata of the bourgeoisie, the rest come from middle sectors but are now integrated into the well-to-do strata.

Nevertheless, it is said that the Head of the Government, General Velasco, is of peasant origin. If this rumor were true it would explain the social sensibility which Velasco seems to have, in contrast to the absence of social emotion which the other members of the Government tend to show. Similarly, such a social background would explain certain [of his] populist attitudes. . . .

According to the declaration of possessions made by the members of the military government. . . . Five of the new rulers possess lands in urban and rural zones, seven possess stocks in companies engaged in mining, in industry, aviation, urban development, or in such exclusive clubs as the Jockey Club, Yacht Club of Ancon, Club de Regatas or the Colegio San Silvestre. All those who evaluate their declared possessions have over one million *soles* each and there is one who declares a fortune of six million. Their compensation as members of the Armed Forces is in the order of 21,000 soles [per month] at a minimum.

Peruvian officers, especially those of the Army, demonstrate a pronounced opposition to the old aristocratic class, something which does not occur in the Navy and in the Air Force, but such a position does not mean identification with popular interests to which they continue to be alien. . . . That is to say they inveigh against the old privileges of the oligarchy, against the class pride which discriminates against the military . . . [an oligarchy] which manifests, often openly, their repudiation of the military institutions. The few officers with aristocratic family names who have entered the military schools are "bad children of good families," they have done so by parental imposition as a correctional device. In general these officers have not reached the top of the hierarchy [Jacques Lambert states that the democratic recruitment of the officers impels them to change the existing political, economic, and social structures.] We consider that exactly the reverse has occurred. While the professional military man tends to combat the strata called aristocratic, they on the other hand defend the bourgeois structures in all the Latin American countries with the exception of Cuba. The Peruvian military in particular acts that way because they are integrated into the higher bourgeoisie; in addition, their professional formation binds them to the defense of the Constitution which legalizes the existence of those structures.

Furthermore, there does not exist an historical antecedent, anywhere in the world, in which a military intervention has transformed the basic structures of the bourgeois capitalist society.

5.
THOSE WHO RULE

JOSÉ LUIS DE IMAZ

> Argentine sociologist José Luis de Imaz did not necessarily
> intend his work to have any relevance to the experiences of
> other Latin American countries. His analysis was limited to
> the domestic Argentine case; however, his findings indicate
> strong parallels to the findings of other studies carried out
> since. Imaz's study, therefore, is a pioneer debunker of pop-
> ular assumptions concerning the structure of the officer corps
> in Argentina, and, by extension, in other Latin American
> countries.

When the contract of the last German professor of the Escuela
Superior de Guerra was cancelled in 1919, "professionalization" in
Argentina had had a clear and undeniable model, a model that had
inculcated its values, had taught discipline, and had given an example
of subjection to the legal authority. Of course, in the Germany of
the Kaiser it was he who interpreted military values.

The generals on active duty in 1943 belonged to the classes graduated from the Military College between 1900 and 1910, which coin-
cides with the height of the influence and prevalence of a professional
consciousness. The senior officers in 1936 had been graduated be-

From *Those Who Rule* by José Luis de Imaz, pp. 52–84, *passim,* footnotes
omitted. Translated by Carlos A. Astiz. Reprinted by permission of the
State University of New York Press. Copyright © 1964 by the State
University of New York Press.

tween 1896 and 1904. In contrast, generals on active duty in 1956 had, with only two exceptions, graduated after 1920, that is, at a time when, after the German military defeat in Europe, its influence had decreased. . . .

The general belief is that most of the Argentine generals come from the traditional families of the interior. Nothing could be less correct. Those born in the Buenos Aires metropolitan area vary, according to the graduating class, from 38 to 47 percent. All those born in the "traditional provinces" amount to only 29 percent of the total. A similar percentage is apparent for generals born in the interior of Buenos Aires Province in La Pampa and Mendoza. . . .

The percentage of those from the city and province of Buenos Aires is greater in the Air Force and in the Navy. Only in this sense could it be said that the Army, at its highest level, is comparatively provincial. . . .

Apparently this pattern has prevailed since the first class graduated from the Military College. In fact, in 1872 when only 58 students were registered at the College, 31 of the 53 scholarship holders were from the Federal Capital, 5 from Cordoba Province, and 4 from Entre Ríos Province. Today as yesterday generals come basically from an urban milieu, half of them from Buenos Aires and environs. . . .

. . . The 1936 and 1941 officers had graduated from the Military College during the last years of the nineteenth century and the beginning of the present one. Five were the sons of Italians who must have come to the country as immigrants at the latest during the first Presidency of Roca. This shows that from its very inception the military establishment was an open group and that recruitment took place as much from the families that had recently settled in the country as from the traditional Creole ones.

Since at that time almost all the cadets were on scholarship, the military career was a channel of upward mobility, even for those coming from the very new middle sectors and the lower-middle class strata. . . .

. . . From these data it is apparent that 73 percent of the Army and Air Force generals studied come from families belonging to the well-to-do bourgeoisie, 25 percent to the petite bourgeoisie, and only 2 percent to families of working-class origin.

Twenty generals are sons of military men, which is not a very high figure compared to those in European countries. In France, where the officer corps is recruited within a provincial milieu, military families are significantly more important. This is not true in Argentina because of the nature of recruitment, which was open from the beginning to people of immigrant stock and was encouraged by the scholarship system. In some years the scholarships covered almost all the available enrollment. . . .

It is difficult to ascertain what percentage of the applicants for admission to the Military College was admitted in each instance. Everything would lead us to suppose that, in selecting among the applicants, universal criteria were applied (such as superior performance in the entrance examination) together with particular criteria with respect to the sons of military personnel. But the number of candidates who applied each year seems to have varied, due, in part, to variations in the popularity of the military in the country. Table 4.3 shows some sample years.

These figures need to be explained. The number of candidates in 1956 was almost the same as in 1920; however, the number of students who could have been candidates in those two years was extremely different. The second consideration is that the opportunities for success and promotion in other fields were much more diversified in 1956 than in 1920. The third factor is that in the 1950's the Air Force School was already in existence and attracted many candidates

Table 4.3. Number of Candidates to Military College by Year

YEAR	TOTAL NUMBER OF CANDIDATES
1920	344
1930	557
1932	688
1933	215
1941	385
1943	1,877
1946	389
1947	799
1952	460
1955	370
1956	354
1961	771

with aviational and technical vocations who had formerly entered the Military College.

The variable of the fluctuating popularity of the armed forces is still apparent, nevertheless, and these figures for the candidates may be valid as indices. Note the increase of candidates during the early days of the military and civilian government led by General Uriburu. On the other hand, the number of candidates decreased in 1933 after the erosion of the popularity of the government.

On the eve of the Revolution in 1943 the highest figure for applicants yet known at the Military College was registered. At the beginning of Perón's presidential term in 1947 the totals were high in relation to the years before and after. Around 1955 and 1956, in the midst of the institutional conflicts the Army was undergoing, the total decreased significantly.

Aside from the objective requirements of recruitment, the continuance of the cadet's career depends upon two factors: his finding that the military career satisfies his vocation and whether the climate existing in the country is favorable or unfavorable to the military group. This too can be ascertained by studying the total number of second lieutenants graduated after four years of study. . . .

Promotions during a military career are made on the basis of a series of strict standards. . . .

. . . In 1946 and 1951, however, "particularist" criteria began to diminish the institutionalization of standards in the services, as did loyalty toward or incompatibility with the established regime. Beyond the official standards of the service, those factors either made easier the promotion of those who did not meet all requirements or speeded them into retirement.

After the Perón period particularism continued, but in reference to an opposite political allegiance. After the Revolution many officers were reinstated and "revolutionary merits," and especially "1951 pre-revolutionary merits" counted for as much or more as objective qualifications, and officers who before 1955 had been retired because of their anti-Perón activity were promoted and permitted to bypass certain grades. These officers were excused from completing higher studies. Although it is understandable that there were special circumstances at the time, these promotions downgraded the institutional standards of the service, producing tensions that would have visible outward effects in 1962 and 1963. . . .

Studies of the origins, backgrounds, and family environments of senior military officers justify discarding the idea that there might be a "military caste." This hypothesis is not acceptable in view of the origins of the officers. Should a "military caste" hypothesis be seriously posited, an explanation must be given using a more liberal meaning of "caste," perhaps by exploring the possibility of a status mentality being created in the military itself. To be called a "caste" in the strict sense of the term, the military establishment would have to be totally closed to outside recruitment, or at least recruitment would have to be conducted as a function of the future officer's ascriptive status. . . .

This is not the case in Argentina; in fact, the situation appears to be the opposite. The Argentine armed forces have always been open groups and have served as channels offering opportunities for upward mobility both to the provincial Creole sectors and to the native-born sons of immigrant parents. The scholarships offered at the Military College, which were especially numerous in the first few years, made higher studies possible for many who could not have afforded them outside the service.

It is a different matter to say that after entering the armed forces, that is, after being recruited from a wide field, a specific status mentality is fostered in the military individual as part of the system of socialization in the services. A boy is taken at a very young age, cast into a specific mould, and taught the belief that a military career, by identifying the individual with the higher degree of patriotism, converts him into a depository of national values. The military does develop a status mentality, then, in its recruits, as do other professional groups. The military status mentality tends to become identified with "national truth," just as that of intellectuals does with "intelligence and critical reason," and that of businessmen with the economic support of society. . . .

The practice of those gentlemanly standards, the collective acceptance of a strict code of honor, and the enduring respect for "good form" lead Navy men to feel personally identified with the highest social stratum, because only the values of this stratum are identifiable with the Navy value system. This identification, as we will see later, takes place through a respect for good form, and it has led many senior officers and Navy ministers in recent years to assume representation of a social stratum which they did not even know. They came to know it after 1955. It was not the service (in itself apolitical), but the new personal relations outside a strictly professional field entered into by some senior Navy officers who, taking advantage of the Navy's political inexperience, involved the institution in doubtful ventures. . . .

. . . But it is also true that many Argentines, minimally interested in public affairs during the last twenty-five years, have hoped at some time for military action, whether to depose Perón or to bring him back to power, that would satisfy their personal point of view on national problems. This strange ambivalence between verbal rationalization and the intimate "living feeling" which has at some time or other been experienced by every uneasy Argentine is one of the many dichotomies which, starting with each individual, split what might otherwise have been a political community.

Since the armed forces have not exercised their manifest function of defending the country in war, the war apparatus of the military has been visualized by all political groups as an instrument potentially useful to satisfy other political objectives. Thus, aside from all the explanations presented, resort to the armed forces as a source of legitimacy has been a tacit rule of the political game in Argentina. This is an aspect of political life of which nobody expressly approves, but from which all the political groups have profited at least once. All will publicly deny this rule, but in private Argentine politicians cannot ignore that, at one time or another during this quarter of a century, they have all knocked on the doors of the garrisons. . . .

. . . In accordance with the latest figures, a third of the generals are military engineers. . . . Military factories, blast furnaces, steel mills, powder magazines, and the manufacture of synthetic toluene require new specialists.

These entrepreneur-generals or military entrepreneurs with ambivalent attitudes towards their status are the ones who can introduce a change of outlook into the armed forces. If it is assumed that the armed forces are an essential instrument for the expression of national cohesion, that the officers as a whole are the depositories of the patriotic legacy of the preceding generations, and that the commanders identify the institutional continuity of the nation, then only the technical-engineers and the engineer-technicians can make the armed forces equal to the solution of the immediate problems of the society in which they live.

6.
THE NEW PERUVIAN SOCIETY

MORALES BERMUDEZ

Since its *coup d'état* against the civilian government of Victor
Andres Belaunde in October 1968, the Peruvian military has
traced a course of nationalist politics some would call revolutionary. Whatever the term implied, by 1970 it had become
apparent that the Peruvian military had evolved a program
of government which many in Latin America, civilian and
military alike, began to regard as a viable alternative model
of development. General Morales Bermudez, at the time Minister of Economy and an influential member of the military
regime, describes the nature of that regime's ideology.

Oiga: During your last speech before the American Chamber of
Commerce you defined the characteristics of the society the Revolu-
tion proposes to build on the basis of humanism and solidarity.
Could you explain the real significance of these terms, Sir?

Minister Morales: This is one of the most difficult problems, and I
must follow up with statements that the President of the Republic
has made. The Peruvian revolutionary process has one characteristic peculiar to it and that is that it has not attempted to define
exactly the type of society that is being constructed. It cannot be
fitted into other established molds. The definitions border on the

From "Morales Bermudez Defines the New Peruvian Society. Why Neither
Capitalist Nor Communist," *Oiga.* No. 414, Año ix (March 12, 1971,
Lima), 11–13. Translated by Consuelo S. Maingot.

simplistic, not so much in the sense of orientation and direction, as in the grammatical, semantic sense. The term "socialist," for example, has diverse meanings throughout the world. It is often applied to dissimilar situations and even contradictory ones.

For this reason we say that the essence, the interesting thing about the Peruvian process is its pragmatic character. In this sense we must depart from some objective historical considerations. Peru has not even been a capitalist country. What we've had here is political opportunism and demagoguery, totally negative factors and obstacles to development and the general welfare. The other complementary factor, which is a consequence of these, is the enormous influence external politics has come to exert. In economic terms: a deterioration in the terms of trade.

When we say that we do not want the capitalist model, we do it because it is obvious that under that system it is not possible to achieve the general welfare of the people. Nor do we want communism. Therefore, we are faced with a reality which must necessarily be met with an essentially pragmatic criterion. There are two concepts, nevertheless, which are fundamental to our process: nationalism and humanism.

It is necessary to clearly define our conception of nationalism. It does not signify for us in any way chauvinism or isolationism. We cannot separate ourselves from the world on the pretext of a purely declarative and insubstantial nationalism. Our nationalism rests on the historical proof that we constitute a national entity, with problems and characteristics peculiar to us. This presents a concrete reality with concrete problems which must be resolved with concrete measures. We cannot import solutions, except to the extent that they are compatible with our reality.

I refer to humanism as the essence of Christianity. Not as eulogizer of any political party, but in its philosophical context. For us humanism is charity, but not in the pejorative and even anti-Christian sense of giving away surplus in order to mitigate conscience, but in its context of social obligation, a conscious bargain to achieve justice and well-being for the people.

Oiga: Sir, we allow ourselves to persist in one aspect. It is known that capitalism is defined as private ownership of the means of production, and that socialism is state ownership of the means of production. Under these terms of reference which is the exact position for the Peruvian model? Could we perhaps speak of a humanistic socialism?

Minister Morales: I shall attempt to answer your question by elimination of the applicable systems, rather than by conceptual definition. I've already indicated that there is a vague concept of the term "socialism" in the world. In accord with the theory of the State, in its classical concept, socialism is a transitory system for attaining communism; it is a superior stage presupposing the total disappearance of the State. . . .

For us this is simply utopian and unrealizable. Socialism would be the antechamber of this Utopia: that is the creation of a total State wherein all means of production and operational resources of society would be under its control. Socialism, so understood, according to this philosophical hypothesis, is clearly *not* the model we aspire to for the new society.

Nevertheless, we can affirm, and we refer to the structure of investments, that in the new Peruvian society the State will play a much more important role than in the past. In mentioning 50 percent of the total investment (it could be 40 or more) as a possible, tentative number in the hands of the public sector, leaving the rest for the private and cooperative sectors, I am giving voice to the express will to restore to the State its principal and dynamic role. If we add to this greater social participation the concept of humanism, we might possibly reach a more precise configuration. Let me make myself clear. It is not that we have set as a goal that State investment reach the 50 percent level, rather it is simply a means to reach a model of a coherent society in which the State fulfills its regulatory role in planning.

Oiga: Within this general context which is an outline of the features of the new society, in your opinion, what role is played by economic planning?

Minister Morales: An essential role, a very central one. I cannot even conceive of development without planning. It is an operational concept, not a descriptive one. To pretend that a developing country can achieve concrete objectives without looking ahead is impossible. Nor is planning a way in itself, it is only a means. Coherence among the three contributory elements of the process—the state, the private, and the cooperative sectors—will be achieved only through planning.

From the operational point of view, the National Institute of Planning is the organization responsible to government for short-, medium-, and long-range plans. We work with it in a flexible, coordinated manner. The process of planning is, in itself, difficult because it is not a static concept, rather it is essentially dynamic. It is necessary to continually measure the effects that are produced. It is, if you wish, a dialectical process, which makes necessary certain adjustments demanded by reality itself. Within this, I particularly am an enthusiast of short-range planning because it is that which can give us the best measure of reality, of projects correctly or erroneously executed. Experience counsels us, for example, of the convenience of setting up a biennial budget.

Oiga: On this same point, is it true there exists a withdrawal of investments or a limitation of our financial capacity which eventually would undermine the present optimism? Should we depend more on external resources than on internal resources?

Minister Morales: The needs of a developing country must be met on the basis of all possible and available resources. We are, therefore, speaking of an external and internal flux. What is destructive to me is for the Nation to resort to the external resources without maximum mobilization of internal resources. This is fundamental because, in so doing, you denationalize what could be a well-structured and solid model of development. The first thing is to mobilize to the maximum your own resources; but as this mobilization does not totally cover the necessities of financial exchange, we need external resources. The essential point is to know how to utilize those resources. The Peruvian model has already changed traditional models of the use of external resources. To verify this, it is enough to mention the case of Cerro Verde in mining, and in the memorandum establishing the groundwork to finance the Chira project which was signed with Yugoslavia. The model for the use of external resources has been changed to reflect the national interest which is in the interest of all. External capital will come, but under new conditions. My optimism is based in reality.

Oiga: We consider state investment to be of great importance. In your opinion, is it advantageous to accelerate these investments to make the revolutionary process more dynamic?

Minister Morales: Obviously, before the revolution the major volume of investments was in the private sector. In the years and months during which this process has been under way, it has been practically impossible to increase in any substantial manner the percentage of state participation in investment. The problem of investments results from situational socioeconomic factors which should change with the speed required of each case. . . .

Nevertheless, and in agreement with the figures we have (subject to correction), the 20 percent that the state possessed for slightly more than 2 years, has been transformed into 25 percent. So, there has been an increase of 5 percent. We must not forget, however, that we have three elements that form the structure: the state, the private sector, and the cooperative sector. For this reason, I am convinced that it is necessary to accelerate state investment. This 25 percent should grow to reach a coherent and balanced position in relation to the purely private sector and the cooperative sector.

Oiga: Can you place a limit on this growth?

Minister Morales: I would venture to say it should grow to 50 percent. This is put in a subjective manner, naturally. But this proportion may be the most convenient; it can be a little less if the cooperative sector participates to a greater degree. In summary, there should be greater state investment, and I attest this not just as a simple belief but as a complete conviction.

7.
THE GREAT CHALLENGE

ALBERTO RUIZ NOVOA

Alberto Ruiz Novoa had been commander of the Colombian batallion—"Batallón Colombia"—in Korea. That experience together with his years combating guerrilla activity in Colombia shaped his vision of the role the military should play in a developing society. As an enormously successful minister of war under two different presidents (1961–1965), General Ruiz Novoa implemented the so-called Plan Lazo, an overall plan of military civic-action, psychological warfare, and counterinsurgency. The ever-increasing politicization of the military, including the noncommissioned officers, and the growing popularity of Ruiz Novoa led to his summary dismissal in early 1965. Whether a conspiracy was uncovered remains a question to this day. This book was an effort to enter the political arena as a presidential candidate, an effort that failed. His military office and uniform removed, Ruiz Novoa became just another ex-military man with political aspirations. His book remains as a testimonial to the aspirations of a progressive military officer. How representative this thought is, is one of the crucial questions in contemporary civil–military relations.

To attest that democracy in Colombia is in a state of crisis is commonplace. What has really happened—with most of national public

From General Alberto Ruiz Novoa, *El gran desafio* (Bogotá: Ediciones Tercer Mundo, 1965), pp. i–iii. Translated by Consuelo S. Maingot.

opinion failing to grasp the point—is that the system defined as democracy has been going through a change for a long time. And so, while among us there has been a standstill in the political system—to the advantage of members of the establishment—in countries which are really democratic permanent reform has been taking place with regard to the structure of the state and to the advantage both of progress and the welfare of the community.

This gap in the political understanding of the Colombian masses, existent also in many important sectors of the middle and upper classes, is as much a product of the control exercised by reactionary members of the ruling classes over the media of communication governing the exchange of ideas, as it is a product of the existence of a formal democracy which creates among the mass of people, politically unsophisticated, the illusion that they enjoy freedom, when in fact the system in no way secures those material and spiritual benefits for the people which should be the purpose of a regime sincerely committed to the welfare of the people. As it was expressed in a *New York Times* editorial which provoked the anger of Colombia's mandarins, Colombia is a country dominated by an oligarchy of great landholders, bankers and businessmen, liberals and conservatives whose interchanges of political power have in no way benefited the working-class poor and the peasantry.

But times have changed. The range and reach of the media of communication have put an end to the isolation of illiterate workers and peasants. Today, those who until quite recently lived in a state of intellectual and material abjection are beginning to emerge from their ignorance thanks to the growing consciousness of their rights and of the possibility of validating those rights. As a consequence of this growing consciousness, the masses are developing a new political sense impelling them to reject those slogans and banners under which in times past they were led to useless sacrifices on political battlefields, and instead, seeking ways leading to economic liberation, to the world of culture, to social security. That is to say, toward true democracy.

That democracy should have a purpose and objective that can be defined as the achievement of social justice. And social justice will only be achieved by emerging from a state of underdevelopment.

According to Germán Arciniegas there exist two Latin Americas: the visible and the invisible. The visible one is comprised of the privileged class, which is a small minority. The invisible are those

140,000,000 abandoned Latin Americans who, "the day they can be heard, will be converted into an all-consuming conflagration or a shining torch."

This is the great challenge facing the peoples south of the Río Grande, the one which confronts Colombia.

We either seek the evolution of our social structure by peaceful means, let us hope in collaboration with the ruling class, or there will be no other recourse than to resort to revolutionary means, because the Colombian people are impatient and are not disposed to bow indefinitely before the myth of a legalism which enslaves them and has them sunk in spiritual and material abjection.

If we fulfill the historical tendency of traditional societies to maintain at all costs its privileges, assuming thereby a blind and suicidal policy, then it will be necessary to call upon what Walter Rostow calls the "modernizing coalition," formed by the army, the intelligentsia, and innovative entrepreneurs who constitute the middle class of the nation, in a coordinated effort to establish the New State. It will be the responsibility of this coalition to assume the task of liberating their country from the "native *encomenderos*" endowed with all the defects and none of the virtues of their Spanish forefathers. As we said before, this is the great challenge the Fatherland presents to its children.

This book sets out to present an overview of Colombia in the struggle against underdevelopment, arguing that it is the best national purpose that the present generation of Colombians can adopt. It hopes to inspire the army, the intelligentsia (professionals, journalists, the clergy, university people, etc.), and the forward-looking entrepreneurial class (industrialists, businessmen and agriculturists not involved in the trafficking in influence) to form the "modernizing coalition," which can take power by taking advantage of the opportunity created by the 1966 election when all the public bodies will be renewed and a President of the Republic elected. Thenceforth, it can bring about the change sought after by the entire nation.

If the middle, working, peasant, and university classes do not possess the bravery, the courage, the decision, the energy, the will, the desire, the virility to launch this battle, if they fail to realize that they can form a political force capable of overthrowing a political machine whose strength is a function of the fear of the oppressed masses, then they will deserve their lot. This is, we repeat, the great challenge.

8.

THE MILITARY IN POLITICS: Changing Patterns in Brazil

ALFRED STEPAN

The questions posed by Alfred Stepan, Associate Professor of Political Science at Yale University, both about the Brazilian case and its possible relevance to the rest of Latin America are a logical conclusion to this unit on the military. His answers will be debated for some time to come. Social change is a complex area of analysis; Latin America a complex area to study social change.

To what extent is the Brazilian experience relevant for other Latin American countries? Are similar patterns of civil–military relations found elsewhere? Some of the most significant system-level variables at work in the shift from the moderator model of civil–military relations to direct military rule are in one degree or another in existence, or coming into existence, in other Latin American countries, most notably Peru. These include the great growth in political demands; the ineffectiveness of parliamentary forms of government in industrializing an increasingly modernized society; the growth of military concern with internal security threats, which the military defines as deriving from an inefficient, corrupt, and unjust middle- and upper-class parliamentary and social system; the belief that their traditional moderator role of system-maintenance does not contribute to the solution of the

From Alfred Stepan, *The Military in Politics: Changing Patterns in Brazil* (copyright © 1971 by the Rand Corporation, published by Princeton University Press), pp. 267–271 *passim,* footnotes omitted. Reprinted by permission of the Rand Corporation and Princeton University Press.

problems of development; and the growth of military confidence that through their Superior War College they have for the first time a cadre of specialists and a development program superior to that of the bankrupt, and therefore illegitimate, politicians. Despite the definite peculiarities of the Brazilian case, it is possible that cross-national, system-level changes are taking place in Latin America that will eventually alter traditional patterns of civil–military relations. Although the Brazilian military to date has been relatively unsuccessful in its new role, the mode of military involvement in Latin American politics may well shift increasingly from that of system-maintenance to that of system-transformation. For example, the Peruvian military has attempted direct rule in the past, but their current effort at system change is of a much more systematic and thorough order, and is directly related to my analysis of the emergence of new patterns of civil–military relations in Latin America along Brazilian lines. From this perspective, the Peruvian experience will merit very close observation.

Military attempts to rule directly in order to transform the political life of a country and hasten development may or may not be nationalistic in style, but they will probably all be authoritarian. The specific working-out of military attempts at system-transformation will vary with the particular set of circumstances in each country. In Brazil, the military institution's experience of FEB in World War II, their intense anti-Communism after 1963, and their fear that labor unions would infiltrate the sergeant corps, together with the soaring inflation, contributed to a pro-American, pro-foreign-capital, antilabor philosophy in the first government of the military regime. In Peru, many of the same system-level changes occurred, but the circumstances were different. The United States' denial of jets to the Peruvian air forces in 1965–1967 and the small allocation of funds from the Alliance for Progress represent both military and political sources of anti-Americanism among Peruvian officers. The military campaign in 1965–1966 against a small guerrilla force added to military interest in changing a political system which they associated with developmental failures and the generation of guerrilla violence. The military doctrines developed in the higher war colleges of both Brazil and Peru stressed the nexus of development and security. The absence of a perceived threat to immediate security when the military actually assumed power in Peru in 1968, however, may have contributed to Peruvian emphasis on development. In Brazil, when the military assumed power in 1964, the emphasis was on security. Similarly, the definition of the class enemy was quite different in the two countries. In Brazil, inflation and the link between the sergeants and the trade unions contributed to an antilabor bias. In Peru, the upper-class landowners and urban middle-class politicians were considered the greatest obstruction to long-term development and security because of their lack of national consciousness. The Peruvian land reform act was aimed as much at eliminating upper-class political and economic power as it was at modernizing the agrarian sector.

I argued in Part II of this work that while the officer corps in Brazil is middle class in social composition, the officers see themselves as without a specific class identity, as above class conflicts, and as having the mission of protecting the national good. To the extent that military men in other Latin American countries are beginning to concern themselves with the failure of parliamentary solutions to the problems of development, and seeking to eliminate obstructions to long-term economic development and social stability, they may come to see other groups as hindering such development. From this perspective, even though the evidence from the Brazilian case clearly indicates that the lower classes have benefited the least from military government, the argument that a military government would necssarily tend to repress the emergence of lower groups because of the military's middle-class composition is not completely valid. The military is above all a *situational* elite, not a *class* elite. The power and prestige of the Latin American military officers derive from their membership in an institution with power. When such an institutional elite feels that middle- and upper-class life styles and political practices impede development by contributing to internal disruption or guerrilla activity which could threaten military power, it is very possible that in their own self-interest the military could take aggressive action against those aspects of middle- and upper-class life which threatened their institutional position. We see this in the Peruvian military's stand on land reform.

If one were to speculate about potential military policy in Latin America in those countries where the military come to power, a more useful framework than that provided by the class analysis, which sees the military restricted in their economic policies because of their allegiance to middle-class values, is to recognize that the military often view their own power as unrelated to the outcome of economic class conflicts. This self-image implies that a wide range of possible positions on economic issues is available to a military regime. The same military institution could shift from far left to far right, and back again, in regard to economic policy.

In political matters, however, the range of the military governments that may emerge in the future will probably be much more limited. In regard to participation, the desire of military radicals for control would tend to conflict with free democratic electoral campaigns, but would be congruent with a military populist plebiscitary style of politics. As regards mobilization, military radicals' preference for order and unity would make them resistant to the proliferation of autonomous lower-class, mass-action groups, but favorably disposed to mass parades. A natural military style might therefore be a populist variant of nationalist socialism, or, to use the phrase of the thirties, fascism.

It is too early to estimate how successful attempts at system-transformation will be. In Part IV of this book, I indicated some of the grave political difficulties that face military government, difficulties that are frequently overlooked. Furthermore, in comparison to new nations, Latin America has a much greater degree of urbanization and industrialization, and much more powerful social groups—such as labor, the intellectuals, the industrialists, and the middle-class interest groups. This makes military control and transformation of the social system a much more politically complicated task than military rule of a less developed social structure. These same conditions make military "radicalism" much more improbable in Brazil than in Peru.

Because military rule is unable to solve the political problems of development, it is unlikely that the military will attempt to retreat to a modified form of the moderator role. However, as I have already indicated, a return to the earlier pattern of civil–military relations is made much more difficult by the experience of military rule, and by the fact that this rule itself reflected system-level changes no longer supportive of a moderator role.

BIBLIOGRAPHIC SUGGESTIONS

The North American pioneers in the field of Latin American civil–military relations are three: Edwin Lieuwen's *Arms and Politics in*

Latin America (New York: Praeger, 1961) was the first full-length study of the subject. With a long section on United States policy toward the military, Lieuwen established himself as a strong critic of United States military assistance to Latin America. Although published in 1957, Lyle N. McAlister's *The 'Fuero Militar' in New Spain* (Gainesville: University of Florida Press, 1957) did not catch the specialist's eye until the field of civil–military relations had become respectable. A brief but pithy and well-documented study of the colonial period, this study became a model of historical scholarship. The third pioneer, John J. Johnson, edited an important reader in 1962, *The Role of the Military in Underdeveloped Countries* (Princeton, N.J.: Princeton University Press, 1962), and in 1964 published his book *The Military and Society in Latin America* (Stanford, Calif.: Stanford University Press, 1964). Johnson, in contrast to Lieuwen, favored continued United States assistance to the Latin American military.

Since these pioneer years the field of civil–military relations has expanded, the scandal surrounding the United States Army–sponsored "Project Camelot" in 1965–1966 notwithstanding. Important country studies include Robert Potash, *The Army and Politics in Argentina, 1928–1945* (Stanford, Calif.: Stanford University Press, 1969), and the study on Brazil by Alfred Stepan, extracted in this unit. Monographic studies of consequence include Martin C. Needler, *Anatomy of a Coup d'État: Ecuador 1963* (Washington, D.C.: Institute for the Comparative Study of Political Systems, 1964); William H. Brill, *Military Intervention in Bolivia: The Overthrow of Paz Estenssoro and the MNR* (Washington, D.C.: Institute for the Comparative Study of Political Systems, 1967); José Nun, *Latin America: The Hegemonic Crisis and the Military Coup* (Berkeley, Calif.: Institute of International Studies, 1969); Liisa North, *Civil-Military Relations in Argentina, Chile, and Peru* (Berkeley, Calif.: Institute of International Studies, 1966).

The student of Latin American history should become acquainted with the considerable literature on the subject by Latin Americans. A good bibliographical essay on the literature in English and Spanish is Lyle N. McAlister, "Recent Research and Writings on the Role of the Military in Latin America," *Latin American Research Review,* Vol. II, No. 1 (Fall 1966), pp. 5–36.

IX.
Revolutionary Ideologies in Latin America

⚑ HOBART A. SPALDING, JR.

Each one has to decide which side he is on—the side of
military violence or guerrilla violence, the side of the violence
that represses or violence that liberates. Crimes in the face
of crimes. Which ones do we choose to be jointly responsible
for, accomplices or accessories to?

It is not individuals that are placed face to face in these
battles, but class interests and ideas; but those who fall in
them, those who die, are persons, are men. We cannot avoid
this contradiction, escape from this pain.

—RÉGIS DEBRAY, at his trial in Camiri, Bolivia

Latin America has been typed as an area of constant revolution. In reality, however, its revolutionary period is
little over a decade old. Only since the successful Cuban
Revolution of 1959, the spread of guerrilla activity, and the
formation of powerful leftist electoral coalitions dedicated
to fundamental change has it become legitimate to speak
about a Latin American Revolution or The Latin American
Revolution. The documents that follow illustrate some facets
of this Revolution, whose main drama lies in the future.

The years prior to 1959, nevertheless, should not be sum-
marily dismissed. The Mexican upheaval of 1910, for example, has been considered the continent's first revolution. That
tumultuous movement, more correctly classed as a popular

explosion, lacked a clear revolutionary ideology, although several interest groups involved in it voiced clear demands. Peasants, notably in the South, clamored for land, the embryonic labor movement for social legislation and greater control over its own destinies, the middle sectors for material benefits, a portion of the elite for political power and the ouster of Dictator Porfirio Díaz, and almost all groups for a curtailing of foreign influence. Although the state that emerged after 1920 placated these demands to a degree, many of them through the Constitution of 1917, the result failed to alter basic relationships between elites and masses. It did partially destroy the traditional landed oligarchy and distribute small plots to peasants, but another large landowning class soon formed. It did pave the way for a measure of industrialization, particularly after 1940, but the conscious choice of development within a capitalistic framework ensured the continuation of elite domination and fundamental inequalities within Mexican society.[1]

Others also struggled for revolutionary causes prior to 1917. Anarchists, anarcho-syndicalists, and socialists perpetrated individual acts against property and the state, activated a burgeoning labor movement, and founded political parties in their attempts to change radically the prevailing system.[2] After the Russian Revolution of 1917, the Leninist variant of Marxist theory gradually emerged as the strongest influence on Latin American revolutionary ideology.

In the 1920s and 1930s reformist and left-leaning groups claiming to be revolutionary did emerge, notably the Alianza Popular Revolucionaria Americana (APRA), centered in

[1]See, for example, Moisés González Navarro, "Mexico: The Lop-Sided Revolution" in Claudio Veliz, ed., *Obstacles in Latin America* (New York: Oxford University Press, 1965), or Pablo González Casanova, *Democracy in Mexico* (New York: Oxford University Press, 1970). The sources from which the documents have been taken provide additional bibliography.

[2]For the Argentine case, generally applicable to all Latin America, see *La clase trabajadora argentina (Documentos para su historia, 1890–1912)* (Buenos Aires: Editorial Galerna, 1970) by the author.

Peru, but not until after World War II did any movements that truly appeared to have revolutionary potential come to the fore.[3] In Guatemala the nationalist government which took power after 1944 had revolutionary overtones. It lacked, however, both a solid base and a coherent ideology, perhaps due to the country's backward economic state and to the amorphous nature of the elements involved in the movement. In the end it proved reformist even though its program of land reform, minimal social legislation, independent foreign policy, and national integration of marginal groups proved sufficient for the United States to support a successful conservative coup in 1954.

The Movimiento Nacional Revolucionario (MNR), which seized power in Bolivia in 1952, seemed more promising. It quickly nationalized the tin mines and promulgated the bases for land reform. Subsequently, however, the movement lost its revolutionary push, and increasingly less progressive elements came into power who often masked their purposes with pseudo-leftist rhetoric while repressing the more revolutionary elements. One of these latter were the tin miners, who hewed to an ultra-left position synthesized in the *Tesis de Pulacayo,* approved at a National Congress of 1946. This document called for worker control, socialization of the entire economy, a virulent anti-imperialism, and working-class internationalism.[4]

The regimes of Getúlio Vargas and Juan Perón cannot be called revolutionary either. Both altered prevailing balances between societal groups, but neither changed basic relationships. Vargas's rule encouraged modernizing sectors and gave organized labor some material and legislative benefits to gain its support while perpetuating its subordinate

[3]On the ideology of APRA see Harry Kantor, *The Program and Ideology of the Peruvian Aprista Party* (Washington, D.C.: Savile, 1964) for the most complete, if overly sympathetic, treatment.

[4]Full text of the *Tesis* in Guillermo Lora, *Documentos políticos de Boliva* (La Paz-Cochabamba: Editorial "Los Amigos del Pueblo," 1970), 361–390.

role. Perón charted an independent course for Argentina and briefly allowed labor to become a favored sector.[5] Revolution, however, involves fundamental changes in political and economic power relationships. Further, today's revolutionary ideology is firmly rooted in a concept of justice which incorporates the equal opportunity for all to develop individual human potential and the equal sharing of existing and future benefits. By these standards, none of the movements previously described can be called revolutionary.

In contrast, Cuba is evolving toward a revolutionary society. It has destroyed those institutions upon which the old state rested and initiated the process of creating new, and in this case, socialist ones. It has, for example, nationalized all foreign property, banned direct foreign penetration of the economy, begun a thorough land reform program, provided for free education and social services, virtually eliminated all class and racial privileges, armed the people, encouraged popular culture and a communal spirit, and is reordering distributive patterns so that all members of the polity get equal opportunities and an equal share of the material goods. Thus, although Cuba's transition to socialism is not complete, its experiment qualifies as revolutionary.[6] The documents that follow show how today's revolutionaries wish to accomplish similar goals.

Prior to 1959 the main lines of revolutionary theory and activity followed a traditionalist line. In this schema, which assumed the inevitability of class struggle, the industrial proletariat, organized into trade unions under the guidance of a centralized Vanguard Party, held the key to revolution. As Latin America entered its industrial phase, feudal structures and the landed oligarchy would be replaced by a na-

[5]Bertram Silverman, for example, notes, "It is remarkable how traditional Peronism was: private enterprise, the market, collective bargaining were accepted institutions," in "Ideology and Economic Development in the Peronist Epoch," in *Studies in Comparative International Development*, Vol. IV, No. 11 (1968–1969), 255.

[6]See, for example, Leo Huberman and Paul Sweezy, *Socialism in Cuba* (New York: Monthly Review, 1969).

tional bourgeoisie attuned to modernization. Its rise, however, would result in a conflict with the representatives of the imperialist countries who competed for control of local resources and markets. In this clash, the revolutionary forces, while continuing to organize the proletariat and to raise its consciousness, would temporarily side with the national bourgeoisie to defeat the imperialists. Then, free from external interference, the proletariat and the bourgeoisie would battle for state power. The workers, more numerous and able to paralyze the economy by strikes and pledged at this point to use armed violence if necessary, would defeat the capitalists and begin the long transition to socialism. After 1959, as we shall see, critics challenged this version, and leading revolutionary groups proposed substantive modifications.

The existence of a revolutionary theory does not guarantee its acceptance, even if it is backed by organized and dedicated advocates. Objective conditions must exist to translate theory into reality. Suffice it here to note that the blatant inequalities that plague Latin America at all levels provide the objective conditions (e.g., see document 3). The revolution of rising expectations, a product of the gradual modernization overtaking traditional society, exercises continual pressures and breeds constant tensions that generate ample sparks for revolutionary fires among workers, peasants, students, intellectuals, middle-group elements, and even frustrated elites.

The directions for change take several courses: against landowning oligarchies and for land reform and modernization of national economies; against rigid social pyramids; against skewed socioeconomic distribution curves; and, a demand common to almost all revolutionary elements, an end to or strict curtailment of foreign domination of local economies. Sentiment on this point is particularly bitter. Foreign companies drain considerable amounts each year, perhaps as much as $2 billion, from Latin America, depriving the area of money that could be used to benefit nationals instead of the international capitalists. As the Second Declaration of Havana stated, in February 1962, in Latin America, four persons per minute die of hunger, curable illness or premature old age; five and a half thousand a day, two million a year . . . for each thousand dollars that leaves, there remains a corpse that is the price of what is called imperialism.[7]

What are the main currents of contemporary revolutionary ideology? Document 1 illustrates aspects of the Cuban Revolution. Written by Ernesto "Che" Guevara, one of the prime architects of the Revolution, the first part shows the ideological bases of the movement and outlines its road to victory, the second indicates how it violated then accepted canons of revolutionary theory. This fact led the French theorist Régis Debray to write a series of essays on the question. In them Debray questioned a total dependence on the industrial proletariat and subservience to a Vanguard Party, suggesting instead that rural elements composed the truly revolutionary sector and proposing that rural guerrillas forming ever-expanding liberated zones, operating independently, could best suit Latin American conditions. Further, in keeping with "new left" ideology Debray endorsed armed struggle and voluntarism, namely the idea that the conditions for revolution could be created.[8]

These challenges to orthodox theory stirred debates throughout Latin America. Documents 2, 3, and 4 illustrate this controversy. Document 2 outlines a compromise position between coalition and guerrilla strategies taken by the newly formed Unified Party of Haitian Communists, then the leading leftist opposition to the Duvalier dictatorship.[9] Document 3 presents the traditionalist-leaning program of the Unión

[7]*Documentos de la revolución cubana* (Montevideo, Uruguay: Nativa Libros, 1967), 74. On imperialism see Harry Magdoff, *The Age of Imperialism* (New York: Monthly Review, 1969), and Andre Gunder Frank, *Capitalism and Underdevelopment in Latin America* (New York: Monthly Review, 1967).

[8]Régis Debray, *Strategy for Revolution: Essays on Latin America* (New York: Monthly Review, 1970).

[9]On contemporary Haiti see Gesner Roc, *Haiti: Tournant Après Duvalier* (Quebec and Ottowa: Editions Jean-Jacques Acaau, 1968) and Gérard Pierre-Charles, *Haiti: Radiografía de una dictadura* (Mexico: Editorial Nuestro Tiempo, 1969).

Popular, the Chilean coalition of Marxists and non-Marxist parties which in 1970 elected Latin America's first Marxist president, Salvador Allende. Document 5, the last of the trio, presents the Chilean Movimiento Izquierdista Revolucionario's (Revolutionary Left Movement, or MIR) critique of that program. The MIR, formed at the University of Concepción in 1967, broke with traditional leftist parties over the issue of armed struggle and went underground only to emerge after Allende's election, and its position summarizes new left attitudes.

Earlier we noted the variety of groups from which revolutionaries have sprung. Documents 5 and 6 show two sides of this phenomenon. The first outlines thinking prevalent among an increasing number of Catholic laymen and clerics, namely that revolution is clearly consonant with Christian principles. The author, Camilo Torres, a Colombian priest trained as a sociologist in Europe, worked within the system to build a United Front composed of varied elements favoring social change. Frustrated by secular and religious elites, he joined the guerrillas in December 1965 and died in action two months later. There follows part of Francisco Julião's letter to Brazilian peasants urging them to join Leagues to defend themselves against the latifundists (document 6). These Leagues and peasant unions, also sponsored by Catholic and Communist elements, grew to some half million members before being destroyed by the reactionary military coup of 1964. Although similar efforts, like that led by Hugo Blanco in Peru's Concepción valley, which flourished until suppressed by the army in 1963, proved more radical, the Brazilian efforts in the countryside organized a previously inert mass for the first time.[10]

[10]Biographical material and collected works of Torres available in Gerassi (see fn document VI) and Oscar Maldonado, Guitemie Oliviéri, and Germán Zabala, *Camilo Torres. Christianismo y revolución* (Mexico: Ediciones Era, 1970). On the new Church in general see *Between Honesty and Hope. Documents From and About the Church in Latin America* (Maryknoll, N.Y.: Maryknoll Publications, 1970) and Alain Gheerbrant, *La iglesia rebelde de América Latina* (Mexico: Siglo XXI, 1970). Docu-

The Cuban success, aside from squarely planting the issue of armed struggle as contrasted with coalition and electoral politics, inspired guerrilla groups across the continent. Since 1958 clearly identified units have operated in Argentina, Bolivia, Brazil, Chile, Colombia, Haiti, Guatemala, Paraguay, Peru, Puerto Rico, and Venezuela—to name only the outstanding cases.[11] This revolutionary activity, however, has not produced another Cuba, but has led to repeated failures, the most publicized being the death of Guevara in October 1967 in Bolivia. Despite these setbacks, rural warfare continues, and today guerrillas fight in several areas throughout Latin America. At the same time, the Cuban victory bred a mystique about guerrilla warfare. Document 7 shows one side of this, presenting a firsthand account of an episode in the life of a fighter and also showing the role played by folk mythology in the struggle.

Why has rural armed insurrection failed up to now? First, while guerrillas proved that small groups could operate and survive in some cases, their effectiveness was limited. Expansion of activities led to armed clashes and, in contrast to the Cuban case, national armies were prepared. As Debray noted, the reactionary forces grasped the lessons of Cuba sooner than the revolutionaries. Once the United States fully perceived the threat involved to its continued continental hegemony, it initiated counterinsurgency training for Latin American forces. Indeed, special ranger corps and United

---

ments on the Brazilian Leagues available in Francisco Julião, ed., *Ligas camponesas, Outubro, 1962–Abril, 1964* (CIDOC, Cuadernos, No. 27, Cuernavaca, Mexico, 1969) and for background see Josue de Castro, *Sete palmos de terra e um caixao* (Lisbon; Serra Nova, 1965). Catholic participation detailed in Emanuel de Kadt, *Catholic Radicals in Brazil* (New York: Oxford University Press, 1970). Material on the Peruvian movement in Víctor Villanueva, *Hugo Blanco y la rebelión campesina* (Lima: Juan Mejia Baca, 1967) and Hugo Niera, *Cuzco: tierra y muerte* (Lima: Popilibros Peruanos, 1964).

[11]The best summary of rural guerrilla activity is Richard Gott, *Guerrilla Movements in Latin America* (Garden City, N.Y.: Doubleday, 1971) and for further reading Gott's bibliography, 555–569.

States advisers as well as military aid (weapons, napalm, planes, etc.) have participated in antiguerrilla efforts in several countries.[12] Second, the romanticization of the guerrilla, and the apparently easy triumph in Cuba, led to an expected instant success which did not materialize. Many groups launched their campaigns without adequate preparation. In addition, rural dwellers, lacking knowledge about the guerrillas and their cause, demonstrated indifference, or even hostility, and failed to join guerrilla forces *en masse*.

These events gradually led revolutionaries to question their tactics. Recently, those pledged to armed struggle have returned to the urban areas they had previously abandoned for the countryside. Documents 8 and 9 show two aspects of this strife. The first, authored by the Uruguayan Movement of National Liberation, popularly known as the Tupamaros, the most active urban guerrilla group in Latin America, shows the nature of popular struggle and its rationale. In the last few years, the Tupamaros, operating almost at will due to their tightly knit organization and base of popular support, have confiscated arms from the police and army, and exposed the oligarchy's corruptness by turning over the contents of company files to the judiciary. To counter government censorship of the press, radio, and television concerning their activities and increasing government repression, they have also seized leading establishment figures. Their most recent exploits along this line include capturing the British ambassador, a North American technician (both released unharmed), and a North American engaged in training the Uruguayan police (executed as a foreign agent). In return for the release of their captives the Tupamaros have

[12]Gott, 104, 116, 450, 487–489. On U.S. complicity in general see North American Congress on Latin America (NACLA) Newsletters, "Supplying the Latin American Military," Vol. III, No. 3, "The Mercenarization of the Third World: Documents on U.S. Military and Police Assistance Programs," Vol. IV, No. 7, "The Pentagon's Counterinsurgency Research Infrastructure," "More on U.S. Military and Police Assistance Programs," Vol. IV, No. 9, and "A.I.D. Police Programs for Latin America, 1971–72," Vol. V, No. 4 (July–August), 1971.

demanded either that the government liberate political prisoners or grant their literature access to the media. They have consistently defied the government's efforts to crush them, and in September of 1971 completed a sensational jail escape that liberated 103 of their members the police had managed to capture. Most notably, consistent with their basic philosophy, they have avoided violence against the people in almost all their operations. Document 10, written by Carlos Marighella, a leading Brazilian urban guerrilla fighter until his death in 1968, expounds on the role of guerrillas within the national political context and on the tactical question of armed warfare.[13]

Outside the areas mentioned above, groups like the CAL in Puerto Rico, the MIR in Chile (at present above ground), and numerous entities in Argentina—all wage urban guerrilla warfare, although several combine this with rural operations. Simultaneously, they work to organize mass bases—in the labor movement, or within the vast reservoir of urban un- and underemployed who inhabit the mushrooming slums around leading cities, or among peasants in the countryside.

What is the future of revolutionary struggle in Latin America? The MIR notes that those who control the wealth, be they national or foreign, will not surrender it peaceably.[14] Meanwhile, factors favoring change grow, as basic dysfunctions cannot be resolved fast enough to reduce tensions accumulated over three centuries. At its present pace, Latin America's population will double within 25 years. To just maintain, let alone improve, standards already grossly inadequate, the number of schools, employment opportunities, houses, and volume of public services will have to be doubled

[13]Material on the Tupamaros in *The Tupamaros: Urban Guerrilla Warfare in Uruguay* (New York: The Liberated Guardian, 1970) and Carlos Nuñez, *Tupamaros: la única vanguardia* (Montevideo: Ediciones Provincias Unidas, 1969). On urban guerrilla warfare in general see Marighella's classic *Minimanual of the Urban Guerrilla* (New World Liberation Front, U.S.A., 1970).

[14]An excellent discussion of the peaceful and armed roads to socialism is "Chile: Peaceful Transition to Socialism?" in *Monthly Review*, Vol. 22, No. 8 (January 1971), 1–18.

in that time, a task impossible under present conditions. Thus as pressures mount, more people will search for alternatives outside the current system, and the appeal of revolutionary alternatives will increase.

Important for the future will be the outcome of Chile's present experiment. If the government can secure Chile's economic independence and significantly alter prevailing distribution patterns, its example will probably be copied. If it fails, those who support violent change will occupy the central place on the political podium of the revolution. Whatever the result, the thrust for change is sure to be anti-imperialist and nationalist in content. At the same time, as document 10 shows, international and intra-Latin American cooperation is increasing, raising the possibility of a united front of leftist elements ranged against the imperialist powers and national elites. In any case, for the United States and its allies, the future is at best fraught with dangers. The potential for another Southeast Asian situation—in the Andes mountains or in the Guatemalan jungles, or in the Brazilian backlands—is real. For revolutionaries the path is clear: either Latin America remains a backward area within the United States' orbit or else it must seek self-determination. This last option may or may not mean socialist societies, although signs at present point to that alternative as the only viable one in view of the international power situation, the foreign policy of the United States, and the inherent nature of world capitalism.

1.
"IDEOLOGY OF THE CUBAN REVOLUTION" AND "LESSONS OF THE CUBAN REVOLUTION"

ERNESTO "CHE" GUEVARA

The author of the first document, Ernesto "Che" Guevara, is one of the best-known Cuban revolutionary leaders. Born in Argentina, he dedicated his life to continental revolution. He formed part of the original force, along with Fidel Castro, which landed in Cuba in 1956, and soon rose to the rank of commander in the revolutionary army. After 1959 he held a number of important positions in the Revolutionary Government and came to be considered one of the regime's spokesmen. He eventually lost his life while leading a guerrilla group in Bolivia during 1967. These two selections show the changing nature of the Cuban struggle after 1956 and suggest some potential lessens to be learned from the Cuban example.

This is a unique revolution which some people maintain contradicts one of the most orthodox premises of the revolutionary movement, expressed by Lenin, "Without a revolutionary theory there is no revolutionary movement." It would be suitable to say that revolutionary theory, as the expression of a social truth, surpasses any declara-

Published originally in *Verde Olivo,* the Cuban armed forces' magazine, October 8, 1960, as "Notes for the Study of the Ideology of the Cuban Revolution." Republished in *Studies on the Left,* 1960, and in George Lavan, ed., *Che Guevara Speaks* (New York: Merit Publishers, 1971), 18–23.

tion of it; that is to say, even if the theory is not known, the revolution can succeed if historical reality is interpreted correctly and if the forces involved are utilized correctly. Every revolution always incorporates elements of very different tendencies which, nevertheless, coincide in action and in the revolution's most immediate objectives.

It is clear that if the leaders have an adequate theoretical knowledge prior to the action, they can avoid trial and error whenever the adopted theory corresponds to the reality.

The principal actors of this revolution had no coherent theoretical criteria; but it cannot be said that they were ignorant of the various concepts of history, society, economics, and revolution which are being discussed in the world today.

Profound knowledge of reality, a close relationship with the people, the firmness of the liberators' objective, and the practical revolutionary experience gave to those leaders the chance to form a more theoretical concept.

The foregoing should be considered an introduction to the explanation of this curious phenomenon that has intrigued the entire world: the Cuban Revolution. It is a deed worthy of study in contemporary world history: the how and the why of a group of men who, scattered by an army enormously superior in technique and equipment, managed first to survive, soon became strong, later became stronger than the enemy in the battle zones, still later moved into new zones of combat, and finally defeated that enemy on the battlefield even though their troops were still very inferior in number.

Naturally we, who often do not show the requisite concern for theory, will not run the risk of expounding the truth of the Cuban Revolution as though we were its masters. We will simply try to give the basis from which one can interpret this truth. In fact, the Cuban Revolution must be separated into two absolutely distinct stages: that of the armed action up to January 1, 1959,[1] and the political, economic and social transformations since then.

Even these two stages deserve further subdivisions; however, we will not take them from the viewpoint of historical exposition, but from the viewpoint of the evolution of the revolutionary thought of

---

[1]The date the revolutionaries took power.—HAS.

its leaders through their contact with the people. Incidentally, here one must introduce a general attitude toward one of the most controversial terms of the modern world: Marxism. When asked whether or not we are Marxists, our position is the same as that of a physicist or biologist when asked if he is a "Newtonian," or if he is a "Pasteurian."

There are truths so evident, so much a part of people's knowledge, that it is now useless to discuss them. One ought to be "Marxist" with the same naturalness with which one is "Newtonian" in physics, or "Pasteurian" in biology, considering that if facts determine new concepts, these new concepts will never divest themselves of that portion of truth possessed by the older concept they have outdated.

The advances in social and political science, as in other fields, belong to a long historical process whose links are connecting, adding up, molding and constantly perfecting themselves. In the origin of peoples, there exists a Chinese, Arab, or Hindu mathematics; today, mathematics has no frontiers. Thus in the field of social and political sciences, from Democritus to Marx, a long series of thinkers added their original investigations and accumulated a body of experience and of doctrines.

The merit of Marx is that he suddenly produces a qualitative change in the history of social thought. He interprets history, understands its dynamic, predicts the future, but in addition to predicting it (which would satisfy his scientific obligation), he expresses a revolutionary concept: The world must not only be interpreted, it must be transformed. Man ceases to be the slave and tool of his environment and converts himself into the architect of his own destiny. At that moment Marx puts himself in a position where he becomes the necessary target of all who have a special interest in maintaining the old. Beginning with the revolutionary Marx, a political group with concrete ideas establishes itself. Basing itself on giants, Marx and Engels, and developing through successive steps with personalities like Lenin, Stalin, Mao Tse-tung and the new Soviet and Chinese rulers, it establishes a body of doctrine and, let us say, examples to follow.

The Cuban Revolution takes up Marx at that point where he himself left science to shoulder his revolutionary rifle. And it takes him up at that point, not in a revisionist spirit, of struggling against that which follows Marx, of reviving "pure Marxism," but simply because up to that point Marx, the scientist, placed himself outside of the history he studied and predicted. From then on Marx, the revolutionary, could fight within history.

We, practical revolutionaries, initiating our own struggle, simply fulfill laws foreseen by Marx, the scientist. We are simply adjusting ourselves to the predictions of the scientific Marx as we travel this road of rebellion, struggling against the old structure of power, supporting ourselves in the people for the destruction of this structure, and having the happiness of this people as the basis of our struggle. This is to say, and it is well to emphasize this again: The laws of Marxism are present in the events of the Cuban Revolution, independently of what its leaders profess or fully know of those laws from a theoretical point of view. . . .

Each of those brief historical moments in the guerrilla warfare framed distinct social concepts and distinct appreciations of the Cuban reality; they outlined the thought of the military leaders of the revolution—those who in time would also take their position as political leaders.

Before the landing of the Granma[2] a mentality predominated that, to some degree, might be called "subjectivist"; blind confidence in a rapid popular explosion, enthusiasm and faith in the power to liquidate the Batista regime by a swift, armed uprising combined with spontaneous revolutionary strikes. . . .

After the landing comes the defeat, the almost total destruction of the forces, and their regrouping and integration as guerrillas. Characteristic of those few survivors, imbued with the spirit of struggle, was the understanding that to count upon spontaneous outbursts throughout the island was a falsehood, an illusion. They understood also that the fight would have to be a long one and that it would need vast *campesino* participation. At this point, the campesinos entered the guerrilla war for the first time.

Two events—hardly important in terms of the number of combatants, but of great psychological value—were unleashed. First, antagonism that the city people, who comprised the central guerrilla group, felt towards the campesinos was erased. The campesinos, in

[2]On December 2, 1956, the boat *Granma* landed 26th of July Movement members from Mexico, including Che and Fidel Castro, initiating the final struggle against Batista's government.—HAS.

turn, distrusted the group and, above all, feared barbarous reprisals of the government. Two things demonstrated themselves at this stage, both very important for the interrelated factors: To the campesinos, the bestialities of the army and all the persecution would not be sufficient to put an end to the guerrilla war, even though the army was certainly capable of liquidating the campesinos' homes, crops, and families. To take refuge with those in hiding was a good solution. In turn, the guerrilla fighters learned the necessity, each time more pointed, of winning the campesino masses. . . .

It may seem strange, incomprehensible, and even incredible that two small columns—without communications, without mobility, without the most elementary arms of modern warfare—could fight against well-trained, and above all, well-armed troops.

Basic [to the victory] is the characteristic of each group: the fewer comforts the guerrilla fighter has, the more he is initiated into the rigors of nature, the more he feels himself at home; his morale is higher, his sense of security greater. At the same time, he has learned to risk his life in every circumstance that might arise, to trust it to luck, like a tossed coin; and in general, as a final result of this kind of combat, it matters little to the individual guerrilla whether or not he survives.

The enemy soldier in the Cuban example is the junior partner of the dictator; he is the man who gets the last crumbs in a long line of profiteers that begins on Wall Street and ends with him. He is disposed to defend his privileges, but he is disposed to defend them only to the degree that they are important to him. His salary and pension are worth some suffering and dangers, but they are never worth his life; if the price of maintaining them will cost it, he is better off giving them up, that is to say, withdrawing from the face of guerrilla danger. From these two concepts and these two morals springs the difference which would cause the crisis of December 31, 1958. . . .

Here ends the insurrection. But the men who arrive in Havana after two years of arduous struggle are not the same men, ideologically, who took part in the first phase of the struggle. Their distrust of the campesino has been converted into affection and respect for his virtues; their total ignorance of life in the country has been converted into a knowledge of the needs of our *guajiros;* their flirtations with statistics and with theory have been fixed by the cement which is practice.

With the banner of Agrarian Reform, these men confront imperialism. They know that Agrarian Reform is the basis upon which the new Cuba must build itself. They know also that Agrarian Reform will give land to all the dispossessed, but that it will dispossess its unjust possessors; and they know that the greatest unjust possessors are also influential men in the State Department or in the government of the United States of America. But they have learned to conquer difficulties with bravery, with audacity, and, above all, with the support of the people; and they have now seen the future of liberation that awaits us on the other side of our sufferings.

The armed victory of the Cuban people over the Batista dictatorship was not only the triumph of heroism as reported by the newspapers of the world; it also forced a change in the old dogmas concerning the conduct of the popular masses of Latin America. It showed plainly the capacity of the people to free themselves by means of guerrilla warfare from a government that oppresses them.

We consider that the Cuban Revolution contributed three fundamental lessons to the conduct of revolutionary movements in America. They are:

1. Popular forces can win a war against the army.
2. It is not necessary to wait until all conditions for making revolution exist: the insurrection can create them.
3. In underdeveloped America the countryside is the basic area for armed fighting.

Of these three propositions, the first two contradict the defeatist attitude of revolutionaries or pseudo-revolutionaries who remain inactive and take refuge in the pretext that against a professional army

From Ernesto Che Guevara, *Guerrilla Warfare,* pp. 1–2. Copyright © 1961 by Monthly Review Press, reprinted by permission.

nothing can be done, who sit down to wait until in some mechanical way all necessary objective and subjective conditions are given without working to accelerate them. These problems were formerly subject of discussion in Cuba, until facts settled the question.

Naturally, it is not to be thought that all conditions for revolution are going to be created through the impulse given to them by guerrilla activity. It must always be kept in mind that there is a necessary minimum without which the establishment and consolidation of the first center is not practicable. People must see clearly the futility of maintaining the fight for social goals within the framework of civil debate. When the forces of oppression come to maintain themselves in power against established law, peace is considered already broken.

In these conditions popular discontent expresses itself in more active forms. An attitude of resistance finally crystallizes in an outbreak of fighting, provoked initially by the conduct of the authorities.

Where a government has come into power through some form of popular vote, fraudulent or not, and maintains at least an appearance of constitutional legality, the guerrilla outbreak cannot be promoted, since the possibilities of peaceful struggle have not yet been exhausted.

The third proposition is a fundamental of strategy. It ought to be noted by those who maintain dogmatically that the struggle of the masses is centered in city movements, entirely forgetting the immense participation of the country people in the life of all the underdeveloped parts of America. Of course, the struggles of the city masses of organized workers should not be underrated, but their real possibilities of engaging in armed struggle must be carefully analyzed where the guarantees which customarily adorn our constitutions are suspended or ignored. In these conditions the illegal workers' movements face enormous dangers. They must function secretly without arms. The situation in the open country is not so difficult. There, in places beyond the reach of the repressive forces, the inhabitants can be supported by armed guerrillas.

2.
CHARTER OF ORGANIC UNITY BETWEEN THE PEP AND THE PUDA AND THE CONSTITUTION OF THE UNIFIED PARTY OF HAITIAN COMMUNISTS (PUCH)

The tyrannical regime of François Duvalier, which ruled the Caribbean island of Haiti from 1957 to 1971, must be considered one of the most brutal in Latin American history. Despite its iron grip over the small republic, and wholesale repression, opposition forces challenged Duvalier in the attempt to liberate the island from both his and foreign control. Document 2, which follows, presents the charter of unification between two revolutionary opposition forces who joined together to better achieve their aims. The analysis takes into consideration the special conditions prevailing within Haiti and adapts to them the theory of armed struggle.

I. The workers' parties known by the designations of Parti D'Entente Populaire (PEP) and Parti Union des Democrates Haitiens (PUDA) have decided to fuse to form the Parti Unifie des Communistes Haitiens (PUCH) on the basis of common ideology, program, tactics, leadership, and statutes.

The elaboration of the program and statutes of the PUCH will be encharged to the new Party's leadership and will be done on the basis of agreements reached through negotiations.

II. The PUCH is the conscious and organized avant-garde of the

From *Boukan,* "Organe du Partie Unifie des Communistes Haitiens (P.U.C.H.)," No. 1 (12 Février, 1969), pp. 1–2. My translation. Footnotes added—HAS.

working class fighting under the banner of Marxist-Leninist ideology. Conceived along the Leninist norms of organization, the PUCH will direct the fight of the proletarian class to make the Haitian revolution, take power, and construct socialism.

III. The unified Party rests on the historical, theoretical, and practical experience of the PUDA and the PEP. It should increase the capacity of its new apparatus by allying itself closely with the working class and peasantry, along with other progressive sectors interested in the democratic revolution of national liberation.

IV. The essential political tasks of the democratic and national revolution consist in overturning the Duvalier dictatorship[1] and taking power in the name of a united front of all the antifeudal and anti-imperialist forces directed by the working class, to destroy the actual social and economic regime and to work the essential transformations of the revolution of national liberation in the social, economic, political, and cultural domains.

V. The democratic and social transformations aspire to conquer full political independence, to promote economic development and to open the way for the establishment of new means of production. These transformations include notably: agrarian reform; nationalization of imperialist property, foreign, principally American; monopoly of foreign commerce; cancellation of public debt; introduction of democratic practices in social life; the liquidation of illiteracy, etc. All these revolutionary measures and their subsequent broadening situate them in the perspectives of the march towards socialism—of which the democratic and national revolution represents an obligatory stage.

VI. The social classes which objectively have an interest in the revolution of national liberation are the working class, the peasantry, the middle sectors, and the fraction of the national bourgeoisie that does not accept the economic and political supremacy of American imperialism. The working class and the peasantry constitute the revolution's fundamental motor forces.

The PUCH will fight for the alliance of these national classes in a united front, realizable essentially in the course of a revolutionary war. The Party will work so that the working class, allied with the peasantry, the principal mass force, will conquer the political leader-

[1]François Duvalier, dictator from 1957 until his death in 1971.

ship of this front which will be created. The principal target of the revolution's motor forces will be the reactionary proimperialist block composed of feudal landed proprietors, the beaureaucratic and comprador bourgeoisie, the *fonctionariste*[2] fraction of the middle strata and the institutions at their service, in particular the army and the militia.

VII. The antifeudal, anti-imperialist fight of the Haitian nation, because of the unique characteristics of the political rule of our feudal dictatorship, poses special exigencies on the plan of political alliances. The PUCH, always keeping its ideological, political, and organizational independence, does not reject specific forms of temporary collaboration with other sociopolitical antidictatorial forces, if these last do not appear as simple lackeys of the United States of North America's imperialist politics vis-à-vis Haiti.

VIII. The reactionary violence of duvalierian *macoutisme* should be opposed by organized revolutionary violence of the classes in struggle for its elimination.[3] The road of the Haitian revolution lies in the armed way. Each phase of this process, which will be long, difficult, and bloody, will be articulated in a combination of nonarmed and armed struggle until it last becomes transformed into the principal form. This way indicates the countryside as the popular war's fundamental theater with the guerrilla as the principal link. Because the macoutist violence expresses itself in a permanent manner, indiscriminate and generalized, the task of armed resistance, in the countryside and in the towns, before the appearance of the guerrillas, is a necessary and opportune political conduit for the creation of the subjective conditions for revolution.

IX. The central link of all the PUCH's present tasks is the preparation for the guerrillas' establishment. The formation of social, political, and military forces for popular war and the national revolution is obligatory for all the organizations of the Unified Party in both rural and urban settings, in the zones suited for guerrilla warfare, and in other regions.

X. The PUCH is the Haitian section of the International Com-

---

[2]*Fonctionariste* refers to the lower-middle or white-collar class, which usually supports the elites' policies.

[3]The *ton ton macoutes* were Duvalier's elite secret police, hatchet men, and bodyguards.

munist Movement. It is engaged in resolving the problems of the national struggle for liberation inside an adhesion to the international discipline of the revolutionary proletariat. The PUCH intends to maintain fraternal links with all the Communist parties. It will fight for unity in world communism's ranks within the framework of respect for the independence of each party and on the basis of fidelity to Marxism-Leninism and to international proletarianism. The PUCH respects the revolutionary traditions of all people in the socialist camp. It will insert itself in the International Communist Movement in full autonomy of judgment in polemic debates. The PUCH considers the critical assimilation of the experience of brother parties as a measure of the revolutionary victory in Haiti. The PUCH declares itself ready to assure the Dominican revolutionary parties, the international and continental revolutionary parties, its militant solidarity.

Haiti, the 18th of January, 1969

3.
THE CHILEAN POPULAR UNITY
GOVERNMENT: Basic Program

The Chilean Popular Unity government, composed of a coalition of Marxist and non-Marxist political parties, came to power in 1970 after the election of its candidate, Salvador Allende, to the presidency. An edited version of its basic program is reproduced here. While the program details the causes of Chile's underdevelopment, the nature of its dependency, and the internal power factors, it proposes basically nationalist and reformist solutions. It stops short of a direct call for revolution and confrontation and emphasizes, at least in the short run, an electoral solution.

Introduction

The parties and movements that make up the Coordinating Committee of Popular Unity,[1] without endangering their own philosophies and political profiles, agree completely in the analysis of national reality explained below and in the programmatic ideas which will be the base for our common action.

1. Chile is living in a profound crisis which manifests itself in

Abridged and reprinted by permission from *NACLA Newsletter,* Vol. V, No. 1 (March 1971), pp. 3–17. Original footnotes omitted.
[1]The Popular Unity, or *Unidad Popular,* is an electoral coalition composed of the following parties: Socialist, Communist, Radical, Social Democratic, Unitary Popular Action Movement (dissident Christian Democrats), and Independent Popular Action.

social and economic stagnation, in generalized poverty and the delays of all kinds suffered by workers, peasants and other exploited classes. It is also seen in the growing difficulties faced by employees, professionals, small and medium businessmen, and in the minimal opportunities available to women and youth.

Chile's problems can be resolved. Our country has great resources such as copper and other materials, a great hydroelectric potential, vast extensions of forests, a long coastland rich in marine species, more than sufficient agricultural lands, and so forth.

What has failed in Chile is a system that does not meet the necessities of our times. Chile is a capitalistic country dependent on imperialism, dominated by bourgeois sectors that are structurally linked to foreign capital and cannot resolve the country's fundamental problems. These are the same problems that derive from class privileges and which will never be renounced voluntarily.

Furthermore, as a consequence of the development of world wide capitalism the surrender by the national monopolistic bourgeoisie to imperialism progressively increases and accentuates its dependence and its role as the minor partner of foreign capital.

2. In Chile the "reformist" and "developmental" solutions that the Alliance for Progress encouraged and that Frei's government made as their own have not succeeded in changing anything important.[2]

3. The development of monopolistic capitalism impedes the widening of democracy and exacerbates antipopular violence.

As the level of people's struggle increases in proportion to the failures of reformism, the position of the most reactionary sectors of the ruling class hardens; in the last analysis, those sectors have recourse only to force.

4. The imperialistic exploitation of backward economies is carried out in many ways. Some are through investment in mining (copper, iron and other) and in industrial, banking, and commercial activities; through the technological control that obliges us to pay extremely high sums for equipment, licenses, and patents; through the usurious North American loans that oblige us to spend in the United States and transport the purchased articles in North American ships, etc.

Since 1952 North Americans have invested 7.473 million dollars in Latin America and they have taken out 16 billion dollars. Impe-

[2]Eduardo Frei, reformist Christian Democrat President, 1964–1970.

rialism has snatched away from Chile large resources equivalent to double the capital invested in our country throughout the whole of its history.

The North American monopolies, with the complicity of the bourgeois government, have succeeded in taking control of almost all our copper, iron, and nitrate. They control foreign trade and dictate our economic policy through the International Monetary Fund and other organizations. They dominate important industrial and service sectors. They enjoy privileged laws at the same time as they impose monetary devaluation, the reduction of salaries, and distort agricultural activity through agricultural surpluses.

They also interfere in education, culture, and communications media. Taking advantage of military and political agreements, they have tried to penetrate the Armed Forces.

5. Chile is governed and legislated in favor of the few. Those who effectively produce are undergoing a difficult situation: half a million families need housing and many others live in terrible conditions with respect to sewer systems, potable water, electricity and health; the necessities of the people with regard to education and health are insufficiently cared for; more than half of Chilean workers receive insufficient remuneration to take care of their minimal living necessities. Unemployment and unstable working conditions are suffered by every family. For innumerable young men the possibility of working is very difficult and uncertain.

Imperialistic capital and a group of privileged people who do not exceed 10 percent of the population monopolize half the national income.

6. The increase in the cost of living is a hell in the homes of the people and especially for the housewife. According to official information, during the past 10 years the cost of living has increased by almost 1,000 percent. The large capitalist on the other hand uses his influence to protect himself from inflation and in fact benefits from it. His property and capital increase in value, his construction contracts with the government are readjusted, and the prices of his products always go up at a higher rate than wage increases.

7. A high number of Chileans are poorly fed. According to official statistics 50 percent of children less than 15 years of age are undernourished. Malnutrition affects their growth and limits their ability to learn and educate themselves. The system of large landholdings is

to blame for Chile's food problems and is responsible for the backward, miserable condition that characterizes the countryside. Infant and adult mortality rates, illiteracy, and a lack of housing and health in rural zones are markedly superior to those of the cities.

8. The growth of our economy is minimal. During recent years we have grown at an annual average rate of 2 percent per capita. Since 1967 we have not grown. This means that in 1966 each Chilean had a larger quantity of goods than he has today.

9. Only the truly popular alternative and consequently the fundamental chore that the government has before it is to end the dominion of the imperialists, the monopolists, and the landholding oligarchy and to begin the construction of Socialism.

The Program
POPULAR POWER

The revolutionary transformation the country needs can be carried out only if the Chilean people take power and exercise it effectively. The popular and revolutionary forces have not united to struggle for the simple substitution of one president of the republic for another, nor to replace one party for another in the government, but to carry out profound changes based on the transfer of power from the old dominant groups to the workers, the peasants, and the progressive sectors of the middle classes of the city and the countryside.

The popular government will guarantee the exercise of democratic rights and will respect the individualism and social guarantees of all people. Freedom of conscience, speech, press, and assembly, the inviolability of the home and the rights of unions and their organizations will rule effectively without the limiting conditions presently established by the dominant classes.

For this to be effective . . . workers will be called upon to intervene at their respective places in the decisions of the organs of power. For example, in the welfare and social security institutions we will establish the administration by depositors themselves, thus assuring them democratic elections and the secret vote for their directive council.

THE NEW ECONOMY

The united popular forces seek as the central objective of their policy to replace the present economic structure, putting an end to the power of national and foreign monopolistic capital and of lati-fundism in order to bring the construction of socialism.

In the new economy, planning will play an extremely important role. The central planning organizations will be at the highest admin-istrative level and their democratically generated decisions will have an executive character.

AREA OF SOCIAL PROPERTY

The process of transforming our economy will begin with a policy destined to make up a dominant state area formed by enterprises that the state presently possesses, along with enterprises that will be ex-propriated. The first step will be to nationalize those basic sources of wealth which are controlled by foreign capital and internal monopolies. Into this area of nationalized activities will be integrated the following sectors: (1) the large mining companies of copper, nitrate, iodine, iron and coal; (2) the country's financial system, especially, private banks and insurance companies; (3) foreign trade; (4) the great distribution enterprises and monopolies; (5) the strategic industrial monopolies; (6) in general all those activities which determine the country's economic and social development. . . .

AREA OF PRIVATE PROPERTY

This area includes all those sectors of industry, mining, agriculture, and services in which the private ownership of the means of produc-tion remains in effect. In numbers, these enterprises will be the majority. The enterprises that make up this sector will be aided by the general planning of the national economy. The state will provide the necessary financial and technical assistance to the enterprises of this area.

MIXED AREA

This sector is called mixed because it will be made up of enter-prises that combine state and private capital.

DEEPENING AND EXTENDING THE AGRARIAN REFORM

The experience that already exists in this field and its vacuums or inconsistencies lead us to reformulate the distribution and organi-zational policies of landownership based on the following directives: (1) Acceleration of the agrarian reform process by expropriating those fields that exceed the maximum established size. . . . The expropriation could include the whole or part of the expropriated fields' assets. (2) The immediate incorporation of abandoned fields and poorly utilized state property into cultivation. (3) The expropriated lands will be organized preferentially as ownership cooperatives. Small farmers will have titles of domain that establish ownership. Lands will also be set aside to create state agricultural enterprises with the most modern technology. (4) In qualified cases land will be assigned to small farmers, tenants, and agricultural employees who are able to do agricultural work. (5) Reorganization of extremely small properties through the progressive introduction of agricultural work cooperatives. (6) Incorporation of small- and medium-size farmers to the advantages and services of cooperatives that operate in their geographical area. (7) Defense of the integrity and amplification as well as the assurance of democratic rule in native Indian communities threatened by usurpation, and assurance to indigenous people of sufficient lands and appropriate technical and credit assistance.

POLICY OF ECONOMIC DEVELOPMENT

Its objectives will be:

1. To resolve the immediate problems of the great majority. For this the country's productive capacity will be turned from superfluous and expensive articles that satisfy high-income groups toward production of articles of popular use of cheap and good quality.

2. To guarantee employment with adequate remuneration to all Chileans of working age.

3. To liberate Chile from her subordination to foreign capital.

4. To assure rapid and decentralized economic growth which tends to develop our productive forces to the maximum and to produce the optimal utilization of resources.

5. To execute a foreign trade policy that tends to develop and diversify our exports, to open new markets, to achieve growing technical and financial independence and to avoid the scandalous devaluation of our currency.

6. To take measures that will lead to monetary stability.

SOCIAL TASKS

The basic points of the government's action will be:

(a) A remunerations policy that proceeds to create immediately the organisms which, with the participation of the workers, will determine the figures that effectively constitute "vital wages" and minimal salaries in the different areas of the country.[3] To establish a minimum wage and a salary system of equal levels for equal jobs (and) in the same way all discrimination between men and women or because of age in relation to wages and salaries will be eliminated.

(b) To unify, improve, and extend the social security system. . . .

(c) To assure both preventive and curative medical and dental attention for all Chileans. . . .

(d) Sufficient funds will be set aside for carrying out an ample plan of housing construction. Each family will eventually own a house. The quotas or monthly rents that house purchasers or renters must pay will not exceed 10 percent of the family income.

(e) Complete civil capability will be established for the married woman as well as for children within or outside of marriage as well as adequate divorce legislation.

(f) The legal division between laborers and employees will be eliminated, the common denomination as "workers" will be established for both, and the right to organize unions for all those who presently do not have the right will be extended.

CULTURE AND EDUCATION

The social process will gradually shape a new culture oriented toward the consideration of human work as the highest value, the expression of the affirmative will and national independence, and the shaping of a critical vision of reality. The new culture will arise from the struggle between brotherhood and individualism. . . . The new state will work for the masses' incorporation into intellectual and artistic activity both through a radically transformed educational system as well as through a national system of popular culture.

INTERNATIONAL POLICY OBJECTIVES

The popular government's international policy will be directed toward affirming the complete political and economic autonomy of Chile. There will be diplomatic relations with all countries of the world irrespective of their ideological and political position on the

[3]The "vital wage" is a minimum legal wage, subject to annual adjustment. Workers and employees receive differing amounts which explains item (f).

basis of respect for self-determination and interests of the people. A strong Latin American and anti-imperialist sense will be promoted through an international policy of peoples rather than chancellories.

Diplomatic relations, interchange, and friendship with the socialist countries will be reinforced.

MORE NATIONAL INDEPENDENCE

The position of active defense of Chilean independence implies denouncing the present Organization of American States as an instrument and agency of North American imperialism and to struggle against all forms of Pan-Americanism implicit in this organization.

INTERNATIONAL SOLIDARITY

Every type of colonialism or neocolonialism will be condemned and the right to rebellion of the people subjected to these systems will be recognized. In the same way the policy will solidify itself effectively with the Cuban revolution, and with the advances of revolution and the construction of socialism on the Latin American continent.

4.
MIR'S RESPONSE TO THE UP

The Revolutionary Left Movement (Movimiento Izquierdista Revolucionario, or MIR) has persistently advocated armed struggle in Chile. Formed under its present leadership in December of 1967 at the University of Concepción in southern Chile, it separated from traditional left parties over the question of tactics. In this selection, the MIR, probably the fastest growing political grouping in the country today, analyzes the meaning of the Unidad Popular's victory. It questions the ultimate validity of electoral politics and concludes that armed confrontation must precede the transition to socialism in Chile.

What is the significance of the electoral victory of the UP? Has the strategy of armed struggle failed in Chile? Must we abandon the present political and military structure of our organizations?

Imperialism and the Latin American Bourgeoisies

Is it possible that today we could have an alliance between important sectors of the national bourgeoisie and the left in order to develop an anti-imperialist policy? The ruling class in Latin America is a social and political conglomerate which includes the North American ruling class and our native bourgeoisies, their economic,

Abridged and reprinted by permission from *NACLA Newsletter,* Vol. V, No. 1 (March 1971), pp. 18–25.

military, and political interests being closely linked. There exist a few contradictions between imperialism and the national bourgeoisies centered around a struggle to obtain a greater share of that which is produced through the exploitation of Latin America. Nevertheless, the common interest of maintaining the system of exploitation and control on which they base their power and their wealth, prevails always above and beyond these lesser contradictions. The contradictions between the bourgeoisie and imperialism increase every time that the share of the bounty decreases significantly for any one of them.

The Latin American bourgeoisie has tried in the last few years to deny imperialism a greater share of the economic surplus that each country produces and this has brought about the so-called "wave of nationalism" in Latin America. This nationalist movement has developed according to the state of mass movements, and according to the extent to which North American interests are willing to divert their investment from the fundamental extractive sectors of the economy to others like the manufacturing industry.

For at least three years mass movements in Chile have been growing and the electoral majority of Allende was based on the heightened aspirations of the workers. The electoral victory is a step forward for the masses in the defense of their interests, and the interests of the national and foreign ruling classes are objectively being threatened. Above and beyond the tactical games of political representation, the Chilean bourgeoisie will try to strengthen its links with imperialism and to present a common front to the masses rising behind the UP.

Imperialism and the Reformist Governments of Latin America

Since World War II, the international situation has been fundamentally defined by a growing colonial revolution and by the struggle of imperialism to prevent it. The North American policy regarding reformist governments of the left has been basically one of open opposition. In spite of this, imperialism has been forced sometimes to accept reformist governments where in the short run it could not intervene because it was tied up in bigger confrontations. In spite of the United States being forced sometimes to allow some local and temporary loosening of control in its empire, it does not seem today that this would be the most probable outcome in Chile in the long run. This does not deny the possibility that some temporary tolerance could be given to a leftist reformist government in Chile, and one must not discard the possibility that the Southeast Asian conflict, the problems of prestige for the "leader of the free world," and the movement within the United States against the Vietnam war may limit political actions for a short period.

It is a mistake to confuse these temporary limitations on imperialist aggression with a strategic tolerance of leftist reformism; either one gives some security to American capitalism or American interests are threatened and a policy of intervention will develop. This does not require direct intervention. It can take the form of aggression from Argentina, or of activating a confrontation between the dominant classes and the working classes in Chile.

The Causes of the Electoral Victory of the UP

The increase in mass movement activity permitted what we thought would be very difficult: the electoral plurality of the UP. The increase in social movement in Chile also means that class struggle has sharpened in the last three years. The electoral majority obtained by the UP is also an expression of the maturity reached by the masses in the last six years.

The Historical Significance of the Electoral Victory of the UP

We are certain that the ruling classes will not give up their privileges free of charge, and therefore the electoral victory assures the legitimacy and the mass character of the confrontation of classes which will precede the seizing of power by the workers.

The Extent of the Electoral Victory of the UP

As long as the state apparatus remains untouched it will not go beyond its present bureaucratic and military structures; it will still be an instrument of oppression and continue fulfilling a class role. Whether or not one can pass from a leftist government to a more advanced phase in the construction of socialism depends on whether or not we destroy the state capitalist apparatus. This depends on the masses' effective participation in this process, on the revolutionary composition of the political forces which lead the process, and on the measures taken in the struggle against imperialism and financial, industrial, and agrarian capital. All of the above involve, with certainty, an armed confrontation between the ruling classes and the workers.

The goal, therefore, is the seizing of power by the workers, which requires the destruction of the state as an instrument of the bourgeoisie; and to place all the state apparatus at the service of the workers' interests. We look for the effective exercise of power by the workers themselves, supported by an armed proletariat, on the local level. All of this is for the purpose of nationalizing foreign capital, and returning all the banks, all the land, and all the factories to all the people.

The Possibilities of the UP Program

We try to determine whether or not the UP program can be coopted by the capitalist system. We begin from the position that it is necessary to destroy the capitalist state . . . we do not believe that sectors of the industrial bourgeoisie exist with whom it would be possible to ally oneself, much less protect. For us the ruling class includes the North Americans and the industrial, financial, and agrarian bourgeoisie as a whole. For us it is not a matter of increasing state control over the economy, allowing sectors of big industry and agribusiness to continue growing.

As the UP program is formulated, it strikes some vital nuclei of capitalism such as foreign enterprise, finance capital, industrial monopolies, and the latifundia. If this program is implemented it will create a bourgeois and imperialist counteroffensive which will bring about a quick radicalization process. For these reasons, although the UP program is not identical to ours, we shall push and support the realization of those measures.

Is the Strategy of Armed Struggle Fundamentally Questioned?

We have always affirmed that the seizing of power by the workers will be possible only through armed struggle. We know that powerful interests must be hurt, interests that the capitalist state apparatus protects; we also know that the ruling classes, as taught by historical experience, will not hesitate to defend their power and wealth with violence.

Furthermore, the armed struggle will take the form of a long and irregular revolutionary war; and it may not take the form of a popular insurrection which in a few hours will turn power definitely to the workers.

None of these fundamental propositions has changed due to the electoral victory of the UP; the confrontation has only been postponed. And when it takes place, it will be more legitimate and massive, which makes the strategy of armed struggle today more valid than ever before.

The Limitations of a UP Government?

The UP will assume the government through legal means, which forces the UP to govern with the capitalist state apparatus remaining untouched. Therefore, it will start governing without any substantial modifications in the armed forces, thus assuring the permanent threat of a reactionary military coup. It will assume power under old structures which will make the exercise of government very difficult, and it will be difficult to modify substantially this limiting legal framework.

Our Politics

For us, the workers have already gained the right to take the foreign enterprises, the banks, the factories, and the land, the property of all the people. The fundamental task of the moment is to defend the electoral victory from the maneuvers of the bourgeoisie and imperialism, to push for mass mobilizations, and to formulate a policy toward the lower rank officers and troops of the armed forces. We shall point out the dangers in the path of seizing power by the workers starting from an electoral majority, with the intention of preparing them for the confrontation that this path necessarily implies.

Afterwards we shall push for the realization of the program, affirming its development in the poorest sectors of society as a way to insure the revolutionary and socialist course of the process.

We will look at the process objectively with socialism as its only goals, with the understanding that our support or our opposition to the UP will not signify opportunist deviations to the extent that we have our objectives and our path very clear.

We shall maintain our political and military structure as long as the capitalist system prevails in Chile and as long as power is not effectively controlled by the workers, the defense of whose interests shall continue to be our sole reason for existence.

National Secretariat of the Movement of the Revolutionary Left
October 1970

5.
"STATEMENT TO THE PRESS" AND "MESSAGE TO COLOMBIANS FROM THE MOUNTAINS"

CAMILO TORRES

> Perhaps no man symbolized the revolutionary New Church in Latin America as much as Camilo Torres. Trained as a priest and sociologist, he attempted to promote basic social change in his native Colombia through United Front politics. Frustrated by the opposition within the Catholic Church and by conservative politicians, he concluded that only violent methods could succeed in bringing social justice to his land. He joined the rural guerrilla movement, but in early 1966 fell to army bullets. These selections present his reasons for believing that revolution is an intimately Christian act and spell out some of the reasons behind his final decision to become a guerrilla.

The Christian priesthood consists not only of officiating at external ritual observances. The Mass, which is at the center of the priesthood, is fundamentally communal. But the Christian community cannot worship in an authentic way unless it has first effectively put into practice the precept of love for fellow man. I chose Christianity because I believed that in it I would find the purest way to serve my fellow man. I was chosen by Christ to be a priest forever because of the desire to consecrate my full time to the love of my fellow man.

From *Revolutionary Priest,* by Camilo Torres, edited by John Gerassi, pp. 324–326, 425–426. Copyright © 1971 by Random House, Inc. Reprinted by permission of the publisher. Also by permission of Brandt and Brandt, London.

As a sociologist, I have wanted this love to be translated into efficient service through technology and science. My analyses of Colombian society made me realize that revolution is necessary to feed the hungry, give drink to the thirsty, clothe the naked, and procure a life of well-being for the needy majority of our people. I believe that the revolutionary struggle is appropriate for the Christian and the priest. Only by revolution, by changing the concrete conditions of our country, can we enable men to practice love for each other.

Throughout my ministry as priest, I have tried in every way possible to persuade the laymen, Catholic or not, to join the revolutionary struggle. In the absence of a massive response, I have resolved to join the revolution myself, thus carrying out part of my work of teaching men to love God by loving each other. I consider this action essential as a Christian, as a priest, and as a Colombian. But such action, at this time, is contrary to the discipline of the present church. I do not want to break the discipline of the church, but I also do not want to betray my conscience.

Therefore, I have asked his Eminence the Cardinal to free me from my obligations as a member of the clergy so that I may serve the people on the temporal level. I forfeit one of the privileges I deeply love—the right to officiate as priest at the external rites of the church. But I do so to create the conditions that will make these rites more authentic.

I believe that my commitment to live a useful life, efficiently fulfilling the precept of love for my fellow man, demands this sacrifice of me. The highest standard by which human decisions must be measured is the all-surpassing love that is true charity. I accept all the risks that this standard demands of me.

Colombians:

I have joined the armed struggle.

From the Colombian mountains I mean to continue the struggle, arms in hand, until power has been won by the people. I have joined the Army of National Liberation because I have found in it the same ideals of the United Front. I found the desire and the attainment of unity at the base, a peasant base, without traditional religious or party differences, and without any interest in combating the revolutionary elements of any sector, movement, or party. And without *caudillismo*. This is a movement that seeks to free the people from exploitation by the oligarchy and imperialism, a movement that will not lay down its arms as long as power is not entirely in the hands of the people, and a movement that, in its goals, accepts the platform of the United Front.

All we Colombian patriots must ready ourselves for war. Little by little, we will emerge ready for war. Little by little, experienced guerrilla leaders will appear in all parts of the country. Meanwhile, we must be alert. We must gather weapons and ammunition, seek guerrilla training, talk with those who are closest to us. We must collect clothing, medical supplies, and provisions in preparation for a protracted struggle.

We must carry out small-scale attacks against the enemy where we can be sure of victory. We must put those who claim to be revolutionaries to the test. We must not refrain from acting, but neither must we grow impatient. In a long, drawn-out war, everyone must go into action at some point. What matters is that the revolution finds them ready and on their guard. We must divide the work. The activists of the United Front must be in the vanguard of action and initiative. We must have patience while we wait and confidence in final victory. The people's struggle must become a national one. We have already begun, and we have a long day's work ahead of us.

Colombians: let us not fail to answer the call of the people and the revolution.

Activists of the United Front: let us turn our watchwords into reality:

For the unity of the popular classes, until death!

For the organization of the popular classes, until death!

For the taking of power for the popular classes, until death!

We say "until death" because we are determined to carry on to the end. We say "until victory" because a people that throws itself into the struggle until death will always achieve victory. We say "until final victory," with the watchwords of the Army of National Liberation:

NOT ONE STEP BACK! LIBERATION OR DEATH!

6.
LETTER OF PEASANT FREEDOM

FRANCISCO JULIÃO

Revolutionary activity has only recently reached the Latin American peasant masses. One of the most powerful peasant movements centered in the backward northeast of Brazil where a network of Peasant Leagues grew to challenge the large landowners for the first time. Francisco Julião, a politician and lawyer, played a fundamental role in organizing the first peasant organizations. This selection is from Julião's letter to the peasants urging them to organize. The simple, direct language and almost liturgical rhythm of the letter shows Julião's conception of how best to communicate with the peasantry. The Leagues, under Communist, Catholic, and Julião's banners, reached almost half a million members before the military government dissolved them in 1964.

I. Unity

From here, from Recife, Pernambuco, the cradle of the Peasant Leagues, I send you this letter, Peasants of Brazil, in the hope that it will reach your home.

You and your brothers are almost all Brazil. It is you who assuages our hunger; and you die of hunger. It is you who clothe us;

Abridged from Francisco Julião, "Carta de alforria do camponês," *Que são as ligas camponesas?* (Rio de Janiero: Ed. Civilização Brasileira, 1962), pp. 69–72. Translated by Karen W. Spalding and Hobart A. Spalding, Jr.

and you live in a loincloth. You are the soldiers who defend the fatherland; and the fatherland forgets you. From your ranks come the straw bosses for the latifundia; and the straw boss crushes you. You give alms to the Church; and the Church preaches resignation in the name of Christ. But Christ was a rebel; and for this he was crucified. And like Christ, the good Francis of Assisi, from Italy, also remained on your side. And two who still live, Mao Tse-tung, of China, and Fidel Castro, of Cuba. All of them triumphed because they were with you and you were with them. You were and are. You are and will be.

This letter, Peasants of Brazil, must reach your hand . . . wherever you groan, night and day, over the hoe, the axe, the scythe, the knife, and the plow. This letter, Peasants of Brazil, that I write from Recife, from the headquarters of the Peasant Leagues, shows you the roads you must follow in search of your freedom.

The journey is difficult and filled with snares, but your victory is as certain as the sunrise every morning. The latifundia is cruel. It hides behind the police, and the straw boss. It uses your worst enemies. To win your vote it uses two means: violence or cunning. With violence it strikes fear into you; with cunning it deceives you. Violence is the straw boss. It is the police. It is the threat to evict you from your land. To pull your house down. To uproot your crops. To kill you of hunger. To call you Communist, and say that God will punish you. As if there could be greater punishment than your present lot. Chained to the latifundia, in the name of a freedom that is not your freedom. And of a God that is not your God.

Cunning enters your house gently as a lamb. With claws sheathed; with venom hidden. And it offers you medicine. And a cart to carry your wife to the hospital. And a little money on loan, or credit at the company store. And it catches you unaware, when the election comes, saying to you: "Prepare your vote. If my candidate wins, things will change." And when the candidate wins things do not change. And if they change it is for the worse. The latifundia distends with fat; you distend with hunger. The years go by. The centuries go by. Listen to what I tell you: what must change, Peasants, is you. But you will only change when you kill fear. And there is only one cure for fear: union. With one finger you cannot hold a hoe, an axe, a knife, or a plow. Nor with an open hand, because the fingers are separated. You must close the hand so that the fingers join together. The League is the closed hand because it is the union of all your brothers. Alone you are a drop of water. United to your brother, you are a cataract. Union creates strength. It is a bundle of rods. It is a river rising. It is the people marching, and the straw boss fleeing. It is the police beaten. It is justice being born. It is freedom coming. With the League our arms, and the syndicate our hands.

II. The Roads

Many are the roads that will carry you to freedom. Freedom means land. It means bread. It means a house. It means medicines. It means schools. It means peace. I will show you these roads. But I tell you and repeat to you: you will not advance in the journey if you attempt it alone. Invite your brother without land or with a little land. And ask him to invite another. In the beginning you will be two. Later, ten. Later, a hundred. Later, a thousand. And in the end you will be everyone. Marching together. As together you go to market, to a fiesta, to mass, to worship, to a burial, to an election. I say and repeat to you: union is the mother of liberty. The roads you can travel with your brothers are many. They begin in different places but they all lead to the same place. What roads are these? These roads are (1) democracy for the peasants; (2) the syndicate for the peasants; (3) cooperatives for the peasants; (4) a human and just law for the peasants; (5) and the vote for the illiterate.

7.
ALVARO "EL CHUNGO"

This story as told by a guerrilla fighter with the Fuerzas Armadas Revolucionaries de Colombia is one part of a larger collection gathered by an anonymous member of the revolutionary forces. He left the university to join the guerrillas and before his death collected a number of case histories of individual guerrillas and actions. This particular selection not only demonstrates the travails of revolutionary fighters but also clearly indicates the relationship between folk mythology and peasant struggle.

"I protected myself, with four other guerrillas, through an old woman who knows all about witchcraft. She protected all of my body but she forgot my right arm. She made me drink a potion. She recited some verses that I did not understand. . . ."

A young peasant from Tolima.[1] Became a guerrilla at 16. Talkative and pleasant, capable of making a dead man laugh. An elongated face, light skin and dancing black eyes that seemed to have an answer to everything. His name is Alvaro. The guerrillas call him Alvaro "El Chungo" (the cripple) because they amputated his right arm. He got used to his new state. He learned to shoot all types of

From *Diario de un guerrillero latinoamericano,* (Montevideo: Editorial Sandino, 1968), pp. 40–45. My translation. Footnotes added.—HAS.
[1]A Colombian town.

weapons. With the help of his stump he shoots and loads with an incredible agility. He has not lost one iota of his courage in the fight.

"It was the second of February of 1963. We were thirteen, we had to attempt an action on the road between Dolores and Prade.[2] They told us that there were military vehicles and not many. Soon after we reached the indicated spot the first car appeared. We installed ourselves. Five in the rearguard, four sharpshooters and we three up front, ready to attack. We had on military uniforms. The terrain was smooth and flat. We waited for them in a curve in the road. We were on top of them when they saw us. The driver stopped short three steps from us. We shouted at them not to move. They answered: "You'll see you sons of bitches." Then we fired. We did not give them time to get away, three fell, another was able to entrench himself behind an embankment, firing like a crazy man so that we would not capture the weapons. When we advanced to take away their rifles, a grenade exploded.

"The chulos[3] had just taken refuge behind an embankment when we heard other explosions, it was a whole convoy. The sharpshooters, seeing that they were attacked from the rear, disbanded, firing in all directions. We, at first, thought it was our rearguard, but when we saw that the bullets whistled by our ears, we understood the situation. We left the field. When I jumped the barbed wire fence I got two bullets in the right arm. The others were able to pass. I dropped my weapon and threw myself on top of it.

"The chulos came after me. Each rifle shot made the dirt fly on top of my head. One tried to jump the barbed wire fence while insulting me. I saw his eyes shining with hatred and with the desire to chop me to pieces as a snake. Upon seeing him so close, I gathered courage and began to run. My arm hung limp and felt like dry wood, it caught in the spines and to free it I had to take the rifle strap in my teeth. A little farther ahead stood another chulo. I fell a second time near a shrub. When I saw them on top of me, I fired. The first fell, the other gave a jump and fell to the ground without ceasing to fire. When they saw that I was still armed

[2]Two towns in Colombia's north central backlands.
[3]Disrespectful name given to government troops.

and that I could shoot, they gave up the chase. I still had to cross their lines. I jumped a fence, fell into a swamp. I got up and kept going toward the rendezvous.

"On the way, I met a comrade bent over from pain. He had cramps, his knees were knots of muscle. He could not take one step. I pissed on his knees, to calm the pain. It worked. When he began to walk, I gave him my knapsack and rifle. He walked behind me to erase the traces of blood.

"I asked him to cut off my arm or kill me. I did not want them to take me alive. I was in bad shape. I could not feel anything in the arm. He tried to cheer me, he told me that it was only a scratch. I could not go farther, I remained hidden behind a bush.

"At last day came. I was soaked, my body bathed in blood. I had only a piece of canvas to cover me. The smell of blood was so strong that at nine in the morning I was amidst a cloud of flies. My arm filled with larvae. I tried to take them out but I could not, I did not even have the strength to move. By afternoon the wound was filled with worms. I managed as best I could, closed my eyes and covered my nose. I was buried, rotting. I felt the worms through all my body as if they were marching through it, in all places. I heard a noise. I thought they were my comrades who had come to look for me. But no, it was the army. I took courage, they passed by.

"Another day. My only company, the worms and the flies. The infection continued spreading. I tried to lift myself but I could not, my body felt like lead. I had new company: vultures circled overhead, they landed close by, at the slightest movement they took off again. Four hours after sunrise they still had not picked out my eyes. They waited for my dead body.

"Near evening, a peasant showed up, attracted by the smell and the vultures. He said that my companions had ordered me searched for but that the patrols which surrounded the zone had made it impossible. I thought that I was going to live again. The peasant, seeing the state in which I was, began to cry. He lifted up my head and took off the blood-stained canvas which covered me. He spilled a small bottle of creosote[4] on the wound. The worms writhed in my arm. Some died but nothing happened to most of them. The peasant

---

[4] A strong antiseptic.

took them out with a small wooden stick that he poked into the wound. My arm became violet and then pure white. A piece of rotten flesh, full of worms. The smell was unbearable.

". . . the comrade left and returned with a canvas to make me a bed. He brought a knife and cut off the clothes full of fly shit that I had on. He washed me, made me put on pants and a clean shirt. He gave me some soup, which I took but vomited it back up. He brought me water in a calabash. I was very thirsty. At night, two more peasants came. They put me in a canvas tied with a branch. They took me to the Magdalena River.[5] They left me a moment at the riverbank. They waited for the boatmen. Someone whistled. A canoe came close, gliding over the water like a serpent. They explained that it had been held up by patrols. One could only hear the noise of the paddles. The river had risen, the boatmen say that it is easier to cross when high. Halfway, the current grabbed us violently, and we went downstream at top speed. At least we gained the other bank.

"That night we walked twelve hours straight. They took turns carrying the bed. It seemed like a procession. In the early morning we reached the village. There they took good care of me. When we arrived at the ravine we realized that the *chulos* were following. At midnight we set out again. At four in the morning they reached the place we had just left.

"A pregnant woman took care of me the next day. I thought I would die. I did not know how much harm that a woman in that condition could do curing a wound. Later they told me she had a fiery look, full of electricity. To play with that is dangerous, especially when one is already in such bad shape.[6]

"As the wound was still full of worms and pus, they washed it again with creosote. The toxin flooded the arm and formed a black sack at the end of the fingers which began to fall off. Every day a comrade gathered them and buried them.

"At last the doctors came, they took me to the city. I saw them cut the bone, clean what was left and put medicine and bandages on it. They left me this stump. They told me not to look and turned

[5]Colombia's main river.
[6]Many peasant cultures consider pregnant women to have strong mystical powers.

my head away. But I saw just the same as there was a large mirror in the room.

"When I got well, I returned to my comrades. They prepared a new action. They agreed to take me along. What happiness to see the *chulos* run, they fell to earth like moles and when the bullets screamed by them they ran like rabbits.

"Here I am back in the mountains, where I belong."

8.

OPEN LETTER TO THE POLICE FROM THE TUPAMAROS

> The Uruguayan Movement for National Liberation (or Tupa-
> maros as they are popularly called) represents the most suc-
> cessful single urban guerrilla group operating in Latin Amer-
> ica. The Tupamaros have consistently defied all government
> attempts to suppress them and have completed numerous
> daring operations. Among these have been the ransoming
> of several prominent Uruguayan and foreign officials in
> return for the release of political prisoners or access to the
> media from which they have been barred. They also have
> seized documents showing the corruption and duplicity of
> the oligarchy and turned them over to public authorities.
> The letter reproduced here outlines the main thrust of the
> Tupamaros analysis and the reasons why they chose revo-
> lutionary methods.

We believe it necessary to communicate to all members of the
police, the army, and other armed forces in the country in an open
letter which we will give the widest circulation possible so that the
greatest quantity of people can witness this kind of dialogue.

From Antonio Mercader and Jorge de Vera, *Tupamaros: estrategia y
acción,* pp. 138–141. Copyright 1969 by Editorial Alfa S.A., Montevideo,
Uruguay. My translation—HAS. Used by permission of the publisher.
   The Montevideo newspaper *Epoca* first published the letter on December
7, 1967, for which the government shut the paper down.

With respect to what happened we wish to manifest the following: you know that you did not confuse us with jewel thieves.[1] At your asking the comrade showed his document of identity and gave you the explanations asked for, unarmed and politely. Even so you detained him, revolvers in hand, and you were going to enter the building despite the fact that said comrade asked for a search warrant which you did not show him. The truth is that the comrade who then came out of the building, weapon in hand, before firing asked you to keep still but you tried to disarm him and fired, wounding him severely. When the policeman fell wounded and asked for his life, his wish was respected and he was attended, examined, and tranquillized by another comrade in view of his serious wound.

All this you know well and so you know that your superiors lie, that the press lies.

With respect to the future we wish to tell you: we tried every way to get out of the situation before having to shoot. And this was because we are not common criminals: because our fight is not against police agents.

Our fight is against those who utilize the armed services and those who shape them to repress the people and maintain their privileges. The same people which accepts and pays for those institutions. Against those, yes, our weapons point without vacilation and they aim also at those who consciously or unconsciously defend them. We have begun a fight in which our life is at stake. A fight which will only end with victory or death. And we have done it because we consider criminal the indifference toward the situation of our country.

Because we have a profound faith in the Uruguayan people, from which we have sprung and which we have seen fooled and exploited freely. Faith in the people, that they will rise up soon together with us.

Because we no longer believe in the laws and institutions that the 600 privileged owners of the country, the political parties, the organs which manipulate public opinion, have created (and which they step on each time it suits them) to defend their interests by starving the people and beating them if they resist.

---

[1] On November 29, 1967, a police patrol encountered some Tupamaros. Later they claimed the episode was a fight with jewel thieves.—HAS.

Because we believe it indispensable that the people organize violence to repress the hidden or open violence·of the oligarchs.

Because we are not ready to witness without a fight the manner in which the country of Artigas is sold to the foreigner.[2]

Because the solutions which without doubt exist to solve the problems of the country will not be reached without a violent fight, because those solutions are contrary to the interests of those who have everything in their own hands and are contrary to the interests of very powerful foreigners.

Because these solutions are also dramatically urgent, life, culture, health, food, the right to work for thousands of men, women, children, and old people depend on them. The country's future depends on them and we are sufficiently mature not to continue waiting indefinitely while the professional politicians, corrupt and bribed, entrenched in power, bring them.

For these reasons we have placed ourselves outside the law. It is the only honest thing to do when the law is not equal for all; when the law exists to defend spurious interests of a minority against the majority; when the law is against the country's progress; when even those who have created it, freely place themselves outside it each time it behooves them.

For us the hour of rebellion has struck, the hour of patience has ended. The hour of action has begun and the responsibility is here and now and the time for talking has ended, the time of theoretical enunciation of goals and unkept promises.

We would not be worthy Uruguayans nor Americans nor worthy of ourselves if we did not listen to the voice of conscience that calls us daily to the fight. Today, no one can deny us the right to follow that voice above all things, no one can take away the sacred right of rebellion and no one can prevent us from dying if necessary for trying to be consistent.

From here on everything is going to be much clearer: with the people or against the people. With the country or against the country. With the revolution or against the revolution.

In this dysfunction the armed forces and those who man them

---

[2]José Gervasio Artigas led Uruguay's fight for independence in the 1810s.—HAS.

are also with the people and the country or with the oligarchy and the foreigners. In short: patriots or sepoys.[3]

To conclude, it is clear hereafter that if we meet again, you or anyone, they will be opting for one side of the dysfunction, and if it is our turn to fall, others will surely occupy our place and then sooner or later you will have to pay the bill.

[3]Sepoys were Indian troops serving the British; here it means natives serving foreign interests.—HAS.

9.

THE ROLE PLAYED BY REVOLUTIONARY
ACTION IN THE ORGANIZATION

CARLOS MARIGHELLA

Carlos Marighella, until his untimely death in 1969, was one
of the leading figures in the Brazilian revolutionary urban
guerrilla struggle against the United States–supported right-
wing military dictatorship that seized power in 1964. A
long-time political activist, Marighella formulated new revolutionary strategies to meet the political realities of the
situation. In this document, an emphasis on practice emerges
as well as the rejection of an immediate need for a political
party or elite groups among revolutionary ranks. Like his
more complete *Minimanual of the Urban Guerrilla,* the passage contains many concrete suggestions for organizing urban
action.

Our organization is the National Liberation Action. Its present
position was not reached in an hour or without sacrifice but rather
as a result of determination and effort. This effort has also been accompanied by the bravery and generosity of those who died fulfilling
their revolutionary duty, those who were arrested and wound up in
reactionary jails where they were savagely tortured, and those who
were murdered by the police.

In 1968 we weren't yet a national organization. We were only a

Abridged from *Carlos Marighella,* pp. 53–81. Copyright 1970 by Tricontinental Publications, Havana, Cuba. Used by permission of the publisher.

revolutionary group in São Paulo with almost no resources, and our ties to the rest of the country were almost nonexistent.

We grew as a result of action, only and exclusively as a result of revolutionary action. Based on the principle that the vanguard is created in action, we began urban guerrilla warfare in fact, but without publicly saying so.

The concrete manifestations of the revolutionary war surged forth in the large cities in Brazil in 1968 through urban guerrilla warfare and psychological warfare—forerunners of the rural guerrillas in our country.

By expropriating property from the government and the wealthy national and foreign capitalists, by seizing arms and explosives, thwarting the dictatorship's initiative and propaganda—as in the case of a bomb in the army's antisubversive exposition in São Paulo—attacking the properties of U.S. imperialists and participating in joint operations aimed at the punishment of U.S. spies, we carried out, by deed not word, a concrete plan of attack against the enemy.

The Brazilian experience concerning the role played by revolutionary action in the organization leads to two important conclusions: (1) A revolutionary organization becomes consolidated as a result of its action. (2) Revolutionary action is what makes the organization and gives it its name.

After a year of armed struggle we can point to the following results: (a) Our growth was the result of revolutionary action. (b) We created our own firepower. (c) We gained a year's advantage over the reactionaries, taking them by surprise with the expropriation and capture of arms and explosives, being careful not to leave behind clues that would reveal our real aims. (d) We spread out the actions of the revolutionary war, beginning with urban guerrilla warfare, instead of beginning with rural guerrilla warfare, which would have drawn a large concentration of enemy forces. (e) We started from zero, and passed from the stage of a group to that of a national organization, which acts on its own and takes responsibility for its actions.

Our struggle and that of the students had one thing in common: we were both working in practice, not theory. Thus, the urban areas were stimulated to action throughout the country, and the enemy forces became involved in fighting a full-scale revolutionary war.

They unleashed a new fascist coup on December 13, 1968, and put into effect fascist laws aimed openly against revolutionary activities.[1] And, for the first time, the dictatorship's law listed terrorism, attacks on banks, the execution of foreign spies, attacks on garrisons, and the detouring and seizing of weapons and explosives as revolutionary actions. The December fascist coup has neither stopped the revolutionary war nor checked our advance, despite political terrorism and the torture and murder of revolutionary militants.

Revolutionary organizations usually grow by two important methods.

One method was traditionally employed in Brazil by those organizations seeking political solutions, agreements, and mutual understandings with bourgeois personalities and groups, its purpose being that of confronting the enemy within the framework of the regime in power and without any intention of modifying that regime in practice. In most cases, the militants recruited through proselytizing work would abandon the ranks once they had been convinced that they had been deceived by words. Those revolutionary organizations that devoted themselves to proselytizing in 1968 made no headway at all.

The other method utilized by revolutionary organizations rejects proselytizing. Instead, it emphasizes revolutionary action; its method is extreme violence and radicalism. As a result of this method those who join our ranks do so because they want to fight and they are aware that the only alternative they will find with us is that of practical, concrete struggle.

Throughout 1968 the enemy utilized an ever-increasing firepower against the student movement and the masses. This resulted in a noticeable increase in the number of losses among those who fought in the streets—most of them unarmed. Experience has shown that our tactics of employing small groups of armed men—tactics which included the expropriation and captures of arms and explosives— were, despite their limitations, the only effective tactics with which to face the enemy's superiority in firepower.

We always had a strategy; if this hadn't been the case we never would have been able to grow from a small group into a national organization with ties in urban and rural areas.

[1]The 1968 coup moved the conservative military government which had seized power in 1964 farther to the right.—HAS.

We said that guerrilla warfare marked a revolutionary strategy for Brazil and that its success depends on rigorously carrying out three phases: the planning and preparation phase, the unleashing and, finally, the shift from guerrilla to conventional warfare and the creation of a revolutionary national liberation army.

From the very moment we appeared on the scene we have been careful not to hide our political and revolutionary objectives pointing out that the fundamental means for attaining power is revolutionary war. (A) We recognize the possibility of the conquest of power and expulsion of the imperialists through a strategy of guerrilla warfare. In the present stage of the general crisis of imperialism, in which we do *not* face a world war, this is the only applicable strategy. (B) We recognize that the guerrillas have been *definitively* incorporated into the life of the people as their own strategy for liberation. For us, the guerrillas have precisely the aim of not allowing any political negotiation for conciliation with the bourgeoisie in detriment to the class interests of the workers, peasants, and their allies and prejudicial to the revolution aimed at expelling the imperialists from the country and eliminating the obstacles on the way to socialism. (C) Our combat against imperialism is being waged on the basis of new forms and with our own characteristics. The road we follow is that of global strategy, whose final aim is the development of the revolutionary war in its threefold aspects of urban guerrillas, psychological warfare, and rural guerrillas. (D) Our struggle is an anti-oligarchic national liberation struggle. Hence it is an anti-capitalist struggle. Our people's principal enemy is Yankee imperialism. However, considering the inter-relationship between the Yankee imperialists and the large Brazilian capitalists and latifundists it is impossible to liberate the country without expelling from power those capitalists and latifundists, replacing them with the armed people and installing a people's revolutionary government.

Under present conditions, there are two different ideas as to work with the masses and relations with the people.

One is that of the organizations that seek immediate social gains and aim their activity at winning over the masses for the revolution through this approach.

Those organizations which limit their activities to work with the masses through the struggle for social gains with a view to transforming that struggle into a political struggle wind up reduced to impotence as a result of the enemy's armed superiority.

The other idea is that of organizations whose main concern is to engage in armed struggle, to face the dictatorship with a firepower which, though limited, will be handled by revolutionaries and the mass movements. Our organization follows that revolutionary idea.

Our organization's revolutionary character is due, above all, to the fact that every one of our actions is a revolutionary action and aims at seizing power through the violence of revolutionary war.

We have eliminated from our organization intermediate echelons and a murderous, topheavy, bureaucratic governing body. In our organization there are no barriers between politicians and soldiers. We have no political commissars to advise the military cadres. Every member is, necessarily, both these things, and is trained for this double role. Those who fail to become both politicians and soldiers do not last long due to the kind of action they must carry out. The same goes for those who are active in our contact with the masses and in our logistics front.

These two fronts are of considerable importance and their militants should make every effort to acquire political and military knowledge, however elementary, lest the organization's rhythm of development be impaired.

The principal defect of the Brazilian revolutionary movement is the dispersion of revolutionary organizations and the dissimilarity of their positions and objectives.

No revolutionary organization takes over the leadership by the simple fact of calling itself the leader or investing itself with such powers. Before we establish the indispensable leadership of the Brazilian revolution we must first increase the number of revolutionary actions until we reach a point where it will be possible to hit the bureaucratic-military machine of the Brazilian State. Such an objective will never be reached by the activity of one single organization.

The revolutionary movement in our country is a very young movement. It dates back to 1968, when urban guerrilla warfare began. It is, moreover, made up totally of young men and women. Among its members can be found women who until then had not participated in revolutionary action but who are now part of it.

Our revolutionary movement also suffers from a lack of technicians, of trained fighters with a knowledge of modern weaponry and its handling. Fighters cannot be trained overnight. This calls for time and is the factor that keeps us from making rapid progress and bringing about a transformation in the quality of the struggle against U.S. imperialism and the military dictatorship.

The perspective is one of a long struggle, one which requires neither speed nor a time schedule.

From urban action we will go on to direct armed struggle against the latifundists through our rural guerrillas. With the armed alliance of workers and peasants, with students, through our mobile guerrillas in the countryside, we will spread in every direction into the interior of Brazil and will bring the revolutionary army of national liberation to a confrontation with the conventional army of the military dictatorship.

Then we will expel the North Americans from Brazil. We will confiscate the property of the latifundists and will bring the agrarian revolution to its culmination, thus liberating the peasants. We will divest Brazil of its condition as a satellite of the politics of the military blocs, so that it will follow a line of unequivocal support for the underdeveloped people in struggle against colonialization.

May 1969

10.
ORGANIZATION OF LATIN AMERICAN
SOLIDARITY: General Declaration

WILLIAM J. POMEROY

The Organization of Latin American Solidarity (OLAS) was
formed at a conference held in Havana, Cuba, in 1967. Delegates representing almost every nation in the Americas endorsed the General Declaration that appears in document 10,
below. It represents a synthesis of the general lines of revolutionary analysis current in Latin America. It clearly shows
the anti-imperialist core of the struggle as well as its foundations in Marxist-Leninist principles.

We, the representatives of the peoples of our America, conscious
of the conditions which prevail on our continent, aware of the existence of a common counter-revolutionary strategy directed by U.S.
imperialism,

PROCLAIM:

1. That making the Revolution is a right and a duty of the people
of Latin America;

2. That the Revolution in Latin America has its deepest historical
roots in the liberation movement against European colonialism in the
19th century and against imperialism of this century. The epic struggle of the peoples of America and the great class battles that our

From William J. Pomeroy, ed., *Guerrilla Warfare and Marxism,* pp. 293–
295. Copyright © 1968 by International Publishers Co., Inc. Reprinted by
permission of the publisher.

people have carried out against imperialism in earlier decades, constitute the source of historical inspiration for the Latin American revolutionary movement;

3. That the essential content of Latin America's Revolution is to be found in its confrontation with imperialism and the bourgeois and landowning oligarchies. Consequently, the character of the Revolution is the struggle for national independence, for emancipation from the oligarchies, and for taking the socialist road to complete economic and social development;

4. That the principles of Marxism-Leninism guide the revolutionary movement of Latin America;

5. That armed revolutionary struggle constitutes the fundamental course of the Revolution in Latin America;

6. That all other forms of struggle must serve to advance and not to retard the development of this fundamental course, which is armed struggle;

7. That, for the majority of the continent's countries, the problems of organizing, initiating, developing and completing the armed struggle now constitute the immediate and fundamental task of the revolutionary movement;

8. That those countries where this task is not included in immediate planning must nevertheless inevitably consider this as a future probability in the development of their revolutionary struggle;

9. That the historic responsibility of furthering revolution in each country belongs to the people and their revolutionary vanguards;

10. That in most of our countries the guerrillas are the embryo of liberation armies and constitute the most efficient way of initiating and carrying out revolutionary struggle;

11. That the leadership of the Revolution requires, as an organizing principle, the existence of a unified political and military command in order to guarantee success;

12. That the most effective type of solidarity that the revolutionary movements can offer each other lies precisely in the development and culmination of their struggle within their own countries;

13. That solidarity with Cuba and cooperation and collaboration with the armed revolutionary movement are imperative duties of an international nature, the duties of all the anti-imperialist organizations of this continent;

14. That the Cuban Revolution, as a symbol of the triumph of the armed revolutionary movement, constitutes the vanguard in the anti-imperialist movement of Latin America. Those peoples that carry out armed struggle will also place themselves in the vanguard as they advance along the road of armed struggle;

15. That the peoples directly colonized by European powers—or subjected to the direct colonial domination of the United States—who are now on the road to liberation must maintain, as their immediate and fundamental objective, their struggle for independence and their close ties with the general struggle on this continent, since this is the only way of preventing their being absorbed into the neo-colonial system of the United States;

16. That the Second Declaration of Havana, a résumé of the great and glorious revolutionary tradition of the past 150 years of Latin American history, serves as a guiding document for the Latin American Revolution, and has been upheld, widened, enriched and made even more radical by the peoples of this continent during the past five years;

17. That the peoples of Latin America harbor no antagonisms toward any peoples of the World and extend their hand of brotherly friendship to the people of the United States itself, encouraging them to fight on against the oppressive policy of imperialist monopolies;

18. That the struggle in Latin America is strengthening its bonds of solidarity with the peoples of Asia and Africa and the socialist countries, especially with the Negroes of the United States, who suffer from class exploitation, poverty, unemployment, racial discrimination and the denial of the most basic human rights and who constitute a force of considerable importance within the revolutionary struggle;

19. That the heroic struggle of the people of Vietnam aids all revolutionary peoples fighting against imperialism to an inestimable degree and constitutes an inspiring example for the people of Latin America;

20. That we have approved the Statutes and created a Permanent Committee with its seat in Havana for the Latin American representation of the peoples of Latin America.

We, the revolutionaries of our America, the America lying south of the Río Bravo,[1] successors of those men who won our first inde-

[1]Latin American name for the Río Grande.—HAS.

pendence, armed with an irrevocable will to struggle and a revolutionary scientific orientation and with nothing to lose but the chains which bind us,

ASSERT:

That our struggle constitutes a decisive contribution to the historic struggle of humanity to liberate itself from slavery and exploitation.

The Duty of Every Revolutionary Is to Make the Revolution!

BIBLIOGRAPHIC SUGGESTIONS

Anonymous. *Diaro de un guerrillero latinoamericano.* Montevideo: Editorial Sandino, 1968. Short selections from the diary of a Latin American rural guerrilla fighter about his comrades and episodes of the struggle.

Anonymous. *Actas Tupamaros.* Buenos Aires: Editorial Shapire, 1971. Accounts of Uruguay's urban guerrillas, the Tupamaros, by a woman participant.

BÉJAR, HÉCTOR. *Peru 1965: Notes on a Guerrilla Experience.* New York: Monthly Review, 1966. A guerrilla leader discusses the unsuccessful Peruvian experience.

DEBRAY, RÉGIS. *Strategy for Revolution: Essays on Latin America.* New York: Monthly Review, 1970. Writings of a major theoretician, with an excellent introduction by Robin Blackburn.

FALS BORDA, ORLANDO. *Subversion and Social Change in Colombia.* New York: Columbia University Press, 1969. An overview showing historical processes of change.

FRANK, ANDRE GUNDER. *Capitalism and Underdevelopment in Latin America: Historical Studies in Chile and Brazil,* Rev. edition. New York: Monthly Review, 1969. An important theoretical contribution to the theory of the historical roots of underdevelopment and the need for revolution to break the cycle.

GALEANO, EDUARDO. *Guatemala: Occupied Country.* New York: Modern Reader, 1968. Observations on revolutionary movements and current events in Guatemala.

GERASSI, JOHN, ed. *Revolutionary Priest.* New York: Random House, 1971. The writing of Camilo Torres, Colombian priest, sociologist, activist, and guerrilla fighter.

GHEERBRANT, ALAIN. *La iglesia rebelde de América Latina*. Mexico: Siglo XXI, 1970. Selections showing the diverse nature of the progressive and revolutionary Latin American church.

GONZÁLEZ CASANOVA, PABLO. *Democracy in Mexico*. New York: Oxford University Press, 1970. A sociological presentation of recent Mexican developments.

GOTT, RICHARD. *Guerrilla Movements in Latin America*. Garden City, N.Y.: Doubleday, 1971. Most complete and best single source on rural guerrilla movements in Latin America, though perhaps overly pessimistic in tone.

GUEVARA, ERNESTO "CHE." *Guerrilla Warfare*. New York: Monthly Review, 1961. Basic handbook on rural warfare.

GUEVARA, ERNESTO "CHE." *Reminiscences of the Cuban Revolutionary War*. New York: Monthly Review, 1972. Personal account of the Cuban struggle.

GUEVARA, ERNESTO "CHE." *Obra revolucionaria*. Mexico: Era, 1969. Complete work of Cuban guerrilla leader.

HUBERMAN, LEO, and PAUL SWEEZY. *Socialism in Cuba*. New York: Monthly Review, 1969. Best single English source on events since 1959.

JULIÃO, FRANCISCO. *Que sao as ligas componeses?* Rió de Janeiro: Editora Civilizacao Brasileira, 1962. Contains documents and commentary by a leading figure behind the peasant leagues in Brazil.

KANTOR, HARRY. *The Ideology and Program of the Peruvian Aprista Party*, Revised edition. Washington, D.C.: Savile Books, 1966. Shows clearly the reformist nature of APRA.

LAVAN, GEORGE, ed. *Che Guevara Speaks*. New York: Merit Publishers, 1971. Contains selections from Guevara's basic writings.

MAGDOFF, HARRY. *The Age of Imperialism*. New York: Monthly Review, 1969. Best single source on new methods of imperialist control after World War II.

MALLOY, JAMES M. *Bolivia: The Unfinished Revolution*. Pittsburgh: University of Pittsburgh Press, 1970. Most recent and best study of Bolivian Revolution in English.

MARIGHELLA, CARLOS. *Minimanual of the Urban Guerrilla*. New World Liberation Front, USA, 1970. A "How to Do It" book for urban guerrillas.

Carlos Marighella. Havana, Cuba: Tricontinental, 1970. Brief biography and most important recent writings of a Brazilian guerrilla leader.

MERCADER, ANTONIO, and JORGE DE VERA. *Tupamaros: estrategia y acción*. Montevideo: Editorial Alfa, 1969. History of the Tupamaros with some documentary material.

MELVILLE, THOMAS, and MARJORIE MELVILLE. *Whose Heaven, Whose Earth?* New York: Knopf, 1970. Personal account and analysis of contemporary Guatamala by two Church people eventually expelled for their activities.

Monthly Review Editors, "Peaceful Transition to Socialism?" *Monthly Review,* Vol. 22 (January 1971), 1–18. A theoretical article on the possibilities in Chile of reaching social change through electoral politics.

NACLA, *New Chile*. Berkeley, Calif., 1971. Best single source on current situation in Chile.

NACLA, *Mexico 1968*. New York, 1968. Documents and commentary on the student uprising in Mexico and role of United States business in the economy.

NIERA, HUGO. *Cuzco: tierra y muerte*. Lima: Popilibros Peruanos, 1964. A newspaperman's reporting on peasant unrest in highland Peru.

PIERRE-CHARLES, GÉRARD. *Haiti, radiografía de una dictadura*. Mexico: Nuestro Tiempo, 1969. Discusses the dictatorship of Duvalier in Haiti.

POMEROY, WILLIAM J. ed. *Guerrilla Warfare and Marxism*. New York: International Publishers, 1968. Discusses guerrilla warfare in several areas of the world including Latin America.

QUARTIM, JOAO. *Dictatorship and Armed Struggle in Brazil*. New York: Monthly Review, 1972. On the Brazilian struggle.

QUIJANO, ANÍBAL. *Nationalism and Capitalism in Peru: A Study in Neo-Imperialism*. New York: Monthly Review, 1971. Clearly shows the nonrevolutionary nature of the Peruvian "revolution" inaugurated by the military.

The Tupamaros, Urban Guerrilla Warfare in Uruguay. New York: The Liberated Guardian, 1970. History of the Tupamaros and their actions.

TORRES, CAMILO. *Cristianismo y revolución*. Mexico City: Ediciones Era, 1970. Collected works of Camilo Torres.

X.
Inter-American Relations

⚜ JOSEPH S. TULCHIN

Foreign powers have played an important role in Latin American history beginning with the imperial domination by Spain and Portugal. The ambitions and weaknesses of the Iberian metropolitan nations often made Latin America a pawn in European power politics. From one point of view, the nations of Latin America are still pawns, still colonies in the sense that they are politically and/or economically dependent on foreign powers.[1] Although the nations of Latin America are at least formally independent and can make decisions for themselves, their independence is inhibited by the need to export, the influence of foreign investments in their midst, the need for hard currency loans, and by the fact that they are held within the confining frame of reference of the cold war. The widespread urge for development, therefore, besides calling for the improvement of certain economic indices, becomes a struggle to establish a national identity, to win national self-respect, to place control of the nation's destiny in the hands of the nation's leaders, and to turn that control to the benefit of the country's citizens.

[1]Stanley J. and Barbara H. Stein, *The Colonial Heritage of Latin America. Essays on Economic Dependence in Perspective* (New York: Oxford University Press, 1970); and F. H. Cardozo and E. Faletto, *Dependência e desenvolvimiento na America Latina; ensaio de interpretação sociológica* (Rio: Zahar, 1970).

Sadly enough, many Latin Americans believe that the greatest single obstacle to their nations' development is the United States. At the same time, they admire the United States for its accomplishments and its political system, so that a peculiar love-hate relationship exists between the Colossus of the North and its brethren in the hemisphere. The latter protest against attempts by the United States to interfere in their affairs and yet they also resent bitterly that the United States is preoccupied with cold war issues, often appearing to ignore Latin American needs when formulating foreign policy. For its part, Latin America cannot ignore the United States: its power is overwhelming, its presence pervasive. "Todo va mejor con Coca Cola" is on every street corner; Hollywood movies play in every neighborhood.

But it was not always thus, and to understand inter-American relations we must look back in time beyond the assumption of U.S. hegemony in the hemisphere. Throughout the nineteenth century Great Britain was the dominant foreign power in Latin America. The British eschewed formal dominance. They preferred to leave local politics to locals and exercised their control through trade and investment. This informal empire established only loose guidelines for international behavior—payment of debts and protection of foreigners.[2]

From the first stirrings of the movements for independence there was some discussion of hemispheric brotherhood and unity. While it never enjoyed commercial or political influence to rival Great Britain, the United States was always present in Latin American thinking as a model, a potential ally or brother. Americans, North and South, saw themselves as part of the brave new world. There were energetic North Americans, like Henry Clay, who saw Latin America as a fruitful field for cooperative enterprise, as part of a great American System (see document 1). On the other hand,

---

[2]J. Gallagher and R. Robinson, "The Imperialism of Free Trade," *Economic History Review* 2nd ser., VI, 1–15; and D. C. M. Platt, *Finance, Trade and Politics in British Foreign Policy, 1815–1914* (New York: Oxford University Press, 1968).

Simón Bolívar expressed a common Latin American attitude when he said, alluding to the North Americans' expansionist tendencies, the United States "seem destined by Providence to plague America with torments in the name of freedom."[3] He sought a confederation of the Spanish American Republics and considered Great Britain's support vital (see document 2). The same disagreement is carried into modern writings on the Pan American movement. Witness Arthur P. Whitaker's emphasis on shared beliefs and experiences in *The Western Hemisphere Idea: Its Rise and Decline* (Ithaca, N.Y.: Cornell University Press, 1954) and the echo of Bolívar's distrust of the United States and his concentration on Latin American unity in Francisco Cuevas Cancino, *Del Congreso de Panamá a la Conferencia de Caracas,* 1826–1954 (Caracas: Sociedad Bolivariana de Venezuela, 1955).

The United States adopted a cautious policy during the Latin American struggle for independence and directed its diplomatic efforts at preventing European nations from exploiting Spain's weakness in America by a concerted intervention or in any manner that might endanger the security of the United States. The nation's leaders were preoccupied with U.S. weakness and vulnerability—especially until the end of the war with Great Britain, in 1815. This was the purpose of President Monroe's message to Congress on December 3, 1823, better known as the Monroe Doctrine (see document 3). It established a pattern that would be followed for many years: that Latin American policy would be formulated in response to the needs of domestic politics and to events outside the hemisphere, generally in Europe, and not with reference, primarily, to events in Latin America.

In the years following 1823 the European threat receded and the United States concentrated its energies on westward expansion. In the course of the movement across the continent, Americans spoke vehemently about their "manifest

[3]Bolívar to Colonel Patrick Campbell, British Chargé D'Affaires, Bogotá, August 5, 1829, in *Selected Writings of Bolívar,* compiled by Vicente Lecuna, edited by Harold A. Bierck, Jr. (New York: Colonial Press, 1951), II, 731–732.

destiny" at the expense of less powerful and less worthy nations in the hemisphere. One nation, Mexico, suffered the very real and painful consequences of American expansion—the loss of half its national territory (see documents 4 and 5). Frightened by American bellicosity the Latin American nations were torn between their fear and hatred of the United States as a grasping predator and their admiration and need for the United States as a model and protector. Colombia went so far as to sign a defense treaty with the United States to guarantee the neutrality of the Isthmus of Panama (the Bidlack Treaty of 1846). Other nations in Latin America, while copying the American Constitution or otherwise using the United States as a model, preferred to keep the United States at a distance. Predictably, when faced with an external threat, many Latin Americans harked back to the teachings of Bolívar and sought protection in unity. None of the efforts to promote Latin American unity through international conferences produced significant results. External threats also had the curious effect of inhibiting the Latin American nations from using force to settle their international differences. If they feared outside intervention, they were inclined to settle disputes with their neighbors by peaceful means. International relations in South America during this period have been characterized as a balance of power.[4]

The situation changed when the United States emerged from a period of internal consolidation following the Civil War. Americans began to concern themselves more insistently with events outside their boundary. Secretary of State James G. Blaine participated energetically in hemispheric diplomacy trying to end the War of the Pacific between Chile and Peru and Bolivia and to mediate several Central American boundary disputes. He also took the initiative in calling the Pan American Conference to encourage hemispheric trade, which met in Washington in 1889 (see document 6). Secretary of State Richard B. Olney's note to the British government in

[4]Robert N. Burr, "The Balance of Power in Nineteenth-Century South America: An Exploratory Essay," *Hispanic American Historical Review*, XXXV (1955), 37–60.

1895 demanding a peaceful settlement of the boundary dispute between the British colony of Guiana and Venezuela expressed a new tone of aggressiveness or bellicosity in dealing with European nations interfering with hemispheric affairs (see document 7).

Americans were ready for overseas expansion at the end of the nineteenth century. They trumpeted many arguments in its favor, and historians ever since have debated their relative importance.[5] As Blaine's scheme for a Pan American Customs Union makes plain, the government was anxious to help businessmen make deeper incursions into the Latin American market. Most observers agreed that the domestic market was no longer capable of absorbing the production of America's dynamic industrial sector. New foreign markets were vital to the nation's well-being. Race and religion figured prominently in the writings of those who justified imperialism on the grounds that the United States had a civilizing mission, a duty to help inferior peoples. Of course, Americans were not the only civilized people; they had observed European powers engage in an orgy of land grabbing in Asia and Africa. Publicists urged the United States to get in on the race for territory and power or the country would be left behind and condemned to a position of inferiority in world politics.

One of the most cogent advocates of a "large policy" was Captain Alfred Thayer Mahan of the U.S. Navy. In a series of influential magazine articles, Mahan outlined his concept of national security based on sea power: a strong fleet, secure lines of communication, and control over certain strategic points such as an isthmian canal were the operational links of a commercial empire by which the United States would exert its civilizing force as a world power.

The debate over American expansion during the 1890s

[5]For a detailed discussion of the issues see Walter LaFeber, *The New Empire* (Ithaca, N.Y.: Cornell University Press, 1963); Ernest R. May, *American Imperialism: A Speculative Essay* (New York: Atheneum, 1968); David Healy, *US Expansionism: The Imperialist Urge in the 1890's* (Madison: University of Wisconsin Press, 1970).

unfolded within a context of what one historian has called a psychic crisis in American history—an unnerving series of economic and social disturbances.[6] The tension produced by the debate rose to unbearable levels and precipitated an armed struggle with Spain over the latter's handling of a sustained uprising in Cuba. As a result of the war—which the United States won easily—the United States gained control over Puerto Rico, Guam, the Philippines, and Cuba, with the self-imposed obligation of helping Cuba to its independence.

In the years following the war with Spain, the United States slowly and painfully came to understand the implications of its new status as the paramount power in the Caribbean. With rather unseemly enthusiasm, President Theodore Roosevelt welcomed the opportunity presented in 1903 by the revolt of the Colombian province of Panama to recognize the independence of the new isthmian republic. With one stroke he realized one of Mahan's cardinal objectives of national security by signing the Hay-Bunau Varilla Treaty giving the United States exclusive rights to construct a canal across the isthmus. Roosevelt believed that strong nations had the right and the duty to teach the benefits of civilization —good government and fiscal responsibility—to weaker and less fortunate nations. He acquiesced in an Anglo-German blockade of Venezuela in 1902–1903 for the purpose of collecting debts, apparently in the belief, as expressed to a German friend, in 1901, that "If any South American state misbehaves toward any European country, let the European country spank it." During the blockade he wrote his friend Albert Shaw that "nothing England and Germany have done . . . has in any way conflicted with . . . the Monroe Doctrine." Roosevelt gradually changed his stance. First, American public opinion surprised him with the intensity of its opposition to the joint blockade. Then, the negotiations be-

[6]Richard A. Hofstadter, "Manifest Destiny and the Philippines," in Daniel Aaron, ed., *America in Crisis* (New York: Knopf, 1952), pp. 173–200, and *The Paranoid Style in American Politics and other Essays* (New York: Knopf, 1966), pp. 145–187.

tween Venezuela and the blockading powers, in which a representative of the United States participated, revealed that, while an intervening power might forswear territorial acquisition, the mere act of intervention accorded a degree of influence over the intervened nation which was as dangerous to U.S. interests in the Caribbean as the acquisition of territory. Finally, the Hague tribunal, to which the Venezuelan dispute was referred, awarded preferential treatment to the blockading powers. This decision put a premium on efforts to collect debts by force. Roosevelt's response, worked out in the course of a dispute between European creditors and the Dominican Republic in 1904, and known as the Roosevelt Corollary to the Monroe Doctrine, was to assume the role of policeman in the hemisphere. He did not question the right of powerful creditors to force weaker nations to behave responsibly. To avoid European intervention in the Caribbean, he would have the United States serve as Europe's bill collector (see document 8).

The presence of a policeman did not by itself put an end to disorder and fiscal irresponsibility. As the problems persisted, William Howard Taft, Roosevelt's successor, thought stability in Latin America would be more likely if the nations' economies were strengthened. He proposed massive doses of United States capital—Dollar Diplomacy—as the means to avoid the unpleasant and unwanted U.S. interventions in the domestic affairs of the nations in the Caribbean Danger Zone. In spite of some initial successes, Dollar Diplomacy led to more interventions, not fewer. President Woodrow Wilson took a new tack. He worked toward the same goals—political stability and fiscal responsibility to forestall European intervention—but was loath to use private capital as the instrumentality of U.S. policy. He preferred to teach the Latin Americans the virtues of democracy and constitutional government. But this too failed, and during Wilson's administration U.S. troops were sent into Mexico, Cuba, Nicaragua, Haiti, and the Dominican Republic, to drive home the lessons of democracy.

Latin Americans were never happy with U.S. dominance.

The struggle against the United States began as soon as the United States made its first aggressive claims to leadership. At the First Pan American Conference in 1889, the Argentine delegation led the opposition to measures for hemispheric cooperation sponsored by the United States. José Enrique Rodo's classic, *Ariel,* published in 1900, was a warning to Latin America not to be taken in by the mechanistic utilitarian drive for progress sponsored by the United States. *Ariel* became the bible of idealists who opposed the wanton exercise of U.S. power in the hemisphere. Critics questioned the benefits of civilization at the end of a bayonet (see document 9). The voices raised against U.S. intervention—and they were not restricted to those who chafed under direct U.S. control—swelled to a crescendo at the Sixth Pan American Conference at Havana in 1928. There, only a dramatic and brilliant oratorical effort by the chief delegate of the United States, Charles Evans Hughes, frustrated a motion to condemn any and all interventions by one state in the affairs of another (see document 10).

Ironically, events already had made Hughes's arguments academic. Changes wrought by World War I in the security position of the United States, together with increasing disillusionment with the fruits of formal responsibilities in the Caribbean, led to efforts to withdraw from existing interventions and to avoid new ones. The war eliminated the possibility that European nations might make a grab for territory in the hemisphere. At the same time, however, the war had forced the United States to expand its concept of strategic necessity to include such items as petroleum (fuel), cables (communications), and bank loans (finance capital). United States policy after the war was directed at establishing informal influence over Latin America, based on trade and investment

As the United States approached its strategic objectives in fuel, communications, and finance capital, it became less hostile to the Latin American position on nonintervention and juridical equality of sovereign states. At first American acceptance was hesitant and inconsistent. President Herbert

Hoover reiterated it in a series of public statements at the end of the 1920s, and President Franklin D. Roosevelt gave it the fortunate appelation the Good Neighbor. The Good Neighbor policy was defined in resolutions at the Pan American Conferences at Montevideo (1933) and Buenos Aires (1936), and worked out during the 1930s in a series of episodes testing the limits of U.S. willingness to allow the Latin American nations to act as they saw fit, even though such action might conflict with traditional interpretations of international law or prejudice U.S. interests. Revisionist historians question the idealism of the Good Neighbor, preferring to see it as another effort by the United States to blunt the force of Latin American nationalism and as mere rhetorical flourish to cover U.S. efforts to expand its markets in Latin America.[7] Whatever the motives behind the Good Neighbor policy, there is no question that most Latin Americans approved of it.[8] (See document 11.) More important, the confidence engendered by the Good Neighbor policy lent legitimacy to U.S. leadership during the war.

World War II drew the nations of the hemisphere together. The United States needed Latin American support and got it. Latin America needed United States protection and got it, although many were unhappy with the sudden escalation of U.S. control over their economies and asked repeatedly for some assurance of postwar cooperation to relieve them of the oppressive burden of dependence on external markets. The tension and bitterness inherent in the love-hate relationship between the paramount nation and its client states surfaced during the conference at Chapultepec in 1945. The United States steadfastly refused to concede to Latin American demands for regional agreements to protect their pri-

[7]For different interpretations of this period see David Green, *The Containment of Latin America. A History of the Myths and Realities of the Good Neighbor Policy* (Chicago: Quadrangle Books, 1971); and Bryce Wood, *The Making of the Good Neighbor Policy* (New York: Columbia University Press, 1961).

[8]Donald M. Dozer, *Are We Good Neighbors? Three Decades of Inter-American Relations, 1930–1960* (Gainesville: University of Florida Press, 1959), pp. 1–70.

mary products or to aid them in meeting the high costs of industrialization. The United States was preoccupied with the shape of the postwar world, and insisted on fitting its relations with Latin America into that broader framework.

Instead of improving when the war ended, inter-American relations deteriorated badly. The cold war distracted the United States from hemispheric events. In a bipolar world, the United States saw Latin America as just another region, another potential victim of Communist subversion, whose problems merited consideration as potential weak points in the struggle against communism (see document 12). Even the Alliance for Progress, in many ways a high-minded and revolutionary enterprise, was a response to the cold war. If the Alliance proved a success, it would offer a satisfactory alternative to the violent socialist revolution led by Fidel Castro. Latin America had to follow the path to progress indicated by the United States.[9] The disaster at the Bay of Pigs and the attitude toward the new socialist regime of Salvador Allende in Chile indicate the limits of U.S. tolerance for aberrant forms of change and the rigidities of cold war policy.

The United States today is still locked into cold war thinking. This means Latin America is low priority for U.S. policymakers and makes it difficult for them to respond with the necessary patience and flexibility to the increasingly nationalistic efforts by Latin Americans to achieve some measure of economic development. The Latin Americans, for their part, believe their plight is desperate and are losing patience with the United States. How can Latin America solve its problems and establish its identity in international relations under the shadow of the United States? The most pessimistic observers feel that the requirements of the capitalistic world economy and the demands of U.S. paramountcy limit the freedom of action of the Latin American nations and condemn them to perpetual dependence and underdevelopment. They see as the only solution a violent revolution to crush American impe-

[9]See, for example, Gregorio Selser, *Alianza Para El Progreso: La Mal Nacida* (Buenos Aires: Ediciones Iguazú, 1964).

rialism (see document 13). Less pessimistic and less hostile commentators, while stressing the need for nationalistic solutions and greater independence, hope that Latin America will not slip into violent, negative rebellion, and see cause for optimism in the potential unity of developing nations. In unity there will be strength to make the voices of weaker powers heard in international affairs.

And what will be the response of the United States to the rising tide of nationalism, the rhetoric of anti-imperialism, and the striving by Latin America for greater independence of action? Will the United States retaliate, as it has in the past, by threatening to cut off aid to nations that expropriate the assets of U.S. companies, or by forcibly overthrowing any government it suspects of Communist leanings? Are there any chances for partnership in the hemisphere? Is there a viable role for the so-called middle powers in world affairs? If there is, can existing international organizations help ease United States nervousness and help the Latin American nations establish an independent posture and gain control over their destinies without having recourse to a suicidal retreat into autarchy or blind opposition to everything stamped "Made in USA"?

1.
HENRY CLAY URGES RECOGNITION OF THE REPUBLICS OF LATIN AMERICA

Henry Clay, of Kentucky, a former "War Hawk" and advocate of energetic participation by the federal government in developing the nation's resources, here speaks against the Monroe administration's cautious policy. Clay speaks from genuine conviction in favor of an American System. He is spurred on also by his rivalry with Secretary of State John Quincy Adams. Later, Clay would be secretary of state in Adams's administration.

After the return of our Commissioners from South America; after they had all agreed in attesting the fact of independent sovereignty being exercised by the Government of Buenos Ayres, the whole nation looked forward to the recognition of the independence of that country as the policy which the Government ought to pursue. . . . Two years ago, Mr. C. said, would in his opinion, have been the proper time for recognising the independence of the South. Then the struggle was somewhat doubtful, and a kind office on the part of this Government would have had a salutary effect. Since that period, what had occurred? Anything to prevent a recognition of their independence, or to make it less expedient? No; every occurrence tended to prove the capacity of that country to maintain its independence. . . .

Reprinted from *The Annals of Congress,* 16 Cong., 1st Sess., pp. 2225–2228 (May 10, 1820).

. . . Here Mr. C. quoted a few passages from the work of the Abbe de Pradt, recently translated by one of our citizens, which, he said, though the author was not very popular among Crowned heads, no man could read without being enlightened and instructed. These passages dwelt on the importance of the commerce of South America, when freed from its present restraints, &c. What would I give, exclaimed Mr. C., could we appreciate the advantages which may be realized by our pursuing the course which I propose! It is in our power to create a system of which we shall be the centre, and in which all South America will act with us. In respect to commerce, we should be most benefited; this country would become the place of deposits of the commerce of the world. Our citizens engaged in foreign trade were at present disheartened by the condition of that trade; they must seek new channels for it, and none so advantageous could be found as those which the trade with South America would afford. . . .

But however important our early recognition of the independence of the South might be to us, as respects our commercial and manufacturing interests, was there not another view of the subject, infinitely more gratifying? We should become the centre of a system which would constitute the rallying point of human wisdom against all the despotism of the Old World. Did any man doubt the feelings of the South towards us? In spite of our coldness towards them, of the rigor of our laws, and the conduct of our officers, their hearts still turned towards us, as to their brethren; and he had no earthly doubt, if our Government would take the lead and recognise them, that they would become yet more anxious to imitate our institutions, and to secure to themselves and to their posterity the same freedom which we enjoy.

On a subject of this sort, Mr. C. asked, was it possible we could be content to remain, as we now were, looking anxiously to Europe, watching the eyes of Lord Castlereagh, and getting scraps of letters doubtfully indicative of his wishes; and sending to the Czar of Russia, and getting another scrap from Count Nesselrode? . . . Mr. C. deprecated this deference for foreign Powers. . . . Our institutions, said Mr. C., now make us free; but, how long shall we continue so, if we mould our opinions on those of Europe? Let us break these commercial and political fetters; let us no longer watch the nod of any European politician; let us become real and true Americans, and place ourselves at the head of the American system.

2.
BOLÍVAR FAVORS A HEMISPHERIC CONFEDERATION

Bolívar was imbued with the notion of an amphictyonic league of Spanish American Republics to bolster the fragile security of the new republics. During the period covered by these two letters, 1824–1826, Bolívar's thinking on the Confederation had evolved to the point where he felt Argentina was not likely to become a useful member. Later at the end of his life, the Liberator would become disillusioned with the entire scheme.

Lima, December 7, 1824

Great and good friend:

After fifteen years of sacrifices devoted to the struggle for American freedom in order to secure a system of guaranties that will be the shield of our new destiny in peace and war, it is time the interests and ties uniting the American republics, formerly Spanish colonies, possessed a fundamental basis to perpetuate, if possible, these governments.

To initiate that system and to concentrate the power of this great political body calls for the exercise of a sublime authority, one capable

Excerpts taken from *Selected Writings of Bolívar*. Compiled by Vicente Lecuna, edited by Harold A. Bierck, Jr., translated by Lewis Bertrand (2 vols.; New York: Colonial Press, 1951), II, pp. 456–459 and 567–570. Reprinted by permission of the Banco de Venezuela, Caracas.

of directing the policy of our governments, whose influence should maintain a uniformity of principles and whose very name alone should put an end to our quarrels. . . .

In 1822, profoundly imbued with these ideas, I, as President of the Republic of Colombia, invited the governments of Mexico, Peru, Chile, and Buenos Aires to form a confederation and to hold at the Isthmus of Panamá, or at some other point agreed upon by the majority, a congress of plenipotentiaries from each state "that should act as a council during periods of great conflicts, to be appealed to in the event of common danger, and to be a faithful interpreter of public treaties when difficulties arise, in brief, to conciliate all our differences." . . .

To defer any longer the meeting of the General Congress of the plenipotentiaries of the Republics that, in fact, are already allied, in order to await the decision of the others would be to deprive ourselves of the advantages which that assembly will afford from its very beginning. . . .

The day when our plenipotentiaries exchange their credentials will mark an immortal epoch in the diplomatic history of the world.

A hundred centuries hence, posterity, searching for the origin of our public law and recalling the compacts that solidified its destiny, will finger with respect the protocols of the Isthmus. In them will be found the plan of the first alliances that will have marked the beginning of our relations with the universe. What, then, will be the Isthmus of Corinth compared with that of Panamá?

God preserve Your Excellency.

Your great and good friend,
Simón Bolívar

José Sánchez Carrión
Minister of Foreign Relations

To José Rafael Revenga, Colombian Minister of Foreign Affairs

Magdalena, February 17, 1826.

My dear Revenga:

I have before me your letters of October 21, November 6, and November 21, in which you write at length respecting the Confederation of the Isthmus and the amendments that you have proposed to its members. I am writing an official letter to the Vice President, giving my opinion of these addenda, and I should like herein to discuss them with you at greater length.

An alliance with Great Britain would give us great prestige and respectability. Under her protection we would grow, and we would later be able to take our place among the stronger civilized nations. Any fears that powerful England might become the arbiter of the counsels and decisions of the assembly, that her voice, her will, and her interests might determine the course of its deliberations are remote fears; and, should they one day materialize, they cannot outweigh the positive, immediate, and tangible benefits that such an alliance would give us at this time. First the Confederation must be born and grow strong, and then the rest will follow. During its infancy we need help so that in manhood we will be able to defend ourselves. At present the alliance can serve our purpose; the future will take care of itself. . . .

. . . I believe as you do that, if the plan were to be adopted by all America and by Great Britain, it would represent an enormous bulwark of power which would inevitably result in stability for the new states. . . .

. . . I shall now add a few words regarding Buenos Aires and Chile. The former will never join the Confederation in good faith. She will in every way attempt to hinder and impede it and will place every possible obstacle in the path of the assembly. This is a forgone conclusion, considering her present organization and the temperament and principles of her ungovernable inhabitants. As for Chile, if she sends plenipotentiaries, she will do so in the best of good faith, and she will be more amenable and useful to the Confederation. . . .

With high esteem, I am yours devotedly,

Bolívar

3.

PRESIDENT MONROE SUMMARIZES U.S. POLICY IN HIS MESSAGE TO CONGRESS, DECEMBER 2, 1823

> After an intensive period of high-level discussion, Secretary of State Adams and President Monroe combined to draft the sections of the annual message to Congress. Two important principles of policy were enunciated: noncolonization and, after an interval of forty paragraphs on miscellaneous subjects, the doctrine of two spheres. The first arose out of consideration of conflicting claims on the northwest coast of North America, and the second out of the apparent threat by the Holy Alliance to intervene in the Latin American struggle for independence on the side of Spain.

In the discussions to which this interest [in the northwest] has given rise and in the arrangements by which they may terminate the occasion has been judged proper for asserting, as a principle in which the rights and interests of the United States are involved, that the American continents, by the free and independent condition which they have assumed and maintain, are henceforth not to be considered as subjects for future colonization by any European powers. . . .

In the wars of the European powers in matters relating to themselves we have never taken any part, nor does it comport with our policy so to do. It is only when our rights are invaded or seriously menaced that we resent injuries or make preparation for our defense.

Messages and Papers of the Presidents, II, pp. 209–219.

With the movements in this hemisphere we are of necessity more immediately connected, and by causes which must be obvious to all enlightened and impartial observers. The political system of the allied powers is essentially different in this respect from that of America. This difference proceeds from that which exists in their respective Governments; and to the defense of our own, which has been achieved by the loss of so much blood and treasure, and matured by the wisdom of their most enlightened citizens, and under which we have enjoyed unexampled felicity, the whole nation is devoted. We owe it, therefore, to candor and to the amicable relations existing between the United States and those powers to declare that we should consider any attempt on their part to extend their system to any portion of this hemisphere as dangerous to our peace and security. With the existing colonies or dependencies of any European power we have not interfered and shall not interfere. But with the Governments who have declared their independence and maintained it, and whose independence we have, on great consideration and on just principles, acknowledged, we could not view any interposition for the purpose of oppressing them, or controlling in any other manner their destiny, by any European power in any other light than as the manifestation of an unfriendly disposition toward the United States. In the war between those new Governments and Spain we declared our neutrality at the time of their recognition, and to this we have adhered, and shall continue to adhere, provided no change shall occur which, in the judgment of the competent authorities of this Government, shall make a corresponding change on the part of the United States indispensable to their security. . . .

If we compare the present condition of our Union with its actual state at the close of our Revolution, the history of the world furnishes no example of a progress in improvement in all the important circumstances which constitute the happiness of a nation which bears any resemblance to it. . . .

The expansion of our population and accession of new States to our Union have had the happiest effect on all its highest interests. That it has eminently augmented our resources and added to our strength and respectability as a power is admitted by all. But it is not in these important circumstances only that this happy effect is felt. It is manifest that by enlarging the basis of our system and increasing the number of States the system itself has been greatly strengthened in both its branches. Consolidation and disunion have thereby been rendered equally impracticable. . . . To what, then, do we owe these blessings? It is known to all that we derive them from the excellence of our institutions. Ought we not, then, to adopt every measure which may be necessary to perpetuate them?

4.
THE UNITED STATES PREPARES FOR WAR WITH MEXICO

The United States had its eye on the territory of California and sought to acquire it, as it had Texas, by indirection and without violence. President Polk, however, was determined to press relentlessly U.S. claims against Mexico. The first selection (Part I) is from the State Department's instructions to its Consul in Monterey, California, Thomas O. Larkin, setting forth the bases for Washington's rather delicate policy. After negotiations with Mexico had failed to settle the differences between the two nations to the satisfaction of the United States, a clash between armed forces at the disputed boundary prompted Polk's demand for war (the second selection, Part II).

Part I

Secretary of State Buchanan to Larkin on October 17, 1845.

I feel much indebted to you for the information which you have communicated to the Department from time to time in relation to

Buchanan to Larkin, October 17, 1845, *Diplomatic Correspondence of the United States: Inter-American Affairs.* Selected and arranged by William R. Manning (8 vols. Washington, D.C.: Carnegie Endowment for International Peace, 1932–1939), VIII, p. 189, and the *Annals of Congress.*

California. The future destiny of that country is a subject of anxious solicitude for the Government and people of the United States. The interests of our commerce and our whale fisheries on the Pacific ocean demand that you should exert the greatest vigilance in discovering and defeating any attempts which may be made by foreign governments to acquire a control over that country. In the contest between Mexico and California we can take no part, unless the former should commence hostilities against the United States; but should California assert and maintain her independence, we shall render her all the kind offices in our power, as a sister Republic. This Government has no ambitious aspirations to gratify and no desire to extend our federal system over more territory than we already possess, unless by the free and spontaneous wish of the independent people of the adjoining territories. The exercise of compulsion or improper influence to accomplish such a result, would be repugnant both to the policy and principles of this Government. But whilst these are the sentiments of the President, he could not view with indifference the transfer of California to Great Britain or any other European Power. The system of colonization by foreign monarchies on the North American continent must and will be resisted by the United States. It could result in nothing but evil to the colonists under their dominion who would naturally desire to secure for themselves the blessings of liberty by means of republican institutions; whilst it must prove highly prejudicial to the best interests of the United States. Nor would it in the end benefit such foreign monarchies. On the contrary, even Great Britain, by the acquisition of California, would sow the seeds of future war and disaster for herself; because there is no political truth more certain than this fine Province could not long be held in vassalage by any European Power. The emigration to it of people from the United States would soon render this impossible.

Whilst the President will make no effort and use no influence to induce California to become one of the free and independent States of this Union, yet if the people should desire to unite their destiny with ours, they would be received as brethren, whenever this can be done without affording Mexico just cause of complaint.

Part II

Polk's message to Congress, Monday, May 11, 1846.

The grievous wrongs perpetrated by Mexico upon our citizens throughout a long period of years remain unredressed, and solemn treaties pledging her public faith for this redress have been disregarded. A government either unable or unwilling to enforce the execution of such treaties fails to perform one of its plainest duties.

Our commerce with Mexico has been almost annihilated. It was formerly highly beneficial to both nations, but our merchants have been deterred from prosecuting it by the system of outrage and extortion which the Mexican authorities have pursued against them, whilst their appeals through their own Government for indemnity have been made in vain. Our forbearance has gone to such an extreme as to be mistaken in its character. Had we acted with vigor in repelling the insults and redressing the injuries inflicted by Mexico at the commencement, we should doubtless have escaped all the difficulties in which we are now involved.

Instead of this, however, we have been exerting our best efforts to propitiate her good will. Upon the pretext that Texas, a nation as independent as herself, thought proper to unite its destinies with our own, she has affected to believe that we have severed her rightful territory, and in official proclamations and manifestoes has repeatedly threatened to make war upon us for the purpose of reconquering Texas. In the meantime we have tried every effort at reconciliation. The cup of forbearance had been exhausted even before the recent information from the frontier of the Del Norte. But now, after reiterated menaces, Mexico has passed the boundary of the United States, has invaded our territory and shed American blood upon American soil. She has proclaimed that hostilities have commenced, and that the two nations are at war.

As war exists, and, notwithstanding all our efforts to avoid it, exists by the act of Mexico herself, we are called upon by every consideration of duty and patriotism to vindicate with decision the honor, the rights, and the interests of our country. . . .

The most energetic and prompt measures and the immediate appearance in arms of a large and overpowering force are recommended to Congress as the most certain and efficient means of bringing the existing collision with Mexico to a speedy and successful termination.

5.

TWO MEXICAN VIEWS OF THE WAR WITH
THE UNITED STATES

Mexico was awake to the danger of United States aggression but powerless to forestall it. The Mexican government was at once outraged by the United States annexation of Texas, anxious to resolve the differences with the United States but not at a cost to the national honor, in severe financial embarrassment, and rendered virtually impotent by internal bickering. Such a combination made for highly emotional responses to events. The war with the United States was a national trauma for Mexico and, like an old wound, the scars still smart. The following excerpts are taken from two works on U.S.–Mexican diplomatic relations. Both historians, Carlos Bosch Garcia and Luis G. Zorilla, strive for objectivity. Dry diplomatic documents as paraphrased by Bosch Garcia appear even drier. Nevertheless, the message is clear: Mexicans were outraged and impotent in the face of United States expansion. Succeeding generations of Mexicans continue to resent U.S. aggression and the failure of their forebears to act decisively to block it.

Part I ⋄ Carlos Bosch Garcia

30 May 1844. Mexico.
J. Bocanegra to B. E. Green.

Upon hearing from Green of the decision to annex Texas to the United States, Bocanegra sent the American a long, vigorous dispatch. In it, he advanced all the considerations due to nations which held territories, the rights by which they maintained these lands, and the ideas on this subject which governments and enlightened men ought to have. He ignored completely the political motives with which Green justified the American action.

Bocanegra commented upon the behavior of the United States during the evolution of the conflict, upon legal titles, and upon the concept of "first settlers" of a region. He asserted that Mexico had always claimed possession of Texas, and that it had never intended to give up the territory. Bocanegra further noted that while Mexico had not intervened to any great extent during the development of the Texan independence movement, the United States had helped the movement in order to assure its success. As for Green's announcement of the annexation decision, which had been intended as an American gesture of respect toward Mexico, Bocanegra observed that it did no more than reveal a consummated, irrevocable act.

Finally, Bocanegra emphasized that Mexico was prepared to defend what it considered its own, and he reminded Green that the dispatch of 28 August 1843 was still in effect. Mexico's only remaining hope, he concluded, was that the American Senate would exercise better judgment and refuse to ratify a treaty which violated reason, law and justice. Otherwise, Mexico would be forced to proceed according to its international rights.

From Carlos Bosch Garcia, *Material Para La Historia Diplomática de Mexico (Mexico y los Estados Unidos, 1824–1848)*, pp. 424–425, 462, 543. Copyright 1957 by Escuela Nacional de Ciencias Políticas y Sociales, UNAM. Translated by Christopher Hunt. Reprinted by permission of the author and the publisher.

January, 1845. Mexico. Congressional
decree in response to the annexation.

The Mexican Congress reacted to the annexation of Texas by denouncing it as a monstruous usurpation of foreign territory, a violation of the sovereignty of nations, and therefore a grave threat to
world peace. In its decree, the Congress accused the United States of
treacherously planning the annexation over a long period of time,
during which it proclaimed its cordial friendship with Mexico. The
appropriation of Texas violated Mexico's rights; besides insulting its
national dignity, the annexation threatened Mexico's independence
and its very political existence. Furthermore, it violated the spirit of
all treaties going back before 1832. The American law of annexation,
the decree continued, had no effect upon Mexican rights to Texas,
which the country was prepared to defend. The injustice of the plun-
dering of Texas gave Mexico the right to retaliate with all its resources; accordingly, the Congress called all citizens to the defense of
Mexican independence. The government would put its entire military
force under arms.

3 December 1845. Mexico.
Article in "La Voz del Pueblo".

In announcing the arrival in Mexico of Slidell, the newspaper "La
Voz del Pueblo" violently attacked the American envoy and his government, which it accused of mendacity. It attributed to the United
States responsibility for every possible kind of villainy in the international field, and commented that there was only one serious offense
which the American government had failed to commit. This last insult
would be delivered by Slidell, who had come on the frigate *Saint Mary*
to arrange for the purchase of Texas, New Mexico and the Californias. The newspaper warned Mexicans that in a few months they
would have no country, for the United States would have taken it
from them. The article concluded by asking if such an atrocity could
be contemplated impassively.

Part II   ⋄   Luis G. Zorilla

An idea of the claims which were so persistently protected by the government in Washington, and which had fallen into the hands of speculators, is given by Ambassador Waddy Thompson in a letter to the Secretary of State, dated that same 20 November: "and [as to] the claims of W. J. Parrott, the Union Land Company, the Trinity Land Company, and Gibert L. Thompson . . . I have examined them thoroughly, and do not hesitate to say that 2 per cent on the amount claimed would be a large allowance, and more than they will ever receive by the decision of any impartial tribunal." All other claims, continues Thompson (who negotiated the treaty), together do not exceed $200,000.00. "I would most gladly have avoided the responsibility of the negotiation. I am thoroughly convinced that much the larger portion of these claims will be rejected by any impartial tribunal," he insists further on in the letter. After the treaty failed to gain ratification, negotiations for a settlement on the claims were dropped, for the poor diplomatic relations between the two countries were aggravated by the arrival of an American naval squadron off Verde Island at Veracruz in June of 1844, and were finally broken off. . . .

The failure of Mexican negotiations over Texas caused the Congress to accuse the administration of José Joaquín de Herrera of negligence, and to refuse to authorize a loan of 15 million pesos which the President had requested in order to begin the war. Despite the country's moral and economic collapse caused by the small clique which had seized power, Herrera managed to build an army of 6,000 men. . . .

Paredes headed north, but on 14 December 1845 he declared that he and his troops, who were supposed to defend the nation, were in

From Luis G. Zorilla, *Historia de las Relaciones Entre Mexico y los Estados Unidos de America, 1800–1958,* 2 vols.; I, pp. 177–182, 209–210. Copyright 1965 by Editorial Porrua, S. A., Mexico. Translated by Christopher Hunt. Reprinted by permission of the publisher.

rebellion against the government. Turning his back on the foreign enemy, he returned to the capital, to assume the presidency which had twice eluded him. At first there were no protests; Paredes gained much support, and the press revived the idea of establishing a monarchy to save the country from chaos. Unrest spread as the enemy advanced across national territory to the banks of the Bravo; there was a series of revolts and military uprisings in Oaxaca, Puebla, Sonora, and other places.

Paredes saw his own course of action imitated: the forces he had sent to defend the Californias, under General Rafael Tellez, declared their opposition to the new President in Mazatlan on 20 May 1846; they appropriated ships and provisions, leaving California undefended. Rebellion spread to Guadaiajara under General Yanez, who, in league with Gómez Farías and López de Santa Ana from his exile abroad, convinced the garrison in the capital to join its chief, Mariano Salas, in revolt as soon as Paredes departed to put down the uprising in Guadalajara. Salas became interim President, and while both quarreling factions appealed to him to save the fatherland, Taylor and 10,000 men dug in at Matamoros, where, since the end of March, they had been building Fort Brown.

Toward the end of 1847 . . . as the political disaster demoralized both liberals and conservatives, our country experienced its most painful moments. Our downfall and disintegration seemed an endless nightmare. The goal of all efforts was the immediate protection of partisan interests. The uprisings of Paredes and the *polkos,* which pretended to be patriotic, were most anti-Mexican in their results, not realizing that actions—not the words which attempt to disguise them —are decisive.

In 1847, the United States of America had more than 21 million inhabitants and natural resources which were superior to Mexico's in every respect. The Mexican population surely did not exceed 8 million, and the country's past was marked by irreconcilable factionalism in both domestic and international affairs, and by thirty-seven years of internal strife. Knowing what we do about the intentions of the government in Washington, and the maneuvers planned and executed by its officials, we need not argue over which country was the aggressor in this war. Although Mexico played into the hands of the United States by accepting its challenge to fight, war was preferable to the only other recourse: handing over without resistance everything that Washington demanded. Conditions for peace such as those offered by Polk are never accepted by a nation—they must be imposed by force of arms. Furthermore, the march of the American army to the Mexican capital was not as glorious as contemporaries pretended; the maneuvers of the State Department were far more brilliant.

Amid such calamities, the greatest of which was the irresponsibility of many of its leaders, it is heartening to see that Mexicans nonetheless put up a resistance.

6.

CONGRESS AUTHORIZES THE PRESIDENT TO CALL A PAN AMERICAN CONFERENCE

Blaine's initial attempt to bring the nations of the hemisphere together in 1881 was frustrated by Garfield's assassination and Arthur's reversal of policy. Seven years later, Blaine was back in office and succeeded in realizing his plan for a hemispheric gathering which would facilitate the expansion of U.S. trade and influence.

An act authorizing the President of the United States to arrange a conference between the United States of America and the Republics of Mexico, Central and South America, Hayti, San Domingo, and the Empire of Brazil, which is in words and figures as follows, to wit:

Be it enacted by the Senate and House of Representatives of the United States of America, in Congress assembled, That the President of the United States be, and he is hereby, requested and authorized to invite the several Governments of the Republics of Mexico, Central and South America, Hayti, San Domingo, and the Empire of Brazil to join the United States in a conference to be held at Washington, in the United States, at such time as he may deem proper, in the year eighteen hundred and eighty-nine, for the purpose of discussing and recommending for adoption to their respective Governments some plan of arbitration for the settlement of disagreements and dis-

Senate Executive Document No. 231, 51 Congress, 1st Session, *Minutes of the International American Conference* (Washington, D.C.: Government Printing Office, 1890), pp. 1–3.

putes that may hereafter arise between them, and for considering questions relating to the improvement of business intercourse and means of direct communication between said countries, and to encourage such reciprocal commercial relations as will be beneficial to all and secure more extensive markets for the products of each of said countries. . . .

Sec. 2. That in forwarding the invitations to the said Governments the President of the United States shall set forth that the Conference is called to consider—

First. Measures that shall tend to preserve the peace and promote the prosperity of the several American States.

Second. Measures toward the formation of an American customs union, under which the trade of the American nations with each other shall, so far as possible and profitable, be promoted.

Third. The establishment of regular and frequent communication between the ports of the several American states and the ports of each other.

Fourth. The establishment of a uniform system of customs regulations in each of the independent American states to govern the mode of importation and exportation of merchandise and port dues and charges, a uniform method of determining the classification and valuation of such merchandise in the ports of each country, and a uniform system of invoices, and the sanitation of ships and quarantine.

Fifth. The adoption of a uniform system of weights and measures, and laws to protect the patent rights, copyrights, and trade-marks of citizens of either country in the other, and for the extradition of criminals.

Sixth. The adoption of a common silver coin, to be issued by each Government, the same to be legal tender in all commercial transactions between the citizens of all of the American States.

Seventh. An agreement upon the recommendation for adoption to their respective Governments of a definite plan of arbitration of all questions, disputes, and differences that may now or hereafter exist between them, to the end that all difficulties and disputes between such nations may be peaceably settled and wars prevented.

Eighth. And to consider such other subjects relating to the welfare of the several States represented as may be presented by any of said States which are hereby invited to participate in said Conference.

7.
SECRETARY OF STATE OLNEY ASSERTS U.S. INFLUENCE IN THE WESTERN HEMISPHERE

President Grover Cleveland was not a friend of the expansionists. Nevertheless, under heavy pressure from domestic forces, he authorized Secretary Olney to take a hard line with Great Britain to pressure the British into submitting their dispute with Venezuela to arbitration. Olney based his position on the principle of international law "under which a nation may justly interpose in a controversy" involving two or more other nations, and on the principles enunciated by George Washington and James Monroe.

That America is in no part open to colonization, though the proposition was not universally admitted at the time of its enunciation, has long been universally conceded. We are now concerned, therefore, only with that other practical application of the Monroe doctrine the disregard of which by an European power is to be deemed an act of unfriendliness towards the United States. The precise scope and limitations of this rule cannot be too clearly apprehended. It does not establish any general protectorate by the United States over other American states. It does not relieve any American state from its obligations as fixed by international law nor prevent any European power directly interested from enforcing such obligations or from inflicting merited punishment for the breach of them. It does not

Olney to Minister Thomas F. Bayard, July 20, 1895, *Papers Relating to the Foreign Relations of the United States, 1895,* Part I (Washington, D.C.: Government Printing Office, 1896), pp. 554–562.

contemplate any interference in the internal affairs of any American state or in the relations between it and other American states. It does not justify any attempt on our part to change the established form of Government of any American state or to prevent the people of such state from altering that form according to their own will and pleasure. The rule in question has but a single purpose and object. It is that no European power or combination of European powers shall forcibly deprive an American state of the right and power of self-government and of shaping for itself its own political fortunes and destinies. . . .

Is it true, then, that the safety and welfare of the United States are so concerned with the maintenance of the independence of every American state as against any European power as to justify and require the interposition of the United States whenever that independence is endangered? The question can be candidly answered in but one way. The states of America, South as well as North, by geographical proximity, by natural sympathy, by similarity of governmental constitutions, are friends and allies, commercially and politically, of the United States. . . . The people of the United States have a vital interest in the cause of popular self-government. They have secured the right for themselves and their posterity at the cost of infinite blood and treasure. . . . It is in that view more than in any other that they believe it not to be tolerated that the political control of an American state shall be forcibly assumed by an European power. . . .

. . . To-day the United States is practically sovereign on this continent, and its fiat is law upon the subjects to which it confines its interposition. Why? It is not because of the pure friendship or good will felt for it. It is not simply by reason of its high character as a civilized state, nor because wisdom and justice and equity are the invariable characteristics of the dealings of the United States. It is because, in addition to all other grounds, its infinite resources combined with its isolated position render it master of the situation and practically invulnerable as against any or all other powers.

All the advantages of this superiority are at once imperiled if the principle be admitted that European powers may convert American states into colonies or provinces of their own. The principle would be eagerly availed of, and every power doing so would immediately acquire a base of military operations against us. What one power was permitted to do could not be denied to another, and it is not inconceivable that the struggle now going on for the acquisition of Africa might be [transferred to] South America. If it were, the weaker countries would unquestionably be soon absorbed, while the ultimate result might be the partition of all South America between the various European powers. The disastrous consequences to the United States of such a condition of things are obvious. The loss of prestige, of authority, and of weight in the councils of the family of nations, would be among the least of them. Our only real rivals in peace as well as enemies in war would be found located at our very doors. . . .

In these circumstances, the duty of the President appears to him unmistakable and imperative. Great Britain's assertion of title to the disputed territory combined with her refusal to have that title investigated being a substantial appropriation of the territory to her own use, not to protest and give warning that the transaction will be regarded as injurious to the interests of the people of the United States as well as oppressive in itself would be to ignore an established policy with which the honor and welfare of this country are closely identified. While the measures necessary or proper for the vindication of that policy are to be determined by another branch of the Government, it is clearly for the Executive to leave nothing undone which may tend to render such determination unnecessary.

8.

THEODORE ROOSEVELT SHOULDERS THE
BURDENS OF POLICEMAN IN THE CARIBBEAN

The Hague Tribunal award in the Venezuelan debt case had immediate repercussions. It was feared in Washington that the award, as a precedent, might threaten American security through developments in the Dominican Republic, where European creditor nations were rumored to be planning an intervention on the grounds that the country was in default on its debts. The series of letters from President Roosevelt and his discussion of foreign policy in his message to Congress reveal his thinking before and after the decision of the Hague Tribunal on the Venezuelan claims and show the steps by which he arrived at the decision to intervene.

February 10, 1904, to Theodore Roosevelt, Jr.

Santo Domingo is drifting into chaos, for after a hundred years of freedom it shows itself utterly incompetent for governmental work. Most reluctantly I have been obliged to take the initial step of interference there. I hope it will be a good while before I have to go further. But sooner or later it seems to me inevitable that the United

Letters to Theodore Roosevelt, Jr., Feb. 10, 1904; to Joseph Bucklin Bishop, Feb. 23, 1904; and to Elihu Root, May 20, 1904, in Elting E. Morison, ed., *The Letters of Theodore Roosevelt* (8 vols; Cambridge, Mass.: Harvard University Press, 1951), vol. 4, pp. 723–724, 734–735, 801. The President's message to Congress is reprinted from *Papers Relating to the Foreign Relations of the United States, 1904* (Washington, D.C.: Government Printing Office, 1905), pp. xli–xlii.

States should assume an attitude of protection and regulation in regard to all these little states in the neighborhood of the Caribbean. I hope it will be deferred as long as possible, but I fear it is inevitable.

February 23, 1904, to Joseph Bucklin Bishop

I have been hoping and praying for three months that the Santo Domingans would behave so that I would not have to act in any way. I want to do nothing but what a policeman has to do in Santo Domingo. As for annexing the island, I have about the same desire to annex it as a gorged boa constrictor might have to swallow a porcupine wrong-end-to. Is that strong enough? I have asked some of our people to go there because, after having refused for three months to do anything, the attitude of the Santo Domingans has become one of half chaotic war towards us. If I possibly can I want to do nothing to them. If it is absolutely necessary to do something, then I want to do as little as possible. Their government has been deviling us to establish some kind of a protectorate over the islands, and take charge of their finances. We have been answering them that we could not possibly go into the subject now at all.

May 20, 1904, to Elihu Root, a public letter read at a banquet in New York

Through you I want to send my heartiest greetings to those gathered to celebrate the second anniversary of the Republic of Cuba. I wish that it were possible to be present with you in person. I rejoice in what Cuba has done and especially in the way in which for the last two years her people have shown their desire and ability to accept in a serious spirit the responsibilities that accompany freedom. Such determination is vital, for those unable or unwilling to shoulder the responsibility of using their liberty aright can never in the long run preserve such liberty.

As for the United States, it must ever be a source of joy and gratification to good American citizens that they were enabled to play the part they did as regards Cuba. . . .

All that we desire is to see all neighboring countries stable, orderly and prosperous. Any country whose people conduct themselves well can count upon our hearty friendliness. If a nation shows that it knows how to act with decency in industrial and political matters, if it keeps order and pays its obligations, then it need fear no interference from the United States. Brutal wrongdoing, or an impotence which results in a general loosening of the ties of civilized society, may finally require intervention by some civilized nation, and in the Western Hemisphere the United States cannot ignore this duty; but it remains true that our interests, and those of our southern neighbors, are in reality identical. All that we ask is that they shall govern themselves well, and be prosperous and orderly. Where this is the case they will find only helpfulness from us.

> After his success in the election of 1904, President Roosevelt moved rapidly in the direction of the policy foreshadowed in his May 20 letter to Elihu Root. The President repeated the phraseology of the Root letter in a major discussion of foreign policy which he included in his annual message to Congress, December 6, 1904. After talking about the need for force and manliness in foreign affairs, and the concept of a righteous war, he said:

Chronic wrongdoing, or an impotence which results in a general loosening of the ties of civilized society, may in America, as elsewhere, ultimately require intervention by some civilized nation, and in the Western Hemisphere the adherence of the United States to the Monroe Doctrine may force the United States, however reluctantly, in flagrant cases of such wrongdoing or impotence, to the exercise of an international police power. If every country washed by the Caribbean Sea would show the progress in stable and just civilization which with the aid of the Platt amendment Cuba has shown since our troops left the island, and which so many of the republics in both Americas are constantly and brilliantly showing, all question of interference by this Nation with their affairs would be at an end. Our interests and those of our southern neighbors are in reality identical. They have great natural riches, and if within their borders the reign of law and justice obtains, prosperity is sure to come to them. While they thus obey the primary laws of civilized society they may rest assured that they will be treated by us in a spirit of cordial and helpful sympathy. We would interfere with them only in the last resort, and then only if it became evident that their inability or unwillingness to do justice at home and abroad had violated the rights of the United

States or had invited foreign aggression to the detriment of the entire body of American nations. It is a mere truism to say that every nation, whether in America or anywhere else, which desires to maintain its freedom, its independence, must ultimately realize that the right of such independence can not be separated from the responsibility of making good use of it.

9.
A LATIN AMERICAN SPEAKS OUT AGAINST IMPERIALISM

JOSÉ INGENIEROS

Many people in Latin America were unhappy with the suffocating preponderance of the United States in hemispheric affairs. Groups in the protectorate nations spoke bitterly against U.S. intervention. And in spite of assurances from Washington that states in South America were "different," not subject to the same policing as Caribbean nations, there were many whose nations had not been intervened who criticized Yankee Imperialism. The following selection is by José Ingenieros (1877–1925) an Argentine writer and *pensador*. It is taken from a speech delivered on October 11, 1922, at a dinner honoring the Mexican man of letters José Vasconcelos. Ingenieros' major works include *Sociología argentina, La evolución de las ideas argentinas,* and *El hombre mediocre.*

We must recognize that in the few years of this century, events have occurred in Latin America which demand serious, even gloomy reflection. And we hope that these words, spoken to this warm fraternal gathering of Argentine writers in honor of a Mexican colleague, will be echoed among the intellectuals of the continent, so that an insistent concern for the future will be awakened in all.

From Miguel Hidalgo et al., *Hispanomerica en lucha por su independencia,* pp. 217–225. Copyright 1962 by Cuadernos Americanos, Mexico. Translated by Christopher Hunt. Reprinted by permission of the publisher.

We are not, we no longer wish to be, we no longer can be pan-americanists. The famous Monroe Doctrine, which for a century seemed to be the guarantee of our political independence against the threat of European conquests, has gradually proved to be a declaration of the American right to protect us and to intervene in our affairs. Our powerful neighbor and meddlesome friend, having developed to its highest level the capitalist mode of production, during the past war has attained world financial hegemony. This development has been accompanied by the growth in voracity of the American privileged caste, which has increasingly pressed for an imperialist policy, and has converted the government into an instrument of its corporations, with no principles other than the capture of sources of wealth and exploitation of the labor of a population already enslaved by an amoral, nationless, inflexible financial elite. Among the ruling classes of this great state, the urge to expand and conquer has grown to the point where the classic, "America for the Americans" actually means, "America—our Latin America—for the North Americans.". . .

This at least is the implication of recent American imperialist policy, the course of which is alarming for all of Latin America. Since the war with Spain, the United States has taken possession of Puerto Rico and imposed upon Cuba the vexatious conditions of the shameful Platt Amendment. It lost little time in amputating from Colombia the Isthmus of Panama, through which the country would join its Atlantic and Pacific coasts. Later, the United States intervened in Nicaragua to secure for itself the route of another possible interoceanic canal. It threaened the sovereignty of Mexico in the unfortunate Veracruz adventure. Under puerile pretexts, it militarily occupied Haiti. Soon afterwards, the United States shamefully occupied Santo Domingo, offering the usual excuse of pacifying the country and restoring its finances. . . .

Only yesterday, and now, as I speak, the United States cripples and dissolves the Central American Federation, knowing that its prey is easy to devour if it is first divided into small bites. Only yesterday, and now, as I speak, it refuses to recognize the constitutional government of Mexico unless it first signs treaties which favor foreign capitalism over national interests. Only yesterday, and now, as I speak, it insults Cuba by imposing on it General Crowder as titular intervenor.

I see on many faces the old objection: Panama is the natural limit of expansion, and capitalist imperialism will stop there. Until a few years ago, many of us believed this; we should admit it, even though this feeling of collective egotism does not honor us. The most distant nations—Brazil, Uruguay, Argentina, and Chile—felt safe from the clutches of the eagle, thinking the torrid zone would arrest its flight.

Lately, some of us have admitted that we were wrong. . . . We know that some governments—we will spare feelings by not naming them—live under a *de facto* tutelage, quite similar to the disgrace sanctioned by law in the Platt Amendment. We know that certain recent loans contain clauses which assure American financial control and imply to some extent the right of intervention. And finally, we know that during the past few years American influence has been felt with increasing intensity in all political, economic and social activities in South America. . . .

The danger does not begin with annexation, as in Puerto Rico, nor with intervention, as in Cuba, nor with a military expedition, as in Mexico, nor with tutelage, as in Nicaragua, nor with territorial secession, as in Colombia, nor with armed occupation, as in Haiti, nor with purchase, as in the Guianas. In its first phase, the danger begins with the progressive mortgaging of national independence through loans destined to grow and to be renewed endlessly, under conditions which are progressively detrimental to the sovereignty of the beneficiaries. . . .

For the peoples of Latin America, the issue is quite simply national defense, although many of our rulers often ignore or hide it. American capitalism seeks to capture the sources of our wealth, with the right to intervene in order to protect its investments and to assure returns on them. In the meantime, we are allowed only an illusion of political independence. As long as a foreign state expressly or surreptitiously possesses the right to intervene, political independence is not effective; as long as it refuses to recognize any government which does not support its policy of privilege and monopoly, it threatens national sovereignty; as long as it does not clearly show that it renounces such policies, it cannot be considered a friendly country. . . .

[Ingenieros proposed a Latin American Union, actually founded in 1925, whose purpose and norms would be:]

To develop in Latin American countries a new consciousness of national and continental interests, promoting all ideological developments which lead to the effective exercise of popular sovereignty, and fighting all dictatorships which oppose reforms inspired by the desire for social justice. . . .

The Latin American Union affirms its commitment to the following principles:

Political solidarity among all Latin American countries, and concerted action in all questions of world interest.

Repudiation of official panamericanism, and suppression of secret diplomacy.

Arbitration, by exclusively Latin American jurisdictions, in any litigation between Latin American nations, and reduction of national armament to the minimum compatible with the maintenance of internal order.

Opposition to any financial policy which compromises national sovereignty, and particularly to the acceptance of loans which sanction or justify the coercive intervention of foreign capitalist states.

Reaffirmation of democratic principles, in accordance with the latest judgments of political science.

Nationalization of sources of wealth, and abolition of economic privilege.

Opposition to any influence of the Church on public life and education.

Extension of free, obligatory secular education, and thorough university reform.

10.
A DEFENSE OF THE UNITED STATES' POSITION

CHARLES EVANS HUGHES

By the end of the 1920s, the United States was coming under increasing attack for its interventions, and from several nations in Latin America, for its protectionist economic policies which hurt inter-American trade. The Sixth Pan American Conference at Havana, 1928, was the forum for the first open debate on interventionism. The State Department was aware of the criticism and had instructed the United States delegation to the Conference to avoid the subject. When that proved impossible, Charles Evans Hughes, the leader of the delegation, defended the U.S. policy and prevented any action by the Conference that might have been embarrassing to the United States. Hughes won debater's points. He did not succeed in settling any issues or stilling the voices of criticism. The following account is taken from a memorandum by Henry C. Beerits, Hughes's private secretary.

In 1927 an International Commission of Jurists had met in Rio de Janeiro to determine the items on public international law to be submitted for consideration at the Sixth Pan American Conference.

Henry C. Beerits Memorandum, "Latin American Conference," pp. 13–14. Papers of Charles Evans Hughes, Manuscript Division Library of Congress, partially reprinted in David J. Danelski and Joseph S. Tulchin, eds., *The Autobiographical Notes of Charles Evans Hughes* (forthcoming). Copyright 1972 by the President and Fellows of Harvard College. Reprinted by permission.

One of the proposals of the commission had been that no American country had the right to intervene in the affairs of any other American country. Hughes did not want to oppose the proposal, but its intent precluded U.S. intervention even to protect American life and property in Latin America. After discussion in a subcommittee of which Hughes was chairman, Dr. Honorio Pueyrredón, Chief of the Argentine delegation, suggested reluctantly that the proposal be dropped because of irreconcilable differences, and it was agreed finally to reconsider the matter at the next Pan American Conference, which was to be held in five years. Pueyrredón stalked out of the Conference in disgust. On the last day of the plenary session of the Conference when the proposal of the Committee on Public International Law came up that the subject of intervention be considered at the next Pan American Conference, Dr. Laurentina Olascoaga of Argentina leapt to his feet and argued in favor of non-intervention.

At once the atmosphere of the Great Hall changed as though a current of electricity had run through it, and the air became charged with tense excitement. Delegate after delegate arose to affirm the ideas of the Argentine delegate. Then Guerrero [of El Salvador], who had promised to drop the matter, arose and said [that] if the Conference were unanimous, as it appeared to him it was, he saw no reason why it should not go on record on the subject of intervention. [Without making a formal motion he proposed the following:]

The Sixth Conference of the American Republics, taking into consideration that each one of the Delegates has expressed his firm decision that the principle of non-intervention and the absolute juridical equality of States should be roundly and categorically stated, resolves: No State has the right to intervene in the internal affairs of another.

At this the Cubans in the gallery broke into thundering applause.

At this point the Great Hall was invaded by the dignitaries of the University, gorgeously gowned, and for an hour learned doctors of law, science and philosophy delivered long speeches. But while the doctors were speaking the delegates were whispering. Fernandez of Brazil and Olaya of Colombia came to Mr. Hughes and protested that this action by Guerrero was a breach of honor, and that it was impossible that it be tolerated. Mr. Hughes replied that he could not be put in the position of stopping discussion on the matter. He sent word to Dr. Antonio Sanchez de Bustamente (Judge of the Permanent Court of International Justice), who was chairman of the Conference, on no account to adjourn the session until the matter was settled.

The interruption in the proceedings of the Conference served only to increase the fierce flame of excitement. After the dignitaries had concluded their addresses, the delegates launched forth into a fierce debate on the non-intervention proposal. It was as tense and exciting a meeting as Mr. Hughes ever witnessed. Maúrtua of Peru arose and attacked Guerrero. One of the Nicaraguan delegates defended the United States. Fiery speech followed upon fiery speech, and the air was becoming more and more tense. Dr. Bustamente at one point found it necessary to call the meeting to order so as to prevent a heated personal exchange between Jesus M. Yepes of Colombia and Guerrero from reaching a stage where nothing but pistols for two would have been acceptable to wounded Latin-American honor.

While all this discussion was taking place, the position of Mr. Hughes was a very delicate one. If the votes were there to defeat the non-intervention resolution, it was better that he did not appear to prevent its passage. If, on the other hand, the votes were not there to prevent its passage, it was essential that he speak in an attempt to defeat it. It was an exceedingly tense experience for him and he never felt more strongly his responsibility for America.

The Great Hall was ringing with violent applause and excited cries each time one of the delegates spoke in favor of the non-intervention proposal. Mr. Hughes finally decided that the time had come when he must speak.

Immediately the room became hushed with eager expectancy. Mr. Hughes started speaking with firm and measured tones. He gave the history of the decision to postpone discussion of the question, in view of the fact that unanimity on the question could not be then attained. Then he took up with great candor the question of intervention, and explained very frankly the policy of his country with respect to this matter. In conclusion he stated:

Let us face the facts. The difficulty, if there is any, in any one of the American Republics, is not of any external aggression. It is an internal difficulty. . . . From time to time there arises a situation most deplorable and regrettable . . . in which sovereignty is not at work, in which for a time in certain areas there is no government at all.

. . . Those are the conditions that create the difficulty with which at times we find ourselves confronted. What are we to do when government breaks down and American citizens are in danger of their lives? Are we to stand by and see them killed because a government in circumstances which it can not control and for which it may not be responsible can no longer afford reasonable protection? I am not speaking of sporadic acts of violence, or of the rising of mobs, or of those distressing incidents which may occur in any country however well administered. I am speaking of the occasions where government itself is unable to function. . . .

Now it is a principle of international law that in such a case a government is fully justified in taking action—I would call it interposition of a temporary character—for the purpose of protecting the lives and property of its nationals. I could say that that is not intervention. One can read in textbooks that that is not intervention. . . . Of course the United States can not forego its right to protect its citizens. No country should forego its right to protect its citizens. International law cannot be changed by the resolutions of this Conference. . . . The rights of nations remain, but nations have duties as well as rights. . . . This very formula, here proposed, is a proposal of duty on the part of a nation. But it is not the only duty. There are other obligations which courts, and tribunals declaring international law, have frequently set forth; and we cannot codify international law and ignore the duties of states, by setting up the impossible reign of self-will without any recognition upon the part of the state of its obligations to its neighbors. . . .

I am too proud of my country to stand before you as in any way suggesting a defense of aggression or of assault upon the sovereignty of independence of any State. I stand before you to tell you that we unite with you in the aspiration for complete sovereignty and the realization of complete independence.

I stand here with you ready to cooperate in every way in establishing the ideals of justice by institutions in every land which will promote fairness of dealing between man and man and nation and nation.

I cannot sacrifice the rights of my country but I will join with you in declaring the law. I will try to help you in coming to a just conclusion as to the law; but it must be the law of justice infused with the spirit which has given us from the days of Grotius this wonderful development of the law of nations, by which we find ourselves bound.

Mr. Hughes never had greater success in his life. When he finished speaking, the galleries rang with applause. A marked change had taken place in the tempo of the audience while he spoke. As the New York *Times* put it, "as Mr. Hughes sat down there was a sudden tension over the whole chamber. It seemed as if everyone realized that the resolution for an immediate decision on the question of intervention was beaten. Mr. Hughes had beaten it by the sheer force of his personality, his eloquence and deep sincerity."

The result was that the Conference voted to postpone consideration of the question of intervention until the meeting of the Seventh Pan American Conference, to be held five years later. Thus the stormy session adjourned, and the delegates finally appeared for their dinner at 10:30 that night.

Mr. Hughes by his masterly speech had prevented the Conference from ending on a harsh note of discord, and thus had saved Pan Americanism from suffering a setback. This was the first Conference at which every one of the twenty-one members of the Pan American Union was represented. It resulted in many tangible achievements, but perhaps its greatest achievement was an increase in Pan American understanding and good will.

11.
AN APPRECIATION OF THE GOOD NEIGHBOR

FRANCISCO CUEVAS CANCINO

Focusing on the motives behind the Good Neighbor policy,
as many North American historians have done, obscures the
fact that most Latin Americans responded warmly to Roosevelt's initiatives. The image of the United States in Latin
America did improve. Latin Americans applauded the New
Deal and were encouraged by an attitude which they thought
would make possible a community of equals. This selection
is taken from the work of a Mexican scholar who is not
always friendly toward the United States.

As the heir to and principal exponent of an established attitude of
sympathy toward Latin America, Franklin Roosevelt cannot justify
his claim of having originated the policy of the Good Neighbor. He
more than compensates for this, however, with that magnificent, innovative ethical element which forms the essence of his Good Neighbor and distinguishes so many of his decisions. This ethical factor
is more evident in his policy toward Latin America than in his attitude toward any other part of the world. One could even assert that
while the principles of Good Neighborhood only slightly affect Roosevelt's general decisions in foreign policy, they dominate his program
toward Latin America.

From Francisco Cuevas Cancino, *Roosevelt y la Buena Vecindad,* pp.
161–163, 231–232, 120, 466–467. Copyright 1954 by Fondo de Cultura
Económica, Mexico. Reprinted by permission of the publisher.

There is another, equally essential element which has not been sufficiently emphasized. Latin American peoples, so frequently governed by corrupt oligarchies, believe in democracy as a system which is personified by a *caudillo* who identifies himself with their aspirations. For them, the ostensible symbol of democracy is a commander who pulls together popular aspirations, an incorruptible leader who will set the political machinery in motion for the benefit of the disinherited.

The austere figure of Hoover, with his ties to financial magnates, could not possibly fit the South American ideal. The words which Hoover spoke during his tour of our continent seemed to come from an impassive heart. Latin Americans were wary of such a cold man; they saw his good deeds as exceptions, and remembered only his mistakes. He did not represent democracy, and consequently even in the best of circumstances his Latin American policy could achieve only limited success.

Roosevelt is the antithesis of Hoover. The conditions under which he reached the White House seem to prove him the champion of the American masses, which like the Latin American people are exploited by an overdeveloped capitalism. And the brilliant beginning of his administration, which shows Roosevelt's commitment to improving conditions for the poor, will surely have profound repercussions in Latin America. His speeches, filled with fiery images, touch the hearts of the countries south of the Bravo, and earn Roosevelt the allegiance of their workers and rural masses. His words seem to spring from a love for mankind, and the affection is returned to him not only by his fellow citizens. The bond of friendship between Roosevelt and Latin America is very strong; it is the fundamental novelty of the Good Neighbor Policy, for before Roosevelt, no American statesman was able to capture the imagination of our continent. Thus it is hardly a surprise that when he visited Rio de Janeiro and Buenos Aires on the occasion of the opening of the Interamerican Conference of 1936, he was received with cries of, "Long live Democracy!" He remembered this greeting affectionately and with deep understanding, for it represents his popular support. It typified his leadership of the disinherited masses of both the United States and the rest of America. . . . Here, in his ability to be seen, both at home and abroad, as the democratic leader *par excellence,* lies Roosevelt's political genius. . . .

[The Buenos Aires Interamerican Conference was important because] for the first time our two civilizations worked together toward continental solidarity. United by democratic aspirations, all the American republics aligned themselves behind a common leader, reaffirming the principle of peace and making possible the agreements which enabled the nations to stand together against aggression: the declarations of Lima and Panama; the meetings of diplomats; and our current panamericanism, which could only be built upon the foundation of spiritual unity laid so masterfully by Roosevelt at Buenos Aires. Because of its foresight, and the role it played in the development of panamericanism, the Buenos Aires Conference must be counted among the most important meetings ever to take place on this continent. . . .

There is something more profound than mere policy in the Good Neighbor program, and it is here that Roosevelt's scheme is vulnerable to criticism. Its principles are of such ethical plentitude that the program cannot avoid violating, to an extent, its own spirit. For as long as man pursues concrete, immediate ends, he can follow a fixed, coherent course of action; but when he aspires to principle, his doubts about directions to follow, individual decisions to make, and the possibility of error begin to grow, even though he remains as eager and purposeful.

Roosevelt's initial formulation of the Good Neighbor Policy confirms this opinion. The fundamental axis of the program is each country's self-respect. If this principle is adopted with conviction, then each action which violates it—whatever the immediate, external results—is harmful to the nation which takes it. Acceptance of this premise will assure respect for the rights of other countries, the moral bases of which limit the action of each nation. . . .

In his inaugural address, Franklin Roosevelt fixed limits for his international policy. In perfectly simple terms, he raised his people above everyday cares and, steeped in moral feeling, explained his policy by means of universals. The relation of his Good Neighbor program to the actions his country would take was clearly outlined. Under Roosevelt, an entire nation accepted the primacy of the great natural laws and, without misunderstanding concrete problems, attempted to resolve all questions ethically. Thus a new international attitude grew as a splendid flower.

Roosevelt's inaugural speech constituted a first, essential step, but it did not in itself transcend all problems. Similar declarations have been made and have proved meaningless; they have been no more than expressions of individual convictions, which the world has heard attentively, but which have not gained the force of law. The case of the Good Neighbor Policy, however, has been different. On numerous occasions, Roosevelt's declaration has been respected, and international problems have been approached in the light of its high standards. The policy has become a reality; the paths down which Roosevelt has guided his country have not been those of mere political accommodation.

The behavior of one country is not in itself strong enough to spread new customs; there are many isolated practices which have not affected the rules which govern the international community. Each member of this community must recognize the freshness and virtue of the new attitude, adopt it as a regulatory norm for its own conduct, and agree to enforce it. This was the final step in the evolution of the Good Neighbor Policy: following the American example, other countries—first a group, then all the rest—agreed that the program encompassed more than policy, that it belonged among the highest rules which guide international conduct. From Roosevelt's declaration in 1933, to its application to American policy, to its acceptance as an international principle, there is an unbroken line of continuity.

12.

THE UNITED STATES AND LATIN AMERICA IN THE COLD WAR

The cold war began almost before the peace had been made to end World War I. In the Western Hemisphere the Rio Defense Treaty (1947) was directed against the Soviet Union, and the United States made its hostility to communism clear on numerous occasions, as evidenced by the following selections.

When the United States government determined that the regime in Guatemala was "about to go Communist" and thus would constitute a threat to the United States, it acted both openly and clandestinely to bring about the Guatemalan government's fall. Secretary of State John Foster Dulles traveled to Caracas in March, 1954, to attend the Tenth Inter-American Conference to line up the OAS behind the U.S. efforts to oust the Guatemalan government. The selections that comprise Part I of this document are taken from Dulles's Address at the Second Plenary Session, March 4, 1954, the statement he made introducing the U.S. draft resolution on Communist Intervention, March 8, and the final text of the Resolution (XCIII) known as The Caracas Declaration.*

*Department of State, Publication 5692, Tenth Inter-American Conference. *Report of the Delegation of United States of America with Related Documents* (Washington, D.C.: Government Printing Office, 1955), pp. 44–55 and 156–157; State Department *Bulletin,* 44, #1141, May 8, 1961, pp. 659–661; and Department of State, *Press Release* No. 241, October 12, 1965.

From Dulles's Address at the Second Plenary Session

We here in the Americas are not immune from that threat of Soviet communism. There is not a single country in this hemisphere which has not been penetrated by the apparatus of international communism acting under orders from Moscow. No one of us knows fully the extent of that conspiracy. From time to time small parts are detected and exposed. . . .

None of us wants to be maneuvered into the position of defending whatever Communists attack. We do not carry on political warfare against ideas or ideals. But equally we must not be blind to the fact that the international conspiracy I describe has, in 15 years, been primarily responsible for turning what were 15 independent nations into Soviet colonies and they would, if they could, duplicate that performance here. . . .

From the earliest days of the independence of our countries, we have all stood resolutely for the integrity of this hemisphere. We have seen that integrity would be endangered unless we stood resolutely against any enlargement here of the colonial domain of the European powers. We have made our position in this matter so clear that it is known to, and accepted by, all the world. What was a great danger has thus receded.

We have not made it equally clear that the integrity of this hemisphere and the peace, safety, and happiness of us all may be endangered by political penetration from without, and that we stand resolutely and unitedly against that form of danger.

Because our position has not been made clear, the danger mounts. I believe that it is time to make it clear with finality that we see that alien despotism is hostile to our ideals, that we unitedly deny it the right to prey upon our hemisphere, and that if it does not heed our warning and keep away, we shall deal with it as a situation that might endanger the peace of America.

What I suggest does not involve any interference in the international affairs of any American Republic. There is ample room for natural differences, and for tolerances, between the political institutions of the different American states. But there is no place here for political institutions which serve alien masters. I hope that we can agree to make that clear.

*Statement by the Secretary of State Introducing the U.S. Draft
Resolution on Communist Intervention*

It may next be asked whether this international Communist apparatus actually seeks to bring this hemisphere, or parts of it, into the
Soviet orbit. The answer must be in the affirmative.

I shall not here accuse any government or any individuals of being
either plotters, or the dupes of plotters. We are not sitting here as a
court to try governments or individuals. We sit rather as legislators.
As such, we need to know what will enable us to take appropriate
action of a general character in the common interest.

Within all the vast area, now embracing one-third of the world's
people, where the military power of the Soviet Union is dominant, no
official can be found who would dare to stand up and openly attack
the Government of the Soviet Union. But in this hemisphere, it takes
no courage for the representative of one of the smallest American
countries openly to attack the government of the most powerful.

I rejoice that that kind of freedom exists in the Americas, even if
it may be at times abused. But the essential is that there be a relationship of sovereign equality. We of the United States want to keep it
that way. We seek no satellites, but only friendly equals. We want
none who come to this table to speak as the tools of non-American
powers. We want to preserve and defend an American society in
which even the weak may speak boldly, because they represent national personalities which, as long as they are free, are equal.

*Declaration of Solidarity for the Preservation of the Political Integrity
of the American States Against the Intervention of International
Communism [The Caracas Declaration]*
WHEREAS:

The American republics at the Ninth International Conference of
American States declared that international communism, by its anti-
democratic nature and its interventionist tendency, is incompatible
with the concept of American freedom, and resolved to adapt within
their respective territories the measures necessary to eradicate and
prevent subversive activities;

The Fourth Meeting of Consultation of Ministers of Foreign Affairs
recognized that, in addition to adequate internal measures in each

state, a high degree of international cooperation is required to eradicate the danger which the subversive activities of international communism pose for the American states; and

The aggressive character of the international communist movement continues to constitute, in the context of world affairs, a special and immediate threat to the national institutions and the peace and security of the American States, and to the right of each state to develop its cultural, political, and economic life freely and naturally without intervention in its internal or external affairs by other states,

The Tenth Inter-American Conference

I

Condemns:

The activities of the international communist movement as constituting intervention in American affairs;

Expresses:

The determination of the American States to take the necessary measures to protect their political independence against the intervention of international communism, acting in the interests of an alien despotism;

Reiterates:

The faith of the peoples of America in the effective exercise of representative democracy as the best means to promote their social and political progress; and

Declares:

That the domination or control of the political institutions of an American State by the international communist movement, extending to this Hemisphere the political system of an extracontinental power, would constitute a threat to the sovereignty and political independence of the American States, endangering the peace of America, and would call for a Meeting of Consultation to consider the adoption of appropriate action in accordance with existing treaties.

II

Recommends:

That, without prejudice to such other measures as they may consider desirable, special attention be given by each of the American governments to the following steps for the purpose of counteracting the subversive activities of the international communist movement within their respective jurisdictions:

1. Measures to require disclosure of the identity, activities, and sources of funds of those who are spreading propaganda of the international communist movement or who travel in the interests of that movement, and of those who act as its agents or in its behalf; and

2. The exchange of information among governments to assist in fulfilling the purpose of the resolutions adopted by the Inter-American Conferences and Meetings of Ministers of Foreign Affairs regarding international communism.

III

This declaration of foreign policy made by the American republics in relations to dangers originating outside this Hemisphere is designed to protect and not to impair the inalienable right of each American State freely to choose its own form of government and economic system and to live its own social and cultural life.

Part II

The Alliance for Progress seemed to mark a significant change in U.S. policy. President Kennedy devoted more attention to Latin America than any president since Franklin Roosevelt. The idealistic tone of his speeches, his willingness to put his government's seal on the call for sweeping social and economic change written into the Charter of Punta del Este (1961), and the State Department's diplomatic interventions in favor of democratic regimes won many supporters in Latin America. But through it all ran the same preoccupation with the cold war, as this speech shows, delivered to the Society of Newspaper Editors on April 20, 1961, just after the tragic debacle at the Bay of Pigs.

The Lesson of Cuba, Address by President Kennedy

The President of a great democracy such as ours, and the editors of great newspapers such as yours, have a common obligation to the people: an obligation to present the facts, to present them with candor, and to present them in perspective. It is with that obligation in mind that I have decided in the last 24 hours to discuss briefly at this time the recent events in Cuba.

On that unhappy island, as in so many other areas of the contest for freedom, the news has grown worse instead of better. I have emphasized before that this was a struggle of Cuban patriots against a Cuban dictator. While we could not be expected to hide our sympathies, we made it repeatedly clear that the armed forces of this country would not intervene in any way.

Any unilateral American intervention, in the absence of an external attack upon ourselves or an ally, would have been contrary to our traditions and to our international obligations. But let the record show that our restraint is not inexhaustible. Should it ever appear that the inter-American doctrine of noninterference merely conceals or excuses a policy of nonaction—if the nations of this hemisphere should fail to meet their commitments against outside Communist penetration—then I want it clearly understood that this Government will not hesitate in meeting its primary obligations, which are to the security of our Nation.

Should that time ever come, we do not intend to be lectured on "intervention" by those whose character was stamped for all time on the bloody streets of Budapest. Nor would we expect or accept the same outcome which this small band of gallant Cuban refugees must have known that they were chancing, determined as they were against heavy odds to pursue their courageous attempts to regain their island's freedom. . . .

Meanwhile we will not accept Mr. Castro's attempts to blame this Nation for the hatred with which his onetime supporters now regard his repression. But there are from this sobering episode useful lessons for all to learn. Some may be still obscure and await further information. Some are clear today.

First, it is clear that the forces of communism are not to be underestimated, in Cuba or anywhere else in the world. The advantages of a police state—its use of mass terror and arrests to prevent the spread of free dissent—cannot be overlooked by those who expect the fall of every fanatic tyrant. If the self-discipline of the free cannot match the iron discipline of the mailed fist—in economic, political, scientific, and all the other kinds of struggles as well as the military— then the peril to freedom will continue to rise.

Secondly, it is clear that this Nation, in concert with all the free nations of this hemisphere, must take an even closer and more realistic look at the menace of external Communist intervention and domination in Cuba. The American people are not complacent about Iron Curtain tanks and planes less than 90 miles from our shores. But a nation of Cuba's size is less a threat to our survival than it is a base for subverting the survival of other free nations throughout the hemisphere. It is not primarily our interest or our security but theirs which is now, today, in the greater peril. It is for their sake as well as our own that we must show our will.

The evidence is clear—and the hour is late. We and our Latin friends will have to face the fact that we cannot postpone any longer the real issue of the survival of freedom in this hemisphere itself. On that issue, unlike perhaps some others, there can be no middle ground. Together we must build a hemisphere where freedom can flourish and where any free nation under outside attack of any kind can be assured that all of our resources stand ready to respond to any request for assistance.

Third, and finally, it is clearer than ever that we face a relentless struggle in every corner of the globe that goes far beyond the clash of armies or even nuclear armaments. The armies are there, and in large number. The nuclear armaments are there. But they serve primarily as the shield behind which subversion, infiltration, and a host of other tactics steadily advance, picking off vulnerable areas one by one in situations which do not permit our own armed intervention.

Power is the hallmark of this offensive—power and discipline and deceit. The legitimate discontent of yearning peoples is exploited. The legitimate trappings of self-determination are employed. But once in power, all talk of discontent is repressed—all self-determination disappears—and the promise of a revolution of hope is betrayed, as in Cuba, into a reign of terror. Those who staged automatic "riots" in the streets of free nations over the effort of a small group of young Cubans to regain their freedom should recall the long roll call of refugees who cannot now go back to Hungary, to North Korea, to North Viet-Nam, to East Germany, or to Poland, or to any of the other lands from which a steady stream of refugees pour forth, in eloquent testimony to the cruel oppression now holding sway in their homelands.

We dare not fail to see the insidious nature of this new and deeper struggle. We dare not fail to grasp the new concepts, the new sense of urgency we will need to combat it—whether in Cuba or [South Viet-Nam]. And we dare not fail to realize that this struggle is taking place every day, without fanfare, in thousands of villages and markets —day and night—and in classrooms all over the globe.

The message of Cuba, of Laos, of the rising din of Communist voices in Asia and Latin America—these messages are all the same. The complacent, the self-indulgent, the soft societies are about to be swept away with the debris of history. Only the strong, only the industrious, only the determined, only the courageous, only the visionary who determine the real nature of our struggle can possibly survive.

No greater task faces this Nation or this administration. No other challenge is more deserving of our every effort and energy. Too long we have fixed our eyes on traditional military needs, on armies prepared to cross borders or missiles poised for flight. Now it should be clear that this is no longer enough—that our security may be lost piece by piece, country by country, without the firing of a single missile or the crossing of a single border.

We intend to profit from this lesson. We intend to reexamine and reorient our forces of all kinds—our tactics and other institutions here in this community. We intend to intensify our efforts for a struggle in many ways more difficult than war, where disappointment will often accompany us.

For I am convinced that we in this country and in the free world possess the necessary resources, and all the skill, and the added strength that comes from a belief in the freedom of man. And I am equally convinced that history will record the fact that this bitter struggle reached its climax in the late 1950's and early 1960's. Let me then make clear as President of the United States that I am determined upon our system's survival and success, regardless of the cost and regardless of the peril.

Part III

> After Kennedy's death, the cold war line seemed to harden, as shown in this speech by Under Secretary of State Thomas C. Mann delivered before the annual meeting of the Inter-American Press Association on October 12, 1965.

It has been suggested that non-intervention is thought by some to be an obsolete doctrine.

I know of no Washington officials who think this way. On the contrary, I believe unilateral intervention by one American state in the internal political affairs of another is not only proscribed in the OAS Charter, but that non-intervention is a keystone of the structure of the inter-American system. American states have a treaty as well as a sovereign right to choose their political, social and economic systems free of all outside interference. . . .

Latin Americans do not want a paternalistic United States deciding which particular political faction should rule their countries. They do not want the United States to launch itself again on what one scholar described as a "civilizing mission" no matter how good its intentions are. This explains why, in the case of the Dominican Republic we refrained, during the first days of violence, from "supporting" the outgoing government or "supporting" either of the factions contending for power.

It explains why we and others thought it best to work for a ceasefire and to encourage the rival Dominican factions to meet together and agree on a Dominican solution to a Dominican problem. It explains why, to use a phrase of international law, we offered our good offices rather than attempting to preside over a meeting for the purpose of proposing political solutions with a "made in USA" label on them.

The second area of confusion concerns the response which an American state, or the Organization of American States as a whole, can make to intervention. When, in other words, a Communist state has intervened in the internal affairs of an American state by training, directing, financing and organizing indigenous Communist elements to take control of the government of an American state by force and violence, should other American states be powerless to lend assistance? Are Communists free to intervene while democratic states are powerless to frustrate the intervention?

This is not so much a question of intervention as it is of whether weak and fragile states should be helped to maintain their independence when they are under attack by subversive elements responding to direction from abroad.

Surely we have learned from the October 1962 missile crisis that the establishment of Communist military bases in this hemisphere threatens the security of every American state. Surely we have learned that political control of an American state by Communists is but the prelude for use of that country as a base for further aggressions.

A number of juridical questions deserve consideration—not in an atmosphere of crisis, demanding an immediate decision, but in an atmosphere of calmness and objectivity. As illustrative of the kind of questions that ought to be considered, I pose these two:

What distinctions ought to be made, on the one hand, between subversive activities which do not constitute an immediate danger to an American state and, on the other, those which, because of their intensity and external direction, do constitute a danger to the peace and security of the country and the hemisphere?

Second, assuming that, as I have suggested, certain subversive activities do constitute a threat to the peace and security of the hemisphere, what response is permitted within the framework of the inter-American system?

I do not offer precise answers to these questions at this time. I only wish to say that the problem of Communist subversion in the hemisphere is a real one. It should not be brushed aside on a false assumption that American states are prohibited by inter-American law from dealing with it.

I turn to a political question: How seriously should we regard Communist subversion in this hemisphere?

I will not take your time to remind you of the expansionist history of the Communist countries in recent years in Eastern Europe and in Asia. The history and the tactics used are well-known. . . .

It is difficult to understand the precise reasons why some appear to be less concerned than others about attempts to expand, by force and violence, areas of Communist domination in this hemisphere.

What we can be certain of is that the greatest danger to freedom and to peace will come when the free world is confused, uncertain, divided and weak—when expansionistic communism comes to believe that new aggressions can be committed without risk.

[Mann went on to clarify some "misconceptions about particular United States actions in the recent Dominican crisis," and concluded with a ringing defense of the American revolutionary traditions and the U.S. commitment to reforms.]

13.
THREE LATIN AMERICANS VIEW THE UNITED STATES

The three selections that comprise this document are intended
to represent a wide spectrum of opinion. Of course, there are
those in Latin America who think everything the United
States does is right or, at the other extreme, wrong. While
the three scholars differ markedly in their vision of the world
and their hopes for the future, they share certain assumptions
about the United States which should interest U.S. readers.

The first selection is by Leopoldo Zea, a renowned Mexican teacher and scholar. Zea has taught for many years at
the National University of Mexico and published several
books on Latin American thinkers and philosophy. His best-
known work in translation is *The Latin American Mind*
(Norman: University of Oklahoma Press, 1963)

I. Latin America and the World   ✧   Leopoldo Zea

The shape that relations between Latin America and the United
States will inevitably take is appearing above the horizon. On one side

From *Latin America and the World,* by Leopoldo Zea, pp. 28–30, 54–58,
96–99. Translated from the Spanish by Frances K. Kendricks and Beatrice
Berler. Copyright 1969 by the University of Oklahoma Press.

is the North America admired by Latin American nations endeavoring to achieve their greatest worth; on the other is the North America repudiated by those same nations who have seen it scheming with forces representative of a past unresigned to being past. On the one side is admiration for the North America that stands for freedom; on the other is repudiation for the North America that incites and supports those who impede freedom in Latin America. Both admiration and repudiation are henceforth going to characterize relations of the two. These attitudes are unrelated to the disputes arising between the United States and the U.S.S.R.; indeed, they are antecedent to them. Problems in relations between Latin America and North America should be resolved with reference to circumstances uncomplicated by those ensuing from the cold war that followed World War II. . . .

I am firmly convinced that our America can greatly assist this emerging world [of developing nations]. Situated between two worlds —the West and the non-West—we continue our efforts to deal with conditions growing out of anxieties we have long experienced and now have in common with many countries. If the countries which provoked these anxieties by their expansion could understand them, then a more responsible and stable world would result. The nations that have learned the lessons of the West now seek to participate in such a world and to find a place of responsibility in it.

*   *   *

What is going to happen in Latin America? Will there be the pretexts offered by the cold war for maintaining the status quo which suits the interests of the United States in this part of the world? Everybody knows—and I emphasize—that the problems discussed in Latin America are the old ones that antedate those growing out of the cold war and, on the whole, antedate the organization of communism as a militant doctrine. The problems of Latin America in its relations with the United States are as old as its history—they appeared almost as soon as the countries of this continent had declared independence.

[Zea goes on to describe Bolívar's attitude to the United States. See above, document 2].

*   *.   *

The cold war between the United States and the U.S.S.R. has been a marvelous pretext for justifying North American intervention in

Latin America in defense of, or for expanding, the interests of its investors. Any action incompatible with these interests is interpreted as an expression of Communist intervention in America and, on that account, a menace to the security of the continent. Efforts that Latin American countries make to improve their economic condition necessarily come up against interests already established or being established by United States investors, provoking the reaction which interferes with the success of those efforts. These countries not only have to struggle against those national interests opposed to any change which would affect their predominance but, what is more, have to face the pressure imposed on them by the representatives of foreign investors whose interests could be affected. Thus a problem as old as that of the land in Latin America is converted into one linked with the cold war which the great powers sustain. Those who resist any agrarian reform will be hailed as supporters of freedom and democracy, while those who dare to proclaim that the land should belong to those who work it will be considered opponents of those principles.

[Zea appeals for hemispheric solidarity to protect the interests of the individual Latin American nations.]

*   *   *

The Iberian community—or Latin America—could be a point of departure for the creation of a world in which the voice of our countries would be effective and would count decisively in world destiny. More than an association, it would be a community of those having something in common—not a society of those uniting their efforts through fear. This community would aim to achieve or to maintain freedom and other human values no less noble; it would not be merely an association necessary for survival. It would be a great community founded through the free will and sovereignty of countries with a common destiny—not an association of frightened sardines that obey the shark, as Arévalo said, for fear of being devoured by the shark or at least postponing the destiny the shark has indicated for them.

*   *   *

Can we realize this dream now that distances have been shortened, now that the interests of all—both the strong and the weak—are closely linked? Can all the Latin American countries create a community that will permit them to enter into discussions and to balance interests with their powerful neighbor of the north as equal with equal in the search for solutions of problems of both our continents? Will the Latin American community, on its part, be effective in finding solutions for all world problems, with its efforts joined by that of other groups, united not by reason of tongue, religion, or culture but by the situation resulting from the common impact of Western influence? Will the Latin American community, united with other groups formed for the same reasons—the Arabs, the Africans, and the Asiatics—have sufficient weight to form another even more powerful group and thus be able to balance their interests with those of the primary powers?

Bolívar held that a community of our countries could be the basis for a wider community that could be extended to the countries of Asia and Africa, in order to make them free and to destroy the yokes that Europe—that is, the Western world—had established over them, in order to form, with all those countries and of course with the others that make up the earth, a new and powerful union that would be comparable only to the one that Iberia dreamed of expanding throughout the world in order to create a great united Christian world in which all men could be equal. "In the march of centuries," said Bolívar, "it might, perhaps, be possible to find only one nation covering the entire earth."

II. Pan-Americanism ❖ Alonso Aguilar

Alonso Aguilar is Professor of Economic Planning and Latin American Economic Development in the School of Economics of the National University of Mexico (UNAM). He has participated in many international economic and political meetings, lectured at universities in Mexico and abroad, and written extensively in his field. Professor Aguilar's latest book is *Latin American Development Theory and Policy*. In the

From Alonso Aguilar, *Pan-Americanism, From Monroe to the Present: A View from the Other Side*, pp. 152–153. Copyright © 1968 by Monthly Review Press; reprinted by permission of Monthly Review Press.

book from which this document is excerpted, his point of
view is Marxist, harshly critical of the United States and
frankly revolutionary. Let it be stated, however that his is
by no means an extreme or radical statement of the Latin
American position.

On April 28, 1965, the President of the United States, Lyndon B.
Johnson, ordered the landing of 400 Marines in Santo Domingo in
order to forestall the imminent triumph of the people in overthrowing
a weak and unpopular military dictatorship. It is possible that many
Latin Americans, although naturally concerned about this development, were momentarily unable to gauge its significance and grave
implications. But only a few days sufficed—one week, actually—for
the aggressive policy of the United States to be exposed and for Latin
America to realize that imperialism was still imperialism despite the
rhetoric of the foreign ministers of the OAS and despite the good
intentions, wishful thinking, and repeated pronouncements endorsing
the principles of self-determination and nonintervention.

When the 400 Marines sent to "protect the lives and property of
U.S. citizens residing in the Dominican Republic" grew into an aggres-
sive force of almost 40,000 fully armed troops, Mr. Johnson's hypocrisy no longer deceived anyone. His motivations, in fact, were basically the same as those which had prompted Mr. Blaine (Secretary of
State during President Harrison's Administration) to propose the first
Pan-American Conference; which caused Theodore Roosevelt to
invent a "revolution" in Panama in order to seize control of the
Isthmus; which led President Taft to use the American flag to protect
United States monopolies seeking raw materials and markets outside
their own country; and the very same which Calvin Coolidge defended
in repeated declarations to the effect that the rights of United States
investors, and the obligation of the government in Washington to protect them, stood above the principles of self-determination and respect
for national sovereignty.

The aggression against the Dominican Republic together with the
so-called Johnson Doctrine, which purports to be its rationale, have
highlighted the profound crisis which the inter-American system is
undergoing, revealing in a single stroke that the policy of anti-Communism inherited from Churchill and Truman, instead of serving the
national interests of Latin America or safeguarding the security of

the continent, constitutes a grave threat to the sovereignty of these nations and is no more than a crude device for maintaining the status quo.

Anti-Communism, favorite weapon of the Pentagon strategists, the U.S. State Department, representatives to the Organization of American States, and the Latin-American oligarchies and "gorillarchies"—its most recent form is the Johnson Doctrine—is not an instrument against armed aggression by a foreign power. It is, rather, the principal weapon being used by imperialism and its allies to hold back social or political progress in Latin America and other parts of the world where the people seem ready to transform present socioeconomic conditions.

For almost a century and a half, the United States had used the Monroe Doctrine to prevent European countries from exporting their political systems to the Americas. By extension, under the Johnson Doctrine, the nations of Latin America are prevented from choosing their form of government and so do not even control their own destinies. As events have dramatically shown in the Dominican Republic and before that in Brazil, Cuba, and Guatemala, Latin Americans are in a sorry plight. If a Latin-American nation, in the full exercise of its sovereignty, chooses a government or type of social organization unfavorable to United States interests or unacceptable to privileged local minorities, the result is either violent unilateral intervention by the United States or the emergence of a politician or army officer disposed to betray his people by crying out for Pan Americanism to enter into immediate action in defense of the indefensible.

[At the third Extraordinary Inter-American Conference convened at Panama in 1966 to consider possible reforms of the OAS charter.]

It was easy to see that two different positions confronted one another; on the one side, the governments wanting to endow the OAS with more effective means of combating "Communist subversion"; on the other, the nations which, though recognizing the "reality of the Communist threat," insisted on incorporating into the Charter of the Organization the principles of the Alliance for Progress and of the World Conference of Trade and Development which had been held in Geneva in 1964. Within a few days, the original and vague agreement of the majority of the Latin-American delegates regarding the problems of development became the first draft of a plan for reforms and additions to those articles of the Charter which contained certain measures tending to accelerate economic growth and to obtain more favorable conditions in international trade. But, unlike other meetings at which the United States accepted various economic demands in exchange for greater political subordination, this time, at Panama, the United States rejection was immediate and flat. The preliminary draft was criticized as "unnecessary," "too long and wordy," and "too far removed from the spirit of inter-American equality of the Charter." And, in a less conventional tone in which his annoyance was evident, Senator Jacob Javits explained his country's rejection by saying, "The United States cannot sign any old piece of paper handed it by the Latin Americans."

While discouragement pervaded Panama and Buenos Aires (where there was at that time a meeting of the Inter-American Economic and Social Council at which the same flat rejection by the United States delegation was to be forthcoming), in Washington, April 14th was declared "Pan-American Day" and Congressman Armistead Selden exhorted the governments of the continent to strengthen the OAS, using the same vehemence with which he had proposed a resolution months before that raised intervention by one country in the affairs of another to the rank of a "right" of United States imperialism to trample the sovereignty of other nations. He declared: "I urge you to recognize that the ultimate objectives of the Alliance for Progress can only be attained if the OAS is ready to meet face to face the constant hostility emanating from the Communist bases in Cuba."

Congressman Dante Fascell, a southern colleague of Selden's, also exhibited his government's absolute lack of understanding of the problems of Latin America, as well as its proverbial ability to see spooks behind every bush, with his statement that the celebration of Pan-American Day in Washington "serves to demonstrate to Latin America that the United States is wholeheartedly on its side in the struggle against Communist usurpation."

Between 1962 and 1966 alone—that is, during the first four years of the "decade of progress"—constitutional law and order in Latin America was broken from eight to ten times by military forces bent on combating Communism and assuring "representative democracy." Frondizi in Argentina; Ydígoras in Guatemala; Arosemena in Ecuador; Bosch in the Dominican Republic; Villeda Morales in Honduras; Goulart in Brazil; and shortly after, Arturo Illía in Argentina, were all to topple ,one after the other, charged with ineptitude and leniency toward Communism. Their removal from office was a reflection of the hard line of Thomas Mann and others in the State Department, who advocated supporting Latin-American military dictatorships as long as they were anti-Communist and protected United States investors.

While the last Panama Conference was in session, Senator William Fulbright, Chairman of the Senate Foreign Relations Committee, said in a speech at the University of Connecticut: "Possibly, it would be more advisable for us to concentrate on our own democracy instead of trying to impose our version of it on all those unfortunate Latin Americans who stubbornly oppose their northern benefactors instead of fighting the real enemy we so graciously found them."

How right he was!

III. National Development Policies and External Dependence in Latin America ∿ Osvaldo Sunkel

> Osvaldo Sunkel is Professor of Economic Development at the Economics Faculty and Research Fellow of the Institute of International Studies of the University of Chile. He was formerly with the UN Economic Commission for Latin America (CEPAL) and the Latin American Institute for Economic and Social Planning. This document is excerpted from a revised version of a lecture delivered on November 17, 1966, at the University of Chile during the series of Inaugural Lectures of the Institute of International Studies. Professor Sunkel's tone is more objective and his posture more "scientific" than Aguilar's. He seems to be describing reality, nothing more. The North American reader should realize, however, that every Latin American understands that the references to an unnamed dominant power means the

From Osvaldo Sunkel, "National Development Policies and External Dependence in Latin America," *Journal of Development Studies*, VI, No. 1, pp. 23, 30–31, 43–46. Reproduced with permission of Frank Cass and Co. Ltd, London.

United States and that Latin America is dependent upon the United States.

The influence which external relations exercise on national development policy derives from the fact that the Latin American countries are enmeshed in the system of international relations of the capitalist world. This system is characterized by the presence of a dominant power, a series of intermediate powers and the underdeveloped countries ascribed to it. Like the domestic situation, this system is also essentially dynamic. Significant variations are experienced both because of changes inside the countries and as a result of the confrontation with the other principal system of international relations, that of the socialist world. Variations in this worldwide confrontation also affect the limits within which national development policy may move.

As a result of the stagnation of traditional agriculture, the structure of foreign trade, the type of industrialization and the function which the State is fulfilling . . . our countries are, from the point of view of the structure and functioning of the economy, entirely dependent on their foreign economic relations. . . . This extreme dependence is rooted in several conditions: the vulnerability and structural deficit of the balance of payments; the type of industrialization and the form of exploitation of the export sector which have not permitted our countries—with a few exceptions—to acquire the ability to adapt and create their own technology; the fact that an important and probably growing part of industry and of the export activities are either foreign owned or depend on licences and foreign technical assistance, all of which weighs heavily on the availability of foreign exchange; and the fact that both the fiscal sector and the balance of payments persistently tend to deficit, which leads to the necessity of foreign financing. In certain conditions this foreign financing can mean the accumulation of such considerable debts and such a structure of maturities that the very servicing of the debt requires resort to additional foreign financing—a genuine vicious circle. It is this aspect—the overbearing and implacable necessity to obtain foreign financing—which finally sums up the situation of dependence; this is the crucial point in the mechanism of dependence. . . .

There remains, however, a last fundamental question: to what extent will the limitations imposed by the web of international relations within which our countries exist, permit us to adopt policies and strategies of national development such as those suggested? Or, in other words, given the repercussions which a policy of national development would necessarily have on the nature of our external relations, would the affected foreign and domestic interests be sufficiently powerful to block these policies?

I believe that, with respect to this, we are in a better position than a few years ago. From the domestic point of view it has already been suggested that conditions could be such that ideas of this nature might form part of a program, a strategy and an ideology of development. With respect to the capitalist world, within which we are, the adoption of strategies and institutional forms such as those which have been suggested would probably have been unacceptable up to eight or ten years ago. But today it is possible to air these problems openly and new solutions seem feasible. There have been fundamental changes in the international scene. These changes relate to the relationship between the two principal world blocs and in particular to the relationship between the two superpowers. Since the Cuban crisis made clear that the direct influence of one of the great powers in the sphere of influence of the other carried the risk of nuclear war, they have arrived at a kind of *détente*. The nuclear balance of power has eliminated the immediate danger of war between the two great powers. This threat having disappeared, the hegemonic powers have lessened their rigid control and the perfect alignment which each had demanded from the intermediate powers and the underdeveloped countries inscribed within their spheres of influence. This has permitted the rise of intermediate countries relatively free of their respective hegemonic powers, and the adoption of important innovations in the development policy of these countries designed to arrive at forms most suited to national conditions. This is the case of the transformations which have occurred in the socialist economies of Eastern Europe and of the reorientation of the policy of international cooperation which the Alliance for Progress represents for Latin America. . . . The program of the Alliance for Progress, at least in its original conception and in the vestiges which remain, approved of this desire to try new formulae. The adoption of positive attitudes towards change in the underdeveloped countries is without doubt linked to the fact that direct nuclear confrontation between the great powers is impossible. What then are the forms in which this confrontation can take place? Obviously one is the ideological struggle, particularly at the level of development policy, each side showing the world that development can best be achieved in a capitalistic or, conversely, a socialist way. Therefore it is now in the interest of the dominant powers, even though they are conscious of running certain risks, to try out formulae which might lead to rapid and satisfactory development *without rupturing the prevailing political system.* This is in fact the argument given by both the U.S. and the U.S.S.R. to justify Santo Domingo and Czechoslovakia. Situations like these are clearly possible but I believe that they are only temporary and partial setbacks in the context of a long-term process of liberalization; internal pressures for liberalization and for decreasing the world-wide commitments of superpowers continue, and nationalistic voices are mounting in the satellite nations and everywhere.

This process has had the effect not only of a thaw within each system, but also led to the rapid proliferation of relationships between the countries of each bloc. The last five or six years show a clear evolution in this direction, both in international trade, in political relations, and also in international cultural relations. The countries of the underdeveloped world, each of which was before directly and exclusively affiliated with its own hegemonic power, have now wider possibilities of international trade, foreign aid, cultural contact, technical assistance and consultation, ideological discussion, exchange of students and professors, and of research, with the countries of the other bloc. . . .

[Because of the nuclear stand-off] revolutionary movements in an underdeveloped country cannot count on open and declared economic or military support from the respective great power, while the government of the country in question will be able to count on massive and declared support from its respective hegemonic power. In other words, the possibility of guerrilla movements expanding and converting themselves into victorious revolutionary movements seems remote, at least in Latin America. Would this mean the maintenance of the *status quo?* I think not. The possibility of implementing progressive policies in Latin America will obviously depend, in the first place, on the social structure and political forces, the degree of national integration, the legitimacy of the government and other internal circumstances. But when positive circumstances are present to a greater or lesser extent, the limits of development policy can, in my opinion, expand considerably beyond the traditional boundaries.

The principal considerations which support this thesis are: [that the danger of internal revolutionary change has been practically eliminated; that tensions in Latin America have their origin in the economic and social structure of these countries; that contact between all nations has been expanding; and that the hegemonic power will try to avoid prerevolutionary situations and promote development].

Finally, then, given the changes in the international political scene, it seems to me that the possibility of carrying out a national development policy depends fundamentally on the domestic situation, that is to say, the degree of differentiation of the social structure, the degree of political participation, and the existence or possible formation of new political movements which would constitute a functional response to the concrete socio-political problems in terms of a program, a strategy and an ideology of national development.

To summarize what I have wanted to suggest in these reflections —the only aim of which is to stimulate a more positive debate on these matters than that which we have had up to now—what I have tried to do is the following: to accept that *national* development is the fundamental objective of the policy of development; second, to indicate that the fulfillment of the objective of reducing external dependence requires very important re-orientations in traditional development strategy, particularly relating to agrarian policy, integration, foreign relations, and industrial policy; third, to indicate that in some countries of Latin America economic, social and political changes and transformations have been occurring which seem to indicate the possibility that such new policies could be formulated and applied; fourth, to suggest that in these particular cases, the changes in the international situation would seem to have created conditions which are sufficiently tolerant and flexible to permit the application of policies of national development.

BIBLIOGRAPHIC SUGGESTIONS

CONNELL-SMITH, GORDON. *The Inter-American System* (New York: Oxford University Press, 1962) is a well-researched study of the OAS and its predecessor organizations which offers a British view of the OAS and U.S. imperialistic behavior.

GIL, FEDERICO G. *Latin American—United States Relations* (New York: Harcourt Brace Jovanovich, 1971) is a sound, perceptive survey that gives balanced attention to the Latin American side of things.

GREEN, DAVID. *The Containment of Latin America: A History of the Myths and Realities of the Good Neighbor Policy* (Chicago: Quadrangle, 1971) is a revisionist account, soundly researched, which argues that U.S. policy was designed to extend U.S. economic influence in the hemisphere and conflicted with Latin American nationalistic aspirations, especially in the period following World War II.

LA FEBER, WALTER. *The New Empire: An Interpretation of American Expansion, 1860–1898* (Ithaca, N. Y.: Cornell University Press, 1963) is a sophisticated analysis of the reasons for America's turning outward at the end of the nineteenth century, particularly useful for its handling of different intellectual currents and its willingness to reach back in time for greater understanding.

MUNRO, DANA G. *Intervention and Dollar Diplomacy in the Caribbean, 1900–1921* (Princeton, N. J.: Princeton University Press, 1964) is a careful, meticulously detailed study based primarily on State Department documents by a former diplomatic officer; it presents the case in favor of gradual, unplanned involvement and against the economic interpretations.

PERKINS, DEXTER. *A History of the Monroe Doctrine* (Boston: Little, Brown, 1963) is a shortened version of the author's classic three-volume history of the Monroe Doctrine; although it may mislead students of foreign policy to focus on the Monroe Doctrine, this book remains valuable for its measured judgments and its information.

PERLOFF, HARVEY S. *Alliance for Progress, A Social Invention in the Making* (Baltimore, Md.: Johns Hopkins Press, 1969) is a sympathetic account which manages to provide a coherent statement of the historical background to the Alliance, the dilemma of Latin American development, the workings of the Alliance and its failings, as well as offering clear detailed suggestions for the future.

TULCHIN, JOSEPH S. *The Aftermath of War: World War I and United States Policy Toward Latin America* (New York: New York University Press, 1971) is a monograph demonstrating the impact of the war on U.S. policy, both in leading to a withdrawal from formal empire and in defining the nature of U.S. strategic interests in the hemisphere during the interwar period.

WAGNER, R. HARRISON. *United States Policy Toward Latin America: A Study in Domestic and International Politics* (Stanford, Calif.: Stanford University Press, 1970) is an effort by a political scientist to explain (and justify) U.S. policy in the period following World War II, asserting that the basic strategic interests of the country and the workings of domestic politics determined the rather narrow limits within which policy might change over time.

WHITAKER, ARTHUR P. *The United States and the Independence of Latin America, 1800–1830* (Baltimore, Md.: The Johns Hopkins University Press, 1941) is a detailed analysis of inter-American relations during the revolutionary period, dealing with culture, economics, politics,and every conceivable facet of international contact.

WHITAKER, ARTHUR P. *The Western Hemisphere Idea: Its Rise and Decline* (Ithaca, N. Y.: Cornell University Press, 1954) is a challenging and subtle interpretation of inter-American relations which traces the rise and decline of the idea that North and South America were united by bonds of geography, politics, history, and by the mere fact of sharing the New World.

WOOD, BRYCE. *The Making of the Good Neighbor Policy* (New York: Columbia University Press, 1961) is a traditional account of the transition in policy from the Hoover to the Roosevelt administration, based on State Department documents and blending juridical issues with economic questions.

6855